# German Colonialism and National Identity

# Routledge Studies in Modern European History

# German Colonialism and National Identity

Edited by Michael Perraudin and
Jürgen Zimmerer

with Katy Heady

Routledge
Taylor & Francis Group
New York   London

First published 2011
by Routledge
270 Madison Avenue, New York, NY 10016

Simultaneously published in the UK
by Routledge
2 Park Square, Milton Park, Abingdon, Oxon OX14 4RN

*Routledge is an imprint of the Taylor & Francis Group, an informa business*

Typeset in Sabon by IBT Global.
Printed in the UK by the MPG Books Group.

*Library of Congress Cataloging-in-Publication Data*
German colonialism and national identity / [edited by] Michael Perraudin and Jürgen
Zimmerer.
    p. cm.—(Routledge studies in modern European history ; 14)
  "Simultaneously published in the UK"—T.p. verso.
  Includes bibliographical references and index.
  1. Germany—Colonies—History.   2. Germany—Foreign relations—19th
century.   3. Germany—Foreign relations—20th century.   4. National characteristics,
German—History.   5. Nationalism—Germany—History.   6. Imperialism—Social
aspects—Germany—History.   7. Popular culture—Germany—History.   8. Political
culture—Germany—History.   9. Germany—Social conditions.   I. Perraudin,
Michael.   II. Zimmerer, Jürgen.
  JV2017.G47 2010
  325'.343—dc22
  2009050513

ISBN13: 978-0-415-96477-7 (hbk)
ISBN13: 978-0-203-85259-0 (ebk)

# Contents

# Figures

# Introduction
## German Colonialism and National Identity

*Michael Perraudin and Jürgen Zimmerer*

For almost 60 years, from the end of World War Two, the German public had forgotten about its colonial empire. Whereas other European powers experienced the traumatic violence of decolonization, Germans believed that they had nothing to do with the colonial exploitation of large parts of Africa, Asia or South America. They were innocent—so many believed—of the devastations brought about by European colonialism and could therefore engage with the new post-colonial world without the dark shadow of a colonial past. Some observers have termed this a "colonial amnesia."

Such suppression was severely shaken in 2004, when the centenary of the genocide of the Herero and Nama peoples confronted a wide German audience with German atrocities of a hundred years before. The first German genocide, as it was called, attracted media coverage, and in August 2004 the then German government officially apologized for the atrocities. After Germany's attempts to come to terms with its Nazi past, this step was seen by many international observers as a major break-through in global attempts to right historic wrongs, especially those committed in a colonial context. In Germany, however, the official apology, far from marking closure on a dark chapter in German history, sparked a variety of agitated responses. Instead of acknowledging the act as a much-needed step in the process of coming to terms with the colonial past, conservative circles denounced the German Minister for Economic Cooperation and Development, Heidemarie Wieczorek-Zeul, who had delivered the apology, as a "traitor." Others worried about claims for reparations by the Herero, and the German tabloid *BILD* asked on its front page, "What will be the cost of the minister's tears?"—deriding her carefully crafted statement as being the result of female sentiment. Wieczorek-Zeul's courageous act had obviously touched a nerve. Whereas some felt encouraged to bring other German colonial atrocities into the limelight—for example, the Maji-Maji war in German East Africa, the centenary of which fell in 2005—others have attempted to rewrite Germany's colonial past by emphasizing the exotic aspects of the German colonial undertaking, and by disconnecting the imperial past from the positive strands of German history. A dubious documentary on prime-time German television, which made repeated use of colonial stereotypes, marked an extreme point of this endeavor.

Nevertheless, the debate showed that Germany had finally arrived at a post-colonial European normality, where its own historical relationship with the world is part of a vigorous debate not only about the past, but also about the future. Migration, multiculturalism and xenophobia are only some of the topics which are substantially shaped by Germany's memory of the past. Colonialism was central to Wilhelminian discourse on national identity and to the country's understanding of itself as a world power; and now discussion about the German empire seems to be resurfacing as part of a German discourse of self-understanding and self-reassurance in the aftermath of Reunification.

The present volume addresses Germany's biased and troubled relationship with its colonial future, present and past over a century and a half. As post-colonial studies have shown, colonial engagement neither began nor ended with formal colonial rule. The 22 chapters of the volume accordingly touch on many aspects of the encounters of Germany and Germans with imagined or real colonial empires from before the colonial epoch to the present day. However, the book is primarily concerned not with the compensatory colonialist fantasies of pre-imperial, particularist Germany, but with reflections and effects of German colonialism from the point in the middle of the nineteenth century when a unified German state with colonial-expansionist capacities became politically feasible. The book mirrors colonial realities from that stage on—German colonial adventure, acquisition and rule, military defeat and dispossession, and German relationships to post-war decolonization; but its principal focus is on the cultural processing of these events, both as they occurred and retrospectively, mainly in the German metropole through the phases of its turbulent history, though also within the colonies and ex-colonies. The individual chapters concern colonial reflections in, among other media, fictional writing, travelogue, journalistic reportage, film, advertising, public statuary and other popular iconography. They touch on a diversity of forms of public discourse as well as issues of political policy at different epochs. What they demonstrate conclusively is not only the powerful impact of the Empire's short-lived colonial engagement on the imagination of its time, but also its continued—and widely underestimated—hold and influence on the German mind of subsequent epochs, from Weimar to the *Wende* and beyond.

The chapters—which are grouped in the first place chronologically and secondly by theme—present a kind of informal narrative of developments in thinking about and utilization of the German colonial idea. The volume's first part focuses on patterns initiated before the imperial phase. It opens with what can be called the political beginnings of unitary Germany's colonializing preoccupations, with Brian Vick's account of debates at the Frankfurt National Assembly during the 1848 Revolution about a German nation state's potential for colonial and quasi-colonial expansion—and characteristic racial understandings already discernible in those deliberations. This is then underpinned by Tracey Reimann-Dawe's discussion of exemplary nineteenth-century travelogues about Africa, from 1848 up to and through the colonial period proper: she shows the African travel narratives evolving and changing in perspective and outlook as a reflection, first, of Germany's progress to nation-state status, and then of its realization of colonial ambitions. Finally, Kristin Kopp, also extending an aspect of Vick's discussion, considers the role of Poland as an object of German imperial desires from the 1850s onward, the developmental continuity from this to Nazi rule in Poland, and modern debates about the application of concepts of colonialism to Germany's dealings with its eastern neighbors.

Part II is a group of essays concentrating specifically on phenomena of the phase of formal colonial rule between 1884 and 1918, as roles and identities for the colonizers and countervailing images of the colonized were created and displayed in metropolitan journalism, commercial iconography and public policy deliberations. First, the myth-making strategies employed in popular press accounts of the course of Germany's misconceived and hubristic engagement in China are analyzed by Yixu Lü. Next, Jeffrey Bowersox examines how middle-class youth magazines combined reportage and fiction about the new German colonies to construct both appealing fantasies of violence and desire and highly gendered moral lessons for their adolescent readerships. David Ciarlo then shows how, in the early years of the twentieth century, advances in the technology and economics of advertising interacted with news of the events of Germany's colonial wars, especially in Africa, to generate a commercial iconography of startling vividness and racial ferocity. In a related vein, Volker Langbehn looks at the expanding medium of the picture postcard, by the turn of the century a dominant medium of popular communication, and analyzes its prevalent use of a grotesque colonial and racial imagery. Finally, an intriguing aspect of German public policy-making and debate vis-à-vis the colonies is examined by Kenneth Orosz, namely, the moves made by colonial experts under the patronage of the German state to establish an officially sanctioned simplified form of German for communication in the African colonies—as a device for bureaucratic efficiency, paternalistic education and ideological control.

Orosz also illustrates how such overt state engagements disappeared after Germany's colonial dispossession in 1918. However, the chapters in the part that follows demonstrate the powerful legacy of the colonial experience for the German imagination and sense of self during the Weimar period and its seamless continuation into the Nazi years. First, Jörg Lehmann studies a series of works of German colonial fiction from the early 1900s to the 1930s and finds a continuity of racial imagery, heroic fantasy and legitimated genocidal violence through this tradition. Michael Pesek examines the way in which, after World War One, elaborate discourses of heroism are constructed around the German campaign failures in East

Africa, myths both of the resolute colonial officer-leader and of the loyal
warrior-native; and these become important elements in German identity-
formation in the aftermath of defeat. The essay by Constant Kpao Sarè
shows how the figure of Germany's arch-colonizer and supposed colonial
martyr Carl Peters is construed in a range of discursive contexts in and
beyond Weimar in support of the types of radical racial thinking which
were central to German fascism. Meanwhile, Britta Schilling's discussion
of Weimar-period images of women in the colonies—in magazine writing
and photography, autobiography and other publications—points to further myth-making tendencies, but also reveals ambiguities that signal new
ideological possibilities: emancipated or masculinized women's roles, and
the beginnings of a questioning of colonialist understandings of blackness.
Finally, Susann Lewerenz examines how colonially conditioned German
constructions of black character—loyal colonial subject or dangerous predator—that prevailed in the post-colonial years in practice affected (that is
to say, ruined) the lives of Germans of African descent.

Whilst World War Two and the demise of the Third Reich mark an obvious hiatus both in the book and in Germany's processing of its colonial
past, the part which follows, on metropolitan receptions from the 1950s
until the present decade, in fact illustrates a complexity of responses. First,
Monika Albrecht examines attitudes in the West German left-liberal press
from the early 1950s to the early 1960s toward the contemporary upheav-
als of decolonization—in which Germans were observers rather than participants—and finds both unreflected colonialist mindsets, symptoms of
the "amnesia" mentioned previously, and energetic challenges to such attitudes. Next, Ingo Cornils shows exemplarily how, in late 1960s Hamburg,
an issue of colonialist memorialization became a focus of spectacular protest and comprehensive ideological critique by radical student groups—a
controversy the resonances of which Cornils then traces through to the
present decade. Kathryn Jones introduces a significant comparative perspective, juxtaposing recent German efforts at acknowledging responsibility for the Herero and Nama genocide with France's in the author's view
less resolved responses to a notable atrocity of its own from the period of
the Algerian war of the early 1960s. Finally, Wolfgang Struck analyzes a
recent, enthusiastically received film drama for German television set in
colonial Namibia around 1900: he demonstrates powerfully how, whatever
the post- and anti-colonial efforts of German policy-makers, colonialist
myths of race and power retain a tenacious hold on the German popular
imagination.

As a final stage of the discussion, the volume's concluding part begins to
shift the focus away from the German metropolis and toward consequences
and recollections of German colonial involvements in the colonial territories themselves. First, Reinhart Kössler studies commemorative practice in
present-day Namibia concerning the colonial wars: the re-enactments and
rituals surrounding the principal memorial days, who takes part, and the

meanings the events hold for participants. Henning Melber's essay complements this with an examination of the political ramifications of modern memorializations of the Herero and Nama genocide, with particular reference to the way the issue is enmeshed with power structures and oppositions in post-independence Namibia. And Dominik Schaller adds a discussion of what he indicates to be the privileging of the Herero genocide in the context of Holocaust analogies emerging in the post-Cold War era around certain episodes of past colonial atrocity: he argues that particular needs and interests in mature post-colonial societies, as well as in and between the former colonizing states, have selectively favored the establishment of such analogies. Next, Denis Laumann turns attention wholly away from Namibia to Germany's territory in what is now Togo, suggesting how a text-fixated scholarship has failed to elicit all the available evidence about the impacts and recollections of German rule, and demonstrating the importance of oral sources in filling this gap. Finally, Arnd Witte brings the discussion full circle with his essay on the intricate development of African *Germanistik*—in the ex-German colonies and elsewhere. A story which began with dreams of imperial acquisition by an as yet unformed Germany concludes with Germany as an object of dispassionate study by scholars in the former colonial domains themselves.

These essays on Germany's colonial engagements and their cultural consequences convey a picture of complexity and consistency, sameness and difference, affirmation and compensation, alibi and guilt. From the first point at which a unified German state began to form, the colonial idea—but also the perception of the nation's lateness and differentness as a colonizer—was constitutive of Germany's sense of self. Once an (overseas) empire had been rather tenuously acquired, basic aspects of German self-understanding articulated themselves through colonially focused discourse and iconography, affirming racial supremacy over the colonized as well as a degree of cultural superiority over other colonizers. After Germany had been violently dispossessed of its colonies, the characteristic resentments of the succeeding era surfaced in relation to the lost colonial realms: Germany as the superior colonial power, unjustly denied; Germany betrayed by foreign trickery; German ethical greatness vindicated and its ethnic identity displayed in its colonial victories and defeats. German colonialism, we see, was complicit in the processes leading to the Holocaust. But after World War Two and in the age of European decolonization, Germany's colonial culpability is largely lost to memory, while myths of the superior colonizer are conserved and a new sense of German distinctiveness emerges. It takes the critical generation of 1968 on their eventual accession to positions of authority, in the aftermath of Unification, to achieve something approaching a frank understanding of the colonial legacy; and even that understanding continues to struggle against the exigencies of political power and prevailing cultural myths. In the former colonies themselves, meanwhile, Germany's colonial presence, however short and inglorious, also leaves

enduring legacies, by which the cultural identities of new nations are endur-
ingly conditioned. This is where both the history and the historiography of
German colonialism are today, and neither is remotely near completion.
That is signaled by the present volume: it points to the breadth of the topic,
underscores its actuality, reveals a diversity of new dimensions, and gestures ahead to the possibilities of dynamic further development which it
undoubtedly contains.

# Part I

# Colonialism From Before the Empire

# 1 Imperialism, Race, and Genocide at the *Paulskirche*
## Origins, Meanings, Trajectories

*Brian Vick*

It might at first seem strange to find an essay on the Frankfurt National Parliament and the 1848 Revolution in a volume on German colonialism, as indeed, for obvious reasons, most histories of German imperialism and colonialism begin in about 1880, or perhaps the late 1870s, at about the same time as the rise of racist doctrines, and at least a couple of decades before the first episodes of modern genocide. Some scholars, however, have attempted to trace the history, or pre-history, of German imperialist thinking back into the early decades of the nineteenth century, and the present discussion is at least in part intended as a contribution to that literature. The 1848 Revolution and, even more particularly, the Frankfurt National Assembly have in this context been seen as the abortive "moment of birth of German imperialism" (in Hermann Hiery's phrase), when plans for extensive expansionist policies overseas and for handling the problem of German mass emigration were for the first time loudly and seriously canvassed in a political setting, if without concrete results. Hans Fenske has even gone so far as to suggest that, had the Frankfurt liberals remained in power at the head of a united German nation state, they would have pursued an imperialist and colonialist course that might have triggered the competitive imperialist land-grab of the 1880s decades earlier.[1]

In what follows, I hope to offer a somewhat more nuanced view of these empire-related debates in Frankfurt in 1848 and at the same time to illuminate the intellectual and cultural background to the emergent discourses of race and of racial conflict—even of genocide—in the German-speaking world. As we shall see, the two areas of focus were intimately related, and often not in the ways one might have expected. The pursuit of empire, and the potential sites of racial conflict, ultimately drew the attention of Frankfurt delegates much more to the east and southeast along the Danube than they did to the farther-flung reaches of the globe or to those who lived there. The Frankfurt delegates applied racialist rhetoric above all to the Slavic-speaking peoples, in fearful expectation of some kind of "Raçenkrieg", or race-war, and in chauvinist hopes of imperial Germanic expansion to the East. Imperialist dreams of world power were therefore certainly present at the *Paulskirche*, as, too, were early iterations of racist civilizing

: radical ethnic conflict, yet they tended to play out within older
ıs of empire and German supremacy of the *Mitteleuropa* sort,
ı in the framework of overseas possessions.

English-speaking world, the semantic and etymological connection between the terms imperialism and empire seems clear enough—perhaps too much so, even confusingly so, to the extent that imperialism and
empire simply seem to go together, with the pursuit of empire entailing the
pursuit of imperialist goals, including the projection of power overseas and
the acquisition of formal or informal overseas colonies and possessions as
a part of the enterprise. In the German context, however, the connections
between the notions of *Reich* and of *Imperialismus*, while still potentially
present, are by no means necessarily so close. Indeed, for Hiery, the problem is rather to explain how, when nineteenth-century nationalists came
to revive the Reich ideal in the decades after 1815, they managed to do so
in ways that incorporated overseas imperialist visions that had never been
prominent in the old Holy Roman Empire, yet without becoming wholly
unfaithful to that older model.[2]

There is, however, both somewhat more and somewhat less to explain
about the nature of "Reich-ism" and imperialism in Germany in the decades
before 1850. The term empire carries connotations of autonomy, self-asser-
tion, and to an extent also of power; the notion of "Reich" does, too, as
well as triggering reminiscences of ostensible German medieval splendor.[3]
In his analysis of German imperialism before 1866, Hans Fenske highlights
three main motives or lines of argumentation behind German imperialist
or colonialist desires in this period, the first having to do with matters of
nationalist prestige and medieval imperial memory, the second with considerations of world power and *Realpolitik,* and the third with problems
of society and economy, particularly overseas trade and mass emigration.
Of these, Fenske thought the second probably the most important.[4] Each
theme can be found in abundance in the Frankfurt debates, but without
adding up to a recipe for overseas expansion. Showing the flag, defending
the rights of Germans abroad, and securing favorable trading concessions
were all part of the program, but desires for the acquisition of colonies were
much less clear, or at least less vocal.

From the literature on the pre-history of German imperialist ideologies,
one would think that there were, to quote Woodruff Smith, "extensive
debates about emigration and colonialism at Frankfurt in 1848." Smith
also asserts that "colonial expansion became in 1848 part of a rather violent and multifaceted formal imperialism that caught hold of the imagination of nationalist liberals"; and he is not alone in this view, as Winfried
Speitkamp's recent survey history *Deutsche Kolonialgeschichte* attests, or
for that matter the studies of Fenske and Hiery.[5] But this was not really the
case. There were significant if brief discussions about the construction of a
German navy, and about the problem of *Auswanderung* or mass emigration that had grown so desperate by the "Hungry Forties," but not about

colonies as such. These two strands of discussion did provide the evidence usually cited in support of the idea that imperial expansion was high on the Frankfurt agenda, but in each case adumbration of colonial acquisitions was relatively by-the-by, and when the issue was raised, it was more likely to involve the German drive into Southeast Europe than the possibility of German possessions in the Americas, Africa or the Pacific.

When the question of the German fleet came up on 8 June 1848, the rapporteur for the newly established Naval Committee, the conservative Prussian general Joseph von Radowitz, did raise the more far-reaching function of a German navy in the projection of power overseas. "The first German warship," he declaimed, "which appears, and lays to before the mouth of the Rio de la Plata, will show the numerous Germans living there that they no longer depend exclusively upon the arbitrary whim of a tyrant, but that rather a people of forty million souls stands behind them." Radowitz's rhetorical flourish earned him a "long-lasting bravo" indicative of the similar sentiments of most other delegates. But, while his statement showed the intent to maintain connections and even a certain national feeling among Germans abroad, he did not actually mention colonies as a part of the plan.[6] Of the speakers in this matter when the report came up for debate on 14 June, in fact only one, the Prussian law professor Johann Ludwig Tellkampf, brought up the colonial question, noting rather in passing among his list of benefits that would follow in the wake of a German navy that a fleet was necessary "for the acquisition and maintenance of a colony." That was all he had to say on the matter, seeming more intrigued by the possible role of a strong navy in keeping a nation "young and powerful," and in supporting its progress in civilization and its liberal-democratic institutions. The other directly imperialist function of a fleet in Tellkampf's speech had more to do with commerce, as he observed that a strong naval presence made it easier to secure favorable trading contracts, as the United States had been able to do in China.[7]

In general during the fleet debate, it was trade and national prestige rather than colonization or settlement that provided the areas of strongest rhetorical consensus; on the whole, this was still an informal type of imperialism. Beyond that, it was, of course, the matter of national defense and the immediate defeat of the minor naval power Denmark in the on-going war over the Duchies of Schleswig and Holstein that figured as the prime concern. Some attention was already given to Great Britain as a potential opponent (hence the desire to learn from the United States about how to compete with the British upon the seas), but most delegates followed the line of the Naval Committee in pushing such plans into a later stage of naval development, and concentrating upon smaller ships rather than ships of the line in the nearer future.

Similarly, in the debate of March 1849 over the proposed law to regulate emigration, the matter of colonies and imperialist rhetoric generally came up rather less than one might imagine given the portrayal of the Frankfurt

Parliament in the literature. The Economics Committee, in charge of drafting the law in this instance, instead emphasized that "the question of colonization" would have to wait for another occasion, and that even the issue of how to support emigrants in their new lands would be excluded from the provisions of the present law. The committee also made it clear that, while they had no intention of attempting to restrict emigration to the Americas, they in theory found it preferable that the wave of *Auswanderung* should travel east and southeast rather than overseas. Until such time as migration could be conscientiously promoted in that direction, however, they simply had to do what they could to cope with the existing problem, namely, improving the lot of those seeking passage across the Atlantic. The committee report did claim that they hoped to bolster the feeling of German nationality among emigrants as a means of maintaining connections with them in future, and profiting from it. Their primary concern was therefore to ensure

> that the powers which are subtracted from the fatherland through it [emigration] are not entirely lost but rather even abroad redound to its benefit, if only indirectly, all the more so as Germany does not possess its own colonies, and therefore preferentially has to concern itself with strengthening and extending its overseas relations and connections as much as possible.[8]

Other accounts of early German imperialism do acknowledge that demands and desires sometimes stopped short of full legal colonization, instead positing autonomous or semi-autonomous areas of contiguous, consciously and nationally German settlement with continued ties to the homeland.[9] The kind of connections envisioned in the Frankfurt committee report, however, seem to fall short even of such a notion of Ersatz-colonies.

Several speakers criticized the lack of provision for colonization in the draft of the *Auswanderungsgesetz*, but primarily with an eye to the East. The Jewish-born Johann Jacob Herz of Vienna, for example, referred to migration along the Danube as "the highest task of German culture," and did not in any case think it likely that the German element in North America would have much chance of influence in face of the predominant English-speaking population there. In this emphasis on southeastern migration, Herz was joined by the Freiburg professor and Catholic spokesman Franz Buß, who was also noted for his related concern with the "Social Question" and pauperism.[10] Even the Gymnasium professor Friedrich Schulz of Weilburg, often rightly cited as among the principal agitators for colonial expansion both in the period generally and at the *Paulskirche*, while still raising the possibility of active German settlements in the United States and even of a German possession in western North America, made it equally clear that the preferred solution was colonization in southeastern Europe. His speech in this debate produced the oft-quoted line, "There on our borders is our

Texas, our Mexico." For that reason, Schulz wanted the new Reich Emigration Office to work with the Austrian government to establish "a regulated colonization system for the lands of the Danube." "The old German oak," Schulz thought, "is still putting forth fresh branches and leaves." The implication of such organicist imagery here clearly seemed to be that planting new German trees elsewhere in the world was less necessary. Moreover, though adverting to the possibility of settlements or colonies of some kind in North America, even Schulz expected a considerable degree of assimilation among German immigrants in America, short of completely forgetting their homeland and mother tongue. In this, he shared the attitudes of the Prussian Party leaders Heinrich von Gagern and Friedrich Dahlmann, Gagern (a strong proponent of eastward migration) having told his father in a letter of 1844 that German emigrants to areas where there was already a "dominant people" should go ahead and "incorporate," rather than form a "Volk im Volke" or "nation within a nation."[11]

Under-State Secretary Johannes Fallati, a member of the Economics Committee and professor of political science, similarly supported the possibility of eastward migration, pointing to feelers in that direction already made by the Reich Ministry, and to a petition from a Wallachian German that had come into his possession inviting the same. When the leader of the Austrian party, Anton von Schmerling, took up the notion of encouraging southeastern emigration with the Provisional Central Power in January 1849, Fallati expressed the government's reservations, citing the need to ensure protection of basic rights (including linguistic rights) for settlers in Hungary or farther east.[12] But this was a question of provisions rather than principle. Nearly all sides in Frankfurt looked eastward in their desire for power, prestige and an outlet for excess population.

In terms of colonization, then, overseas possessions really did not feature prominently even in the emigration debate, very much taking a back seat to the prospect of German eastward expansion (hence more like the contemporary American example of Manifest Destiny and westward expansion than like Kaiser Wilhelm's later "place in the sun"). Imperialism and *Weltpolitik* tended much more to mean the assertion of German power overseas in the interests of putting Germany on an equal footing with other large nations, of maintaining national sentiment among emigrants and of enhancing trading opportunities abroad, both in areas where Germans had settled and in areas where they had not. As the Bremen merchant and Economics Committee rapporteur Carl Gevekoht emphasized in his final summation before voting on the draft emigration bill, the law was important not just for the settlers themselves, but also politically, in allowing the new Germany to strengthen "national feeling" and "like other Great Powers to secure and maintain nationhood."[13]

Or, looked at another way, imperialist desires and visions of a German *Weltpolitik* concentrated primarily upon the idea of consolidating a Central and Eastern European German hegemonic realm, or *Mitteleuropa*, as described in Günther Wollstein's fine work *Das Grossdeutschland der Paulskirche*, or in my own study of the nationalist thought-world of the Frankfurt Parliament.[14] It was this *Mitteleuropa* that rested at the heart of both Little German and Greater German plans for the future shape of Germany, and for the establishment of a new German Reich, or Empire (that is, of those who preferred a Prussia-focused Germany, and those who desired the inclusion of the Austrian Habsburg possessions). For this reason, it is no surprise to find that most mentions of German colonization and expansion occurred not in the handling of the fleet or emigration questions, but rather in the lengthy and hard-fought constitutional debates about the relationship of the new German state to Austria and about the nature of the future German head of state (intended by most delegates to be a German Kaiser at the head of a German Reich—the disagreement centered around the issue of whether that Kaiser would be Prussian or Austrian, Catholic or Protestant). The grandiose visions of a "Reich of 70 Millions" that would incorporate all of the Habsburg Empire and more, propounded by the Bavarian Johann Sepp, the Bohemian Count Friedrich Deym, and the Viennese Karl Moering, never had a very large following, but the ideas of Prussian-Party leaders such as the Assembly President, Heinrich von Gagern of Hessen, or the Prussian historian Johann Gustav Droysen, or of Greater Germany adherents such as the Austrian Schmerling or the Badenese Carl Theodor Welcker, were in the present context not very different. It may suffice here to quote Gagern's famous tag about the "mission" of the German Volk, "to incorporate those peoples who, along the Danube, have neither the calling nor the claim to independence, like satellites in our planetary system." Or one could add the example of the Darmstadt attorney Wilhelm Schulz, who, from his Greater German democratic perspective, proclaimed that he would accept a Prussian hereditary emperor only on condition of an immediate declaration of war that would carry the borders of Germany to the shores of the Black Sea.[15]

Giving consideration to notions of race in the Frankfurt debates might seem even more out of place than discussing the role of imperialism and colonialism, particularly if the foregoing part of this essay is correct in downplaying the prominence of demands for overseas colonization. Race in the 1840s, however, was a much more flexible concept or category than is usually recognized. Various typologies of three or four or five racial groups certainly already existed, in which the differences between Caucasians, Asians, Africans and so on were given priority; but there were other schemes available that allowed for much finer differentiations, even within these larger-scale groupings. For present purposes, the significant point is that notions of race were also applied within Europe, above all in referring to the Romance, Germanic, and Slavic groupings (to the extent that Romance and Germanic peoples were often lumped together, the difference between Teutonic and Slavic became all the more fundamental). And as with notions of race in our own times, racial conceptions then also carried with them a raft of stereotypes and value judgments, typically favorable toward one's own group, and derogatory toward others.

In this case, Slavic peoples were acknowledged to possess some noteworthy talents and creativity, but on the whole they were deemed lacking in comparison to Western Europeans of Germanic descent, less well adapted to the needs of progressive modern life in building states and cities and industry. As such, they were thought to be fair game for assimilation into the progressive, and expanding, German cultural realm. Ultimately, attitudes toward Slavic-speaking nationalities brought together the worst of both worlds and sowed the seeds of potential ethnic—or racial—conflict. Germans tended to denigrate the Slavs, but at the same time still feared them, given their numbers, their connection to the powerful Russian empire, and also a certain alleged barbarism. The Young Hegelian Wilhelm Jordan was perhaps the most extreme exponent of such views, and has certainly been the most quoted (above all in his infamous Poland Speech of 24 July 1848), but he was by no means alone in them. Even the normally quite cosmopolitan leftist Arnold Ruge warned against "unleashing upon us the hatred of the entire Slavic element, of this monstrous family of peoples."[16] Germans, and indeed other Europeans at the time, tended to cast their political thinking not just in national categories, but also in transnational or proto-racial ones: Romance and Teutonic, Pan-German and Pan-Slavic. Ethnic affinity and international relations were typically thought to shape one another, in ways that offered both threats and opportunities. The most famous instance of such thinking at the *Paulskirche* was probably the "Völkerlager" or "ethnic camps" speech of Karl Moering, in which he proposed a grand Germanic alliance to counterbalance the aggregate weight of numbers among the Romance and Slavic peoples, an alliance extending to Britain and the United States. But in doing so, Moering was merely running further with a widespread idea.[17]

Such racialist rhetoric appeared primarily in those contexts where there was real ethnic conflict during the Revolution, above all in the debates relating to Slavic-speaking peoples: about the Prussian Duchy of Poznania, where fighting broke out between Germans and Poles, but also in those about the situation in Bohemia, and particularly in Prague, where German nationalists had come up against Czech nationalists who preferred to stay within a federal Austrian monarchy rather than cooperate with a new Frankfurt-centered German nation-state. Despite the war with Denmark, the Danes were still considered a "brother-people" with the Germans, and the conflict there seemed somehow unnatural, destined to end with a return to Teutonic cooperation at some point in the future. As the Schleswig activist and moderate liberal leader Georg Beseler observed in the border debates of October, "I have always regretted the struggle between the Danes and the Duchies, because I saw here in enmity Germanic peoples who have a common enemy, against whom they should stand together in solidarity."[18]

More disturbingly, the invocation of race was already bound up with thoughts of genocide and ethnic cleansing (surprisingly early, given the usual understanding of the subject in the literature on ethnic cleansing). In the treatment of the Czech question, for example, both Arnold Ruge and the democrat Jakob Venedey actually used the term *Raçenkrieg* (race-war) to describe the potential for conflict there, while the Austrian delegates Carl Giskra, Ernst Schilling, and Johann Berger used the more frequently encountered formulation of a "national battle of extermination," or *Vertilgungskampf*.[19] Regarding the situation in Poland, Wilhelm Jordan predicted a "life and death struggle" of Germans versus Poles and Russians, while two local Poznanian delegates referred respectively to the "real battle of annihilation against Germans" and the "most frightful war of extermination against Germans" undertaken in 1848 by the Poles in Poznania. It should be noted here as well that the only Polish representative from Poznania in the Assembly, the Catholic cleric and professor Jan Janiszewski, for his part asked if the Germans intended conducting a full-scale "war of annihilation" against Poles.[20]

It cannot be stressed enough that these thoughts of genocide applied to fears of what the other side might do, not to the desirability of such an approach as a matter of policy on one's own part. There is still a wide gulf between these ideas and those of later periods where such gruesome fantasies were actively promoted. Yet, the mere fact that notions of colonial expansion, pejorative racial difference, population-changing or -eradicating ethnic conflict, and German national identity were all brought together in such close juxtaposition still seems both troubling and significant.

In the context of racist discourse more generally, it is well to consider Winfried Speitkamp's observation that a shift in terminology occurred in the manner of referring to African peoples, with travelers from the 1840s and even as late as the 1870s still tending to use terms like "states," "kingdoms" and *Nationen*, while later on, one increasingly heard only of *Stämme* or "tribes" in need of education (if thought to be capable of improvement) or of control (if thought incapable of it). My own work on perceptions and conceptions of racial difference in the first half of the nineteenth century suggests that, while pejorative racial stereotypes were certainly already in place for the major non-Caucasian groups, racial discourse also typically still emphasized common humanity and the potential for improvement; it was indeed later in the century that a shift seems to have occurred, to a more biologically determinist view of racial difference as something that could not be changed.[21] Clearly, however, even in the intellectual constellation before 1850, notions of white, or Germanic, supremacy still shaped German nationalist views of the world, and of Europe itself, with the idea of a German assimilatory drive to the East that would bring civilization and progress to the Slavic peoples. The whole project of a German-dominated *Mitteleuropa* was in that sense once again an imperialist venture, if one that envisioned the expansion of empire and power into adjacent areas of the Eurasian landmass rather than overseas.

At this point, I hope we have come full circle in the discussion, having shown that while German imperialism and an associated language of race and genocide did play an important role in 1848, they did so in a rather different context than in 1884 and thereafter. It was not Africa, Asia, or even the Americas that was the prime goal of imperialist aspirations, and it was not Africans, Asians, or Native Americans who featured most prominently in the racist discourse. Rather, these ideas were in both cases applied to the Slavic-settled lands of Eastern and Southeastern Europe. This does, however, raise two important issues. First, it begs the question of ideological continuity between 1848 and later racist, imperialist, and colonialist movements and thinking. Did later German imperialists reflect back upon the ideas of continental imperialism and anti-Slavic racial thinking when they were devising plans for overseas colonial expansion three decades further on, or were they more influenced by the imperialist and racist models of discourse afforded by other contemporary nations? And second, to the extent that the study of German imperialism has since 1945 always been bedeviled by the added complication of having to account for the specific nature of Nazi imperialism during World War Two, the conclusions presented here also bear thinking about in that regard. In as far as the German colonial experience may have helped shape German mentalities in the twentieth century and the experience of war in Eastern Europe, it may also be the case that the patterns of thought acted upon there still bore some affinity with those first explored at the *Paulskirche* in 1848, in an imperial venture which, while open to the possibility of overseas expansion, was first and foremost directed to the East and to the struggle for *Lebensraum* between supposed Germanic and Slavic racial groups (as well as embedding another racist-inspired conflict against European Jewry). In general, I tend not to read too much of the Frankfurt experience of 1848 into the later history of radical conservative nationalism and National Socialism, preferring instead to emphasize the more open-minded, liberal, and tolerant dimension of mid-century German nationalism (a tolerance which was certainly applied to German Jews, and to some extent to Slavic minorities), as well as the more open-ended nature of historical development generally. Much would have to change to transform the rather fearful racialist and imperialist rhetoric of 1848 into the megalomaniacal policy initiatives of racial resettlement and racial cleansing during World War Two. But the question of non-teleological continuities still remains.

The conclusions presented here also need not automatically translate into support for the thesis of Woodruff Smith, according to which Nazi imperialism drew upon two separate ideological traditions of German imperialism, one, "economic imperialism," pointing toward overseas economic expansion and liberal *Weltpolitik*, and the other, "migrationist colonialism," pointing toward the radical conservative ideology of *Lebensraum*, with its emphasis on settlement colonies, including overseas, but above all in Eastern Europe. Both directions seem implicated in the imperialist thinking of the Frankfurt parliamentarians, and the distinction therefore seems problematic.[22] Mid-century imperialism as much as anything seems characterized by an opportunistic flexibility of power-political and imperial goals, or indeed those of informal imperialism of a Gallagher and Robinson sort. The Frankfurt experience does, however, at least suggest the importance of making the analytical distinction between the different types and directions of imperialism and colonialism when one is attempting to account for the history, or the pre-history, of colonialist imperialism, as well as of racial thinking and genocide, in nineteenth- and twentieth-century Germany.

## NOTES

1. Hermann Hiery, "Der Kaiser, das Reich und der Kolonialismus. Anmerkungen zur Entstehung des deutschen Imperialismus im 19. Jahrhundert," <http:// www.uni-bayreuth.de/departments/neueste/Imperium-Beitrag-Hiery.htm> [accessed 26 June 2006]; Hans Fenske, "Imperialistische Tendenzen in Deutschland vor 1866. Auswanderung, überseeische Bestrebungen, Weltmachtträume," *Historisches Jahrbuch*, 97–98 (1978), 336–83 (p. 382); and Fenske, "Ungeduldige Zuschauer. Die Deutschen und die europäische Expansion 1815–1880," in *Imperialistische Kontinuität und nationale Ungeduld im 19. Jahrhundert*, ed. by Wolfgang Reinhard (Frankfurt/M.: Fischer, 1991), pp. 87–123, 136–40 (p. 122). Cf. Frank Lorenz Müller, "Imperialist Ambitions in *Vormärz* and Revolutionary Germany: The Agitation for German Settlement Colonies Overseas, 1840–1849," *German History*, 17.3 (1999), 346–68, which also makes strong claims for the breadth and depth of colonialist imperialism in this earlier period, and for its relationship to later Wilhelmine imperialism.
2. Hiery, "Der Kaiser," p. 2.
3. The term "Imperium" already carried with it connotations of size and expansionism in Roman and medieval times, not just of acknowledging no higher sovereign than God: see "Imperialismus," in *Geschichtliche Grundbegriffe*, ed. by Reinhart Koselleck et al., 8 vols (Stuttgart: Klett, 1972–97), vol. 3, pp. 171–236, section by Jörg Fisch, pp. 171–175 (pp. 172, 175).
4. Fenske, "Ungeduldige Zuschauer," p. 88f.; cf. Fenske, "Imperialistische Tendenzen," pp. 366, 377f.
5. Woodruff D. Smith, *The Ideological Origins of Nazi Imperialism* (New York: Oxford University Press, 1986), p. 24 ("extensive debates") and p. 26 ("violent and multifaceted formal imperialism"); Winfried Speitkamp, *Deutsche Kolonialgeschichte* (Stuttgart: Reclam, 2005), p. 17.
6. Franz Wigard, *Stenographische Berichte über die Verhandlungen der deutschen konstituierenden Nationalversammlung zu Frankfurt a. M.*, 9 vols (Frankfurt/M.: Sauerländer, 1848–9), vol. 1, pp. 251–3, quotation p. 251 (hereafter as StB, with volume and page numbers).
7. StB 1: 309; for the entire debate on that day, StB 1: 305–19.
8. StB 8: 5716.
9. Fenske, "Ungeduldige Zuschauer," p. 94f.; Fenske "Imperialistische Tendenzen," pp. 346, 353f.; Smith, *The Ideological Origins*, p. 24. Müller tends, on the other hand, to conflate the various levels of discussion of colonization

and emigration, and thus overestimates efforts to establish independent colonies overseas.

10. StB 8: 5722f. for Herz, 5718–20 for Buß.
11. StB 8: 5720–2 for Schulz; "oak" and "Colonisationssystem" at 5722; 5721 for the possibility of settlements in North America. On Gagern, see *Deutscher Liberalismus im Vormärz. Heinrich von Gagern: Briefe und Reden 1815–1848*, ed. by Paul Wentzcke and Wolfgang Klötzer (Göttingen: Musterschmidt, 1959), p. 278 (18 August 1844); for Dahlmann, *Verhandlungen der Germanisten zu Lübeck am 27., 28. und 30. September 1847* (Lübeck: Boldemann, 1848), p. 47.
12. StB 8: 5723–6 for Fallati's intervention in the debate; for the petition and the proposal to establish consulates in the Romanian principalities, see *Die Protokolle des Volkswirtschaftlichen Ausschusses der deutschen Nationalversammlung 1848/49*, ed. by Werner Conze and Wolfgang Zorn (Boppard am Rhein: Boldt, 1992), pp. 458–60. On Schmerling, see Hans Fenske, "Die Deutsche Auswanderung in der Mitte des 19. Jahrhunderts—Öffentliche Meinung und amtliche Politik," in *Preussentum und Liberalismus. Aufsätze zur preussischen und deutschen Geschichte des 19. und 20. Jahrhunderts*, ed. by Hermann Hiery (Dettelbach: Röhl, 2002), pp. 415–28 (p. 421f.).
13. StB 8: 5726.
14. Günter Wollstein, *Das "Grossdeutschland" der Paulskirche. Nationale Ziele in der bürgerlichen Revolution 1848/49* (Düsseldorf: Droste, 1977); Brian E. Vick, *Defining Germany: The 1848 Frankfurt Parliamentarians and National Identity* (Cambridge, MA: Harvard University Press, 2002).
15. StB 4: 2898 for Gagern; 8: 5834 for Wilhelm Schulz.
16. StB 2: 1145–8 for Jordan; 1187 for Ruge.
17. StB 2: 1113f. for Moering.
18. StB 4: 2759. Cf. Vick, *Defining Germany*, pp. 193–5, and Wollstein, *Grossdeutschland*, p. 319f.; "Brudervolk" is a term used by Ernst Moritz Arndt, from a speech of 14 September on the Malmö armistice with Denmark: StB 3: 2050.
19. StB 1: 419 for Venedey, Berger and Schilling, and StB 1: 671 for Ruge and Giskra. Venedey and Ruge both still hoped to prevent such a conflict, and Venedey notably also thought it would be a "Bürgerkrieg" or "civil war" as well as a "Rassenkrieg," suggesting both the closeness and the distance of Czechs and Germans, depending on how one looked at it.
20. StB 2: 1137f. for Adolph Goeden ("real battle of annihilation") and 2: 1170 for Samuel Kerst ("war of extermination"); 2: 1145 for Jordan; 2: 1169 for Janiszewski ("Vernichtungskampf"). Referring generally to the situation in Southeastern Europe, the historian Droysen in private correspondence harbored expectations of a healthy *Rassenkrieg* between Germans and Russians along the Danube: see *Johann Gustav Droysen. Briefwechsel*, ed. by Rudolf Hübner, 2 vols (Stuttgart: Deutsche Verlags-Anstalt, 1924), vol. 1, pp. 496 (December 16 1848) and 529 (March 15 1849).
21. On changing terminology and attitudes regarding race, see Speitkamp, *Deutsche Kolonialgeschichte*, p. 16; Vick, *Defining Germany*, pp. 33–9, 230f. n. 16; and Brian Vick, "Arndt and German Ideas of Race: Between Kant and Social Darwinism," in *Ernst Moritz Arndt (1769–1860): Deutscher Nationalismus—Europa—Transatlantische Perspektiven*, ed. by Walter Erhart and Arne Koch (Tübingen: Niemeyer, 2007), pp. 65–76. This last piece situates Arndt's racial views in wider contexts of German racial thought. Cf. also H. Glenn Penny, *Objects of Culture: Ethnology and Ethnographic Museums in Imperial Germany* (Chapel Hill: University North Carolina Press, 2002).

22. Smith, *The Ideological Origins*, pp. 18–20, and passim. Müller, "Imperialist Ambitions," p. 348, associates the imperialism of Forty-Eighter liberals with the "migrationist colonialism" strand.

# 2 Time, Identity and Colonialism in German Travel Writing on Africa, 1848–1914

*Tracey Reimann-Dawe*

This chapter argues that cross-cultural encounter between Germans and Africans in late nineteenth-century travel narratives is characterized by a dialectical combination of impulses: first, an interest in alternative regions of human experience and appreciation of cultural heterogeneity, and, second, expansionist aspirations fueled by growing German nationalism and inter-European rivalry. As we shall see, the incorporation of these contradictory tendencies in travel writing reflects and influences not only the authors' understanding of their own identity, but also, on a wider scale, Germany's evolving national identity and the nature of German colonial experience. For the narratives were written during a period of extensive internal political turmoil, which saw the unification of the German Reich in 1871 and its emergence as a colonial power in Africa in 1884. The travel narratives therefore not only document events in German colonial history, but they also tell the story of changes in German national self-understanding as it evolved in the repeated encounter with the "dark" continent.

The travel narratives are part of a generation of macrotext which documents German academic explorers' passage through Africa on scientific expeditions of discovery. The Prussian geographer Heinrich Barth's first German-led African expedition in 1848 sparked a wave of German expeditions to the African continent and their subsequent publication in narrative form. This study focuses on three characteristic works from this body of material which epitomize developments in Germanic national self-understanding. Gerhard Rohlfs's *Quer durch Afrika* and Gustav Nachtigal's *Sahara und Sudan* exemplify concepts of identity pre-1871.[1] Leo Frobenius's *Und Afrika sprach*, in contrast, highlights changing notions of national identity after German unification and during the colonial period.[2] The travel narratives have often been misconstrued as mere scientific reports, devoid of literary substance and critical merit. They are in reality, however, a mélange of scientific data, adventure novel, autobiography and poetics which documents German–African encounter throughout a turbulent political era.

Let us begin chronologically with Rohlfs's narrative account of his journey from Tripoli through the Sahara to Lagos, undertaken from 1865 to 1867. Considering himself representative of the latest developments in Western knowledge and its attendant technological achievements, Rohlfs epitomizes the early, "scientific" explorer.[3] In the absence of an established national identity, "scientific discovery" united German explorers during their passage through Africa pre-1871. German pluralist ideologies which influenced scientific discourse of the era also affected the reception and definition of culture and alterity and consequently the scientific character of African exploration.[4] But the most notable cultural reference and expression of the explorers' occidental-Germanic identity when in Africa was their adherence to a Western, 'scientized' concept of rational, measurable, linear time.[5] For the early explorers employed the Western time-set more than any other feature both to structure their travel narratives and to distinguish themselves from the African "Other." This time-set reflected the revolutionary processes of industrialization, mechanization and capitalism;[6] and those processes were themselves manifested in the greatest feat of technological achievement, the railway.[7] As a tool of industrialization, the railway, with its linearity, reliance on speed and adherence to standardized, measurable time, introduced new values to nineteenth-century society.[8] As Hans Maier states in *Die christliche Zeitrechnung*, technology and its link to rational, measurable time increasingly became the mediating force between humankind and nature, leading to a belief in man's capacity for ever-greater control of his surroundings.[9] The pace of life accelerated as the minimum size of measurable time-units decreased and the importance attached to each one grew. Time in Western society thus became a valuable, measurable commodity which could be gained, lost or wasted.

Linear, measurable time was, moreover, not only synonymous with technological advancement: a linear-historicist mind-set also dominated theories of racial, historical and cultural development evident in the earlier travel narratives.[10] Consequently, the Western time-set presented a prime feature of cultural reference for explorers during the pre-unification era, for it signified the major elements of the nineteenth-century Western mind-set: a belief in scientific rationalism, technological advancement and linear progress.

As the following excerpt demonstrates, the Western time-set is a continual feature both of Rohlfs's expedition and of the narrative process in his text. During the early stages of his journey, Rohlfs spends six weeks in the town of Rhadames. Dissatisfied with this interruption of his speedy and dynamic passage, Rohlfs finally receives word that he can continue his journey with a Tuareg chief called Si-Othman and his caravan. However, Rohlfs's hopes are dashed when the caravan fails to arrive:

> It would have been a sheer waste of time to remain in Rhadames any longer, as Si-Othman's arrival from Algiers would have meant waiting several months at least. He had, according to our definition, broken his

promise. He, of course, would take the whole thing more lightly, for, like all of his countrymen, he had no concept of the value of time.[11]

Assuming a shared temporal ideology with his readers, Rohlfs employs temporal concepts to highlight the importance of time to his expedition and to consolidate his believed superiority over the African "Other." Time-wasting is the ultimate sin, since pedantic time-keeping is as much a psychological instrument of orientation in a seemingly unchanging desert landscape as an instrument of navigation. Western, linear clock-time enables the measurement of both distance covered and progress made, becoming a key to survival in unknown territories. Like all explorers, Rohlfs employs native guides, yet they are in fact portrayed as hindrances, for, like Si-Othman, they apparently have no concept of the value of time. Rohlfs equates this with intellectual inferiority, for he emphasizes that these "Others" are not merely unwilling, but are also apparently incapable of understanding the concept. Thus Rohlfs also categorizes Si-Othman and his people as culturally inferior, for he measures levels of cultural advancement temporally on a Hegelian, linear-historicist scale.[12] Rohlfs's a priori confidence places his own culture at the top of this scale as the most advanced. Other cultures can be equated to a past era of Western history and consequently represent an inferior level of cultural development.

Rohlfs's movement through African terrain and his sojourn within it are similarly defined by opposing temporal ideologies. During periods of transit, his narrative reinforces the imagery of traversal with an unhindered, mechanical precision of style. Transforming Africa into a comprehensible set of time-units, Rohlfs intentionally demystifies the "dark continent," removing any sense of the exotic: "After climbing a ridge of hills, we came to the Dendal-Galaima valley at two o'clock, the Meschru valley at four o'clock . . . and Meschru well at six o' clock."[13] The favoring of a pared-down narrative syntax of simple verbs and proper nouns, with little supplementary description or expression of personal sentiment, stresses the factual nature of the experience. The rhythmic repetition of the preposition "at" (*um*) suggests the regulated, mechanical consumption of terrain, while the meticulous notation of hours creates and maintains an occidental sense of order. Effective time-keeping here becomes equated with superior control over foreign terrain. The narrative structuring is manipulated to reflect this level of control.

Periods of extended sojourn, however, present a striking contrast. Undertaken in populated areas, periods of residence are significantly devoid of references to time and date—these examples of pre-structured African space become timeless voids. As time does not seem to pass in these places, they become sites of darkness, disorientation and therefore danger. The "labyrinth" of narrow, dark and winding streets in the town of Kuka creates an eerie sense of foreboding—who knows what dangers lurk in the unquantifiable darkness?[14] Rohlfs attempts to counteract this potential threat by maintaining strict daily routines: he rises every day at seven, studies Barth's works, receives visitors till midday and takes walks in the afternoons. This suggests that there is no pre-existing African temporal structure with which he could measure the cumulative passage of time. By acting in such a way, however, Rohlfs unintentionally demonstrates the extent to which his purely mathematical understanding of time has alienated him from other possible means of structuring it.

As Rohlfs's sense of self is so irretrievably linked to a linear-progressive time-set, any evidence that this time-set may not be superior and authoritative leaves him particularly vulnerable. He cannot voluntarily open himself to alternative concepts for fear of proving the fallibility of the very mindset on which his believed superiority rests. Yet, in spite of his rigid timekeeping, Rohlfs is none the less overcome by an unavoidable experience of alterity, with dramatic results. After traversing North Africa disguised as a Muslim Arab, Rohlfs reaches the Sahara desert and perceives it as a place of relief, freedom and familiarity. Finally able to remove his disguise, Rohlfs metamorphoses back to his European, Christian self. However, this symbolic re-imposition of European culture and apparent control on to Africa is quickly marred by an ensuing sand-storm. Rohlfs is utterly powerless, as clouds of whirling dust and sand subject him to temporary blindness. He is consumed by the landscape and plunged into sudden darkness, narrating images of unstoppable submersion with an uncharacteristic intensity and immediacy that appeal to all the senses:

> An eerie closeness shivered through the air, although there was not a trace of wind, but a pitch-black cloud, churning majestically towards us, left no doubt that a hurricane was about to break forth over us. The sun became even redder, the heat even more oppressive, the hot, dry air made it almost impossible to breathe. The specter came rushing towards us . . . Complete darkness enclosed us, the whirling dust reached several hundred feet and darkened the sun like an eclipse.[15]

Although this episode might be read as constructed exoticism, the significant break in the text which the sudden change in narrative style presents strongly suggests that the encounter has had a deeper effect on Rohlfs. Alternative narrative techniques indicate the involuntary counter-penetration of "otherness," for the episode stands in stark contrast to Rohlfs's otherwise barren portrayals of transit. The large number of compounds intensifies the episode's complexity and evocative power. Unable to portray the phenomenon in familiar terms, Rohlfs's text allows the storm, now personified as a "specter," to signal the realms of the supernatural. As the party awaits the approaching hurricane, the desert's alienating silence seems to increase, enhancing the feeling of dread and foreboding, for silence is indicative of lack of movement, disorientation and ultimately death. Loss of direction is the most fearsome of threats, as it would, with great certainty, prove fatal. This fear is combined

with a sense of disbelief as Rohlfs then proceeds to tell us—repeatedly—
that his camels, acting "without command," simultaneously turn away from
the approaching hurricane and crouch down. These symbols of nature, over
which Rohlfs has assumed he has control, suddenly become autonomous.
The images of fire and darkness which follow are on an apocalyptic scale.
The silence is broken by the rush of wind, carrying with it whirling clouds of
sand and dust as the combined forces of terrain and climate seize all power
and control from human influence. Rohlfs can neither prevent nor flee from
the unprecedented strength of this nightmarish occurrence. Rohlfs's scientific
instruments are stripped of all function and power, as he finds himself equal
to his entourage in the face of omnipotent nature.

After the storm has passed, Rohlfs notes that the whole episode—his
brush with death and return to normality—lasted barely more than 20 minutes. During the storm, he was unable to read his watch and keep time, and
therefore had no semblance of control over it and was momentarily stripped
of his pre-existing identity. Unable to enclose alterity in Western temporal
structures, Rohlfs is forced to open himself to the unfamiliar—a change
that is reflected in his particularly uncharacteristic narrative style. The
storm, so it would seem, becomes a threshold experience, induced when the
familiar rhythms of Western time and space are neither definable nor recog-
nizable. Instead, they are replaced by an alternative temporality: the natural
rhythm of the storm. Its cyclical movement—for Rohlfs, synonymous with
stagnation and lack of progress—links alternative temporal consciousness
with non-linearity and absolute difference. Although Rohlfs employs the
Western time-set as a disjunctive device with which to maintain distance
from African alterity, such periods of unavoidable encounter unintentionally expose that time-set's cognitive limits. In spite of his attempts to the
contrary, Rohlfs cannot but narrate qualitatively new experiences.

Let us compare Rohlfs's experiences with those of his successor, Nachtigal. A Prussian physician residing in Tunis, Nachtigal began his expedition in 1869, traveling along the same route as his predecessors, Barth
and Rohlfs, before proceeding eastward through Sudan to arrive at his
final destination, Khartoum, in 1874.[16] Like Rohlfs, Nachtigal initially
encounters Africa with a priori confidence in the authority of his mind-
set and its irretrievable link to linear, progressive time. Yet Nachtigal's
initial desert encounter soon erodes the power of this imported knowledge. As was the case for his predecessor, the episode proves to be a profound and significant moment in his journey. Confronted by the desert's
majesty and awed by the extreme sense of solitude and emphatic silence
surrounding him, Nachtigal falls (so his narrative says) into a dream-like
state during which he symbolically recognizes the constraints of his previous temporal conceptions:

> Images of the past melted into those of the present, my North-German
> home into the African-Mediterranean coast. The mighty Carthage,

Roman Africa, Cyrenaic Empires, Turks and Christians, Negroes and
Vandals, Arabs, Garamantes, Berbers and Ancient Egyptians all tum-
bled through my dreaming mind. I unraveled the varied fates of these
nations and thought back to the time when, sitting on a school bench,
I had often wished to live through these events, no matter how terri-
fying, rather than pedantically force their innumerable dates into my
rebellious memory. The images became gradually unclear and increasingly confused, until at last, just before morning, a deep sleep dissolved
them away.[17]

This dream prepares Nachtigal for his journey by symbolically collapsing
the cultural laws of time and space which govern the preformed interpretation of information. Rejecting them as inappropriate, distorted categories,
his dream instead creates a synthesis of common experience which blurs
the border between self and other. Although separated geographically and
culturally, Nachtigal's German home and Africa are present both equally
and simultaneously in the chaotic, illogical patterns of his imagination and
subconscious. Nachtigal's longing for Africa is a longing for the freedom
denied him by the artificial structures of thought imposed on him since
childhood. His images of childlike innocence and returning to nature are
not associated with inferior knowledge but with unconstrained thought.
In contrast to the widely accepted Western temporal epistemology we saw
in Rohlfs's narrative, Nachtigal revalidates the romantic, individual, subjective dream-experience as an alternative form of consciousness and pre-
empts later modernist explorations. His dream-like state unifies apparent
tensions, creates a synthesis of awareness and marks a new beginning.

The dream-like state is evoked again a short time later. Only four months
into the expedition, Nachtigal's party loses its way while traveling through
the Sahara. Desperation intensifies as water-rations run dangerously low.
Losing the last glimmer of hope, Nachtigal resigns himself to death. He
depicts his near-death experience as a dream-like condition in which the
past and present, home and Africa again merge into one. The threat of
imminent death increases the intensity of this episode. It seems unlikely that
the confused images in Nachtigal's mind will end in a deep, peaceful sleep
as before, for this unfamiliar state of awareness blurs the borders between
waking and unconsciousness. The dream-like state is both illogical and
disorientating, yet, unlike Rohlfs's nightmarish threshold experience, there
is a sense of exhilaration and excitement as Nachtigal is pulled between
the poles of life and death. His intense journey, which requires no physical
movement, overturns the linearity of travel propounded by Rohlfs.

Although brought back to reality shortly afterward with life-saving
water, Nachtigal accepts the dream-like sensation as the only way to experience Africa. The same evening, the "magical" light at dusk invigorates his
imagination, as the gigantic, majestic rock-formations create the "strang-
est" images on the horizon. They draw Nachtigal willingly back into his

new-found form of consciousness—"the most wonderful dreams."[18] In contrast to Rohlfs's dualistic analogies of darkness and mystery with cultural inferiority, Nachtigal's submersion into dream-time produces a sense of enlightenment and understanding. He acknowledges that his pre-existing, Western mind-set cannot master Africa and he gradually accepts alien influences—from this point onward his narrative becomes significantly devoid of references to Western time. Our explorers' encounters with alterity thus reveal an unintended and dialectical reverse-influence of Africa on the German, by disclosing the cognitive limits of their nineteenth-century, Western time-set. Nachtigal's recognition of this fact creates a narrative of exploration and discovery which documents cultural plurality and universal humanity.

Notwithstanding aspects of his writing, Nachtigal went on to play a major role in the German colonial project. On his return from his expedition, Nachtigal's public lectures and involvement with geographical societies won him recognition as an Africa specialist. Reports of French and British intrigues endangering established German trading operations on the Guinea coast prompted requests for official protection of German interests; after much hesitation, Bismarck agreed and entrusted the project to Nachtigal. Greatly weakened by recurring tropical illness, Nachtigal knew that this would be his final mission. Yet, asserting that it was his "duty," he hoisted the German flag through large areas of Togo and Cameroon, winning the race against the British for control of the region.[19] Nachtigal completed his humanistic travel narrative while undertaking this expansionist mission. It is only possible to speculate on these seemingly conflicting aspects, as Nachtigal composed no personal account of his colonial involvement. However, the reference to "duty" does seem to suggest the beginnings of a new sense of German patriotism which was absent from pre-unification works and, as we shall see, becomes increasingly relevant in later travel narratives.

Our final text sheds substantial further light on such developments in German national self-understanding post-1871. As Germany's national identity became increasingly consolidated, the significance of time as a means of self-identification receded, as did its function as a navigational tool. On the other hand, an appreciation of cultural diversity, as seen in Nachtigal's narrative, was far from being dismissed, and remained very much an aspect of German exploration. Acknowledging both "primitive" and complex social forms and characteristics in all cultures, many explorers attempted to identify universal human traits.[20] This history of cultural openness raises the question of why the German Reich embarked on colonial ventures at all: the devastating effects of colonial wars were common knowledge. The established economist and colonial advocate Paul Rohrbach's work *Das deutsche Kolonialwesen* suggests that there was also little real expectation of economic gain from African territories.[21] However, later narratives simultaneously illustrate other significant developments in the nature of African cross-cultural encounters. As European presence in Africa increased throughout the nineteenth century, inter-European rivalries were played out on African soil.[22] The narration of such clashes in the travel narrative highlights the rise of German nationalism as a new factor in German national self-understanding which fueled the German colonial project.

Let us see how our last work illustrates these conflicting aspects of German national identity. Frobenius's ethnographic expedition took him to Nigeria, Cameroon, Sudan and Ethiopia between 1910 and 1912. In contrast to our earlier narratives, Frobenius begins his work by challenging Western preconceptions with a monumental assertion: oral culture is in fact the superior method of preserving history over written documentation. Pointing to the widespread belief that written documentation is to be equated with cultural advancement, and the fact that it is the only method of recording history acknowledged by his own culture, Frobenius maintains that historical awareness was in fact stronger before the existence of the written word.[23] Frobenius continues by stating that writing does not merely distort the representation of historical events, but completely destroys human "Gedächtnisarchive" (memory archives) and consequently the true nature of historical awareness.[24] In a complete negation of Hegelian historicism, Frobenius maintains that historical awareness is carried within the human mind by those closest to their natural environment. Attempts to temporalize cultures on a scale of more or less civilized development merely mask this universal inter-cultural connection, for, as in Africa, folklore, dismissed as primitive, actually led to important archaeological discoveries:

> The traveler to Northern European shores encounters small hills and unevenness of terrain about which naive local inhabitants speak with reverence, just like the peasants around the River Niger speak of theirs . . . In long periods of blissful peace, year after year, hoes furrowed the land and heavy ears of corn swayed upon it. Generation after generation passed over and ignored them. The art of writing came and, in neighboring towns, endless chronicles were written, were printed, decayed and were lost. Meanwhile, ivy cracked and destroyed written inscriptions engraved into headstones in the church graveyard. But for almost two thousand years, the knowledge remained in peoples' minds.[25]

The cyclical corn harvest preserves the subject of local folklore; unlike Rohlfs's association of cyclical temporality with stagnation and lack of progress, this folklore becomes increasingly ingrained into local memory and culture with each passing year and each repetition. Nature protects and nurtures myth while modifying and even destroying written inscriptions. Frobenius's ivy strangles and silences engraved words, just as the voice of the "African Other" has been silenced in Western European narrative. Frobenius takes Nachtigal's rejection of history one step further and returns to Europe with a revalorized image of African culture.

Yet Frobenius's work also continues a narrative of Anglo–German rivalry which, despite his anti-colonial sentiment, parallels developments in German nineteenth-century pro-colonial discourse.[26] Frobenius's introduction, while preparing the reader for the positive image of African culture to come, simultaneously begins his increasingly negative portrayal of the British. Stating that the British should not transfer their inter-European rivalries on to Europeans in Africa, and hinting at coming conflicts, Frobenius names national pride and self-assurance as the prime causes of British aggression. These British attributes are "intensively inculcated"—they have been learned and perfected over time.[27] Germany, a comparatively "new" nation, cannot possibly have reached a comparable level of national self-understanding and consequently is not prepared to defend its national interests at all costs. However, Frobenius claims moral superiority over the British, citing science pursued for the greater good of humankind as the German priority. Although Germany had eventually caught up with its industrialized neighbors, a narrative of national inferiority toward other European nation-states—Britain in particular—was well established in German literature and discourse.[28] Despite claims of moral and intellectual superiority, this narrative of national inferiority contained an underlying longing for a strong national self-belief like that of the British, for this was regarded as the key to international success.[29] As we shall see, Frobenius's interactions with the British expose this conflict.

The cause of Frobenius's negativity toward the British soon becomes clear. Residing in the British administrative center of Ibadan in Nigeria, Frobenius has plans to travel to the holy city of Ife, which are continually— and, as he suggests, deliberately—sabotaged by British officials. Rumors abound that the German party's archaeological successes irritate the British authorities, who wish to claim academic esteem for their own nation.[30] Finally receiving permission to travel, Frobenius discovers important artifacts in a ruined temple on the outskirts of Ife. He attributes his find to "German thoroughness."[31] He notes that the British had also examined the ruins, yet missed the most important pieces; not only are the British portrayed as underhand, but they are also apparently inferior scientists. Elated by his find, Frobenius and his expedition leave the city, only to be stopped en route by British officials, arrested, imprisoned and put on trial for stealing archaeological remains.

Frobenius initially narrates the proceedings with a note of sarcasm, expecting this to be another mere time-consuming ruse to sabotage his success—he insists that all artifacts were obtained legally. Yet events take a more sinister turn as the trial and, consequently, the German party's incarceration last several weeks. Frobenius states that he and his colleagues were neither cross-examined nor permitted to speak during the trial. Partridge, the British official heading the proceedings, suddenly metamorphoses from a laughable caricature of the officious bureaucrat into a real threat, as Frobenius realizes he is both physically and judicially impotent. In fact, Partridge becomes the embodiment of the stereotypical despotic African potentate, as portrayed by numerous earlier explorers.[32] Partridge combines the utmost power and authority in one figure, and appears devoid of such qualities as morality, reason and wisdom. Instead, the British representative embodies negative characteristics generally reserved for "primitive" cultures in Western discourse.[33] Partridge's dishonesty and underhandedness are in evidence long after the episode. Frobenius notes that all the artifacts confiscated from his party and supposedly returned to the locals subsequently appear on display in the British Museum. Reinforcing his earlier comments about British national self-interest, Frobenius maintains that Partridge's "misguided national sentiments" were a deliberate attempt to sabotage German interests.[34] When narrating incidents that took place immediately after the trial, Frobenius creates a deliberate contrast with the British, emphasizing character traits such as loyalty, intellect, friendship and trust as inherently German.[35]

Frobenius's obviously biased account cannot be taken as fact, yet it highlights a development in German national self-understanding—a sense of German nationalism which is entirely absent in earlier pre-unification travel narratives. Although Frobenius presents a remarkable picture of African cultural diversity and openly criticizes colonial expansion, his portrayal of the British paradoxically calls for an aggressive defense of German national interests—in the process echoing social-Darwinist justifications for colonial expansion into African territories. Thus, the travel narratives describe phases in Germanic national self-understanding which move from Rohlfs's fragile and fragmented notion of belonging based on scientific and cultural affiliation to Nachtigal's openly pluralist, humanistic conception, and culminate in Frobenius's revalorization of non-Western cultures, negation of Western cultural superiority, yet distinctly nationalist self-understanding. Although German–African encounter resulted in positive images of African culture, Anglo–German encounter in Africa proved to be more significant. In a reversal of roles, the British and not the Africans become the "threatening Others," as inter-European rivalries are played out in Africa. Frobenius completed his narrative shortly before the outbreak of World War One. His portrayal of long-standing national inferiority complexes and new-found nationalism not only sheds light on German expansionist motives, but his work also suggests, even pre-empts, the escalation of conflicts on European soil.

## NOTES

1. Gerhard Rohlfs, *Quer durch Afrika: Reise vom Mittelmeer nach dem Tschad-See und zum Golf von Guinea*, 2 vols (Leipzig: Brockhaus, 1874);

Gustav Nachtigal, *Sahara und Sudan: Ergebnisse sechsjähriger Reisen in Afrika*, 3 vols (Berlin: Verlagsgesellschaft M.B.H, 1879–89).

2. Leo Frobenius, *Und Afrika sprach: Bericht über den Verlauf der dritten Reiseperiode der Deutschen Innerafrikanischen Forschungsexpedition in den Jahren 1910–1912*, 3 vols (Berlin, 1912).

3. Although barely qualified, Rohlfs considered himself a scientist by his cultural affiliation.

4. For example, Herder's cultural pluralism, Goethe's cosmopolitanism and Hegel's linear historicism.

5. "Western" refers to areas in the sphere of Western European cultural influence, including the United States.

6. See Germano Pàttaro, "The Christian Conception of Time," in *Cultures and Time*, ed. by Louis Gardet et al. (Paris: Unesco, 1976), pp. 169–97.

7. Wolfgang Schivelbusch, *Die Geschichte der Eisenbahnreise: Zur Industrialisierung von Raum und Zeit im 19. Jahrhundert*, 2nd edn (Frankfurt/M.: Fischer, 2000), p. 16.

8. Ibid., p. 37. The expansion of the railway necessitated the introduction of standardized time. Railway companies, and not governments, were the first to instate standard time to improve inefficiencies in their time-tabling resulting from localized time-zones. As railways extended over national boundaries, the process repeated itself on a larger scale.

9. Hans Maier, *Die christliche Zeitrechnung*, 5th edn (Freiburg/Br.: Herder, 1991), p. 42f.

10. Although the texts discussed all post-date Darwin, the influence of Darwinian theory is not yet evident in the earlier works. These works instead demonstrate pre-Darwinian views of racial, historical and cultural development which are dominated by a linear-historicist mind-set. Heinrich Barth's travel narrative *Reisen und Entdeckungen in Nord- und Central-Afrika in den Jahren 1849 bis 1855: Tagebuch seiner im Auftrag der Britischen Regierung unternommenen Reise*, 5 vols (Gotha: Perthes, 1849–55), is a further, particularly striking example. Darwinian influence does not come to the fore until such later works as Georg Schweinfurth's *Im Herzen von Afrika: Reisen und Entdeckungen im zentralen Äquatorial-Afrika während der Jahre 1868–1871; ein Beitrag zur Entdeckungsgeschichte von Afrika*, 2 vols (Leipzig: Brockhaus, 1874).

11. Rohlfs, *Quer durch Afrika*, vol. 1, p. 81. This and subsequent translated passages are my own.

12. See G.W.F. Hegel, *Lectures on the Philosophy of World History*, trans. by H.B. Nisbet (Cambridge: Cambridge University Press, 1975), pp.148–50.

13. Rohlfs, *Quer durch Afrika*, vol. 1, p. 221.

14. Ibid., vol. 1, p. 338.

15. Ibid., vol. 1, p. 94f.

16. Nachtigal remained unaware of German unification until after his expedition.

17. Nachtigal, *Sahara und Sudan*, vol. 1, p. 12.

18. Ibid., vol. 1, p. 64.

19. Gustav Nachtigal, *Tibesti: Die Erstdurchquerung des Sudan 1869–1874* (Tübingen: Erdmann, 1978), p. 24.

20. This trend parallels developments in German anthropological and ethnographic discourse of the time. See *Worldly Provincialism: German Anthropology in the Age of Empire*, ed. by H. Glenn Penny and M. Bunzl, 4th edn (Ann Arbor: University of Michigan Press, 2006), p. 2.

21. See Paul Rohrbach, *Das deutsche Kolonialwesen* (Leipzig: Gloeckner, 1911), p. 7.

22. Frobenius's travel narrative is characteristic of such developments, which are also evident in works such as Capitän-Lieutenant F. Rust a.D, *Die deutsche Emin Pascha Expedition* (Berlin: Luckhardt, 1890), and Franz Stuhlmann, *Mit Emin Pascha ins Herz von Afrika: Ein Reisebericht mit Beiträgen von Emin Pascha*, 2 vols (Berlin: Reimer, 1894).
23. Frobenius, *Und Afrika sprach*, vol. 1, p. xiii.
24. Ibid., vol. 1, p. 26.
25. Ibid., vol. 1, p. 26f.
26. See Rohrbach, *Das deutsche Kolonialwesen*, p. 11, and Gerhard Rohlfs, *Angra Pequena: Die erste deutsche Kolonie in Afrika* (Bielefeld: Belhagen & Klafing, 1884), p. 5.
27. Frobenius, *Und Afrika sprach*, vol. 1, p. xxii.
28. See, for example, Carl Peters, "Deutsche Kolonialpolitik aus englischer Perspektive," *Die Gegenwart*, 1 (March 1884), p. 229.
29. See Wilhelm Hübbe-Schleiden, *Deutsche Colonisation* (Hamburg: Friederichsen, 1881), p. 3f.
30. Frobenius, *Und Afrika sprach*, vol. 1, p. 67.
31. Ibid., vol. 1, p. 85.
32. See, for example, Franz Stuhlmann's portrayal of the former Ugandan king, in Franz Stuhlmann, *Mit Emin Pascha ins Herz von Afrika*, vol. 1, p. 162.
33. See for example Walter Bagehot's characterization of "primitive races" in Walter Bagehot, *Physics and Politics, or Thoughts on the Application of the Principles of "Natural Selection" and "Inheritance" to Political Society* (London: King, 1872), p. 115f.
34. Frobenius, *Und Afrika sprach*, vol. 1, p. 126.
35. Ibid., vol. 1, p. 128.

# 3   Gray Zones
## On the Inclusion of "Poland" in the Study of German Colonialism

*Kristin Kopp*

During the winter of 1939–40, Heinrich Himmler's secretary, Hanns Johst, traveled with the *Reichsführer* of the SS through Poland and made the following observation:

> The Poles are not a state-building nation. They lack even the most elementary preconditions for it. I drove alongside the Reichsführer-SS up and down that country. A country which has so little feeling for systematic settlement, that is not even up to dealing with the style of a village, has no claim to any sort of independent political status within the European area. *It is a colonial country!*[1]

During World War Two, the National Socialists planned a fundamental reorganization of Eastern European space that would involve the creation of German settlement colonies there. When Germany invaded Poland, it divided the territory it occupied into various administrative units, most significantly the *Wartheland* and the *Generalgouvernement*. Various government institutions produced competing models for the form a settlement project might ultimately take in these territories, but, overall, the plan was to move the Poles out of the western *Wartheland* into the eastern *Generalgouvernement*, to move ethnic Germans (for example, those being brought "home to the Reich" from the Baltic states) into the *Wartheland*, and then subsequently to reintroduce the Slavic population as either an enslaved or a disenfranchised agricultural labor force in a plantation system that, in some versions, was to look more or less like Virginia prior to the American Civil War.[2] The first stages of this plan were carried out, in that hundreds of thousands of Germans were relocated into a space from which over a million ethnic Poles and Jews had been violently evicted. Further steps, however, were prevented by the demands of the war.

This episode has been largely excluded from most narratives of both German colonial history and the history of World War Two, because it was short, truncated, and ultimately eclipsed by events that subsequently took place in the same geographic sphere. Götz Aly has advocated a renewed look at this specific history, going so far as to argue that these forced relocations created a demographic pressure that accelerated into a spiral of violence and resulted in the mass killings of the Polish intellectual, political, and religious elites in addition to the mass killings of Jews.[3] Yet, whether or not we accept Aly's account of these events as aggravating the Holocaust, we must still make sense of the colonial project(s) planned and set into motion in Eastern Europe.[4] Such depictions as Johst's, which presented the region in colonial terms—as chaotic and backward, unable to keep pace with modernity, and requiring external intervention in order to progress—became key components of the rhetoric used to legitimize these plans. In Johst's claim that he was traveling through a "colonial country" lies the invitation to map centuries' worth of European overseas colonial experience on to adjacent space in Eastern Europe, and to structure German–Polish affairs according to conventional expectations of relationships between colonizers and the colonized.

In recent years, scholars of both German colonial history and National Socialism have increasingly returned to Hannah Arendt's interrogation from 1951 of the ways in which these two historical experiences might have been linked.[5] They question whether it is possible—and debate to what extent it is useful—to draw connections between the 1904 mass murder of the Herero and Nama peoples in German South-West Africa, on the one hand, and National Socialist atrocities on the European continent, on the other.[6] There are several ways in which this question is approached: some scholars investigate whether racist ideologies or specific elimination-ist practices deriving from the overseas colonial experience also found expression in National Socialist continental expansionism. In this context, some studies have found continuities in specific governing practices and even in certain responsible individuals that were directly transplanted from Africa to the European continent.[7] Other scholars challenge this "continuity thesis" through close studies of particular institutional practices, and argue that connections found between Nazism and colonialism represent misguided readings of similarities that, upon closer examination, prove to be too superficial to serve as the basis of useful comparison.[8] The stakes in these debates are high, and the arguments accordingly polarized. Are we to understand that colonial-style genocidal warfare in Africa paved the way for the Holocaust? If so, was the mass murder of Jews and Slavs in Eastern Europe a continuation of European colonial settlement practices, and thus in some way analogous to the decimation of Native tribes on the North American continent or of the Aboriginal populations in Australia? The debate surrounding these questions has seemingly reached an impasse, in which one side makes accusations of relativism, while the other attacks the emergence of a version of the *Sonderweg* thesis, the assertion of an inherent German propensity to genocide.[9]

Recently, the work of the historian Frederick Cooper has been introduced into this discussion, and I would like to take the opportunity to clarify the difference in our positions. In his *Colonialism in Question*, from

2005, Cooper warns that contemporary scholarship has extended the category of the colonial too far, and as a result runs the risk of "making colonialism appear everywhere—and hence nowhere."[10] As a scholar working to include the history of German interventions in Eastern Europe within a colonial-studies paradigm, I understand myself to belong to the group at which this admonition is targeted, and I do not accept the implied criticism as valid in this case.

Cooper draws a strong line between what he considers to be the legitimate object of historical research, namely, institutions and institutional policies, and what he excludes, namely, discourse, societal attitudes, ideology, and so on—in a word, "culture."[11] I do not underestimate the importance of studying specific institutions, their structures and histories, but I do take issue with the notion that such studies could possibly tell us all that we need to know about colonial history, much less colonialism as social practice. Despite the extended reflection on (inter-)disciplinarity in the introductory section of *Colonialism in Question*, Cooper none the less seems to lay proprietary claim to the colonial object on behalf of the historical discipline, narrowly defined.

My research on German constructions of Poland as colonial space would seem to offer a corrective to Cooper's categories, while also approaching the question of colonial–National Socialist continuities from a new angle. I have shown that such colonial constructions of Poland had been in prominent cultural and political circulation long before Hanns Johst and Heinrich Himmler made their journey eastward.[12] Indeed, since the mid-nineteenth century, various groups and individuals promoting German eastward expansion had represented Eastern Europe in racial and spatial terms derived from an overarching European colonial idiom. Quite aside from questions regarding the colonial nature of any of the various German interventions in Polish space—institutional or otherwise—the colonial constructions exist, and must be accounted for.

There are two sets of questions I find it important to address in interpreting this finding. First, the discourse must be historically contextualized, for it first appeared at a particular historical juncture, and the intensity of its use was greatest at specific moments and in response to specific socio-political needs. Second, the discourse must be internally analyzed, its distinctive features identified, and the changes it underwent over time addressed. This colonial discourse vis-à-vis Poland was adapted to suit the rhetorical needs of various particular historical, cultural, and political contexts. Hanns Johst could therefore appeal to a rich set of pre-existing representational models to depict the East as colonial space, and it is important to explain which of these he gravitated toward, and why.

Johst's claim that the Poles lacked the ability to generate a modern state on their own (and thus required colonial intervention in order to achieve and maintain this level of civilized development) strongly echoes a very similar assertion made in the best-selling German novel of the nineteenth century, Gustav Freytag's *Soll und Haben* (1855).[13] In the pivotal scene of this text, the protagonist, Anton Wohlfart, travels into Polish lands with his employer on a mission to rescue a convoy of goods from hordes of wild, dark-skinned Polish "natives," who have attacked it. As they travel toward their destination, Wohlfart's employer assesses the nature of the Poles and their ability to form their own state:

> "There is no race more lacking in the prerequisites of social progress and no race more unable to use their capital to achieve civilized development than the Slavic race . . . There, the privileged class claims to represent the people. As if the nobility and their indentured servants could establish a state! They don't have any more right to do so than this flock of sparrows in the trees . . ." "They don't have a middle class," concurred Anton eagerly.
> "That means they don't have any culture." The merchant continued: "it is incredible how incapable they are of generating for themselves the social class that could bring about civilization and progress, and that could unite a heap of scattered farmsteads into a proper state."[14]

Both Wohlfart's employer and Himmler's employee appeal to the same concept of autonomous civilizational development. That they both depict this capacity as absent in their representations of Polish space is indicative of a discursive continuity I have found to have spanned a century of German rhetoric on the East.

Freytag's novel of 1855 is an important starting point, because it is the first literary text in which German colonial intervention in Poland was thematically presented as a contemporary phenomenon. *Soll und Haben* presents a classic tale of European colonization, mobilizing the structuring conventions of racial difference and spatial under-development to do so: Anton Wohlfart travels into Poland as a self-proclaimed German colonist, cultivates a barren piece of land to make it fruitful, protects this developed territory from the attacks of primitive warring natives, and creates the conditions under which future generations of his ethnic cohort can expand and consolidate their hold over the region.

A central tenet of European colonial ideology held that non-European peoples lagged behind European civilization because, due to their intrinsically static nature, they lacked the ability to change and progress on their own. As J. M. Blaut usefully synthesizes it, the belief of the colonizer centered on the notion that European civilization had "some unique historical advantage" that gave "this human community a permanent superiority over all other communities."[15] While this special quality was variously cast in racial, cultural, environmental, or spiritual terms, it was always understood as that which enabled Europeans to progress while the rest of the world lingered in a state of stagnation. This self-identity of the Europeans translated into geographical terms: the world featured "a permanent geographical center and a permanent periphery: an Inside and an Outside."[16] Inside led, Outside lagged; Inside innovated, Outside imitated. Blaut labels this conceptual model "Eurocentric diffusionism," and he uses it to explain how civilizational developments were understood to move across the surface of the world as a whole: they tended to originate in European space and flow toward non-European space. Understood as such, diffusionism legitimized colonial intervention: where Europe positioned itself as the source of diffusions with non-Europe as their passive recipient, colonization could be seen as the primary vector facilitating the flow of progress to the rest of the world.

Blaut's model is central to my understanding of the way in which Eastern Europe might have been positioned within German colonial discourse. This world region was identified as non-European, as existing in the Outside and thus just as dependent upon European diffusions as, for example, Africa would have been—except that Eastern Europe was *closer* to the source of diffusionist flow. This proximity meant that the contact of Eastern Europeans with these diffusions was more frequent and more concentrated than that of populations located overseas. It would, therefore, have been possible within colonial discourse to acknowledge a higher level of civilization in Poland than would be found in Germany's African colonies, for example, without necessarily granting the Poles any higher potential for indigenous autonomous development than Africans possessed.

Most considerations of European colonial ideologies begin with the unexamined assumption that a colonial relationship must be founded upon "Manichean dichotomies" of race (black versus white) and space (European center versus distant overseas periphery).[17] An investigation of German constructions of Poland as colonial space demands an expansion of Blaut's model that focuses attention on the gray zones between these two sets of extremes. It is indeed possible to find ideological continuities linking German interventions in Africa and in Eastern Europe, but only after we account for the effects of adjacency—of perceived racial and spatial proximity to the European center—and the differences this introduces for the way Poland was cast in colonial discourse.

Within the scholarship on German colonialism and German colonial literature, the literary and social-discursive construction of Poland has been overlooked because Poland's adjacent status challenges the conventions of racial and spatial difference which are uncritically presumed to be a prerequisite of colonial relationships, and thus of colonial discourse itself. Ironically, this adjacency also posed conceptual problems for those who used colonial rhetoric to promote their agendas in the East, and it is important that we examine critically the strategies they enlisted to compensate for this perceived lack of structuring dichotomies. In order to construct conceptual borders of difference across the historically fluid German–Polish frontier, for example, writers initially rendered Poles as racially "black" or "Indian." In many of the earlier novels I examine, Polish characters have black hair, black eyes, and "bronze skin like the North American Indians." Yet, given the reality of the spatial and racial adjacencies extending across Germany and Poland and Germans and Poles, such easy dichotomies of racial "black and white" and spatial "here and there" were ultimately replaced by complex models of dangerous racial and spatial ambiguity. For example, Polish characters were introduced whose external "whiteness" rendered their hidden essential "blackness" all the more insidious because they were able to infiltrate into German cultural space, where they worked to undermine the colonial project (Clara Viebig's *Das schlafende Heer*, of 1904, is a prominent example of this narrative strategy). In the project from which this chapter is taken, I examine a range of such conceptual intricacies in order to develop a model of "colonial adjacency" which outlines the ways in which colonial categories taken from an overseas context were adapted to meet the contingencies of contiguous continental space.

"Poland" was reinvented as German colonial space over the second half of the nineteenth century, beginning in the context of the liberal revolutionary activity of 1848–9. In his contribution to the present volume, Brian Vick shows that in 1848, at the moment when educated Germans were envisioning what their hoped-for German state would look like and anticipating the role it might play on the global stage, they did not in their proto-colonial or imperial imaginings primarily reference the overseas acquisition of colonial space, but instead focused upon expansion into the lands of Eastern Europe.

There were three factors that led to the discursive re-invention of Poland at this time. First, liberals were seeking to create a unified German state according to an ethnically defined category of nationhood. They envisioned the borders of the new state as circumscribing those areas where ethnic Germans lived. But this created a problem at the peripheries of this territory that were populated by other ethnic majorities. Would Germans have to relinquish this space? Many argued that it was only right to cede Polish ethnic regions to the Poles, who also desired the establishment of their own ethnically defined nation state. Others desired a continued German hold over these Polish territories, but they struggled with a lack of moral justification for such an aspiration.[18]

The dynamics of this debate were dramatically shifted through the casting of the Poles into the category of the non-European within a colonial paradigm. If the Poles were unable to generate and maintain their own state, and if they were indeed dependent upon a superior people to manage their affairs for them (as Freytag's subsequent novel only too clearly depicts), then Germans were justified in their desire to keep Polish space under German control.

Such a protective role created an imperial identity for the German nation, such that Germans could imagine joining the ranks of the European imperial empires, even without overseas colonies. And it also provided the promise of an answer to the emigration crisis. The 1840s saw waves of

Germans abandoning German space and heading for overseas destinations, most notably North America. A colonial identity for Poland provided a rhetorical alternative: Germans should head not to Texas, but to Posen—where their colonial endeavors would continue to serve the German nation instead of other European empires.

Decades later, Bismarck launched his "inner colonization" campaign to promote the settlement of ethnic Germans in predominantly Polish regions of Prussia. But he faced problems of attractiveness: how could potential settlers be persuaded to head east, when tales of adventure in the "Wild West" were so successfully luring them to North America? Representations of Poland as exciting colonial space in which Germans could seek their fortunes reflect these pragmatic needs. Various literary works, such as Freytag's *Soll und Haben* (1855), Theodor Fontane's *Effi Briest* (1895), and Clara Viebig's *Das schlafende Heer* (1904), as well as a broad selection of colonial novels set in Polish regions—the so-called *Ostmarkenromane*—participated in generating and maintaining this colonial discourse.[19] Together with representations delivered in the popular press, these texts offered readers images of an under-developed, even wild landscape populated by an inferior and antagonistic race existing outside of civilized Europe. Poland became the "Wild East"—a domain which offered Germans the promise of challenge and adventure and the chance to serve the German nation (instead of the Americans) with their colonial endeavors. The authors of the *Ostmarkenromane* were socially positioned actors, supported in their literary activities either financially or politically (or both) by nationalist interest groups such as the *Ostmarken-Verein* and the *Alldeutscher Verband*.

In the period following World War One, Germany was dispossessed of its overseas colonies and forced to cede 13 per cent of its continental expanse, much of which became part of a reinstated Polish state. In this context, it is interesting to explore the rhetoric deployed by those attempting to regain the lost region in the East. At this historical juncture, the pre-war colonial discourse is reconfigured along two partially overlapping lines of argumentation. The first insists upon the need to regain the lost eastern territories as a means of pre-empting the threatening movement of Eastern subjects into German space, while the second employs the geopolitical concept of "deutscher Kulturboden" to claim Germany's inherent right to the territory it had cultivated in the East. While both of these sets of arguments are familiar to scholars of inter-war Germany, I would argue that they are best understood as being derived from *pre-war* colonial constructions of the East.

Within the first line of argument, the shifting of power into the hands of Poles (understood now as former colonial subjects) was met with an "anxiety of reverse colonization"[20]—the fear that (visually unidentifiable) Polish subjects would infiltrate into the heart of the German metropolis, which they would contaminate with regressive, even barbaric elements in a backward diffusionary flow.[21] Germans, it was argued, could only defend themselves against such violation of their space through the erection of impermeable borders, preferably along the former state demarcation lines in the East, where they would allegedly be easier to patrol.[22]

The second line of argument arose out of a popularization of inter-war geo-political theories according to which any territory in Poland that had been cultivated was, in reality, "deutscher Kulturboden". This space belonged back in German hands, it was argued, because it had only been brought into the era of human progress and development due to past German colonial intervention. Allowing Poles to control this land, it followed, was not only an injustice to the Germans who had invested their colonial labor in the civilizing of this space, but was also an injustice to the agricultural and architectural products they left behind, which would certainly only fall into decay and misuse under Slavic control.

In the post-war climate, the interest in territorial recovery and eastward expansion involved ever-larger segments of the German population, and these two reconfigured colonial arguments found expression in a wide variety of popular cultural productions. Both "trivial" novels (for example, Hans von Saltzwedel's *Der schwarze Lupno* from 1926, a rewriting of the *Nibelungen* epic as a tale of German–Polish intrigue) and canonized literature (for example, Alfred Döblin's *Reise in Polen*, of 1926, and Arnolt Bronnen's *O.S.*, of 1929) manifest elements of this reconfigured post-war colonial discourse. The two main lines of argument, meanwhile, also structure meaning in several well-known Weimar-era films set in Eastern Europe (for instance, Carl Boese's and Paul Wegener's *Der Golem, wie er in die Welt kam*, 1920, F. W. Murnau's *Nosferatu*, from 1922, and Fritz Lang's 1924 *Nibelungen* films), find direct expression in school textbooks, and appear prominently in the popular press.

While historians increasingly address the question of the National Socialist colonization plans for Eastern Europe and attempt to explain the ideology behind this project, I would argue that the understanding of this ideology can be greatly enhanced by contextualizing it within the history of German colonial constructions of Eastern Europe. When National Socialist military officials gave speeches to the troops about the need to reclaim "ancient German land that was ripped away" in the east after World War One, when Hitler asserted the German right to *Lebensraum* (living space) in Eastern Europe, or when Poles were rendered as *Untermenschen* (subhumans) in National Socialist rhetoric, we are seeing the reconfiguration of colonial tropes developed in the nineteenth century to accommodate the desire for eastward expansion.

## NOTES

1. Jürgen Zimmerer, "The Birth of the *Ostland* out of the Spirit of Colonialism: A Postcolonial Perspective on the Nazi Policy of Conquest and Extermination," *Patterns of Prejudice*, 39.2 (2005), 197–219 (p. 205). My emphasis.

2. For the history of this colonial project, see Michael A. Hartenstein, *Neue Dorf-landschaften: nationalsozialistische Siedlungsplanung in den "eingegliederten Ostgebieten" 1939 bis 1944* (Berlin: Köster, 1998); and *Vom Generalplan Ost zum Generalsiedlungsplan*, ed. by Czeslaw Madajczyk (Munich: Saur, 1994).
3. Götz Aly, *"Final Solution": Nazi Population Policy and the Murder of the European Jews* (London: Oxford University Press, 1999).
4. Important contributions to this discussion include David Furber, *Going East: Colonialism and German Life in Nazi-Occupied Poland* (PhD diss., University of New York, Buffalo, 2003); Elizabeth Harvey, *Women and the Nazi East: Agents and Witnesses of Germanization* (New Haven, CT: Yale University Press, 2003); Wendy Lower, *Nazi Empire-Building and the Holocaust in Ukraine* (Chapel Hill: University of North Carolina Press, 2005).
5. Hannah Arendt, *The Origins of Totalitarianism* (New York: Harcourt, Brace, 1951).
6. See Pascal Grosse, "What Does German Colonialism Have to Do with National Socialism? A Conceptual Framework," in *Germany's Colonial Pasts*, ed. by Eric Ames et al. (Lincoln: Nebraska University Press, 2005), pp. 115–34; Marcia Klotz, "Global Visions: From the Colonial to the National Socialist World," *European Studies Journal*, 16.2 (1999), 37–68; Woodruff D. Smith, *The Ideological Origins of Nazi Imperialism* (New York: Oxford University Press, 1986).
7. Jürgen Zimmerer, "Colonial Genocide and the Holocaust: Towards an Archaeology of Genocide," in *Genocide and Settler Society: Frontier Violence and Stolen Indigenous Children in Australian History*, ed. by A. Dirk Moses (New York: Berghahn, 2004), pp. 49–76.
8. Birthe Kundrus, "Von Windhoek nach Nürnberg?: Koloniale 'Mischehenverbote' und die nationalsozialistische Rassengesetzgebung," in *Phantasiereiche: Zur Kulturgeschichte des deutschen Kolonialismus*, ed. by Birthe Kundrus (Frankfurt/M.: Campus, 2003), pp. 110–31. See also Jürgen Zimmerer's response to Kundrus: "Von Windhuk nach Warschau. Die rassische Privilegiengesellschaft in Deutsch-Südwestafrika—ein Modell mit Zukunft?," in *Rassenmischehen—Mischlinge—Rassentrennung: Zur Politik der Rasse im deutschen Kolonialreich*, ed. by Frank Becker (Stuttgart: Steiner, 2004), pp. 97–123.
9. Cf. *Von Windhuk nach Auschwitz? Beiträge zum Verhältnis von Kolonialismus und Holocaust*, ed. by Jürgen Zimmerer (Münster: LIT 2008).
10. Frederick Cooper, *Colonialism in Question: Theory, Knowledge, History* (Berkeley: University of California Press, 2005), p. 47.
11. The full quotation thus reads: "Looking for a 'textual colonization' or a 'metaphoric colonization' distinct from the institutions through which colonial power is exercised risks making colonialism appear everywhere—and hence nowhere." See Cooper, *Colonialism in Question*, p. 47.
12. Kristin Kopp, "Constructing Racial Difference in Colonial Poland," in *Germany's Colonial Pasts*, ed. by Eric Ames et al. (Lincoln: University of Nebraska Press, 2005), pp. 76–96; Kopp, "'Ich stehe jetzt hier als einer von den Eroberern': *Soll und Haben* als Kolonialroman," in *150 Jahre "Soll und Haben" (1855). Studien zu Gustav Freytags kontroversem Roman*, ed. by Florian Krobb (Würzburg: Königshausen & Neumann, 2005), pp. 225–37; Kopp, "Cartographic Claims: Colonial Mappings of Poland in German Territorial Revisionism," in *The Text as Spectacle: Visual Culture in Twentieth-Century Germany*, ed. by Gail Finney (Bloomington: Indiana University Press, 2006), pp. 199–213.
13. For a further analysis of Freytag's colonial novel, see Kopp, "*Soll und Haben* als Kolonialroman."

14. Gustav Freytag, *Soll und Haben*, 58th edn (Leipzig: Hirzel, 1902), p. 383. My translation.
15. J. M. Blaut, *The Colonizer's Model of the World: Geographic Diffusionism and Eurocentric History* (New York: Guilford, 1993), p. 1. Blaut introduces his model in order to explain his criticism of much historical work undertaken today, which he sees as uncritically reproducing Eurocentric diffusionism, especially in accounts of the rise of Western hegemony over the colonized world.
16. Ibid.
17. Abdul R. JanMohamed, "The Economy of Manichean Allegory: The Function of Racial Difference in Colonialist Literature," in *"Race," Writing and Difference*, ed. by Henry Louis Gates, Jr. (Chicago: University of Chicago Press, 1985), pp. 78–106.
18. See Michael G. Müller et al., *Die "Polen-Debatte" in der Frankfurter Paulskirche: Darstellung, Lernziele, Materialien* (Frankfurt/M.: Diesterweg, 1995).
19. See Maria Wojtczak, *Literatur der Ostmark: Posener Heimatliteratur, 1890–1918* (Poznan: Wydawnictwo Naukowe Uniwersytetu im. Adama Mickiewicza, 1998).
20. Stephen D. Arata, "The Occidental Tourist: *Dracula* and the Anxiety of Reverse Colonization," *Victorian Studies*, 33 (1990), 621–44.
21. J. M. Blaut, *The Colonizer's Model of the World*, p. 16f.
22. Annemarie Sammartino, "The Frustration and Failures of Border Control in Early Weimar Germany," paper presented at the German Studies Association Conference, 2006, Pittsburgh, PA.

# Part II

# Colonialism and Popular Utterance in the Imperial Phase

# 4 The War That Scarcely Was

## The *Berliner Morgenpost* and the Boxer Uprising

*Yixu Lü*

The twentieth century began with an armed conflict between China and the foreign powers that were engaged there in colonial exploitation or missionary activity, or both. The conflict began with a series of guerrilla attacks carried out by the "Boxers" ("Fists for Harmony and Righteousness") against foreigners and the technology they had introduced, but escalated to involve the army of the Qing regime and the siege of the foreign legations in Beijing. After eight weeks, the siege was lifted by an allied force under the British General Gaselee. Subsequently, the reinforced occupation troops were placed under the command of the German *Generalfeldmarschall* Graf von Waldersee, although no German troops had been involved in freeing the legations.[1] While this brief war was soon overshadowed by greater conflicts on the world stage, it was perceived in Germany in 1900 as the most momentous military and political event to have occurred since the foundation of the German *Reich*. For it was not only the first war in which Germany had been engaged since 1871, but also the first time that Germany, as a new colonial power, had had the chance to assert and strengthen its position, interacting with established colonial nations in a common military undertaking. As a result, the Boxer Uprising became a phenomenon in the German print media that was out of all proportion to the small German role in the actual fighting. An important factor that contributed to this process was the technical innovation of reporting by telegraph, which gave distant events an immediacy that journalism had hitherto lacked. The German reading public could thus be engaged emotionally in a conflict on a faraway continent. Such a mode of reporting bore the stamp of "authenticity" and also served to raise nationalist feeling to extravagantly new levels. As I have shown elsewhere, the dramatic and often fictitious way in which the war was reported in fact amounted to a covert re-enactment in print of the foundation myth of the *Reich*, namely the defeat of France at Sedan.[2]

The present chapter sets out to explore one specific perspective on this process. Its chief concern is with the political aspects of the creation of a German middle-class version of the Boxer uprising through the popular print media. My aim is to redress the imbalances which have been caused in scholarship to date. These have arisen, on the one hand, through an er-emphasis on the part of some scholars on the supposed effects of the Emperor's spectacular rhetoric in his speech of 27 July to departing troops, in which he urged they imitate the Huns under Attila in their manner of dealing with the Chinese.[3] On the other hand, there has also been a contrary tendency in the relevant literature to be too strongly influenced by the counter-strategies of those Social Democratic papers, such as *Vorwärts*, which collected and published first-hand accounts by German soldiers of atrocities committed by German troops in China in order to attack government policy.[4]

There is a middle ground, which has its own intrinsic interest. It is documented by a wealth of newspapers which have been preserved in archives. If one excludes those newspapers whose political stance is explicitly supportive or critical of government policy, a vast quantity of material still remains. For the purposes of this chapter, it is necessary to narrow the focus while preserving coherence and continuity. This may best be done by examining the coverage of the Boxer Uprising in a single highly successful German newspaper that did not have any explicit political affiliation but, instead, was produced for mass consumption by an urban readership without aiming to sway readers toward one side of party politics or another. Rudolf Stöber estimates that, around the turn of the century, about 55 per cent of the more than 3,000 newspapers then appearing in Germany did have an explicit affiliation, be it political or religious, while the remaining 45 per cent could be termed *parteilos* (not committed to any party).[5] This is not an absolute category, but it indicates that a particular newspaper's prime agenda was commercial rather than tendentious. The *Berliner Morgenpost* belonged to this group. With circulation figures of around 250,000 copies per day, it was one of the most successful of the mass-circulation papers that exemplified the new and increasingly prominent enterprise of the *Generalanzeiger* (General Gazette), *parteilos* but unashamedly appealing to a middlebrow readership.[6] The circulation figures of the *Berliner Morgenpost* and the target readership to which it was addressed are thus such as to permit a degree of generalization about the creation of a middle-class version of the conflict in China by the German print media. Werner Faulstich has estimated a total newspaper readership of 9 million for all of Germany, so the interaction of the *Morgenpost* with its readership of a quarter of a million permits a credible exploration of aspects of the middle ground of public opinion.[7]

Given that the global reporting of these events was often contradictory or required subsequent correction, all German newspapers faced the challenge of making sense of this material for their readers. The method common both to papers which were aimed at a more sophisticated readership, such as the *Frankfurter Zeitung* or the *Kölnische Zeitung*, and also to the populist newspapers, exemplified by the *Berliner Morgenpost*, was to shape the raw material into continuous narratives. These were steered by an ongoing concern to identify and separate the defining events—as they unfolded—from amid the mass of conjecture, rumor and false information coming from China. In the reporting of the Boxer uprising in 1900, the German press as a whole appears in retrospect to have been subject to an imperative to anticipate outcomes, so as to impress the readership as being more "authoritative" and as having a better grasp of their raw material than their competitors.

Considering that many German newspapers were preoccupied with the Boxers for the whole of 1900, it is advisable to narrow the focus of this enquiry and examine how the *Berliner Morgenpost* treated the following three phases of the war: events prior to the murder of the German envoy, von Ketteler, on 20 June; the siege of the diplomatic quarter in Beijing, which ended on 14 August; and the punitive forays of the allied troops under the command of Graf von Waldersee, starting in October and extending into February 1901. It is also important to stress, before we proceed to these specific instances as they figure in the *Morgenpost*, that the *whole* German mainstream press displays from the outset some of the contradictions inherent in any colonialist view of the world. In this case, a distinct contradiction emerges between an allegedly benevolent colonial mission to "civilize" the Chinese and an enterprise unashamedly bent on the commercial exploitation of China. These contradictory attitudes are displayed with a lack of critical self-awareness that anticipates the crass discrepancy between the exhortations to genocide in the main part of Wilhelm II's "Hunnenrede" (Hun Speech) of 27 July and its astonishing conclusion: "Öffnet der Kultur den Weg ein für allemal!" (Clear the way for Culture once and for all!).[8] The uneasy coexistence of the myth of a duty to "civilize" the Chinese with the avowed need to make a profit while doing so becomes more and more manifest in newspapers as anxiety about the threat posed by the Boxers grows. Thus, the *Kölnische Zeitung*, a non-partisan journal aimed at a highly educated readership, writes on 8 June,

> Already the damage the Boxers have inflicted on the railways, the means of disseminating Occidental Culture . . . has cost 20 million marks, already the lifeline of Western interests, the railway and road from Beijing to Tianjin, is in the power of the fanatical rebels, already a number of Europeans, missionaries and engineers, pioneers of Culture and trade, have fallen prey to fanaticism—and still we have no word that there is any resolve on the part of the colonial powers . . . to protect themselves and their future in East Asia.

This newspaper was esteemed throughout Germany for its sophistication, so its blatant materialism is surprising. More importantly, the passages show that the tacit identification of "Cultur" with the armed force needed to sustain it was already part of the semantics of militant German colonialism—long before Wilhelm II's *Hunnenrede* gave it center stage as an international embarrassment. Once the murder of von Ketteler had outraged national pride, the sensationalism of German newspapers—of whatever persuasion—knew no bounds. Yet the essential point is that the mode of discourse that conflated profits with culture and morality had—well in advance—paved the way for later rhetoric that justified looting, the wholesale murder of Chinese civilians and the demands for huge financial compensation in the peace settlement as a justifiable response to the depredations of the Boxers and their support by Chinese government forces.

In the light of what was to follow, it is remarkable how low-key and sporadic the reports on China in the *Berliner Morgenpost* in the first five months of 1900 remained. This is in part because the conflict between the British and the Boers in South Africa interested the newspaper's readership much more. Articles bearing the bold headline "*Der Krieg*" are limited to detailed accounts of the South African conflict. When, on 27 January, there is a report to the effect that the Chinese Emperor has committed suicide, it is brief and buried among a wealth of other foreign news items in the columns headed "Political News of the Day."[9] The same applies to the follow-up pieces in which it is revealed that the Emperor is not dead at all, but has simply appointed another successor. By 11 March, "the alleged coup in China" is explicitly written off, partly as an example of the untrustworthiness of English reporting, and partly as typical of the obscure and eccentric goings-on at the court of the Dowager Empress. By contrast, the *Kölnische Zeitung* gave great prominence to the same series of dubious events, with an in-depth historical review of the failure of attempts by the young Chinese Emperor to reform the bureaucracy. Reports that he is dead or, at least, imprisoned are accompanied by extensive and highly dramatized commentaries which compare him to the mythical Icarus and turn him into a tragic figure, using the template of Schiller's *Don Carlos*.[10]

The *Berliner Morgenpost* also makes no attempt to forge the intermittent reports of Boxer activity into a coherent narrative of a kind which would have given them the ideological subtext evident in the reports from the *Kölnische Zeitung* quoted previously. Instead, military actions by "anti-Christian secret societies" or "murderous arsonists" and their clashes with either the Qing army or colonial troops are reported piecemeal and with no attempt to analyze underlying causes. Through March, April and May, reports from China remain brief bulletins among a mass of other oddities.

It is not until 1 June that the *Morgenpost*, under the heading "The Boxer Uprising," begins to question the seriousness of the Qing court's edict deeming membership of the Boxers was punishable by death. Suspicions of complicity between the Qing court and the Boxers are thus aired very late by the *Morgenpost*; but the length of the report shows that events in China are finally beginning to be treated more earnestly. This approach is the opposite of the detailed commentaries the *Kölnische Zeitung* had devoted to the same topics since January. But the readerships of the two papers were quite different. The *Kölnische Zeitung* was read throughout Germany, while the readership of the *Morgenpost* was local, less educated but very much larger, so that a sensation from China was needed to make a lengthy front-page story. Nevertheless, in this first phase, the casual use of negative stereotypes, when briefly reporting events in China, paved the way for the characterization of all Chinese as barbarians in the much more detailed reporting that the *Morgenpost* was to undertake in the phase to come.

On 10 June, the telegraph line between Beijing and Tianjin was severed by Boxers. This had major consequences for the way in which the world press reported events in Beijing in the coming months, since the legations were now almost entirely cut off from the outside world, and newspapers had to fill their columns as best they could, often with quite inaccurate material, in which scanty information was inextricably mixed with rumor and conjecture. Without mentioning how unreliable reports from the Chinese capital had now become, the *Morgenpost* declares on 16 June, with great aplomb but no basis in fact, "The Boxer Uprising has in recent days increasingly become a general revolt by the Chinese against the foreign powers; it has spread much more swiftly than expected to all regions of this by no means heavenly kingdom." In reality, Boxer violence was virtually limited to the provinces of Shandong and Zhili; but the populist press now had the bit between its teeth, and so the *Morgenpost* had no hesitation in proclaiming a full-scale "Chinese revolution," at a time when the only significant military action in China was that of the allied relief column sent to Beijing under Vice-Admiral Seymour, now in severe difficulties in Tianjin.

In this context, it was ironic but unsurprising that the first time events in China provided the *Morgenpost* with a leading front-page story was on 17 June. The article in question was an erroneous account of the "murder" of the German envoy in Beijing. Baron von Ketteler was shot by a Manchu soldier; but this did not occur until 20 June, and it remains a mystery why his death was reported world-wide at a time when he was still alive and a forceful voice in the councils of the besieged diplomats. However, the tone of the commentary in the *Morgenpost* anticipates much of the rhetoric to come: "A German envoy murdered? Impossible, that *cannot* be true! The report is like a slap in the face." Here the paper is, in effect, dictating its own readers' response—a technique which would be increasingly employed in subsequent months. Only after strong patriotic emotions have been aroused does the article mention in passing that the telegraph line to Beijing had been cut some days before, so that the atrocity cannot be verified. It was to take no less than 16 days after the real event for von Ketteler's death to become widely accepted as fact—an ironic proof that "authentic" reporting from China was now, in reality, highly unreliable and would remain so till early August.

Nonetheless, the *Morgenpost* compensated energetically for its previous offhand treatment of events in China, now filling the front page on a daily basis with stories enhanced by hand-drawn illustrations. On 20 June, all international wars of recent years are listed as a lead-up to the surprising conclusion: "But how insignificant all those bloody events are compared to the war that has now got underway between the infinitely populous Asiatic empire and the Western powers, allied with Japan!" China has finally revealed its potential as a domain in which German nationalist sentiment may be invested with an expectation of enhanced returns, and so the *Berliner Morgenpost* casts away all skepticism and simply reports all rumors from China, so long as they are dramatic enough, as having a roughly equal chance of having occurred. Moreover, the still unconfirmed death of von Ketteler has the effect of intensifying the image of the Chinese as cruel and perfidious barbarians.

This is shown by another sensational—and erroneous—disclosure in the *Morgenpost* of 5 July. "Chinese newspapers," quoted third hand, are named as the source for a report that, following a massacre in the legations, there are no foreigners at all left alive in Beijing. On 5 July, the paper lends credence to equally unconfirmed reports from London:

> It is reported that the Europeans in the English legation maintained a long resistance against vastly superior numbers. When they saw that all was lost, they themselves first killed the women and children, so as to spare them tortures inflicted by the Chinese, and then all fell in a heroic last-ditch struggle . . . There is a rumor stemming from Peking that 5,000 Chinese Christians have been murdered.

On 8 July, the *Morgenpost* further confirms the butchering of all the diplomats, their womenfolk, their children and the soldiers defending them after they had held out for 18 days: "When all ammunition and provisions had been used up, the Chinese forced their way into the legation, killed those still living . . . and incinerated the wounded and dead."

Although nothing certain was known at this point in July about events in Beijing, the *Morgenpost* is happy to accept the massacre as fact, since it provides a welcome opportunity to demonize the Chinese. For the conflict to have the magnitude already claimed for it in the commentary of 20 June, it must be made consistent with the established paradigm of an epoch-making and mortal conflict between civilization and barbarism, with Germany in the vanguard of *Cultur*.

The *Berliner Morgenpost* was not alone in believing the diplomats and their families were dead. Although the American Envoy, Edwin Conger, had managed to get a telegram through to Washington on 16 July, giving sparse details of the continuing siege and appealing for "quick relief," the State Department suspected that this proof that the legations were still holding out was a Chinese forgery.[11] It was not until late July that, in the absence of further confirmation of the massacre, Conger's report gained credibility, and only in early August did reports from other besieged diplomats reveal the slaughter of all foreigners to be a fiction. It is important to note that, in the meantime, some other German papers, such as the *Frankfurter*

*Zeitung*, had remained skeptical of the quality of the reports from China and refrained from embellishing them, whereas the *Morgenpost* was happy to concoct a set-piece tale of "heroic" Westerners killing their wives and children in order to save them from a worse fate.

The logical extension of the process begun with the first reports of von Ketteler's death was to make credible the image of an enemy so savage that there was no limit to the violence which might be justified in reply. The genuine weakness of the Qing regime and the obsolete equipment of most of its army had been proverbial in the German press long before it became evident that the Chinese government had thrown in its lot with the Boxers. It was thus scarcely credible that China could withstand for long the combined might of the colonial nations that was now being mobilized. The print media in Germany, however, had successfully created another reality, in which civilization itself was at stake in a war of apocalyptic proportions and one bloodbath in Beijing called for an unlimited number of further atrocities in reprisal. The *Morgenpost* stands out in this context only by its belated recognition of the Boxer Uprising as an ideal means of engaging its readership in a patriotic cause, and by the vehemence with which it caricatured the enemy. China was real in this context only to the extent that it offered a means to glorify German national identity.

In fact, the second allied relief force under General Gaselee had won a victory at Tianjin on 13 July, and this altered the balance of factions within the Qing court, with the result that a truce was offered to the besieged diplomats on 17 July. This was to endure, with minor intermittent hostilities, until the allied troops invaded Beijing on 14 August. Without such a respite, the siege would have ended very differently, since the besieged legations simply lacked enough ammunition to hold out any longer. However, it was not until around 7 August that the German press could assure its readership that most of the besieged were still alive and well.

In the last days of July, while the *Morgenpost* was still asking whether Conger's telegram was a forgery and was styling the fate of the diplomats "the Peking Enigma," Wilhelm II delivered his notorious *Hunnenrede* to troops departing for China from Bremerhaven on 27 July. As is well known, the speech was printed in two versions. The first, an official press-release, toned down or in some cases simply omitted the more bloodthirsty locutions; the second, an authentic shorthand transcription by a reporter who was present, not only exhorted the troops to give no quarter and take no prisoners, but went on to urge them to emulate the horrific exploits of Attila the Hun to such effect "that no Chinese will ever again dare even to look askance at a German."[12]

From today's perspective, the whole *Hunnenrede* appears less as a revealing blunder on the Emperor's part than as simply a shriller version of attitudes most of the German press had been propagating since well before von Ketteler's murder, apparently with its readership's approval. Certainly, the speech was an *international* embarrassment—precisely because such tones were expected from popular journalism and not from a head of state. The treatment of it in the *Morgenpost* indicates, however, that the speech did not shock middlebrow German readers at all. On 29 July, the paper prints *both* versions of the most sensational passages, and—surprisingly— abstains from any direct editorial comment comparing their content. Rather, it merely points out that the euphemistic interpretation of these passages in the *Kreuz-Zeitung*, a paper on the far right, was just as much a criticism of the Emperor's words as the polemics against them in journals on the left. For the *Morgenpost*, Wilhelm II had said what he had said, and there was no cause to expect its readers to have trouble digesting it. Later editions of the *Morgenpost* did not revisit the topic, which suggests that the *Hunnenrede* had simply become part of a broad rhetoric of aggressive patriotism with which its readers had come to feel at ease.

In similar vein, the *Morgenpost* had no difficulty, once the true fate of the diplomats in Beijing was known, in ignoring the fact that it had long been feeding its readership lurid fictions of their having been massacred: retractions do not sell papers. While, in the first days of August, the *Frankfurter Zeitung* comments in scathing terms on the sensationalist misreporting that had filled the populist press during the siege, the commentary in the *Morgenpost* on 5 August simply avoids the issue and finds a fresh target in allied disunity: "the solidarity of the civilized nations in the face of the Yellow Peril"—now that the bloodbath in Beijing has turned out not to have taken place—has regrettably given way to squabbling.

The formula that the *Morgenpost* had copied from other papers for anything happening in China, "die chinesischen Wirren" (the Chinese turmoil) thus became an implicit excuse for all kinds of past inaccuracy. The severing of telegraph lines in China and the obscurity of what dictated the conduct of the Qing court had created a climate in the world press in which any news from Beijing seemed credible, and the prime goal of the *Morgenpost* was to give its readers what they wanted. Essentially, this was a further heightening of those nationalist feelings that were already inflamed.

The only obstacle—once the "turmoil" had given way to clarity—to celebrating the bloody feats Wilhelm II had demanded was the awkward fact that the German contingent in Gaselee's relief column had not withstood the rigors of the march to Beijing, and had turned back to Tianjin. As the *Morgenpost* admits on 18 August, German troops played no part in the final relief action. This, it hastily adds, should not lessen its readers' joy at the event. In reality, however, there was an emotional vacuum demanding to be filled by tangible German heroism. Such a role now fell to the German commander of the allied mopping-up operations in China, Graf von Waldersee.

Waldersee's appointment had every appearance of being what the German press needed at this juncture, as the *Morgenpost* led, on 9 August, with the banner headline: "Germany has Supreme Command." Since the distinction could in no way have been earned by German feats of arms, it was lauded instead as a tribute to German political integrity. Unlike the other colonial powers, Germany was above petty in-fighting and had thus earned the accolade. But all was not to go smoothly. On 12 August, the same paper was obliged to concede that the announcement had been premature. Four days later, it reports frictions between Czar Nicholas and the Kaiser. On 19 August, jubilant once more, it quotes a speech in which Wilhelm II formally announces von Waldersee's appointment, attributing it in grandiose terms to "the instigation and express wish of His Majesty the Emperor of all Russians."

However, three days later, matters have changed again as a result of a contradictory account in the *Petersburger Regierungsbote*. The *Morgenpost* is obliged to admit as diplomatically as possible that it was Wilhelm II who had had to go begging: "Kaiser Wilhelm appealed directly by telegram to Czar Nicholas and to all governments involved, and placed Field Marshall Graf Waldersee at their disposal." Thus a sense of anticlimax overshadowed what had first appeared a gratifying, spontaneous recognition of Germany's enhanced status among the colonial powers. Clearly, the *Morgenpost* would have preferred to adhere to its first, triumphant announcement. But the fact that its competitors were reporting the impediments to von Waldersee's appointment gave it no choice. The two weeks of uncertainty and the sobering dénouement, however, took the gloss off the event and were an unfavorable omen for Germany's punitive mission in China.

For what was there left to do? The Qing court had fled Beijing on 15 August; their army was dispersed. The capital had been comprehensively looted, and a number of Boxer strongholds had been attacked and taken while von Waldersee was still at sea. Speaking about the operations he directed from October onward, the American Major General Chaffee stated, "[W]here one real Boxer has been killed . . . fifteen harmless coolies or laborers on the farms, including not a few women and children, have been slain."[13] Even in Germany, von Waldersee's punitive expeditions failed to meet the demand for heroic exploits—so much so that the *Morgenpost*, on 30 November, quotes at length August Bebel's eloquent and ferocious attack on them during the debate on China in the *Reichstag* the day before:

> All foreign nations laughed at Waldersee's departure, at the speeches, at the hordes of photographers and cinematographers and so on. But the abundant examples in letters from troops in China, which are all over every newspaper, only serve to prove: Graf Waldersee is not a marshal of world stature but rather a marshal of executions.

Once more, the *Morgenpost* had no choice but to report this, since its competitors not only printed the same text, but had also been publishing numerous "Hunnenbriefe" (Hun Letters), first-hand accounts by German soldiers of atrocities against Chinese civilians.

Great hopes had been placed by the German patriotic press in the punitive expedition to take the former Boxer stronghold of Baodingfu, and the *Morgenpost* was able to trumpet, on 27 October, a minor German victory in a skirmish on the way there. But once again, anticlimax was the order of the day. Not only had all Chinese militants abandoned the city in advance, but—worst of all—a French detachment had reached it first, indeed five days earlier, and had taken over, as the paper sourly notes on 30 October. Some prominent Chinese officials were executed, but this was no substitute for a glorious feat of arms.

Graf Waldersee was becoming a lost cause to a readership hungry for major battles won by German bravery. This is all too clear from a revealing passage in the *Morgenpost* of 1 November, in which the Supreme Commander complains to the British envoy. The main point at issue was the railways, and Graf Waldersee admits to having trouble asserting his authority in the matter. The *Morgenpost* continues to report loyally any positive news from von Waldersee's command post, such as the defeat of a thousand Chinese troops by Germans under Major Förster, the hoisting of the German flag on the Great Wall to mark the victory, and the restoration of some railway links. But equal space is given in the same reports, under the heading "Bad News From China," to the ravages of dysentery and typhus among German soldiers.

Wilhelm II's speech from the throne at the opening of the *Reichstag* on 14 November revives his earlier rhetoric against Chinese "atrocities against the advance guard of Western civilization and Christian culture dwelling peaceably among them," but proceeds to demand nothing more dramatic than "as rapid a restoration of order as possible" and punishment of the worst offenders. Visions of great battles in the apocalyptic mode of the *Hunnenrede* of 27 July are conspicuously absent from his vision of future events.

Peace negotiations between the colonial powers and China were, in fact, to drag on till the signing of a treaty on 7 September 1901. These delays had, as Diana Preston writes, "less to do with Chinese intransigence than with allied squabbling about the conditions to be imposed on China."[14] As far as the *Berliner Morgenpost* is concerned, with the end of the debate in the *Reichstag* the potential of the *chinesische Wirren* to engage its readership with bold and exciting accounts had been exhausted, and its reports revert to the laconic style of the first five months of 1900.

Comparing the journalism of the *Berliner Morgenpost* in this instance with that of its more highbrow counterparts, it becomes clear that even the patriotism it so pompously espouses is subject to commercial considerations. In the first phase I examined, the murders of German missionaries and other civilians are briefly reported without any attempt to forge a grand narrative. Only when events take a sufficiently dramatic turn in early June does the *Morgenpost* set about exploiting the Boxer Uprising. Its narrative constructs abandon all restraint when stories show promise of stimulating nationalist anger among readers: the most obvious example is the newspaper's treatment of the Beijing massacre that did not occur. This second phase is forced to a conclusion in early August when the newspaper's fictions are exposed. The third phase, which takes up the appointment of Graf von Waldersee as Supreme Allied Commander, is launched with great panache on 9 August. However, it fails to provide the drama and excitement demanded by the readership, and is consequently allowed to trail off into occasional, brief bulletins.

Two points should be made in conclusion. First, apart from the lavish illustrations of Chinese scenes accompanying stories in the phase of high drama, there is no attempt by the *Morgenpost* to provide in-depth commentary or background information on China. The result was a poorly defined image of China, which allowed the middle-class readers to imagine the details as they chose. By implementing the reciprocal principle of offering the public what it is inclined to think anyway, the main sub-text of reports in the *Morgenpost* was an unquestioning conflation of militant patriotism with colonialism. Secondly, the strong element of nationalist fantasy in the *Morgenpost*'s treatment of the second phase may be seen as emotionally potent, though neither informed nor informative. I conclude, however, that its very vagueness did much to create a fertile climate for the immense wave of German popular fiction that was inspired by the Boxer Uprising. I have dealt with this literary phenomenon in detail elsewhere.[15]

## NOTES

1. Paul A. Cohen, *History in Three Keys: The Boxers as Event, Experience and Myth* (New York: Columbia University Press, 1997), p. 54f.
2. See Yixu Lü, "Geschichte und Fiktion: Der Boxer-Aufstand in der zeitgenössischen deutschen Kolonialliteratur," *Jahrbuch für internationale Germanistik*, Series A 84 (2007), 229–34.
3. See, for example, Tim Trampedach, "'Yellow Peril'? German Public Opinion and the Chinese Boxer Movement," *Berliner China-Hefte*, 23 (2002), 71–81.
4. See, for example, Ute Wielandt and Michael Kaschner, "Die Reichstagsdebatten über den deutschen Kriegseinsatz in China: August Bebel und die 'Hunnenbriefe'," in *Das deutsche Reich und der Boxeraufstand*, ed. by Susanne Kuß and Bernd Martin (Munich: iudicium, 2002), pp. 183–202.
5. Rudolf Stöber, *Deutsche Pressegeschichte. Einführung, Systematik, Glossar* (Konstanz: UVK Medien, 2000), p. 209f.
6. Werner Faulstich, *Medienwandel im Industriezeitalter* (Göttingen: Vandenhoeck & Ruprecht, 2004), pp. 31–45; Jürgen Wilke, *Grundzüge der Medien- und Kommunikationsgeschichte: Von den Anfängen bis ins 20. Jahrhundert* (Cologne: Böhlau, 2000), p. 269.
7. Faulstich, *Medienwandel im Industriezeitalter*, p. 31.
8. *Reden des Kaisers: Ansprachen, Predigten und Trinksprüche Wilhelms II*, ed. by Ernst Johann (Munich: DTV, 1966), p. 91.

9. Since, in what follows, all German papers are quoted from the original editions—there are no reprints—only the date of each issue will be given. All translations from the German are my own.
10. *Kölnische Zeitung*, 26 January 1900.
11. Diana Preston, *The Boxer Rebellion* (New York: Berkeley, 2000), p. 172.
12. *Reden des Kaisers*, p. 141.
13. Cohen, *History in Three Keys*, p. 57.
14. Preston, *The Boxer Rebellion*, p. 309.
15. Yixu Lü, "German Colonial Fiction on China: the Boxer Uprising of 1900," *German Life and Letters*, 59.1 (2006), 78–100.

# 5 Boy's and Girl's Own Empires[1]
## Gender and the Uses of the Colonial World in *Kaiserreich* Youth Magazines

*Jeff Bowersox*

The era of Germany's "unification" and rise to Great Power status in the late nineteenth and early twentieth centuries coincided with an age of unprecedented global interaction. At the same time that residents of the recently formed nation-state struggled to define their nation, who belonged to it, and what roles they would play in maintaining it, they also became ever more aware of the world beyond Germany's and Europe's borders. Dramatic advances in transportation, expanding commercial and communications networks, and the various foreign interventions and adventures that these facilitated brought distant corners of the globe into Germans' everyday lives. A developing mass culture provided media—books, periodicals, toys, advertisements, museums, exhibitions, zoos, panoramas and eventually films, as well as myriad other products and productions—for making sense of it all. As the exercise of formal and informal colonial influence increasingly defined the nature of these global encounters, colonial references came to structure the idioms through which Germans across lines of class, gender, and region understood their place in the wider world.

While Germans were increasingly interested in efforts to maintain and develop their own, recently acquired colonial possessions, this interest was predicated on and intimately intertwined with Germans' familiarity with a larger world order defined by empire. They defined their world in terms of hierarchies of relative civilization, and in this world it was generally assumed that the civilized, however defined, had a right and duty to intervene in the affairs of the less civilized. Indeed, the very measure of a society's vitality was its ability to spread progress, however defined, to those in need of it. Just as social reformers argued for the need to mould the unruly working classes in a more "respectable" image and nationalists demanded the Germanization of backward national minorities within Germany's borders, so did this conception reference, explain, and justify the expansion of European influence around the globe by establishing a fundamental opposition between civilized and uncivilized. The expressions of this worldview in the media of mass culture were not monolithic and consistent, but they were no less important for their flexibility. As producers shaped their products to appeal and apply to specific audiences, they referenced empire in various and sometimes contradictory ways, always inflected by notions of gender, race, class, confession, nation, and *Kultur*.

In an effort to illustrate the prevalence and utility of empire in German popular culture around the turn of the century, I focus on media aimed at German youth. Such products are particularly instructive because they illustrate more than simply the prevailing cultural reference points of the day. Given pervasive fears of declining national virility in an era defined by national competition and the survival of the fittest, raising a generation capable of building a strong community at home and promoting its interests abroad was a central social concern. A host of reform movements aimed at educating and invigorating young Germans turned their attention to ameliorating perceived degenerative influences, in particular the baleful effects of industrialization and the *Tingel-Tangel* of mass culture. In line with the most progressive pedagogical practices of the day, reformers demanded that products for children contain entertaining yet enriching content, content that engaged imaginations as it conveyed practical lessons and encouraged appropriate behavior. Although profit was usually the primary motive for producers, many sought to distance themselves from trashy commercial culture by infusing their products for youth with self-consciously instructional intentions. A critical reading of these materials provides a glimpse not only of the terms in which young Germans came to understand their world but also of how various adults *wanted* the world to appear to their children.

Producers of media for youth faced exigencies that were sometimes difficult to reconcile. Young readers wanted entertaining content; pedagogues, politicians, and many parents insisted on educational material; and all demanded relevant and current topics. Using empire, producers could address all of these, specifically by directing young Germans' interest in the exotic world down pedagogically responsible avenues, providing lessons to boys and girls about their respective roles in German society and in the wider world. In this chapter, I examine the utility of colonial references in two mainstream youth periodicals, one for boys and one for girls. Both journals relied on a fundamental opposition between a civilized European world and a chaotic colonial world, but their details differed according to contemporary gender ideals. Ultimately, the image of a colonial world defined by chaos and backwardness could provide both boys and girls with spaces for adventure and personal development not available within the confines of the civilized metropole. It was a space for independent and heroic action and for the illustration of the ultimate superiority of European civilization.

This vision, shaped to suit current events and the growing interest in Germany's own colonial efforts, remained relatively constant in media aimed at German boys over the course of the period. In media aimed at girls, by contrast, the colonial world was initially far less adventurous and chaotic. Instead, it provided tamed, exotic decoration or examples of

foreign barbarity that reinforced European notions of civilized femininity. However, under the influence of the middle-class women's movement,
empire became something more. Just as the adventure found on the frontier could entertain while promoting an active masculinity, so did publishers and contributors eventually try to promote an active, yet still domestic
femininity through the example of women struggling at the margins of
civilization. This project found its clearest expression when focusing on
Germany's mission in its own colonies. By serving in their natural roles as
bearers of *Kultur* to those most in need of it, female colonizers proved the
necessity of capable women for ensuring Germany's vitality both at home
and abroad.

*Der gute Kamerad* (The Good Pal) and *Das Kränzchen* (The Friendship
Circle) were two of the most popular youth journals of the period and were
eminently mainstream, middle-of-the-road publications; even their Social
Democratic competitors, who were not shy of ascribing bias to other publications, considered them politically "neutral."[2] The Stuttgart publisher
Wilhelm Spemann began publishing *Der gute Kamerad* in 1887 in an effort
to reach primarily middle-class boys between the ages of 10 and 14. In the
following year, he established its sister journal to reach girls of the same age
and class.[3] Their institutional interconnectedness makes them especially
useful for illustrating the gendering of the colonial frontier in media aimed
at German youth. The two publications shared publishers and editors, but
they also shared a common mission: they aimed to prepare their respective
readerships for their future roles as men and women capable of promoting
the well-being of Germany, and they sought to do so in an entertaining
manner. To this end, both combined fictional features with general interest
stories containing self-consciously educational content. Serial stories were
accompanied by reports on current events, famous personages, and technological advancements as well as informational articles on various topics in ethnography, geography, and natural history, such as readers would
have encountered in their classrooms. By paying close attention, readers
could learn how they could best contribute to German society at home and
abroad. However, despite their links and shared goals, *Der gute Kamerad*
and *Das Kränzchen* were very different in content and emphasis according to prevailing notions of masculinity and femininity—specifically, the
public roles of each. Like most youth literature, they generally followed the
dictum that "the girl stays at home, the boy ventures out into the world,"
and their visions of the colonial world followed suit.[4]

*Der gute Kamerad* focused on attracting boys with serialized tales of
exotic adventure and informational reports on technological and military
marvels or discoveries in the fields of ethnography and geography. Imagined as a frontier ripe with excitement, the colonial world fits well into *Der
gute Kamerad*'s general mission. An appealingly wild setting for adventure
literature, the colonial context also provided authors the opportunity to
portray men wrestling, training, and improving that disordered space. In

this realm readers found examples of such stereotypically masculine qualities as bravery and daring but also respectability, humility, diligence, an appreciation for hard work, and intelligence. In *Der gute Kamerad*, boys were to engage imaginatively in the colonial world as hunters, explorers, adventurers, and agents of European civilization.

*Das Kränzchen* initially encouraged a different way of relating to the colonial world through its focus on the domestic sphere and "woman's work." The journal did encourage girls to be aware of the colonial world but only insofar as it related directly to their lives and presumed roles in the civilized metropole. Rather than active participation in civilizing efforts and the adventure that came along with it, for most of the period under consideration, *Das Kränzchen* encouraged readers only to observe a colonial world defined in terms of domesticity and civility. Readers encountered a safely exotic world, shorn of the chaos that produced the excitement and opportunities for personal development that characterized boys' literature in general.

A few examples can illustrate this dichotomy. From its founding in 1887, *Der gute Kamerad* made an exoticized colonial world a central part of its offerings to readers first and foremost through the serialized adventure stories included in every issue. Roughly 10 stories appeared each year between 1887 and 1914, and fewer than a handful of these took Europe as their setting. The rest took place in Africa, the South Pacific, China, Latin America, the American frontier, or on the high seas. Karl May, whom Wilhelm Spemann helped to make one of the most popular authors of the period, contributed seven novels within the journal's first 11 years.[5] May's *Die Sklavenkarawane* is typical of *Der gute Kamerad*'s standard fare, with its tale of hardy European frontiersmen and their loyal native subordinates who wrestle with chaotic environments and savage peoples.[6] In this story, Emil Schwartz, a blond-haired and blue-eyed German professor of natural history, travels through Sudan to collect local flora and fauna for museums and his own research. Along the way the fearless scholar-warrior is drawn into conflict with the murderous Arab slave-trader Abu el Mot, who raids local towns and enslaves the poor black population as well as any Europeans, including Schwartz's own brother, who get in the way. Through exceptional resourcefulness, courage, and skill with their fists and firearms, Schwartz and his comrades succeed in defeating the slavers and freeing their prisoners.

By contrast, only on very few occasions did readers of *Das Kränzchen*'s serialized stories get a glimpse of the world beyond Europe's boundaries, and that world was far from adventurous. Luise Glaß's *Annele* was one of only a handful of stories over the entire period that included non-European settings and, like virtually all of the stories in the journal, was a sentimental *Backfischroman* in which the plot revolves around the female protagonist coming to terms with her domestic responsibilities.[7] Egypt serves as the setting for a tame travel report wrapped around an extended discourse on national identity and the necessity of maintaining it in a foreign space. The dramatic tension comes not from any threat but rather from the question of whether Annele can help convince a German who has "gone native" during his long stay in the Orient to reclaim his national identity. Glaß's Egypt is sufficiently strange, wondrous, and chaotic to provide an exotic flavor to her tale, but it is also sufficiently domesticated not to frighten or over-excite her apparently impressionable girl readers. The passive heroine encounters no physical danger during her stay abroad; even when she walks through the disorderly streets of Cairo, German men chaperone her at all times. The limits of feminine respectability meant that Glaß's Annele, unlike May's heroic Emil Schwartz, could become nothing more than a tourist unprepared to survive in this exotic environment on her own.

The distinction between these two perspectives on the colonial world—dangerous versus safe, active participation versus passive observation, masculine versus feminine—becomes particularly clear if we look at informational reports, similar to classroom readings, that served as the journals' educational content. Both journals relied on a fundamental opposition—between a progressive and civilized European world, on the one hand, and a more or less backward colonial domain in need of European assistance, on the other—to situate their readers in the wider world and to entertain them; but they used very different details to establish this binary and, in turn, put this binary to very different ends.

Compare, for example, the engagement with exotic animals in Figures 1 and 2 (respectively "The lioness attacks," *Der gute Kamerad*, 1893/94, and "Playmates," *Das Kränzchen*, 1898/99[8]).

Die Löwin im Angriff.

*Figure 5.1*   "The lioness attacks," *Der gute Kamerad*, 1893–4.

*Figure 5.2*   "Playmates," *Das Kränzchen* 1898–9.

Figure 5.1 embodies the masculine engagement with the colonial world promoted in *Der gute Kamerad*. The lioness marks this space as a wild frontier ruled not by civilized rules of decorum but by a Darwinian struggle for survival, and its cultivation requires the efforts of capable men with reserves of bravery. Appropriately, the stalwart hunter stands tall and proud as he faces down the prowling predator, while the natives, marked as subordinates by their dress and fearful postures, look to their white master for leadership and protection.[9] *Der gute Kamerad* regularly used portrayals of freely roaming animals to emphasize the rawness and danger inherent in the colonial world, a danger faced most often in the form of a thrilling hunt such as this. By contrast, not a single story in *Das Kränzchen* described the hunting of wild animals or the threat that they could pose to humans. *Das Kränzchen* recognized and played to an interest among its readers in the very same exotic creatures portrayed in *Der gute Kamerad*, but offered stories that examined them in controlled environments like ranches, circuses, and zoos. As Figure 5.2 demonstrates, girls encountered a colonial world that need not be so dangerous after all. The accompanying article explains that lions are the "dearest" creatures when born; for months, they are tame enough to play with toddlers.[10]

The purpose of such distinctions becomes clearer with an examination of ethnographic reports on the habits and characteristics of non-European peoples. *Der gute Kamerad* taught a relatively straightforward lesson through factual reportage focused primarily on the activities of men—hunting, fighting, trade and other economic activities; the use of technology; and forms of political organization. As in Figure 5.1, these portrayals suggested that European men possess particular virtues lacking to varying degrees in most of the colonial peoples they encounter, and this disparity requires European men to bring order and prosperity to the colonial world. Stories of native simplicity, superstition, and corruption—for example, the humorous tale of a tyrannical "nigger king" confounded by a European trader able to create fire with a magnifying glass—encouraged readers to value intelligence, bravery, independence, selflessness, and command of the advances of European civilization.[11] The protagonists in these stories and reports embodied the virtues that German men needed to build a stronger nation at home. Editors of and contributors to *Der gute Kamerad* tried to teach boys to develop these virtues through an imaginative engagement with a chaotic colonial world.

*Das Kränzchen* constructed a more ambivalent relationship between its readers and the colonial world, one built around passive observation of circumstances among colonial peoples rather than models of feminine behavior constructively promoting the cause of civilization. However, the editors and contributors put this observation to good use to promote a domestic femininity that accorded with the goals of the middle-class women's movement in Germany. Particularly in its first decade and a half, *Das Kränzchen* offered a virtual ethnographic world tour of fashion and manners among peoples scattered across the spectrum of civilization. Contributors used pieces on clothing styles to plead for more simplicity and practicality in German women's dress. One writer used the tastes of "savages"—specifically the "gigantic" ear piercings of the Masai or the "splendid *chignons*" in which the Papuans and Greenlanders wore their hair—to mock the elaborate costuming of European high fashion.[12] Frequent articles outlining the horrors of foot-binding among the Chinese offered more extreme examples of the ways that fashion could constrict and confine women unnecessarily. Likewise, the lifestyles of women and children among the Japanese, Chinese, Mexicans, Native Americans, Indians, North Africans, and even black Americans provided opportunities for the readers of *Das Kränzchen* to place their own, comparatively more civilized everyday lives in a global context. The emphasis on efforts to educate these peoples on a European model paralleled the journal's frequent pieces promoting the efforts of the middle-class women's movement to increase educational opportunities for German women at home.

Where *Der gute Kamerad* encouraged its readers to identify with the main characters of its stories and reports, before the turn of the century *Das Kränzchen*'s portrayals of the colonial world only encouraged readers to compare their experiences. Such articles entertained insofar as they gave girls a glimpse of strange and horrifying situations and practices around the world, but they did so in a way presumed appropriate for feminine sensibilities. These were patently not exciting. Germany's future men needed to take part in imaginative adventures in the colonial world in order to develop manly virtues, while such adventures risked over-stimulating the nation's future wives and mothers and also threatened a dangerous blurring of gender boundaries. Nevertheless, despite contemporary concerns, it became apparent that many German girls were also interested in the very same adventure literature that pedagogues believed could develop maturity and independence in German boys.[13] Because reformist pedagogy advised that the most effective education made use of the media and themes that fired youngsters' imaginations, this realization led *Das Kränzchen*'s editors and contributors to encourage readers to relate to the colonial world in new ways.

In these two journals, this shift was facilitated by the rising public interest in Germany's own colonial possessions overseas, an interest spurred in particular by wars fought in China (1900) and South-West and East Africa (1904–8). *Der gute Kamerad* responded by devoting more space to Germany's colonial affairs relative to the colonial world more generally. Before 1900, South-West Africa or Togo had merited no more attention than Somalia or Bolivia, but thereafter Germany's *Schutzgebiete* increasingly became the focal point of the journal's factual reports on the non-European world. By reporting on the twin aims of colonial administration—suppressing opposition and building schools and infrastructure—*Der gute Kamerad* increasingly tied the effort to raise capable men at home with an effort to establish the capability of the German nation on the world stage. *Das Kränzchen* also capitalized on the heightened attention to colonial affairs, for its part, to promote the goals of the middle-class women's movement. In 1904, the girls' journal suddenly began reporting on colonizing efforts, like *Der gute Kamerad* with a special emphasis on Germans' good works. As editors and contributors tried to demonstrate to their female readers that German women, too, had a role to play in nation-building both at home and abroad, they increasingly appropriated the colonial adventure that hitherto had been an exclusively masculine preserve. The eventual result was a dramatic change from the journal's previous fare.

Indeed, there was a noticeable and consistent effort in *Das Kränzchen* after 1904 to reconcile prevailing notions of domestic femininity with an active role in the colonial sphere. While the emphasis in the journal's stories remained on domestic, "women's" concerns, editors and contributors began using the colonial sphere to promote a new range of feminine virtues and activities. They did so by educating readers about the ways that women had played and must continue to play a central role in German civilizing efforts. Especially in roles where women could show off their particular domestic talents—nursing, teaching, or housekeeping—they also could fulfill their role as bearers of German *Kultur*. Readers could look to such models as "the heroine of Cameroon," Anna Margarete Hesse née Leue, for examples of a distinctively feminine bravery, wit, and altruism honed under extreme circumstances. A true "Samaritan" honored posthumously by the *Kaiser* himself, Hesse was a nurse who had selflessly defended her European patients against tropical diseases and barbaric savages before meeting an untimely death.[14] These stories proved that girls, too, could bear and benefit from the challenges to be faced and the sacrifices to be made in putting the chaotic and adventurous frontier in order.

Although not on the same scale as in *Der gute Kamerad*, *Das Kränzchen* nonetheless began promoting character development among readers by encouraging them to imagine themselves actively participating in the civilizing of the colonial world together with their male counterparts. This shift is perhaps best illustrated by the first and only colonialist fiction to appear in the journal before the outbreak of the Great War. In a radical departure from the fiction that had previously appeared in the publication, the editors chose in 1913–14 to serialize Henny Koch's *Die Vollrads in Süd-west*.[15] The story is similar to other *Backfischromane* insofar as it follows the development of the main character, Hanna Vollrad, from a naïve, inno-cent 15-year-old "into a true woman," capable of efficiently and effectively running a household.[16]

However, her development takes place in South-West Africa, where the family hopes to make a new start after the death of Hanna's mother. There they set up a farm and begin taming the colonial landscape around them. Not only must Hanna take on her mother's responsibilities; she must also persuade her father and three brothers, who often refer to her using the boy's name Hänsel, that they cannot do without her feminine qualities. As in literature for boys, Koch's colonial frontier features as an uncertain chaotic setting in need of order, but she makes clear that European men cannot accomplish this task without the help of women. The adventurous colonial frontier matures Hanna and allows her to prove her worth as a bearer and promoter of German *Kultur*. She, and only she, can perform the domestic tasks necessary to establishing a German home: running a clear, orderly, civilized household that is a model for the indig-enous population; caring for sick relatives in the absence of any medical assistance; cultivating a vegetable and flower garden to create a sort of tropical paradise out of the barren landscape. At the same time, facing down the challenges of the frontier allows her to grow as an individual. She acclimatizes to the harsh climate, hunts and tracks animals, and even fights against murderous natives in defense of her new German homeland. Unlike in boys' literature, however, Koch's embrace of colonial adventure could not be absolute. To make the story appropriate for the staid pages of *Das Kränzchen*, she injects a certain ambivalence: one moment Hanna thrills at firing a gun or riding a horse and in the next shudders with remorse at her apparent transgression.

Nevertheless, *Vollrads* represented the culmination of a dramatic change for *Das Kränzchen*, as a comparison of Figure 5.3[17] with Figures 5.1 and 5.2 reveals. In an obvious metaphor for the necessary role that German women must play in colonial affairs, Hanna offers her shoulder as support so that her wounded brother can kill a leopard that threatens them and their herds. Beyond its evident symbolism, though, the image also evokes the previously forbidden danger of the lioness attack rather than the tamed exoticism of the lion cubs, and Koch emphasizes that this young woman had benefited from her adventurous encounter. In so doing, she directs an uplifting message at her female readership, namely, that women are strong and valuable *because* of their feminine, domesticating abilities. Hanna's father makes this lesson explicit through his eventual realization that "in certain circumstances a real woman is worth more than some men."[18]

By 1914, *Das Kränzchen*'s editors and contributors had accepted the widespread interest in colonial adventure and used it to promote their vision of an active, middle-class, domestic femininity that complemented the active masculinity promoted in *Der gute Kamerad*. Although they offered different perspectives to their respective audiences, both tried to profit from a self-evident distinction between the European and non-European worlds,

... Sie bog den Kopf zur Seite, so weit sie konnte; da krachte der Schuß ...

*Figure 5.3* "She bent her head to the side as far as she could; then the shot rang out," *Das Kränzchen*, 1913–14.

using the narrative of a civilizing mission to mediate the encounter between the two. The different developments of colonial entertainment in these publications helps us to understand why such colonial references became and remained a common part of Germans' everyday lives during this period.

Empire was far from being a matter of marginal interest for Germans; rather, it was a defining feature of how they understood themselves as a modern, powerful, civilized nation within a globalizing world. In the commercial youth literature developing in Germany from the 1880s, the interplay between consumers and producers determined the various forms of young Germans' colonial encounters. Young readers turned to portrayals of the colonial world because they offered opportunities to escape into exotic domains where different rules applied from those that governed their mundane *Alltag*. Editors and contributors both responded to and tried to shape this interest. In *Der gute Kamerad* and *Das Kränzchen*, colonial encounters offered familiar, popular, and appropriate sets of references for entertaining and for conveying specific lessons to their respective readerships about their place in the modern world. The specific details may have varied over the Imperial Period according to shifts in context and audience, but the enduring utility and attraction of colonial references did not wane. If anything, their prominence and allure grew, as cultural producers used them to reach new audiences. The flexibility of this popular colonialism, the fact that various colonial perspectives could coexist and compete in media aimed at young Germans, both reflects its appeal and helps to explain its prevalence.

## NOTES

1. My title alludes to the British "Boy's Own Paper" and "Girl's Own Paper"— which were certainly models of sorts for the publishers of the journals with which the present article is concerned.
2. Paul Böttcher, "Die Leipziger Jugendschriftenausstellung," *Arbeiter-Jugend*, 1.14 (9 October 1909), p. 222.
3. In 1891, Spemann's publishing house joined with others to create the *Union Deutsche Verlagsgesellschaft*, a conglomerate that dominated the production of youth literature. See Hubert Göbels, *Zeitschriften für die deutschen Jugend: Eine Chronographie 1772–1960* (Dortmund: Harenberg, 1986), pp. 168–77.
4. Valentin Marquardt, *Sozialdemokratische Jugendzeitschriftendiskussion um die Jahrhundertwende: Ein Ansatz zur Grundlegung der Erziehung von proletarischen Kindern und Jugendlichen mit Hilfe des Mediums "Literatur"* (Bielefeld: Kleine, 1986), p. 159.
5. The stories first published in *Der gute Kamerad* were *Sohn des Bärenjägers* (1887); *Kong-Kheou, das Ehrenwort* (1888–9); *Die Sklavenkarawane* (1889–90); *Der Schatz im Silbersee* (1891); *Das Vermächtnis des Inka* (1891–2); *Der Ölprinz* (1892–3); and *Der schwarze Mustang* (1896).
6. Karl May, *Die Sklavenkarawane*, serialized in *Der gute Kamerad*, 4.1–4.52 (1889–90).
7. Luise Glaß, *Annele*, serialized in *Das Kränzchen*, 11.25–11.52 (1898–9).

8. Images by courtesy of the Universitäts- und Landesbibliothek Darmstadt (Figure 5.1) and the Württembergische Landesbibliothek, Stuttgart (Figure 5.2).

9. "Die Löwin im Angriff," *Der gute Kamerad*, 6.47 (1893–4), p. 667.

10. "Spielkameraden," *Das Kränzchen*, 11.37 (1898–9), pp. 340 and 346.

11. "Ein Niggerkönig," *Der gute Kamerad*, 3.51 (1889), p. 815.

12. "Was die wilden Völker schön finden," *Das Kränzchen*, 9.29 (1896–7), p. 405.

13. See, for example, "Neues vom Weihnachtsbüchertisch," *Das Kränzchen* 19.14 (1906–7), p. 220f.

14. Incidentally, this was *Das Kränzchen*'s first substantial article on a German colony. "Die Heldin von Kamerun," *Das Kränzchen*, 17.48 (1904–5), p. 767f.

15. Henny Koch, *Die Vollrads in Südwest*, serialized in *Das Kränzchen* 26.1–26.39 (1913–14). The story was published as a stand-alone novel in 1916 but had reached its 11th edition by 1919. "Literaturverzeichnis," in *Mädchenliteratur der Kaiserzeit: Zwischen weiblicher Identifizierung und Grenzüberschreitung*, ed. by Gisela Wilkending (Stuttgart: Metzler, 2003), p. 323.

16. Henny Koch, *Die Vollrads in Südwest*, *Das Kränzchen*, 26.1 (1913–14), p. 1.

17. Image by courtesy of the Württembergische Landesbibliothek, Stuttgart.

18. Koch, *Vollrads*, *Das Kränzchen*, 26.29 (1913–14), p. 455.

# 6 Picturing Genocide in German Consumer Culture, 1904–10

*David Ciarlo*

Compared with the gravity of events like war, massacre or genocide, the topic of consumer culture might seem trivial. The ubiquity of mass-produced commercial imagery, however, makes it crucial. Pictorial advertising (*Bildreklame* in German) first emerged in the *Kaiserreich* in the last decades of the nineteenth century, but only two decades later had developed into a flood of images. By the time of the Herero war, virtually every person in Germany saw commercial imagery on a daily basis. In fact, many more Germans saw illustrated advertisements than scrutinized the half-tone photographs in the new illustrated tabloids (*Illustrierte*). Advertising imagery circulated not just in the tabloids, but also papered city walls and *Litfaßsäulen*, decorated window displays, and adorned cardboard packaging that was carried back into the home. While the various German print media—whether the colonialist bulletins, bourgeois family magazines, socialist newsletters, or even cosmopolitan tabloids—each had their own political slant and reached their own section of a socially stratified readership, the visual appeals of advertising were not bound to a particular social class or political standpoint. Instead, mass-disseminated commercial imagery strove to speak to a depoliticized, "classless" consumer.[1] Its omnipresence and its social reach therefore makes commercial imagery a significant field for scholarly investigation. One way to glimpse how everyday Germans in the metropole looked upon the events perpetrated by their military and colonial authorities is to discover what they actually *saw*.

In discussions of German colonialism, the Herero war looms large. It has often been recognized that the war reverberated through the German metropole, particularly in the so-called Hottentot election of 1907, where nationalist parties gained seats by tapping into wartime patriotism—and by underscoring the "racial" nature of this threat to the German nation.[2] There can be no doubt that the military campaign in South-West Africa was approached as a "race war" by those that waged it.[3] Scholars have also pointed to an escalation of racist rhetoric and imagery in the German metropole during and after the war in literature, magazines, memoirs, and children's books.[4] Yet many scholars approach the escalating racism in the German public sphere as if it were an almost inevitable extension of the colonial war itself—as if the violence in the colonies was simply channeled back into the metropole. The commercial context of advertising, however, complicates any such direct connection. Advertisers had their own aims and ambitions, and pursued their own agendas, even as the new forces of mechanical reproduction broadcast this agenda to a viewing public of unprecedented scope.

In the years before the war, the nascent consumer imaginary in Germany offered a sprawling tapestry of illustrative motifs. Maternal figures made earnest recommendations; pictorial puns caught the eye of passers-by; national icons played upon patriotic feelings; and panoramas of distant landscapes offered exotic allure.[5] One thread of this mass-produced, commercialized image-world is particularly relevant to the Herero war, namely, the figure of the African. Right around 1900, Africans began to appear frequently in German advertising and product packaging across a whole range of products, including many that had only the most tenuous connection to official colonialism[6].

This motif often depicted an African carrying a burden of supposed "colonial" goods or wares, as in a Zuntz coffee ad from 1901 (see Figure 6.1). (Such "natives," it should be noted, were attached to products from the global commodities market; the tiny handful of goods actually exported from the German colonies themselves were generally marketed with more conservative

*Figure 6.1*   A. Zuntz, Berlin: "Roasted Coffee."

themes, such as a German flag or a drawing of the prize medallion "won" by the product.) As I have argued elsewhere, the new presence of this figure arose more from purely domestic commercial needs than from the imagery or activities of the institutions of German colonialism: for the figure of the African native allowed the advertiser to couple the allure of tropical exoticism succinctly and efficiently to a power-laden appeal to the German viewer's ego, all within a single, concise illustration.[7] After 1900, the new technologies of cheap image reproduction then standardized the depictions of Africans into a colonial subordinate laboring under a heavy burden. I might even speculate here (without the luxury of evidence) that the increasing prevalence of commercial images of Africans—laboring dutifully on German product packaging—may have contributed to the disbelief that met the news of the initial success of the Herero uprising.

Entrepreneurial interests greeted the Herero uprising and the subsequent military campaign with enthusiasm and, in the process, disseminated very different visions of Africans from those of dutiful laborers. In 1904, the commercial press in Germany threw itself into the fray by recounting the atrocities of the Herero, glorifying the brave lieutenants of the colonial forces (*Schutztruppe*), berating the government for inaction, and boasting of exclusive access to up-to-date information (including photographs) from the battlefield. This thrilling current event presented businesses with a new field of opportunity. Almost immediately, a pay-for-admission panorama of the Herero uprising appeared in Berlin.[8] Entertainment personalities became involved: the *Völkerschau* impresario Carl Hagenbeck sent 2,000 camels to South-West Africa in a well-publicized contribution to the war effort.[9] (An advertisement from 1907 by a Hamburg import/export firm illustrates this marketing coup: it depicts three lines of German colonial troops riding in formation on camelback.)[10] Firms like Gustav Kühn and Oehmigke & Riemschneider churned out *Bilderbogen* depicting heroic scenes of courageous German colonial troops battling relentless hordes of fierce African warriors.[11] The satirical humor magazines, from the venerable *Kladderadatsch* and the fashionable *Simplicissimus* to the socialist *Der wahre Jacob*, offered cartoons of the conflict; although they offered pointed and bitter critiques of European and German colonial policy, their caricatures of Africans as savage cannibals were equally sharp.[12] Finally, a surge of soldiers' and settlers' memoirs appeared right after the war, capitalizing on "eyewitness" accounts; many of these books (including Gustav Frenssen's fictional account, *Peter Moors Fahrt nach Südwest*) feature cover illustrations of a threatening, looming or staring Herero savage, or a triumphant German colonial soldier smiting a cowering brute.[13] Impelled by commercial opportunism, two different visions of Africans circulated: illustrations of rebellious, murderous savages and photographs of defeated Africans in chains or in prison camps.[14] Each of these pictorial motifs contrasted strikingly with the illustrations of natives cheerfully carrying burdens before 1904.

## LIONIZING THE *SCHUTZTRUPPE*

To what degree did imagery associated directly with the war appear as *commodity* imagery—as advertising to sell products? First, advertisers began to deploy motifs of the uniformed *Schutztruppe*—the colonial forces. This incarnation of the "white hero in the tropics" differed from the pith helm-wearing explorer long seen in *Liebigbilder* or in the back pages of colonial enthusiast publications—not the least because the colonial trooper appeared in ads by firms with very different habits of pictorial advertising. The small Westphalian cigar manufacturer Carl Warmann & Co, for instance, had long deployed military themes: one of their typical ads might show a discriminating Prussian officer with monocle and riding crop enjoying one of Warmann's cigars. Early in the decade, Warmann also trademarked a "Chinakämpfer" cigarette brand to celebrate the German marines' part in suppressing the Boxer rebellion.[15] So it was not surprising that the South-West African campaign, the German army's largest military action since 1870, emerged in Warmann's advertising, as we see in this dramatic cavalry charge of the *Schutztruppe* trademarked in 1909 (see Figure 6.2).

*Figure 6.2*   Carl Warmann & Co. cigars: "German Riders."

Yet even the large, mass-market firms with a vastly different pictorial inventory participated in marketing the German heroes in the African war. The Dresden cigarette giant Jasmatzi had deployed orientalist themes for its brands such as Cheops, Sphinx, and Ramses from the 1880s onward; but they leapt on to the colonial bandwagon in 1908, introducing a "Südwest-Afrika" brand that featured a colonial officer (see Figure 6.3).[16]

Of course, those companies that had some connection to the German colonial troops found it effective advertising to market this fact to their domestic consumers, as with an ad by the *Conservenfabrik Standard* of Berlin (see Figure 6.4).

*Figure 6.3* Jasmatzi, Dresden: "South-West Africa Cigarettes."

*Figure 6.4 Conservenfabrik* Standard, Berlin: "Standard Tropic-Resistant [Products]."

In 1906, with the nationalistic fervor of the Hottentot election reaching its greatest intensity, this ad's mere depiction of a German colonial soldier might have been enough to capture the attention of patriotic German viewers. But, on closer inspection, we can see that the *Standard* company's pictorial composition displays a great deal of sophistication. First, the officer's own evident fascination draws a viewer's attention directly to the can—and thereby directly to the company logo. By placing the can label upside-down, moreover, the curious viewer is encouraged to crane his head, to get the viewer to read the company name for a second time. Finally, the trooper's facial expression is one of bliss; the contents of the tin are far more than just another bit of potted meat kept fresh by modern technology; they are a little taste of home—perhaps even the essence of German civilization—packaged neatly as a durable, transportable commodity. Overall, this is a tranquil rather than bellicose scene. The rising sun in the background conveys a sense of optimism; modern civilization in the form of well-equipped troops *and* well-sealed tins will bring a new dawn to the dark continent.

An early ad from 1905, by the Mainz champagne manufacturing giant Kupferberg, presents a similarly peaceful theme (see Figure 6.5).

GRUSS AUS DER
HEIMAT

*Figure 6.5* Kupferberg wines, Mainz: "Greetings from Home."

The colonial soldier here, identifiable as such only by his Southwester hat, is in the role of pioneer in repose; without a visible weapon at hand, he relaxes, as horses graze in the background. He raises a toast, either to those who dispatched such a civilized drink to this frontier or to acknowledge the distant *Heimat* that produced it. As with the Standard firm's tins, the commodity takes on an added gravitas, distilling the very essence of modern civilization. If the colonial troops far from home can find such contentment in the product, then surely those Germans safely back in the metropole will appreciate it as well.

Some visual advertising also sought to evoke the courage and martial heroism of the colonial forces but in a way that effaced the harsh realities of war and the brutality of their actions. A hunting scene for "German-South-West" cigarettes, trademarked by a small Berlin company in 1910, shows a rifleman taking aim at a menacing lion in a typical "white hunter in the tropics" safari tableau (see Figure 6.6).

Yet a devil lies in the details. This hunter wears the uniform of the colonial forces and thereby stands for German military power in the South-West African colony; but the presence of the lion recasts that power to confront hostile *nature* rather than to crush indigenous rebellion. Significantly, the lion menaces the soldier from atop a pile of the brand-name cigarettes themselves. This implies, visually, that the cigarettes or the tobacco to make them can be found in abundance in German South-West. (In point of fact, tobacco was never exported from South-West Africa in significant quantities.) The scene further implies that the "lion," or any "untamed" threat that bars access to this colonial product, needs to be dealt with forcefully and with finality.

The lion as a stand-in for the threat of the Herero was also a theme with products that actually came from the German colony of South-West (see Figure 6.7).

*Figure 6.6*   "German South-West [Africa]" cigarettes, Berlin.

*Figure 6.7* Fischer, Reutlingen: "Fischer's German South-West [Africa] Wool."

In an ad trademarked by a small company in Reutlingen, the colonial trooper uses the colonial wool to lasso a lion. The German-produced colonial commodity, in short, can tame the savage beast. (In a more sinister reading, the trooper is pulling the very wool itself out of the lion's whisker's—using the very body of the savage beast as a raw material.) Either interpretation taps into the trooper's heroism, for he and the modern (German) commodity jointly confront the savagery of nature.

## REFASHIONING THE NATIVE

What of the images of Africans in advertising during and after the war? Were they shown as opponents of the *Schutztruppe*—as the ruthless, savage hordes illustrated in the *Bilderbogen*—or as defeated, beaten prisoners seen in the photo-pages of the *Illustrierten*? In fact, images of Africans had become so highly charged that they were irresistible to advertisers. Older patterns of depiction were less tenable, however. A trademark showing a Herero warrior, by the import/export company Carl Henckell, stands as a case in point (see Figure 6.8).

The surprisingly placid pose echoes many of the established conventions of ethnographic drawings (such as those found in popular magazines like *Über Land und Meer* in the 1880s) that emphasized the nobility of

*Figure 6.8*  Carl Henckell import/export: "Herero."

the native subject. Registered in 1905, however, the intent of the image is ambiguous, particularly when placed among the sensationalized savages appearing in other media. Perhaps the allure of Henckell's image was to be its "authenticity." More likely, it was simply taken over from an earlier ethnography tome in the rush to trademark a "Herero" image and capitalize on the topicality of the war. Indeed, it looks almost identical to the figure on the cover of Friedrich Meister's 1904 *Muhérer riKárra* (Beware, Herero), which itself appears to be pilfered from earlier ethnographic drawings.[17] Regardless, static images such as Henckell's became less common after 1905. The competition from more striking or titillating depictions may well have made such ethnographic-style images easy to overlook; and to be overlooked was the fear of every advertiser.

*Figure 6.9*   "Herero" schnapps, Stettin.

At the other end of the spectrum, some ads celebrated the German victory over the Herero with downright venom. A bottle label from a small liquor manufacturer in Stettin, for instance, features a racist caricature of a "Herero" dancing for the amusement of a German sailor as he prepares to swig the advertised product (see Figure 6.9). The lips of the black "native" are massively oversized for German advertising of 1904; indeed, the facial features are not so much caricatured as they are deformed in an apparent attempt to illustrate racial degeneracy. It is unclear as to whether the cross-hatching on the arms and legs is meant to represent filth or hair; both would serve in the effort to animalize the figure. One can infer from the amateurish composition of this ad that it involved a hasty rush by a smaller business to capitalize on post-victory jingoism. Its most dehumanizing elements, particularly the attempt to illustrate "dirtiness," are extremely unusual for product labels. Even when advertisements presented the most exaggerated racial stereotypes, they generally did so in a style that was as crisp and clean in its delineations as in its discriminations. This is quite understandable: consumer imagery was meant to entice, not disgust.

Illustrations of questionable taste or morality could enjoy a greater degree of latitude from the authorities when they played into patriotic nationalism. In the most startling example that I have found, a Dresden cigar firm trademarked a photograph of a supine and totally nude black woman in a pose that abandoned any pretense at artistic demur in favor of blatant eroticism (see Figure 6.10). Semi-nude erotic photographs of African or South Pacific women were common in ethnographic books or journals, of course.[18] But publicly circulated imagery was held to a far stricter standard and subject to police censorship.[19] A copyrighted trademark, moreover, had to pass through a lengthy bureaucratic registration process. This image of a "Herero Girl" is the first full nude photograph—ever—to appear as a trademark in the German imperial Trademark Registration Rolls. The cigars, a house brand from a tobacconist in Dresden, were named "Swakopmund" after the coastal town in German South-West Africa (an accurate

*Figure 6.10*  *Cigarrenhaus* "Swakomund," Dresden: "Own Brand 'Herero Girls'."

detail that suggests the tobacconist catered to colonial enthusiasts). The registrant was one Frau Taeß, whose gender may have helped to slip this image past the censors. But the image remains startling: in the context of war, reprisal, repression, and genocide—in Swakopmund, the survivors of Trotha's genocidal policy were at this point suffering forced labor, starvation, and disease in concentration camps—the proffered nudity and sexual access of the "Herero Girl" cannot help but be evocative of symbolic rape.[20] It was not imitated, however.

A far more typical engagement of advertising with the Herero, at least among the capitalized firms and businesses that invested large sums in advertising, played in a more indefinite realm. Given that marketers had little wish to alienate prospective purchasers, the perfect advertisement would stimulate popular interest with its topicality, yet avoid taking a position on an issue that was potentially divisive. After all, potential customers included the working class, a broad swath of which was organized by Social Democrats who were explicitly opposed to the colonial policy of the German state. Over the first decade of the twentieth century, advertisers increasingly sought to address Germans as (theoretically) classless consumers and thereby avoided divisive political statements; yet the thrill of political events offered unparalleled opportunity. One seemingly safe avenue through these competing demands was that of humor.

A 1905 advertisement by the Chemische Fabriken Meer for photography products offers a case in point (see Figure 6.11). A black man-child whips and lectures a coy and somewhat embarrassed baboon that appears to wear a monocle. The implicit violence of the image might very well arrest attention. (The illustration also plays upon popular German children's comics like Wilhelm Busch's *Phipps der Affe*.) The image itself can be interpreted in a variety of ways. It could be read as a visual narrative where the Prussian baboon is learning a "lesson" at the hands of the African native— and thus could be viewed as a satirical critique of military policy. Another interpretation, however, could instead read the scene as an illustration of natural hierarchy, where the native scolds and punishes his biological inferior, the thieving monkey, who has stolen an object from him. *This* African can punish a thieving inferior, just as the German can similarly punish his unruly inferiors. These two interpretations (and others) contradict each other; which is correct?

I would argue that this question is not really important for the advertisement to work. Instead, the crucial element of the image is what all of the possible interpretations *share*. Regardless of the political valence or meaning derived from the image, the viewer is confronted with the graphic racialization of the bodily features of the native. The lips are absurdly, comically exaggerated; the figure is manifestly immature (he is not really a child—but not really an adult, either); and his bare feet and curly hair are both emphasized. These details are all deliberately deployed by the graphic artist to make it difficult, if not impossible, to see the native as similar to

*Figure 6.11   Chemische Fabriken* Meer photography products.

the European viewer. The interpretation of the scene might be ambivalent, but the most elemental, graphic message cannot be mistaken: the body of the African is fundamentally different.

   Such graphic racialization of African figures in advertising began before the Herero uprising; but it is after 1905 that this pattern of depiction really gathers momentum.[21] Is this a result of the war, or even a post factum justification of the genocide? In fact, a whole host of factors came together right at mid-decade around this thorny issue of race, and only some were directly related to the war in South-West Africa. For instance, Andrew Zimmerman, Pascal Grosse, and others have skillfully charted the rapid ascendancy of "race science" in professional disciplines, with the middle of the decade similarly emerging as a pivotal moment.[22] Advertisers and graphic artists were largely oblivious to these academic debates about race, however. Instead, advertisers' own professional concerns, coupled with the expectations of their viewing public, ultimately drove their own pictorial production.

   The racialization of black figures was one pictorial strategy that spoke the new language of the mass market. Professional advertising writers increasingly insisted that an ad should make bold statements; it should force its way into the attention—into the psyche—of the casual passer-by. A 1904 insecticide advertisement by the Berlin company Hermann Bardorf illustrates this vividly (see Figure 6.12).

This particular ad was certainly *not* crafted as a direct response to the Herero uprising; although the illustration was issued in 1904, the company trademarked the brand name "Massenmord" (Mass Murder) back in 1896. But even though Bardorf's brand is not crafted as a reference to colonial genocide, it is indicative of a new cultural syntax—a dramatic way of presenting power to the broad public in a stark visual form. Advertisements like this were unthinkable in the German public sphere of the 1880s; yet by World War One, they were everywhere. They came with a new creed among the makers of mass culture—a creed that insisted that sensationalism sells and that presentations of power persuade.[23] At the same time, brutal, total, even genocidal solutions to "problems" were being casually advocated in the political realm. I would suggest that these two streams—stark, dramatic, and aggressive presentations of power in commercial culture, on the one hand, and a stark, dramatic, and aggressive political rhetoric of "solutions," on the other—are more closely interlaced than we commonly recognize.

If Bardorf's insecticide did not directly reference the war in South-West Africa, then an image for Müller's Ink-Remover certainly did (see Figure 6.13). Registered by an office-supply firm in Stettin, the advertisement

*Figure 6.12*   Hermann Bardorf insecticide, Berlin: "Bardorf's Mass Murder. The Best Remedy against Bedbugs."

*Figure 6.13*   Müller ink-remover, Stettin: "Eradicate all your Spelling Mistakes and Blots with Müller's Ink Remover."

exhorted, "Eradicate your Spelling Mistakes and Blots with Müller's Ink Remover." The advertisement attempts to deploy humor by drawing both on the adage of the *Mohrenwäsche* and on the visual puns of advertising that related the blackness of "black" products (such as ink, coffee, or shoe polish) to "black" people.[24] The illustration ties into these long-established twin pictorial lineages of blackness, which then serves (rather paradoxically) to *de*politicize the figure's "Africanness."

The implications of the ad, however, are striking. First, its language is quite sinister. News of the war in South-West Africa saturated the mass media in 1904, and the choice of words—*vertilgen* (destroy, eradicate, exterminate) for correcting the "mistake" of too much blackness—cannot be accidental. Even more ominous are its visual elements: the ink is literally dissolving the blackness of the African. In a startling (and powerful) visual gesture, the figure has inadvertently transferred some of the ink-remover to his neck—a mistake that has left, quite literally, a white hand grasping the black figure's throat. Finally, the figure is graphically racialized. The figure's skull is deliberately elongated with a receding hairline to emphasize it better, the eyes are drawn wide, and the size of the lips is exaggerated.

By 1910, such pictorial conventions underscoring physiognomic and bodily differences had become ubiquitous with African figures. One can trace this ongoing racialization even in the ads of a single firm (see Figure 6.14).

# Nama

*Figure 6.14* Henkelmann groceries, Magdeburg: "Nama" I.

A mail-order grocery company in Magdeburg registered an illustration for *Kolonialwaren*—groceries of a certain sort, namely, coffee, cocoa, tobacco, spices, and the like. Registered in 1911, the trademark is clearly amateurish and decidedly odd. There is no indication why they chose to name their brand "Nama," after one of the peoples destroyed by the German colonial forces in South-West Africa. (The firm is not likely to have been a colonial company, for such would have registered instead under the category "Produkte aus den deutschen Kolonien.") An ad from just two years later, however, is revealing (see Figure 6.15).

First of all, the artistic execution is more professional, if nonetheless still a bit cluttered. It clearly shifts the trademark to a more "humorous" plane: the lion is anthropomorphized, for instance, and the figure is drawn as a caricature. The graphic racialization of the Nama figure,

*Figure 6.15*   Henkelmann groceries, Magdeburg: "Nama" II.

however, is sensationalistic; it dramatizes by gross exaggeration, thereby calling attention to the composition as a whole. The caricature of man and beast also seeks to draw upon humor to temper the political implications of the image and its brand name. Finally, the seemingly good-natured humor of the caricature draws attention away from illustrations of bloodthirsty, savage Africans that had so saturated the public sphere during the war. This caricatured "Nama" cannot be the same as those fearsome foes who waged guerilla war for three long years, for this figure is clearly foolish. In a way, then, racialization offered one means by which to continue to use the figures of Africans in commercial culture— but without calling to mind the more threatening images circulating in other media and further contexts.

There is no simple, cause-and-effect relationship between the Herero war and the stereotypes that circulated during and afterward: racist advertising did not flow naturally from the colonies as a byproduct of racially motivated warfare. Rather, the ultimate arbiter of this imagery—and its motor for change—was the dynamic commercial and consumer forces in the German metropole. In the short term, amateurs registered images of virulently racist jingoism; but the professional designers looked more to the (German) colonial trooper as a way to capitalize on the public's attentions. In their portrayals of Africans, meanwhile, professional advertisers turned to ambiguity and to "humor"—in part, I argue, to lend their images broad appeal that would cross class and especially political boundaries. During the Herero revolt and subsequent genocide, stylistic conventions of graphic racialization accelerated and intensified in German consumer culture. This was not so much because advertisers were politically committed to convincing the German public—in the fashion of propaganda—that Africans far away in the German colonies were racially inferior and therefore deserving of brutal treatment. Instead, I would suggest that, for German advertisers, the motif of the African was simply too useful to abandon. The figure of the African native had proved too adept at arousing curiosity with exoticism, too useful at seizing attention through sensationalistic exaggeration, and too powerful in demonstrating the significance of the product by juxtaposing it against a representation of the "uncivilized." In short, images of African subjects could flatter the German viewer with a presentation of power that was (to them) inoffensive. After 1904, advertisers racialized the figures of Africans, in order to continue to exploit them.

## NOTES

1. Cf. Peter Borscheid and Clemens Wischermann, *Bilderwelt des Alltags. Werbung in der Konsumgesellschaft des 19. und 20. Jahrhunderts* (Stuttgart: Steiner, 1995).
2. See Ulrich van der Heyden, "Die 'Hottentottenwahlen' von 1907," in *Völkermord in Deutsch-Südwestafrika*, ed. by Jürgen Zimmerer and Joachim Zeller (Berlin: Links, 2003), pp. 97–102. See also Woodruff D. Smith, *The German Colonial Empire* (Chapel Hill: University of North Carolina Press, 1978), pp. 183–91.
3. See *Genozid und Gedenken*, ed. by Henning Melber (Frankfurt/M.: Brandes & Apsel, 2005); Helmut Bley, *South-West Africa under German Rule, 1894–1914* (London: Heinemann, 1971), p. 165; Pascal Grosse, *Kolonialismus, Eugenik und bürgerliche Gesellschaft in Deutschland 1850–1918* (Frankfurt/M.: Campus, 2000); Gesine Krüger, *Kriegsbewältigung und Geschichtsbewußtsein. Realität, Deutung und Verarbeitung des Deutschen Kolonialkriegs in Namibia 1904 bis 1907* (Göttingen: Vandenhoeck & Ruprecht, 1999), p. 84f.
4. See, for example, Jörg Wassink, *Auf den Spuren des deutschen Völkermordes in Südwestafrika* (Munich: Meidenbauer, 2004); *Kolonialismus, Kolonialdiskurs und Genozid*, ed. by Mihran Dabag, Horst Gründer and

Uwe-K. Ketelsen (Munich: Fink, 2004); Marieluise Christadler, "Zwischen Gartenlaube und Genozid. Kolonialistische Jugendbücher im Kaiserreich," in *Die Menschen sind arm, weil sie arm sind*, ed. by Jörg Becker and Charlotte Oberfeld (Frankfurt/M.: Haag & Herchen, 1978), pp. 61–98.

5. For examples, see *Reklame: Produktwerbung im Plakat 1890 bis 1918*, DVD-Rom (Berlin: Deutsches Historisches Museum, 2005); *Selling Modernity: Advertising in Twentieth-Century Germany*, ed. by Pamela E. Swett, S. Jonathan Wiesen and Jonathan R. Zatlin (Durham, NC: Duke University Press, 2007); Detlef Lorenz, *Reklamekunst um 1900* (Berlin: Reimer, 2000); Jeremy Aynsley, *Graphic Design in Germany, 1890–1945* (Berkeley: University of California Press, 2000); Jürgen Schwarz, *Bildannoncen aus der Jahrhundertwende* (Frankfurt/M.: Kunstgeschichtliches Institut, 1990); *Das frühe Plakat in Europa und den USA*, vol. 3: *Deutschland*, ed. by Helga Hollmann et al. (Berlin: Mann, 1980).

6. Claims about the prevalence of certain imagery or the larger patterns of commercial motifs are based on my research into the trademark registration rolls (*Warenzeichenblatt*, henceforth WZB) of the *Kaiserliches Patentamt*. In fin-de-siècle Germany, ads and packaging were often registered as trademarks as a form of copyright. From 2,000 to 4,000 images were registered every year before 1914, providing an enormous pool of imagery, all precisely dated.

7. See David Ciarlo, *Advertising Empire, Consuming Race: Colonialism, Commerce and Visual Culture in Germany, 1887–1914* (Cambridge, MA: Harvard University Press, forthcoming).

8. See *Schilder, Bilder, Moritaten. Sonderschau des Museums für Volkskunde im Pergamonmuseum*, ed. by Erika Karasek et al. (Berlin: Staatliche Museen, 1987), appendix.

9. See Carl Hagenbeck, *Von Tieren und Menschen* (Berlin: Vita, 1909). Cf. also Eric Ames, "Where the Wild Things Are: Locating the Exotic in German Modernity" (PhD diss., University of California, Berkeley, 2000), p. 6.

10. F. Reddaway & Co. (Hamburg): see WZB (1907), p. 2253, no. 102005.

11. For *Bilderbogen*, the caricatured buffoonery of colonial natives in the late 1880s gave way to scenes of heroic German soldiers fighting hordes of tough and merciless Africans. See Astrid Frevert, Gisela Rautenstrauch, and Matthias Rickling, "Kolonialismus und Darstellungen aus den Kolonien," in *Neuruppiner Bilderbogen. Ein Massenmedium des 19. Jahrhunderts*, ed. by Stefan Brakensiek, Regina Krull, and Irina Rockel (Bielefeld: Verlag für Regionalgeschichte, 1993), pp. 137–55; and Theodor Kohlmann, *Neuruppiner Bilderbogen* (Berlin: Staatliche Museen, 1981).

12. See the "Kolonial-Nummer" of *Simplicissimus*, 9.6 (1904). See also Edward Graham Norris and Arnold Beuke, "Kolonialkrieg und Karikatur in Deutschland," in *Studien zur Geschichte des deutschen Kolonialismus in Afrika*, ed. by Peter Heine and Ulrich van der Heyden (Pfaffenweiler: Centaurus, 1995), pp. 377–98.

13. See Medardus Brehl, "Die Vernichtung der Herero und Nama in der deutschen (Populär-) Literatur," in *Völkermord*, ed. by Zimmerer and Zeller, pp. 86–96.

14. Cf. Joachim Zeller, "Images of the South West African War: Reflections of the 1904–1907 Colonial War in Contemporary Photo Reportage and Book Illustration," in *Hues Between Black and White*, ed. by Wolfram Hartmann (Windhoek: Out of Africa, 2004), pp. 309–23.

15. Carl Warmann & Co (Bünde i.W.): see WZB (1904), p. 317, no. 66474.

16. Cf. *Historische Plakate 1890–1914*, ed. by Susanne Anna (Stuttgart: Daco, 1995), p. 265f. On the orientalism of German cigarette advertising, see *Smoke*, ed. by Sander Gilman and Zhou Xun (London: Reaktion, 2004);

Michael Weisser, *Cigaretten-Reclame* (Münster: Coppenrath, 1980); and David Ciarlo, "Consuming Race, Envisioning Empire: Colonialism and German Mass Culture, 1887–1914" (PhD diss., University of Wisconsin, Madison, 2003), pp. 169–183.

17. See the cover of *Muhérer riKárra* (*Beware, Herero*), reproduced in Brehl, "Die Vernichtung," p. 89.
18. See Jutta Engelhard and Peter Mesenhöller, *Bilder aus dem Paradies* (Cologne: Jonas, 1995); Michael Wiener, *Ikonographie des Wilden. Menschen-Bilder in Ethnographie und Photographie zwischen 1850 und 1918* (Munich: Trickster, 1990); *Prehistories of the Future: The Primitivist Project and the Culture of Modernism*, ed. by Elazar Barkan and Ronald Bush (Stanford: Stanford University Press, 1995), p. 86f; Raymond Corbey, "Alterity: the Colonial Nude," *Critique of Anthropology*, 8 (1988), 75–92.
19. See Lynn Abrams, "From Control to Commercialization: The Triumph of Mass Entertainment in Germany, 1900–1925," *German History*, 8 (1990), 278–93; Robin Lenman, "Control of the Visual Image in Imperial Germany," in *Zensur und Kultur*, ed. by John McCarthy and Werner von der Ohe (Tübingen: Niemeyer, 1995), 111–22.
20. The Herero war facilitated a broader relaxation of mores in conservative circles. The German Colonial Society, for one, moved away rather suddenly from its ethnographic gaze, and began to print blatantly erotic or shockingly violent imagery. See Ciarlo, "Consuming Race, Envisioning Empire," Ch. 5. On the concentration camp at Swakopmund, see Zimmerer and Zeller, *Völkermord*, pp. 64–79.
21. Cf. Ciarlo, *Advertising Empire*, Chs 5 and 6.
22. Andrew Zimmerman, *Anthropology and Antihumanism in Imperial Germany* (Chicago: University of Chicago Press, 2001); Wolfgang U. Eckart, *Medizin und Kolonialimperialismus* (Paderborn: Schöningh, 1997).
23. Professional advertising writers insisted on decorum and urged tasteful designs to legitimize advertising with the cachet of *Kunst*. See Christiane Lamberty, *Reklame in Deutschland 1890–1914. Wahrnehmung, Professionalisierung und Kritik der Wirtschaftswerbung* (Berlin: Duncker & Humblot, 2000). The visual record of early German advertising practice, however, strongly contradicts such discursive invocations.
24. See, for example, Michael Scholz-Hänsel, *Das exotische Plakat* (Stuttgart: Cantz, 1987); Hermann Pollig, *Exotische Welten: europäische Phantasien* (Stuttgart: Cantz, 1987); Peter Martin, *Schwarze Teufel, edle Mohren. Afrikaner in Bewußtsein und Geschichte der Deutschen* (Hamburg: Junius, 1993). The *Mohrenwäsche* was a venerable popular folk saying about the futility of attempting to wash the color off an Ethiopian; see Jean Michel Massing, "From Greek Proverb to Soap Advert: Washing the Ethiopian," *Journal of the Warburg and Courtauld Institutes*, 58 (1995), 180–201.

# 7 The Visual Representation of Blackness During German Imperialism Around 1900

*Volker Langbehn*

Germany's principal engagement as a colonial power, in the epoch around 1900, coincides with the rise of postcards as a medium of communication.[1] As important cultural and historical artifacts, and seen from the perspective of a post-colonial age, postcards represent a form of forgotten "collective colonial memory" that has received little critical attention in the context of German colonialism.[2] As a form of perception and representation of the foreign, postcards assumed a role as witness of and instrument in the production of cultural knowledge at the period.[3] Knowledge about cultures outside of Europe and the self-perception of Western European civilization as *culture* mutually conditioned each other, creating an interdependent binary structure between identity and alterity. Like many other contributions to the cultural history of colonialism in the Wilhelminian era, postcards supply evidence of popular images of alterity that circulated among the public, disseminated by, among others, newspapers, satirical magazines, journals, posters, museums, scientific societies and world fairs. Germany's quest to become a colonial power found significant support in the vast array of colonial images that were spread in postcard representations.

I argue that postcards played a central identity-forming role within German culture and society during the Wilhelminian era. Viewed as part of a wider pattern of cultural expression, postcards can provide an important understanding of the pervasive and persistent set of cultural attitudes that informed Germany's position toward the rest of the world, and especially toward its colonies. In addressing the visual representation of Germany's colonialism, I shall additionally seek to link the visual culture of postcards to the fascination with new modes of seeing and the enigmas of visual experience that have become one of the trademarks of modernity. By considering vision and visuality as culturally inflected practices, I shall interrogate the hidden effects of visual metaphors, or what Walter Benjamin has called the optical unconscious.[4] Rather like the so-called "linguistic turn" identified by twentieth-century philosophers, a "pictorial turn" can be discerned, which provokes—as Martin Jay puts it—"historical investigations of the entanglement of the political and the visual."[5] To illuminate the complexity of this process, I would quote W. J. T. Mitchell's definition:

[I]t is rather a postlinguistic, postsemiotic rediscovery of the picture as a complex interplay between visuality, apparatus, institutions, discourse, bodies, and figurality. It is the realization that *spectatorship* (the look, the gaze, the glance, the practices of observation, surveillance, and visual pleasure) may be as deep a problem as various forms of *reading* (decipherment, decoding, interpretation, etc.) and that visual experience or "visual literacy" might not be fully explicable on the model of textuality.[6]

Mitchell's characterization of our contemporary era of video and cybernetic technology, the age of electronic reproduction, and its new development and control of visual stimulation and illusion, invites us to revisit the decades around 1900 and establish the links between the pictorial turn, colonialism and postcards.[7] This period saw the development of the picture postcard, the rapid refinement of photographic technology and the emergence of myriad new printing processes.[8] The new repertoire for describing and representing intercultural encounter dramatically expanded and reconfigured the knowledge of alterity.[9] The development of new disciplines such as anthropology, sociology and ethnology, as described by Michel Foucault, contributed to the production of discursive knowledge about locales outside of Europe.[10]

While mass culture and mass consumer society threatened the existing social and political order, it concurrently favored a fundamentally new articulation of German identity by representing images of alterity.[11] Hence such private groupings as the printing industry could usurp the role of a political community of citizens. However, creating a national consciousness was not without disagreements, since institutional ways of creating such consciousness differed significantly from advocacy by an authentic political community of citizens of their own nationalist ideas and ambitions.[12] The new mass culture stressed visuality as a central component in its self-definition without governmental approval. Visual appeal became a central characteristic in a vast array of industries, especially in advertising.

During the process of national identity formation, the medium of the letter post assumed an important role in advancing Germany's colonial politics. Under the guidance of the General Director of Posts, Heinrich von Stephan (1831–97), whose book *Geschichte der preußischen Post* (1859) set the guidelines for the reorganization of the German postal services, Germany introduced postcards in 1870, and they quickly became a crucial method of communication in the early days of the German Empire.[13] Early in his career, Heinrich von Stephan pushed for the standardization and internationalization of the postal services, which—among other developments—led to the establishment of the Universal Postal Union in 1874, an international organization that, even today, coordinates postal policies among member nations. As Oliver Simons has convincingly demonstrated, von Stephan linked his national and international postal ambitions with Germany's national interests in the conquering and securing of new space.[14]

With the introduction of picture postcards, or *Ansichtskarten*, in 1875, the revolution in technical communication received a further dramatic impulse, which led through various further stages to what was in effect a golden age between 1895 and 1914–18.[15] The manufacture and distribution of picture postcards remained under the control of the postal services themselves in most member countries of the Postal Union until 1885, and in some states until the mid-1890s, whereupon private companies were permitted to produce their own picture postcards for postal communication. This new form of mass culture and mass consumption then experienced a dramatic increase in popularity, and postcards gained the status of the principal communication method of the masses, aided by the delivery of mail several times a day.[16] In contrast to letter-writing, which required leisure and a certain degree of education—thus appealing more to the bourgeoisie—writing postcards liberated the masses from the stifling requirements of epistolary etiquette, and enabled them to enter the flow of public communication on their own terms. The popularity of postcards ultimately sealed the victory of postcards over letter writing, reflecting the industrialization of communication.[17] Their victory also signaled a radical alteration of previous temporal and spatial consciousness, creating and provoking an array of new aesthetic responses. In conjunction with the emergence of inexpensive photography, postcards began to shape people's response to the world and their representation in it. As one of the main suppliers of postcards, Germany's printing industry participated in the historical changes that subverted the prevailing sense of temporality and of spatial and existential presence. Space assumes a central element in Germany's colonial discourse, because, as Thomas Molden puts it,

> the element of space and the structure of spatial relationships are among the features that define the hierarchical organization of the imagined community and that differentiate between those who are within it and those who are not, between those at its center and those at—or beyond—its margins.[18]

Picture postcards in fact provided the ultimate medium to illustrate Germany's imperial story, with images of its many characters and events shared with the rest of the world thanks to Heinrich von Stephan's global communication system. The *Ansichtskarten*, literally translated as "cards to be looked at," had been transformed into an international spectacle, a collective celebration of Germany's imperial superiority. Postcards displaced letter writing from its position as the dominant method of communication, and the describing of the world took place in the form of free-floating images transmitted by the post office.[19]

The following picture postcards present images of children, one of the most widely circulated themes around 1900. My discussion will seek to outline the system by which alterity is represented in such images, with a particular focus on the use of color—central to the binary structuring of the world in literature specifically and the arts in general—and the pictorial strategy or iconographic codification this represents. The most obvious visual characteristic of postcards is the contrast between dark and light. One of the many strategies employed to capture the attention of the viewer was the composition of an image based on a specific format which would supply interpretive guidance. At first glance, the postcards seem to have very little to do with colonialism per se; instead, they reveal the mental disposition of Germans vis-à-vis people of different skin color.

In the postcard entitled "Mohrenwäsche" (Blackamoor washing), sent from Berlin to Munich on 25 July 1913, what the viewer sees is an image of a toddler taking a bath (see Figure 7.1).[20] Formally speaking, we see the interior of a bathroom, including a towel on a rack, a chair, and, in the center, a portable tub with a handle and spout, which is being used as a bath. We also notice square black and white tiles, a gray wall and a toddler and tub which

„ Mohrenwäsche"

*Figure 7.1*  "Mohrenwäsche" I.

are both *brown* (unfortunately not apparent in this volume's monochrome reproduction). Without any further information, we know that this bathroom belongs to a certain historical period, namely, the turn of the century, and that the arrangement of objects in the room exemplifies cleanliness and order. Around 1900, Germans took shower baths, using large sponges, in special bowls called *Sitzwannen*. Only affluent people had separate bathrooms, which did not become widespread until after World War Two; before then, they were seen as a luxury. The formal structuring of the picture thus implies and relates to certain norms in household management practice.

The attention paid to colors becomes important when we examine the location and skin color of the toddler in relation to his attempt to clean himself. In comparing the *brown* toddler with the arrangement of the bathroom, a viewer might associate the clean and orderly bathroom with what were held to be specifically German traits and, by extension, with being white. By presenting this binary opposition between white and brown, the artist creates a web of references that are connected to the idea of racial difference. The depiction of the toddler in a German bathroom invokes the Western European distinction between civilized Europeans and uncivilized native Africans. The toddler sits alone in the bathtub with eyes closed, holding an oversized sponge over his head. We perceive that size is significant, because the objects in the bathroom are oversized in relation to the brown body. Read as a visual metaphor, the toddler appears to be overwhelmed by modern civilization while yet unable, on account of his inescapable difference, to become white and clean. His implied desire to be part of the existing Western order is overwhelmed by the sea of whiteness—so the disproportion between the toddler's size and the volume of water in the tub suggests. The task of becoming white is literally too big.

The power of contrast is illuminated further when we analyze the physiognomic traits given to the toddler. His exaggerated physical features, huge lips and curly hair, reinforce the image of alterity and present the antithesis of an idealized German self-image. In the visual system of alterity, the fascination with racial difference, from skin color to physiognomy, results in its association with pathology and sexuality, as Sander Gilman has succinctly argued when examining the stereotypes of sexuality, race, and madness.[21] The art historian Ernst Hans Gombrich (among others) has described how the contrast between light and darkness functions as a symbol for the opposition of good and evil in Western iconography: as he puts it, the "notion of light as the visible symbol of the good is important in philosophy, from Plato to the Enlightenment, as it is also within the Christian tradition."[22] Allowing for a shift from religious to political symbolism and an association with pathological traits, the same basic aesthetic applies to our postcard—suggesting that the toddler is essentially evil and the implied white Germans are saints. The equation of sense perceptions and moral qualities, fusing the mythical and the real, creates a synthesis in which the physiognomic creatures of light, here the implied Germans, are contrasted with the traditional physiognomic type of Africans. The artists provide a system of co-ordinates for reading and feeling that appeals to a mindset that has been socially and politically conditioned in the viewer. The postcard condenses a whole chain of signifiers into a single image. This image feeds into the European fiction of irreconcilable antinomies—notions such as the impossibility of civilizing the noble savage or of bridging the gap between nature and civilization—which it implicitly portrays as biologically grounded.[23]

The picture postcard provides further clues to the relationship between image and language. The title "Mohrenwäsche" serves as a determinate message or referential sign.[24] Here, the artist uses language literally: the title, "Mohrenwäsche," activates the habit we have of talking about the images of things as if they were the things themselves. The status of language means that the title becomes true: we read what we see; we see what we read. The verbal figure is customary and conventional, lending authority to the image. The word correlates with the image and vice versa, thereby activating a set of practices which are second nature, and enacting a form of verbal and visual discipline. The image aims at viewers whose "natural attitude" enables them to subscribe to the transparency of images that represent objects.[25] Hence, the significance of picture postcards for Germany's colonial project hinged upon a general notion of image in conjunction with one or more of a number of specific rhetorical processes (*convenientia*, *aemulatio*, analogy, sympathy); this is a fundamental principle that, according to Foucault, secures the "order of things" and controls the world with "figures of knowledge."[26] Postcards engage the viewers' self-knowledge and their socially and politically conditioned experience of alterity.[27] They activate the viewer's fantasies of being a sovereign subject or white European, and they nourish an imaginary colonialism.[28] The invitation to the viewer to participate in an act of imaginary text production generates a network of meanings that confirm the interdependent binary structure between identity and alterity.

Artists used the theme of "Mohrenwäsche" in different variations; and, as suggested in the case of the image just discussed, the representation of children played a significant role. More often than not, images of alterity such that illustrated in my second example (Figure 7.2) thematized the relationship between Germans and natives, or represented a meeting—an unequal meeting—between cultures.[29] Because Germany was a colonial power, postcards forced Germans to think about the relationship between Germanness, whiteness, and color. Such romanticized encounters often reinforced a kind of *Berührungsangst* (fear of contact) with indigenous people, offering the viewer a kind of imaginary surface to relate to the experience depicted in the image. The notion of *Heimat* also assumed a central place in the depiction of alterity, in that it provided a sense of security and belonging vis-à-vis the emerging forces of modernity. By juxtaposing black and white, the artist here appropriates the conventional imagery of innocence as a means of naturalizing an arbitrary racial hierarchy that

Figure 7.2   "Mohrenwäsche" II.

is under threat. Especially when taken in conjunction with the notion of *Heimat* as a physical space, the imagery of innocence as exemplified by children could serve as a vehicle for distinguishing between the self and the other. As an "intrinsically conservative value connoting originary or primary factors in identity," *Heimat* and childhood both express the desire for "absolute foundation or unchanging essence."[30] The art historian Anne Higonnet develops this argument by observing that our "modern concept of childhood was an invented cultural ideal," and that images played an important role in consolidating this idealized vision.[31] Both *Heimat* and childhood signify the process of myth-making.[32] To adapt Higonnet's argument, the modern (Wilhelminian) images in German postcards catered to an idealized image of childhood as defined by the eighteenth century, in which "innocence must be an edenic state from which all adults fall, never to return. Nor can Romantic children know adults: they are by definition unconscious of adult desires, including adults' desires for childhood."[33] The special clothing of the white girl and her posture unconsciously prefigure gendered adult roles, and her superiority in the encounter with the indigenous boy is demonstrated by the fact that she is in charge of the action, that is, by washing off the boy's skin color. He, by contrast, looks scared and uncomfortable. While the girl is properly dressed and thereby associated with normality, German tradition, and prosperity, the boy's clothing and physical posture suggest the opposite: both his dress and his fearful reaction to the girl identify him as an outsider in a foreign culture, a message further emphasized here by the background of a German pastoral land-scape. Also in conformity with Higonnet's argument, the gesture of the white girl solicits immediate empathy, because she appears to be an honest child who wishes to help. With her red, irresistibly round cheeks and her facial expression suggesting she does not know how to deal with the indigenous boy, the girl displays the kind of naivety or innocence which Higonnet describes.

This second "Mohrenwäsche" postcard displays a sentimental image of the innocent child in its (her) first encounter with otherness, while simultaneously suggesting the metaphorical maternal value of *Heimat*. The combination of a landscape of *Heimat* with the innocence of the girl in juxtaposition with the indigenous boy connotes a loss of childhood. Considering that, in patriarchal discourse around 1900, women were traditionally viewed as the embodiment of *Heimat*, the image on the postcard invites a dualistic mode of reading in terms of identity and difference and of belonging and exclusion. Thus, the idyllic image invokes what is literally a dark side, a threat or a change to this state of existence. For Higonnet, "romantic images of childhood gain power not only from their charms, but also from their menace."[34] Here, the indigenous boy acts as an intruder, a threat to tranquility and to the balance of the existing naturalized white landscape that *Heimat* signifies. We might speculate that, in the context of modernity and of the continuous technological and mechanical transformation of German society, the boy signals precisely this transformation. Hence, by emphasizing the rural setting and the innocence of childhood, the image underlines the tensions between tradition and modernity. The stress placed on innocence thus applies both to the girl and to Germany, insofar as the child is always "the sign of a bygone era, of a past which is necessarily the past of adults," and is understood only through nostalgia.[35] Similarly, Germany's transformation creates an increased longing for the past, its traditions and its social harmony. The card can therefore be read as an attempt at a form of retrospection and a yearning for a homogeneous German nation.

In following the notion of the image suggested by Foucault, a viewer of these picture postcards encounters another interesting phenomenon, namely the absence of presence. The images on postcards lure the reader into a multiplicity of reading operations. My brief reading of these images suggests that viewing postcards forces the reader into an act of reception which, in turn, implies that the designer and artist of postcards has considered the role of the viewer. As a text, the image reveals numerous strands of information about German perceptions of alterity. Viewing postcards triggers—consciously or unconsciously—associations and connections which constitute a signifying chain of affiliations between ideas related to colonialism. Reading postcards becomes a disseminative activity, one in which the image is a tissue of signs. As a reader of the image, the viewer assumes the role of an extended author, developing and extrapolating from the initial image. Thus, the images represent a dissolution of the artist's original meaning and intention, and generate a matrix of signification, albeit a limited one. Consequently, the colonial image has the potential to generate multiple readings. If, in Lacan's famous formulation, "man's desire is the desire of the Other," then this also holds true for colonial images on picture postcards, where the artist's desire becomes that of the viewer and reader, and vice versa.[36] To read or to view is to repeat images rather than to understand them fully. Images germinate and are disseminated through the reader's imaginative response. The artist and printing press engage the reader in a dialogue of creation and recreation.

In conclusion, the postcard industry in Germany around 1900 aligned itself with cultural developments—themselves the result of aspects of the evolution of capitalism in the nineteenth century—that were characterized by simultaneous processes of unification and differentiation. By stressing unity and German identity, the postcard industry contributed to the increasing anxiety that was apparent as an effect of colonialism and the processes of modernity. The anthropologist and historian Ann Stoler has maintained—albeit with a different focus—that the (cultural) politics of exclusion (which I have also sought to outline in the present article) followed, whether deliberately or not, a "nationalist discourse that drew on and gave force to a wider politics of exclusion."[37]

## NOTES

1. For a brief history of postcards, see Herbert Leclerc, "Ansichten über Ansichtskarten," *Archiv für Postgeschichte*, 2 (1986), 5–65, and Robert Lebeck, "Die Postkarte im Spiegel der Kultur und Gesellschaft," in *Viele Grüße . . . Eine Kulturgeschichte der Postkarte*, ed. by Robert Lebeck and Gerhard Kaufmann (Dortmund: Harenberg, 1985), pp. 399–437.
2. James Ryan, *Picturing Empire: Photography and the Visualization of the British Empire* (Chicago: University of Chicago Press, 1997), p. 12. See also Felix Axster, "Die Angst vor dem *Verkaffern*—Politiken der Reinigung im deutschen Kolonialismus," *Werkstattgeschichte*, 39 (2005), 39–53.
3. See Alexander Honold and Klaus Scherpe, "Einleitung," in *Das Fremde: Reiseerfahrungen, Schreibformen und kulturelles Wissen*, ed. by Alexander Honold and Klaus Scherpe (Bern: Lang, 1999), pp. 7–11, and "Einleitung: Für eine deutsche Kulturgeschichte des Fremden," in *Mit Deutschland um die Welt: Eine Kulturgeschichte des Fremden in der Kolonialzeit*, ed. by Alexander Honold and Klaus Scherpe (Stuttgart: Metzler, 2004), pp. 1–25.
4. For an explanation of both terms, see Hal Foster, "Preface," in *Vision and Visuality*, ed. by Hal Foster (Seattle: Bay Press, 1988), pp. ix–xiv. Walter Benjamin, "Kleine Geschichte der Photographie," in *Angelus Novus, Ausgewählte Schriften 2* (Frankfurt/M.: Suhrkamp, 1988), pp. 229–247 (p. 232).
5. See Richard Rorty, *Philosophy and the Mirror of Nature* (Princeton: Princeton University Press, 1979), p. 263; W.J.T. Mitchell, *Picture Theory* (Chicago: University of Chicago Press, 1994); Martin Jay, "Vision in Context:

Reflections and Refractions," in *Vision in Context: Historical and Contemporary Perspectives on Sight*, ed. by Teresa Brennan (New York: Routledge, 1996), pp. 3–12 (p. 4).

6. Mitchell, *Picture Theory*, p. 16.

7. Ibid., p. 15.

8. For a historical overview of the printing industry, see Howard Woody, "International Postcards: Their Histories, Production, and Distribution (Circa 1895 to 1915)," in *Delivering Views: Distant Cultures in Early Postcards*, ed. by Christraud Geary and Virginia-Lee Webb (Washington: Smithsonian Institution, 1998), pp. 13–45.

9. On exoticism around 1900, see Thomas Schwarz, "'Die Tropen bin ich!' Der exotische Diskurs der Jahrhundertwende," *KultuRRevolution*, 32–33 (1995), 11–21.

10. Michel Foucault, *The Order of Things: An Archaeology of the Human Sciences* (New York: Vintage, 1994).

11. See Robert Rydell, "Souvenirs of Imperialism: World's Fair Postcards," in *Delivering Views: Distant Cultures in Early Postcards*, ed. by Geary and Webb, pp. 47–63.

12. See Geoff Eley, "Making a Place in the Nation: Meanings of 'Citizenship' in Wilhelmine Germany," in *Wilhelminism and its Legacies: German Modernities, Imperialism, and the Meanings of Reform, 1890–1930*, ed. by Geoff Eley and James Retallack (New York: Berghahn, 2003), pp. 16–33.

13. Heinrich von Stephan, *Geschichte der preußischen Post von ihrem Ursprung bis auf die Gegenwart* (Berlin, 1859; reprinted Heidelberg, 1987).

14. Oliver Simons, "Dichter am Kanal," in *Kolonialismus als Kultur: Literatur, Medien, Wissenschaft in der deutschen Gründerzeit des Fremden*, ed. by Alexander Honold and Oliver Simons (Tübingen: Francke, 2002), pp. 243–62. See also Simons's essay, "Heinrich von Stephan und die Idee der Weltpost," in *Mit Deutschland um die Welt*, ed. by Honold and Scherpe, pp. 26–35.

15. See Robert Lebeck, "Die Postkarte im Spiegel der Kultur und Gesellschaft," p. 411.

16. Christraud Geary and Virginia-Lee Webb, "Introduction: Views on Postcards," in *Delivering Views: Distant Cultures in Early Postcards*, ed. by Geary and Webb, pp. 1–12 (p. 4).

17. Helmut Hartwig, "Weiter nichts neues andermal mehr—Kommunikation per Postkarte," in *Massenmedium Bildpostkarte*, vol. 1, ed. by Karl Riha (Siegen: Veröffentlichungen der Forschungsschwerpunkte Massenmedien und Kommunikation, 1979), pp. 1–42 (p. 5).

18. Thomas Nolden, "On Colonial Spaces and Bodies: Hans Grimm's *Geschichten aus Südwestafrika*," in *The Imperialist Imagination: German Colonialism and its Legacy*, ed. by Sara Friedrichmeyer, Sara Lenox, and Susanne Zantop (Ann Arbor: University of Michigan Press, 1998), pp. 125–40 (p. 127).

19. Bernhard Siegert, *Relais: Geschichte der Literatur als Epoche der Post, 1751–1913* (Berlin: Brinkmann & Bose, 1993), p. 177.

20. Image © Peter Weiss, <http://www.postcard-museum.com/> [accessed 26 February 2008].

21. Sander Gilman, *Difference and Pathology: Stereotypes of Sexuality, Race, and Madness* (Ithaca, NY: Cornell University Press, 1985).

22. Ernst Hans Gombrich, "The Cartoonist's Armoury," in *Meditations on a Hobby Horse*, ed. by Gombrich (London: Phaidon, 1963), pp. 127–42 (p. 138).

23. Jan Nederveen Pieterse, *White on Black: Images of Africa and Blacks in Western Popular Culture* (New Haven, CT: Yale University Press, 1992), p. 98.

24. For a detailed historical overview of the "Mohr," see Peter Martin, *Schwarze Teufel, edle Mohren: Afrikaner in Bewußtsein und Geschichte der Deutschen* (Hamburg: Junius, 1993).

25. The use of the term "natural attitude" in relation to pictures is drawn from Norman Bryson, *Vision and Painting: The Logic of the Gaze* (New Haven, CT: Yale University Press, 1983); see Ch. 1.

26. See Michel Foucault, *The Order of Things*, Ch. 2.

27. On responses to images, see David Freedberg, *The Power of Images: Studies in the History and Theory of Response* (Chicago: University of Chicago Press, 1989).

28. See W.J.T. Mitchell's discussion of Velázquez's *Las Meninas*, in *Picture Theory*, pp. 58–64.

29. Image © Peter Weiss, <http://www.postcard-museum.com/> [accessed 26 February 2008].

30. *Heimat—A German Dream: Regional Loyalties and National Identity in German Culture 1890–1990*, ed. by Elizabeth Boa and Rachel Palfreyman (London: Oxford University Press, 2000), p. 23.

31. Anne Higonnet, *Pictures of Innocence: The History and Crisis of Ideal Childhood* (New York: Thames & Hudson, 1998), p. 8.

32. See Roland Barthes, *Mythologies* (New York: Hill & Wang, 1972).

33. Higonnet, *Pictures of Innocence*, p. 28.

34. Ibid., p. 29.

35. Ibid., p. 27.

36. Jacques Lacan, *Écrits: A Selection* (New York: Norton, 2002), p. 264.

37. Laura Ann Stoler, *Race and the Education of Desire: Foucault's "History of Sexuality" and the Colonial Order of Things* (Durham, NC: Duke University Press, 1995), p. 8.

# 8 Colonialism and the Simplification of Language
## Germany's *Kolonial-Deutsch* Experiment

*Kenneth J. Orosz*

When the Germans began acquiring colonies in the mid-1880s, Bismarck's clear expectation was that the new possessions would be administered by the commercial firms whose business interests had motivated the annexations.[1] The subsequent failure of these private interests to provide effective government forced Berlin's hand and, within a few years, led to the creation of official colonial administrations in all of Germany's overseas holdings. One of the results of this rapid transfer of responsibility was the failure to develop a coherent language policy, an omission that soon led Germans at home and abroad to begin agonizing over whether it was better to use local vernaculars or German to communicate with the inhabitants of their colonies. While the ongoing debate remained unresolved prior to the onset of World War One, all participants agreed that the persistent use of foreign languages like English and Pidgin English within German colonies was an embarrassment that threatened to open the door to foreign meddling in German colonial affairs. These views only intensified after the outbreak of hostilities in 1914, eventually leading German colonial authorities seriously to consider the creation and implementation of a new, simplified German dialect for use in the colonies.

## DEBATES ABOUT LANGUAGE IN GERMAN COLONIES, 1884–1914

German colonization unfolded against a backdrop of growing metropolitan interest in the creation of artificial languages, like Volapük and Esperanto, that were designed to facilitate international communication and cooperation.[2] Volapük, which was created in 1878 by a German priest named Johann Schleyer, combined phonetically spelled, simplified words taken primarily from English with a modified grammatical structure based on German. On the other hand, Esperanto, founded in 1887 by a Pole named Ludwig Zamenhof, was built on a phonetic vocabulary drawn largely from Romance languages and used much simpler and more regular grammatical structures. Although both artificial languages enjoyed some popularity in Germany during the final decade of the nineteenth century, neither was ever seriously proposed for use in her new colonial empire. Moreover, by the turn of the century, a combination of rising nationalism and concerns that German language and culture were losing ground to those of other nations weakened metropolitan interest in both of these artificial language movements, while simultaneously triggering concern about the linguistic situation inside the far-flung German colonies.

My own work builds on that of Sherida Altehenger-Smith, Anne Brumfit and Wolfgang Mehnert to show that the debates about language policy in the German colonies which emerged after 1895 were the result of a unique combination of seemingly unrelated issues and events.[3] During the first decade of German colonial rule, Berlin was far too preoccupied with domestic affairs and the problems of establishing colonial administrations to pay any attention to the issue of language or education policy in its new overseas holdings. Lacking any official guidance from home, local administrators in each colony opened a handful of official schools to train German-literate clerical staff for government service. All other educational and linguistic efforts were left in the hands of missionaries, who had their own interests and their own approach to language issues. In particular, since Protestant mission theology held that evangelical efforts were best conducted in the vernacular, mission schools rarely provided more than a cursory introduction to German.

Although government officials remained essentially content with this state of affairs during the first decade of German colonial rule, by 1895, the fall of the Caprivi government over the issue of restoring Polish language instruction on a voluntary basis to the curriculum in Prussian Poland led to a new and growing interest in language policy throughout the German territories.[4] Despite calls by nationalists, some colonial administrators, and a variety of metropolitan-based colonial theorists for a switch from vernacular to German-based education systems, Protestant missions over the next decades successfully resisted these demands on the grounds that implementing them would hinder their evangelical efforts, alienate Africans from their environment, and discourage them from manual labor. Some even argued that teaching Africans German was politically dangerous, since it would enable colonized peoples to unite, share grievances and possibly even turn to socialism.[5] The issue of colonial language policy did not, however, disappear. Colonial congresses in 1905 and 1910, the 1906 school strikes in Prussian Poland and the Dernburg Reforms of the following year meant that language policy continued to be debated right up to the onset of World War One, with a gradually emerging consensus that, despite Protestant objections, greater efforts had to be made to expand the use of German in the colonies.

## THE DEVELOPMENT OF *KOLONIAL-DEUTSCH*

Emil Schwörer, lawyer and former *Schutztruppe* captain in German South-West Africa, entered this debate in early 1916 with a presentation to the Munich branch of the German Colonial Society, followed by an article in the *Deutsche Kolonialzeitung* (DKZ) and a separately published pamphlet that appeared later that year.[6] His decision to become involved in the discussions was motivated by several observations. According to Schwörer, the absence of an official colonial language policy had led to the persistent use of Pidgin English as the de facto lingua franca in West Africa and Polynesia, a situation that was both embarrassing and potentially dangerous, since it opened the door to possible foreign intervention in German colonial affairs. Schwörer also felt that Germany's long-term political and economic goals were seriously compromised by the ongoing linguistic chaos in her colonies. Although war-time censorship prevented him from revealing precisely what he thought those goals to be, Schwörer in his writings hinted at the hope that the future would bring additional colonial annexations, and discussed how these would be easier to acquire if Germany resolved its long running debate about language policy and adopted a lingua franca. More importantly, he repeatedly argued that the German colonies had not lived up to their full economic potential, a failure he blamed on communication problems between ruler and ruled. Schwörer openly expressed the fear that, unless drastic steps were taken to rectify this situation, Germany would lose control of what he argued was a coming economic world war later in the century.[7] Finally, he argued that the lack of linguistic cohesion in the colonies was not only unaesthetic, but that it also complicated unnecessarily the already difficult task of colonial administration and wasted much energy, as colonial officials scrambled to learn a multitude of colonial vernaculars.[8]

Consequently, Schwörer was convinced that Germany needed immediately to adopt a lingua franca for use throughout its colonial empire. The only question was which one to pick. The use of an indigenous language was, he concluded, problematic on multiple levels. Not only were there far too many to choose from, but, even worse, many vernaculars were specific to individual colonies and often covered only a fraction of that colony.[9] Although Swahili was often proposed as the leading contender to be Germany's colonial lingua franca, Schwörer argued that national, political and practical considerations made this impossible. After all, the use of an African language rather than German implied a degree of equality between ruler and ruled. Moreover, he said, "it is a mistake to describe the uncommonly form-rich, even complicated, Kiswahili as an 'easy' language, as people often do who think, after little study, that they have 'mastered' it, but generally only know it very superficially"; and he warned that it therefore presented the possibility of exposing German colonizers to mockery, if they acquired a clumsy and inferior Pidgin Swahili.[10] Furthermore, according to Schwörer, Swahili was not as widespread as many people in the metropole believed; hence, if it was chosen, large numbers of Arabs, Asians, and Bantus living in East Africa would also have to learn Swahili, in addition to inhabitants of other colonies and the Germans themselves.

As problematic as Swahili was, other African vernaculars were even worse. Not only were they even less widespread than Swahili, but in Schwörer's view their lack of a connection to higher culture or meaningful literature effectively rendered them useless as agents of the process of moral improvement.[11] Moreover, the link between some of the more common vernaculars and ethnic groups deemed inimical to German rule, like the Duala of Cameroon, rendered them too dangerous to use as a lingua franca, as their adoption threatened to undermine local efforts to break the power of those groups.[12] Finally, experience in colonies like Cameroon showed that Africans often resented having another regional language forced upon them and frequently resisted, thereby creating additional headaches for local German authorities.[13]

In the light of these problems, Schwörer concluded that the clear choice for a German colonial lingua franca was therefore "obviously German and nothing else."[14] His desire to see the systematic introduction of German throughout the colonies was ultimately motivated by a variety of patriotic and practical issues. In particular, he was offended that German was not already more widespread in the colonies and felt it was self-evident that German officials and businessmen should speak to each other in their mother tongue while in German colonies. Echoing comments made in a 1913 issue of the official government journal in Cameroon, he noted that it was unpleasant and unnatural that, 20 years after Germany had established her colonies, people everywhere except South-West Africa automatically resorted to Pidgin English when speaking with the natives.[15] The pernicious influence of this state of affairs was described best by Dr. Hans Meyer, who lamented on behalf of the colonial administration in Cameroon that not only did 90 per cent of the natives still speak Pidgin, but English words were constantly infiltrating official reports and threatened to create a "bastardized version of German akin to that used in North America."[16] Schwörer naturally felt that the immediate introduction of German on a systematic basis would put a halt to this trend. Furthermore, since German was the language of the conqueror, colonized peoples would welcome its introduction, as seemed to be indicated by their readiness to attend schools where it was taught. Better still, exposure to German language and literature would have a civilizing effect, make the natives more reliable, tie them more closely to Germany, and ease periodic labor shortages by removing linguistic barriers to labor migration.[17] Finally, the use of German would eliminate the need to train colonial officials in multiple vernaculars, something which he felt was a tremendous waste of time and energy, since officials went home on leave or were assigned to new colonial districts using new dialects before they had mastered the one that they had been studying.[18] Hence, Schwörer believed that "the introduction of the German language will . . . gradually create a considerable saving in time and work, provide essential relief to administration and trade, and in a certain sense will uplift and integrate the black population, and strengthen German authority."[19]

Accordingly, German was the clear choice as colonial lingua franca. However, a further important consideration remained for Schwörer:

> The German language is known as one of the hardest, something which all foreigners agree upon and confirm. Apart from the pronunciation difficulties and the complexity of the sentence structure, the unusually large number of irregularities . . . the . . . enormous vocabulary (with numerous synonyms) and many further obstacles inhibit the learning of our mother tongue by foreigners.[20]

As hard as Europeans found it to learn, Schwörer argued, it was much worse for Africans, who were wholly ignorant of European linguistic concepts and therefore could not be expected to learn the fundamentals of correct written or spoken German. Although a few, through systematic schooling, eventually perfected their German language skills, they were the clear exception, as the majority were destined to remain manual laborers with limited formal education. Moreover, since most Africans tended to learn by word of mouth, efforts to teach complex subjects like grammar, let alone proper pronunciation, were doomed.

In the light of these limitations and, on the other hand, the clear need for a lingua franca, Schwörer proposed a practical solution in the form of a simplified *Kolonial-Deutsch* (KD) which would be easier both to learn and to understand. Although clearly influenced by earlier attempts to create a simplified universal German, Schwörer's proposal was unique in that it was intended only for use in the German colonies. It was to consist of a drastically curtailed vocabulary of 500–600 "useful," easily pronounceable words designed to advance German interests.[21] Synonyms, extraneous words, and abstract terms would all be eliminated in favor of simple descriptors, nouns, and verbs relevant to commerce, plantations and the needs of local colonial authorities. Although the selection of these words, which were to be compiled in an official dictionary that could only be amended by local authorities in order to reflect local needs better, was to be left to a formal commission, Schwörer's suggestions make it clear that there was no room for vocabulary which expressed abstract principles such as on political topics, as these might confuse the natives and might possibly lead to the development of anti-German sentiments.

In addition to a reduced vocabulary, Schwörer also proposed significant grammatical changes, including the abolition of umlauts, the reduction of nouns to a single gender and the elimination of all cases.[22] Instead, KD was to have only two direct articles, "de" for singular nouns and "die" for plural, with "eine" serving as the only indirect article. All plural nouns were to be further indicated by adding the suffix "-en", or "-n" in the case of words ending in "-el." Possessives were to be indicated by the insertion of "von" wherever necessary. In order to simplify conjugation, all verbs were to be left in the infinitive; time was to be indicated by conjugating the auxiliary verbs to do, want, have, must, can, and be (*tun, wollen, haben, müssen, können*, and *sein*) in either the present or past tenses. Future actions were to be illustrated by the addition of appropriate phrases like "tomorrow" (*morgen*). Sentence structure was to be simplified via a simple, clear and natural word order and the use of short, main-clause sentences. Lastly, although it pained him to do so, Schwörer proposed the substitution of Latin characters in place of their German or Gothic counterparts.

## IN DEFENSE OF *KOLONIAL-DEUTSCH*

Aware that his proposal was likely to be controversial, Schwörer took pains both to underscore the advantages of his proposed KD and to anticipate potential criticisms. In terms of advantages, he argued that KD would enable Germany to counter British, French and Belgian influence in Africa while cementing her own colonial claims.[23] Furthermore, he argued that KD was inherently "practical and, above all, German."[24] In addition, since KD was in his estimation 90 per cent easier to learn than *Hochdeutsch* (HD), it would spread quickly and would do invaluable service in containing and then supplanting English and Pidgin. He also argued that the use of KD as a new colonial lingua franca would, in the process, greatly facilitate colonial development, by fostering greater awareness of colonial issues among inhabitants of the metropole and by improving communication between white employers and their colonial employees. Consequently, he envisioned KD as a powerful linguistic weapon in the coming economic struggle which he was sure would erupt after the conclusion of peace in Europe.[25]

As for potential critics of his proposal, Schwörer rejected out of hand arguments against the use of any form of the German language (either KD or HD). For example, he mocked as completely unfounded the claims of some older business firms that making Africans learn German might actually hinder trade by creating new language problems.[26] According to Schwörer, KD would in fact have the opposite effect, since its simplicity would enhance communications by eliminating the current reliance on Pidgin, which he described as an "ugly, corrupted . . . as well as illogical and frequently even ridiculous dialect."[27] He similarly rejected the notion that denying colonized peoples access to German provided an important, useful and necessary linguistic barrier to the creation of inappropriate intimate relations between whites and blacks.[28] In fact, Schwörer argued, such barriers only hurt Germany by complicating colonial administration, delaying economic development and alienating the native peoples.

Schwörer reserved the bulk of his comments, however, for potential critics who might argue that the German language was too beautiful and too important a cultural inheritance to experiment with. While he shared their love for the German language—indeed, he made a point of warning his readers about the dangers of importing foreign words into the HD spoken at home in Germany—Schwörer wrote that, "impelled by the relentless necessities of the battle of peoples for survival [in the modern world] . . . we must . . . apply our powers of organization to what hitherto appeared sacrosanct" and consider modifying the German language for use in the colonies.[29] He went on to argue that "the opposing voices of those critics who fight colonial language reform with spurious reasons or with the weapon of mockery and perhaps speak of . . . the 'ruin' of the German language shall not be heard."[30] KD was, he pointed out, only to be used in the colonies to communicate with racial inferiors. Since the colonized peoples were not free to travel at will to the metropole, there was no chance that KD would be imported and replace HD at home. Moreover, KD could hardly be a contagion or potential disaster since it was inherently German, employed German words and grammar, and was no more dangerous than other linguistic variants. After all, he argued, if one were to follow the logic of the most vociferous linguistic defenders and insist that the structure of the German language must remain sacrosanct, then one would have to acknowledge that stenography, slang, dialects like Swabian, and the use of "Kindersprache" between mothers and children had already destroyed German.[31] Schwörer went on to say that not only was it rational to adapt German to African surroundings, but failure to do so would be to make Africans learn a correct form of German that the Germans themselves did not speak. Finally, he similarly discounted the notion that KD was in any way a form of Pidgin German, because, unlike Pidgins, which are ad hoc creations of native peoples lacking guidance, rules or coherence, KD was a specially constructed language, created and controlled by whites.[32] Moreover, because KD was German, using purely German words and a modified German grammar, it was merely another German dialect—but one which had the added benefit of greatly advancing the twin goals of colonial development and expanding the number of German speakers.

## REACTIONS TO *KOLONIAL-DEUTSCH*

Schwörer's proposal met with cautious interest. In a letter of 18 February 1916, Duke Johann Albrecht von Mecklenburg, President of the German Colonial Society, revealed that Colonial Secretary Wilhelm Solf was aware of the proposal but had some questions.[33] Although Solf felt that KD would increase the distortion of German, he recognized that it would also simultaneously stop the spread of Pidgin and therefore felt that it had to be considered seriously, sentiments that Mecklenburg himself shared. As a result, the German Colonial Society commissioned a special panel, as Schwörer had intended, to examine the issue in greater detail.

While awaiting the panel's first meeting, the DKZ ran an editorial encouraging genuine discussion of Schwörer's proposal.[34] Although the DKZ noted the benefits of creating a lingua franca in all German territories and repeated Schwörer's lament about the persistent use of Pidgin English in German colonies, the journal also expressed caution regarding the Germanization of verbal communications between ruler and ruled. According to the editors, "[O]nly a precise knowledge of the language of the natives, that is, Kiswahili, [opens] the door to understanding the native mentality."[35] Nevertheless, the editors concluded that Schwörer's proposal "undoubtedly [deserves] further consideration if German colonies [are] in the future truly to become part of the German lands."[36]

The seven-person committee, which was deliberately composed of members with backgrounds in government, commerce, and missionary work, finally met in early June 1916.[37] During the course of their two meetings, the committee members listened to an outline of Schwörer's proposal and then, after expressing some cautious support, began adding a few slight modifications. Rather than implement KD as a final resolution of the language question, the committee discussed introducing it in colonial schools as a means of laying the groundwork for the later introduction of HD at some unspecified time in the future. The committee also proposed additional meetings with members of the Oriental Seminar and the Hamburg *Kolonialinstitut* in order to obtain additional expert opinions and eliminate potential opposition to the proposal.[38] Arrangements were also made to form a sub-committee to examine which words should be included in an official KD lexicon. Throughout these meetings, the tone of the discussion and the focus on the practical ramifications of implementing KD seem to indicate genuine and serious interest in Schwörer's ideas.

At the very least, the committee felt strongly enough about the matter to present its findings in October 1916 to the *Allgemeiner Deutscher Sprachverein* (ADS), an organization devoted to preserving the purity of the German language.[39] Predictably, the ADS announced its opposition to Schwörer's proposal, writing in its newspaper that, while the elimination of English from the German colonies was clearly a laudable goal, it did not think KD was either an appropriate or a viable means to that end. For example, it argued that legal proceedings in this "German" dialect would be a farce. Worse yet, its implementation had the potential to turn the German people into a joke and would do nothing to stop the encroachment of other European languages. As a result, the ADS emphasized that, instead of meddling with the structure and content of the German language, the most important step in resolving the colonial language question was "to make [the natives] able in the first instance to express their thoughts sufficiently to be comprehensible; the rest will follow."[40] This is a carefully argued response; yet the tone of the piece suggests significant concern that the government was continuing to give Schwörer's proposal serious consideration during the fall of 1916.

Due to the fragmentary and ultimately inconclusive nature of the documentary evidence in the Potsdam archive, it is impossible to determine what conclusions, if any, the German government ultimately reached in regard to KD. The fact that it was discussed at all, particularly in the midst of a war, seems to indicate that it was considered a genuine possibility, and is illustrative of how insecure the Germans felt in their colonies. Nevertheless, the decision by the victorious allies at the end of World War One permanently to deprive Berlin of her colonies rendered further discussion of Schwörer's proposal moot and caused it quickly to become forgotten. Many of the issues Schwörer raised, however, have subsequently been revisited in post-1945 debates—about the use of *Fraktur* versus *Antiqua* typeface, the development of a simplified *Gastarbeiterdeutsch* among imported Turkish laborers, and the hotly contested German orthography reforms of the last decade.[41] Thus, despite its inglorious end, Schwörer's proposed KD was in many ways ahead of its time.

# NOTES

1. Woodruff Smith, *The German Colonial Empire* (Chapel Hill: University of North Carolina Press, 1978), pp. 42–7; and W. O. Henderson, *The German Colonial Empire 1884–1919* (London: Cass, 1993), p. 33f.
2. Susanne Mühleisen, "Emil Schwörers Kolonial-Deutsch (1916): Sprachliche und historische Anmerkungen zu einem 'geplanten Pidgin' im kolonialen Deutsch Südwest Afrika," *Philologie im Netz*, 31 (2005), <http://web.fu-berlin.de/phin/phin31/p31t3.htm> [accessed 30 August 2007], p. 31. For an overview of efforts to create international languages, including both Volapük and Esperanto, see Peter G. Forster, *The Esperanto Movement* (New York: Mouton, 1982), Ch. 2.
3. Sherida Altehenger-Smith, "Language Planning and Language Policy in Tanzania During the German Colonial Period," *Swahili: The Journal of the East African Swahili Committee*, 48.2 (1968), 73–80; Anne Brumfit, "The Rise and Development of a Language Policy in German East Africa," *Sprache und Geschichte in Afrika*, 2 (1980), 219–331; Wolfgang Mehnert, "The Language Question in the Colonial Policy of German Imperialism," in *African Studies—Afrika-Studien*, ed. by Thea Büttner and Gerhard Brehme (Berlin: Akademie, 1973), pp. 383–97; and Kenneth J. Orosz, *Religious Conflict and the Evolution of Language Policy in German and French Cameroon, 1885–1939* (New York: Lang, 2008).
4. John J. Kulczycki, *School Strikes in Prussian Poland, 1901–1907: The Struggle Over Bilingual Education* (New York: Columbia University Press, 1981), pp. 45–52; Richard Blanke, *Prussian Poland in the German Empire (1871–1900)* (New York: Columbia University Press, 1981), pp. 130–2; Josef Miaso, "Educational Policy and Educational Development in the Polish Territories under Austrian, Russian and German Rule 1850–1918," in *Schooling, Educational Policy and Ethnic Identity*, ed. by Janusz J. Tomiak (New York: New York University Press, 1991), pp. 163–84; and Part 3 of Helmut Walser Smith, *German Nationalism and Religious Conflict* (Princeton, NJ: Princeton University Press, 1995).
5. Wolfgang Mehnert, "Education Policy," in *German Imperialism in Africa*, ed. by Helmuth Stoecker (London: Hurst, 1986), pp. 223–6.
6. Newspaper clipping entitled "Kolonial-Deutsch," *Münchener Neueste Nachrichten*, 27 February 1916, in *Deutsche Kolonial-Gesellschaft*, 944, p. 43, Bundesarchiv, Potsdam (hereafter cited as DKG 944); Emil Schwörer,

"Zur künftigen Sprachenfrage in den deutschen Kolonien," Parts 1 and 2, *Deutsche Kolonialzeitung*, 33.1 (20 January 1916), pp. 10–12; 33.2 (20 February 1916), p. 25; and Emil Schwörer, *Kolonial-Deutsch: Vorschläge einer künftigen deutschen Kolonialsprache in systematisch-grammatikalischer Darstellung und Begründung* (Diessen: Huber, 1916).

7. Schwörer, *Kolonial-Deutsch*, p. 6.

8. Schwörer, "Zur künftigen Sprachenfrage," Part 1, p. 10.

9. Schwörer, *Kolonial-Deutsch*, pp. 9–11.

10. Ibid, p. 21, n. 2, and p. 24, n. 1.

11. Ibid., p. 11.

12. See Ralph Austen and Jonathan Derrick, *Middlemen of the Cameroon Rivers: The Duala and their Hinterland c. 1600–c. 1960* (Cambridge: Cambridge University Press, 1999), Ch. 4; and Mehnert, "Education Policy," p. 223.

13. Rudolf Stumpf, *La Politique Linguistique au Cameroun de 1884 à 1960* (Bern: Lang, 1979), p. 55f.

14. Schwörer, "Zur künftigen Sprachenfrage," Part 1, p. 10.

15. Schwörer, *Kolonial-Deutsch*, p. 11f.; and Hans Meyer, "Verfügung des Gouverneurs über das Neger-Englisch (pidgin-english)," *Amtsblatt für das Schutzgebiet Kamerun*, 6.14 (1 May 1913), p. 166.

16. Ibid., p. 167.

17. Schwörer, *Kolonial-Deutsch*, p. 13.

18. Ibid., p. 12.

19. Ibid., p. 13.

20. Ibid, p. 14.

21. John M. Lipski, "'Me Want Cookie': Foreigner Talk as Monster Talk", unpublished article of 29 March 2005, <http://www.personal.psu.edu/jml34/monster.pdf> [accessed 30 August 2007], p. 7; see also Oswald Salzmann, *Das vereinfachte Deutsch: Die Sprache aller Völker* (Leipzig: Salzmann, 1913), and Adalbert Baumann, *Das neue, leichte Weltdeutsch (das Verbesserte wedé) für unsere Bundesgenossen und Freunde! Seine Notwendigkeit und seine wirtschaftliche Bedeutung* (Diessen: Jos. C. Huber, 1916). The details of Schwörer's proposal can be found in Schwörer, "Zur künftigen Sprachenfrage," Part 1, p. 12; Part 2, p. 25; and Schwörer, *Kolonial-Deutsch*, pp. 17–20.

22. Schwörer, *Kolonial-Deutsch*, pp. 17–20. For a summary of these grammatical changes, see Matthias Perl, "Kolonial-Deutsch as restructured German," in *"Was ich noch sagen wollte": A Multi-Lingual Festschrift for Norbert Boretzky on Occasion of His 65th Birthday*, ed. by Birgit Igla, Thomas Stolz and Norbert Boretzky (Berlin: Akademie, 2001), pp. 240–3.

23. Schwörer, *Kolonial-Deutsch*, p. 23.

24. Ibid., p. 20.

25. Ibid., p. 6.

26. Ibid., p. 23.

27. Ibid., p. 16.

28. Ibid., p. 12.

29. Ibid., p. 5.

30. Ibid., p. 25.

31. Ibid., p. 25, n. 1.

32. Ibid., p. 26.

33. Johann Albrecht von Mecklenburg to Kontreadmiral Strauch, 18 February 1916, DKG 944, p. 52.

34. "Kolonialdeutsch," *Deutsche Kolonialzeitung*, 20 May 1916 (no. 33.5), p. 74.

35. Ibid.
36. Ibid.
37. Members included Schwörer, Albert Hahl (former Governor of New Guinea), Father Hermann Nekes of the Pallotine mission, Oskar Hintrager (former Deputy Governor of South-West Africa), Dr Oskar Karstedt (former administrator in East Africa), Major Göring, and Ernst Kliemke (President of the German Esperanto Society). "Sitzung der Kommission Kolonial-Deutsch im Reichskolonialamt, 5. Juni 1916," DKG 944, p. 16; and "Bericht über die Sitzung der Kommission betreffend Kolonial Deutsch 2. Juni," DKG 944, p. 17.
38. Both institutions provided expert training to colonial civil servants. See L. H. Gann and Peter Duignan, *The Rulers of German Africa 1884–1914* (Stanford: Stanford University Press, 1977), p. 54f.
39. Richard Pallesker, "Kolonial-Deutsch," *Zeitschrift des Allgemeinen Deutschen Sprachvereins*, October 1916 (no. 31.10), p. 324. For background information on the ADS, see Roger Chickering, "Language and the Social Foundations of Radical Nationalism in the Wilhelmine Era," in *1870/71–1989/90: German Unifications and the Change of Literary Discourse*, ed. by Walter Pape (New York: de Gruyter, 1993), pp. 61–78.
40. Pallesker, "Kolonial-Deutsch," p. 324.
41. Gerald Newton, "Deutsche Schrift: The Demise and Rise of German Black Letter," *German Life and Letters*, 56.2 (April 2003), 183–204; Johanna Watzinger-Tharp, "Turkish-German Language: An Innovative Style of Communication and its Implications for Citizenship and Identity," *Journal of Muslim Minority Affairs*, 24.2 (October 2004), 285–94; Sally Johnson, "The Cultural Politics of the 1998 Reform of German Orthography," *German Life and Letters*, 55.1 (January 2000), 106–25; Elke Philburn, "Rechtschreibreform Still Spells Controversy," *Debatte* 11.1 (May 2003), 60–9.

# Part III

# Colonialism and the End of Empire

# 9 Fraternity, Frenzy, and Genocide in German War Literature, 1906–36

## Jörg Lehmann

The best-known book on the genocide of the Herero and Nama peoples from the era itself is a small text entitled *Peter Moors Fahrt nach Südwest* (Peter Moor's Journey to South-West Africa), published in 1906.[1] This work was a classic long-time seller: by 1940, more than 400,000 copies had been sold. Its author was the German pastor Gustav Frenssen, a representative of the *Heimatkunst* movement who had previously written "regional" novels. Because *Peter Moor* reached not only an audience interested in colonial topics but also a broader social stratum of bourgeois readers of the time, it can be understood as the representative narrative on this topic written before World War One.

*Peter Moor* is designed as an *Entwicklungsroman* (developmental novel), and, against this backdrop, two notions are developed: the events are shown in the context of history, and they serve to construct a collective German identity. The war against another race—and the extermination of that race—enhances the title character's self-understanding as a German, just as his comradeship with his fellow soldiers creates a feeling of belonging and community. The protagonist, Peter Moor, exemplifies the return to a German identity within an evolving German *Volksgemeinschaft* (racial community).[2]

In two passages dealing with justifications for the extermination of the colonized blacks, themes of both fraternity and annihilation of the "Other" surface:

> They are not our brothers, but our servants, whom we should treat humanely but sternly! These should be our brothers? Maybe they will be in the future, in one or two hundred years! First let them learn what we have learned for ourselves: build dams and wells, dig and plant corn, build houses and weave cloth. Afterwards they may become our brothers. Nobody is accepted as a member of a fellowship unless he has paid his dues.[3]

In the second passage, at the end of the book, the topic of fraternity arises again: a member of the colonial *Schutztruppe* has caught a native carrying a German gun. After interrogating him, the *Schutztruppler* says, "A missionary once told me: 'My friend, don't forget that the blacks are our brothers.' Now I want to give my brother his wages";[4] and he shoots him. What follows is a discussion between the soldiers. A lieutenant says,

> These blacks have earned their death before God and man, not because they have murdered two hundred farmers and have rebelled against us, but because they didn't build houses and didn't dig wells . . . The world belongs to those who are superior, those who are more alert. That is God's justice.[5]

The protagonist then objects to this "fratricide," and the lieutenant answers, "We have to remain tough-minded for a while and kill; but as both individuals and as a people, we must strive for lofty thoughts and noble deeds in order to contribute our share to the future brotherhood of man."[6] These examples display Frenssen's two-fold strategy. On the one hand, the deeds of the *Schutztruppe* are legitimated even when they obviously result in murder and genocide. On the other hand, the war against the Hereros is justified through ideology as a kind of pedagogic measure, as a means to teach German virtues and values and to achieve fraternity in the distant future. The military campaign is thus set into the wider context of a historical development that aims at cultural progress, and the final destination of this struggle for identity in the historical process is the German *Volksgemeinschaft*.

Manuel Köppen has discussed how such references to a dirty, cruel and "wild" style of warfare have to be seen in the larger context of military discourse around 1900. He argues that the rules of war usually in force for armed hostilities between "civilized" nations do not apply to warfare in the colonies.[7] The "wild" Hereros themselves did not adhere to these rules, the argument goes, so they are not under the protection of international law. Consequently, a military campaign that annihilated the Hereros was seen as a legitimate course of action.[8]

Frenssen's depiction of the campaign against the Herero and Nama peoples fits not only into the context of contemporary literary production,[9] but also into the wider discourse of the time, which has only recently been analyzed by Medardus Brehl.[10] Brehl is able to show how discursive structures provided meaning and legitimacy for historical events, how these structures resulted in public consent, and how they served to motivate and prepare for the genocide of the Herero and Nama. Brehl identifies the relationship between discursive strategies of exclusion and the execution of the genocide. But these discursive structures changed completely with the eruption of World War One and the loss of the colonies. Defeat in World War One not only inflicted a serious blow on the German self-image as a world power, but the retrospective tendencies of the 1920s also changed the patterns of justification. The colonial enterprise was judged in pedagogical terms, and German accomplishments were described as being the result of the fact that Germans were the best colonizers.

It is therefore not surprising to find the topic of fraternity returning in numerous accounts published during the Weimar Republic and written by veterans who experienced the war in the colonies. The most famous account is probably that of Paul von Lettow-Vorbeck, whose *Heia Safari* was published in 1920. Here, the report of the Askaris' loyalty, devotion, and willingness to sacrifice leads Lettow-Vorbeck to highlight the community of German and native soldiers:

> What kept us together was simply the good relationships among the men. This was what is meant by loyalty and devotion in the best sense of the word, because the blacks also knew and saw and experienced, in distress and death, that we served a just cause and tried to be just towards each other as well as towards the enemy.[11]

This kind of propaganda was an answer to the claim that Germans were not able to colonize properly. The war in the colonies seemed to be the appropriate topic to describe the positive effects of German education and its most efficient institution, the military system. The accounts from the war in the colonies show how German virtues and values had been adopted by the Askaris and how, in the extreme situation of the war, the success of this colonial achievement can be seen. In the rhetoric of these books, the native soldiers gain the status of brothers in arms, or, to use the contemporary parlance, of *Kameraden*: "Our Askaris were our comrades at all times. The Englishman, who almost never speaks his language, always presents himself as the master, whereas we Germans tried to learn the language of our brothers in arms."[12]

Another author, Hans Reck, who published his book *Buschteufel* on the war in German East Africa in 1926, reports on his comradeship with the native soldiers, but with the following qualification:

> —here the white man stood in front, together with the black, in the line of battle. Necessity taught the white man gladly to share the last mouthful with his loyal black brothers in arms—yet without relinquishing his race, the authority of his superior leadership.[13]

Brotherhood at the front became a commonplace in war accounts of the 1920s and is often linked to the issue of the pay that the Askaris received. This topos is double-edged: it is directed not only against the assertion that Germans cannot colonize, but also against the fact that Weimar politicians refused to remunerate the Askaris, who had not been paid during World War One. There is no mention of the German defeat in World War One and its blow to national identity. On the contrary, Germans as well as Askaris are shown as moral victors who were loyal to each other and to their convictions. In 1936, 30 years after Frenssen's book, an anthology with the title *Deutsche Flagge über Sand und Palmen* (German Flag over Sand and Palms) was published by a renowned author of war novels, Werner von Langsdorff.[14] It was a collection of 53 texts covering the period from Carl Peters in the late nineteenth century to the loss of the colonies before 1920. At least four of these texts explicitly deal with the topos of the loyal Askari, and the last one is even entitled *Schwarze Kameraden* (Black Comrades). This is remarkable not because German virtues like loyalty, courage in war, or readiness to make sacrifices are praised, but rather because, since the Nazi burning of the books in 1933, terms such as "comrades" and "comradeship" had been exclusively connected to the nationalist vision of a community without classes and races, and to the "spirit of the front." This notion of comradeship with natives was necessarily in conflict with the contemporary vision of an Aryan master race. Though the accounts of fraternity seem at first sight to be mostly of propagandistic value, serving the interests of colonial revisionists, they are connected to an imagined community of equals and are thus an exaggerated fantasy. Viewed from this angle, fraternity is a moral or symbolic compensation for the loss of identity manifested in the accusations made in the treaty of Versailles.

If one looks at the body of German war literature produced after the end of World War One, more than 600 books are to be found. Within this plethora of texts, accounts of the war in the colonies occupy only a marginal position. Obviously, there was little of importance to be told from the colonies—in comparison to accounts from the Western or Eastern Front. Except in the case of authors as famous as Lettow-Vorbeck, veterans' publications were generally—like those of the aforementioned Hans Reck—collections of anecdotes drawn from various colonial settings, in an effort to assemble enough material to be worth reporting. This is one of the reasons that authors did not limit themselves to reporting on native soldiers and relations with them in the way characterized previously. Rather, they looked for events or themes that promised to attract readers beyond the few who were directly interested in the fate of the colonies. One of these recurrent topics is the different culture of war among native soldiers. They were said not to adhere to the rules and restraints developed by modern Western military training. The native soldiers' cruelty and barbaric treatment of enemies are especially emphasized. Even Lettow-Vorbeck addresses this theme alongside his description of loyalty and comradeship: "And with loud cries of victory, our good blacks raced into the frightened Indians, and their gleaming German bayonets did terrible work."[15]

As other texts report, native soldiers were eager to behead their enemies or devour them after killing.[16] Here, the stereotype of the primitive, cruel, bloodthirsty, and cannibalistic black is used to create suspense and attract readers. But it is astonishing to find that these descriptions are not confined to native soldiers alone. At the very end of a diary published in 1925, a lieutenant of the *Schutztruppe* in Cameroon, Conrad Harder, describes his feelings during battle:

> [F]irst it creeps up slowly to the heart, then faster into the brain, this feeling of a beast, a bloodthirsty beast, greedy for murder. / You are driven forward, further and further, as if a magnetic force is pulling you into the jaws of death. Comrades fall to your right and left. You do not see it. Only afterwards, while collecting the injured and the dead, do you think: I was standing there too. / Each man has only one thought: "Kill!"—[17]

In this German author-veteran's report of blood-lust and the desire to kill, the division between German and native soldiers—or between "us" and "them"—is explicitly suspended, whereas previously the desire to kill had essentially been confined to the native soldiers. However, from 1930 onward—12 years after the end of World War One—battle scenes in which German soldiers fight against native colonial soldiers on the Western Front are a regular feature in war literature. The following report from the Western Front, written by Georg Bucher and published in 1930, purports to be autobiographical:

> Let anyone advance as we did to get back our lost position. Forward, through the trench and through everything. From trench to trench. Murder in front of us, roaring Senegalese soldiers, whom we drove before us to the old trench . . . where those of our comrades who failed to keep up during the last rushed withdrawal still lay, twitching and bestially mutilated. And how they were mutilated: eyes gone and mud and excrement in their mouths and noses—bayonets through their wrists and cheeks! To see this . . . see it! / Of course, we did not take it lightly—we went mad. But "we" [sic] did not murder—we just dealt out raging retribution and extermination—we drove drunken, roaring and stinking black monsters into blocked trenches from which there was no escape. And into foxholes. There was and could be no mercy: our fury and our hand grenades turned the holes into mass graves! / . . . / At Loretto we avenged our poor comrades. But we could only avenge them against the black beasts.[18]

Scenes of this kind can be found in about a half dozen texts, and the setting is always the Western Front.[19] To understand this phenomenon, one has to recall the debate on the *Schwarze Schmach* (Black Disgrace) in the early 1920s and the occupation of parts of the German Reich, which was accomplished with the aid of French colonial soldiers.[20] In the mid-1920s, this debate drew much attention to the topic of soldiers from the colonies and reinforced the stereotypes about them. So it is no surprise that encounters with French colonial soldiers were also incorporated into war literature. As passages of this kind cannot be found in war literature published before 1930, however, the authenticity of such "reports" must be seriously questioned—why were they not recounted earlier?[21] It is more likely that they represent collectively shared genocidal fantasms,[22] and that such an aesthetic of horror is being employed to attract readers. These texts present murder and genocide as event.

A close look at what happens in the cited scenes reveals a tension between two forces: on the one hand, a frenzy triggered by soldiers from the colonies and a pleasure in their extermination; on the other hand, a resemblance between German and native soldiers as regards uncivilized, unconstrained and barbaric behavior in war. Since all the books cited are by authors known to have been radical nationalists, the question should be posed: how is national identity tied here to the existence of the racial "Other"? The German self-image had been severely damaged by Germany's defeat in World War One and by the loss of the German colonies. The examples cited previously present fantasmagoric scenes in which genocidal fantasies are merged with a euphoric feeling of victory. Thus the old hierarchy between the races is re-established, and the defeat in World War One and the loss of the colonies are redeemed on a symbolic level.

This interpretation may be supported by another example. In 1936, Karl Angebauer, an author who had previously written around a dozen books on hunting and the life of farmers in South-West Africa, published an account of the campaign against the Hereros entitled *Kameraden in Südwest* (Comrades in South-West Africa). This book merges fact and fiction in what is sub-titled a *Tatsachenroman* (factual novel), a form typical of fascist literature of the 1930s. In the novel, a very similar depiction of emotions such as anger, fury and pleasure in killing, together with an aesthetic of barbarism, can be found.[23] In the part that deals with the campaign, historical figures like Oberst Leutwein or Major von Estorff act side by side with unknown characters, whose thoughts and feelings are recounted as if the author could have known them. The Herero rebellion is described as "the battle of race against race."[24] There are numerous descriptions of atrocities, including the mutilation, torture and murder of German men, women, and children by Hereros. After a call for retaliation, the campaign begins. The battle at the Leutweinsberg is described as follows:

> God knows, the kaffirs are tenacious today. They have retaken their former defensive positions and have started firing again from there. / We cannot have that! Now, while the enemy is still shaken, has not yet fully recovered from his last fright, right now is the time for a counter-attack. Lieutenant Epp's command rings out: / "Fix bayonets—attack!" / With a loud shout, Lieutenant von Wurmb, the only surviving platoon commander, leaps forward in front of the company. On the left flank, First Lieutenant Epp leads the attack. Following them, the fourth company, with a thunderous hurrah, with a burning thirst for revenge. /

Now let the dogs see what a real attack is like! / The enemy position is reached. The bayonet does its work. Any resistance is cut down. We follow close on the heels of the fugitives. Anyone who turns to defend himself is cut down! Anyone who is overtaken is cut down![25]

As the examples cited show, the discourse on war and the colonies represented in texts of the mid-1930s has two facets: anecdotes of fraternity and "brothers in arms" such as those collected in Werner von Langsdorff's book; and genocidal fantasms such as those in Angebauer's "factual" novel. But should we understand these two topics as two sides of a single coin? There is one book that brings together fraternity and frenzy. In 1931, Carl Wilhelm Heinrich Koch published *Im Tropenhelm: Kriegstagebuch eines Kamerunkämpfers* (In a Pith-Helmet: War-Diary of a Cameroon Veteran). Though the flyleaf tells us that Carl Koch is the editor of this diary, a short biography given at the end of Langsdorff's *Deutsche Flagge über Sand und Palmen* refers to Koch as the author of the text. Koch's biography is remarkable: after having fought in Cameroon, he was a prisoner of war in Spain and Great Britain, joined the *Eiserne Division* (Iron Division) in the Baltic in 1919, lived as a farmer in Angola from 1924 to 1930, joined the *Sturmabteilung* (SA) (storm troopers) in 1932, and worked as an assistant in the *Kolonialpolitisches Amt der Reichsleitung* (Hitler's Colonial Office). In 1934, he published the *Ehrenbuch der SA* (Roll of Honor of the SA).

At the beginning of the diary, published in 1931, the first-person narrator describes modern, "civilized" warfare as superfluous in the case of the colonies:

Yes, today the enemy is the prey. And we are predators. With constraints which may be applicable in Europe but not for us here in this distant, peaceless land, where death marches in step with us wherever we go. Why the hypocrisy?[26]

Further on, he confesses his pleasure in barbarity and blood-lust:

I looked at the young lad. He belongs to the man-eating Maka tribe. In his eyes I saw the great animal that was suppressed in us and that had now also taken possession of me . . . Frighteningly and dishearteningly, I recognized that I now loved to kill and did so with heedless savagery.[27]

What follows is a constant stream of descriptions of the experience of war as ecstasy and frenzy, as in the following example:

We are all just beasts. We want to kill and not be killed. A wild intoxication of blood and murder and, here and there, sudden fear. It can suddenly seize the heart. Courage? It doesn't exist. Duty? Yes. And self-discipline.[28]

After 200 pages of descriptions of this kind, the first-person narrator sums up his experience. He admits to having become like his native comrades. The narrator confesses to having conducted a style of warfare similar to that of the natives. But he never questions his leadership or the fact that he belongs to the master race:

> The whites of that time regarded the campaign—in purely human and personal respects—as a great, wild and dangerous adventure. If something happened, they overcame their scruples, cast aside their European identity, and said: "Damn it, we'll crush that crew into the dirt." They took aim cold-bloodedly or with self-control, rejoices at the death of every opponent who had come to take our new territory from us and destroy with blood and cruelty our ascendant mastery and power.[29]
>
> If doubt and incomprehension overcome these men and their coloreds, who shared the same spirit, what is to happen to them? The last strength they have in their sickly bodies and weary minds is the free self-mastery of the foot-soldier within the iron, lashing ring of the columns of enemy conquerors. And are they now to become slaves?[30]

Koch's text is outstanding in its merging of the themes of fraternity and frenzy. His protagonist longs to slip into barbarity and resembles his native soldiers in behavior and perception; he perpetrates the same cruel style of warfare, and thus they become true comrades. Koch seems to echo the Nietzschean appraisal of war as an intensifier of cultural development through barbarization. Read as a process of identity-construction, the barbarity of the "Others" is presented as an object of desire for the protagonist. The pictures of "Self" and "Other" become mutually dependent, and each bears the imprint of the other. Unlike the texts cited earlier, Koch describes this grasping for the superiority of the beast as a path to a new *Herrentum* (racial mastery). His protagonist does not succumb to the danger of total immersion in the racial "Other".

If this is the core of the fantasms presented in the accounts from the colonies and the Western Front, the dialectic between the desire for the "Other" and the fear of becoming "other" is laid open. Fraternity, as well as likeness in frenzy, can be read as a form of intimacy and identification with the racial "Other." But there is also the danger of blurring the dividing lines between "us" and "them." This creates an uncertainty that can only be overcome by an annihilation, be it imagined or real, of the "Other." Annihilation is a way to end uncertainty, through violence. Violence provides orientation,[31] even though (or because) the desired "Other" is being extinguished. In this sense, Mihran Dabag's thesis that annihilation is a means to create identity is validated.[32] If fraternity and frenzy are linked within the same discourse, the racial "Other" is, for German nationalists, at once an object of desire and something that must be exterminated.

Is there a link between the desire for annihilation of the "Other" in the cited texts and the Holocaust? Certainly, there is no direct connection. These fantasms neither influenced Nazi plans to exterminate Gypsies and Jews, nor did the texts function to produce meaning or legitimacy, as was the case with the discourses examined by Brehl. In Brehl's analysis, literature fulfills the task of interpreting events and bears a mark of belatedness.[33] But in the case of the literary production of the early 1930s, the texts have to be interpreted in a narrow sense: the references to fraternity re-establish German accomplishments as a colonizing power and are thus directed against the treaty of Versailles; and the accounts that describe the annihilation of the racial "Other" imaginatively restore the hierarchy of the races and, in the case of Angebauer, present an imaginary reconquering of the colonies. Only in a very broad sense do these texts serve as conduits for communicating ideas of the pleasure of extermination to the Nazi era that followed.[34]

## NOTES

1. Gustav Frenssen, *Peter Moors Fahrt nach Südwest. Ein Feldzugsbericht* (Berlin: Grote, 1906).
2. A more detailed analysis of this ideology can be found in Medardus Brehl, "'Das Drama spielte sich auf der dunklen Bühne des Sandfeldes ab': Die Vernichtung der Herero und Nama in der deutschen (Populär-)Literatur," in *Völkermord in Deutsch-Südwestafrika: Der Kolonialkrieg (1904–1908) in Namibia und seine Folgen*, ed. by Jürgen Zimmerer and Joachim Zeller (Berlin: Links, 2003), pp. 86–96 (pp. 88–92).
3. Frenssen, *Peter Moor*, p. 68. All translations are mine.
4. Ibid., p. 198.
5. Ibid., p. 200.
6. Ibid., p. 201.
7. Manuel Köppen, "Im Krieg mit dem Fremden. Barbarentum und Kulturkampf," in *Kolonialismus als Kultur. Literatur, Medien, Wissenschaft in der deutschen Gründerzeit des Fremden*, ed. by Alexander Honold and Oliver Simons (Tübingen: Francke, 2002), pp. 263–87, esp. pp. 267–72.
8. See also Medardus Brehl, "'Diese Schwarzen haben vor Gott und den Menschen den Tod verdient'," *Völkermord und Kriegsverbrechen in der 1. Hälfte des 20. Jahrhunderts*, ed. by Irmtrud Wojak and Susanne Meinl (Frankfurt/M.: Campus 2004), pp. 77–97 (p. 91f.).
9. A valuable compilation of this material is to be found in Jörg Wassink, *Auf den Spuren des deutschen Völkermordes in Südwestafrika. Der Herero-/Nama-Aufstand der deutschen Kolonialliteratur. Eine literarhistorische Analyse* (Munich: M-Press, 2004).
10. Medardus Brehl, *Vernichtung der Herero. Diskurse der Gewalt in der deutschen Kolonialliteratur* (Paderborn: Fink, 2007).
11. Paul von Lettow-Vorbeck, *Heia Safari! Deutschlands Kampf in Ostafrika* (Leipzig: Koehler, 1920), pp. 179–80.
12. Ibid., p. 159.

13. Hans Reck, *Buschteufel. Deutsch-Ostafrikanisches* (Berlin: Reimer/Vohsen, 1926), p. 19.
14. Werner von Langsdorff, *Deutsche Flagge über Sand und Palmen. 53 Kolonialkrieger erzählen* (Gütersloh: Bertelsmann, 1936).
15. Lettow-Vorbeck, *Heia Safari*, p. 41.
16. Examples can be found in Carl W.H. Koch, *Kamerun. Erlebtes und Empfundenes* (imprint 9,000–13,000, Leipzig: Voigtländer, 1924), p. 24f.; Hermann Consten, "... *und ich weine um dich, Deutsch-Afrika*" (Stuttgart: Strecker & Schröder, 1926), p. 175; Hans Surén, *Kampf um Kamerun. Garua* (Berlin: Scherl, 1934), p. 21.
17. Conrad Harder, *In Busch und Steppe. Erlebnisse eines Kamerunkämpfers aus den letzten Jahren unserer Kolonie* (Berlin: Weltenberg, 1925), p. 212.
18. Georg Bucher, *Westfront 1914–1918. Das Buch vom Frontkameraden* (Wien: Konegen, 1930), p. 18f.
19. Hans Zöberlein, *Der Glaube an Deutschland. Ein Kriegserleben von Verdun bis zum Umsturz* (Munich: Eher, 1931), pp. 657 and 774; Franz Schauwecker, *Aufbruch der Nation* (Berlin: Frundsberg, 1930), pp. 253–6; Joseph Magnus Wehner, *Sieben vor Verdun. Ein Kriegsroman* (Hamburg: Deutsche Hausbücherei, 1930), pp. 235 and 282; Erhard Wittek, *Durchbruch anno achtzehn. Ein Fronterlebnis*, 3rd edn (Stuttgart: Franckh, 1933), pp. 148–55; Joachim von der Goltz, *Der Baum von Cléry. Roman* (Berlin: Gutenberg, 1934), p. 189; Paul C. Ettighoffer, *Eine Armee meutert. Schicksalstag Frankreich 1917. Ein Bericht* (Gütersloh: Bertelsmann, 1937), p. 122.
20. Gisela Lebzelter, "Die 'Schwarze Schmach'. Vorurteile—Propaganda—Mythos," *Geschichte und Gesellschaft*, 11 (1985), 37–58.
21. Christian Koller denies that significant contraventions of the *ius in bellum* were committed by soldiers from the colonies: Christian Koller, "*Von Wilden aller Rassen niedergemetzelt*": Die Diskussion um die Verwendung von Kolonialtruppen in Europa zwischen Rassismus, Kolonial- und Militärpolitik (1914–1930)* (Stuttgart: Steiner, 2001), p. 102.
22. The term "fantasm" designates an imagined scenario in which the subject is present and displays its relations to others. This scenario can be the product of real-life experiences as well as the representation of desires. For a discussion of the concept "fantasm," see Herman Rapaport, "Theories of the Fantasm," in Rapaport, *Between the Sign & the Gaze* (Ithaca, NY: Cornell University Press, 1994), pp. 17–90. The concept is introduced as a methodological approach in my PhD thesis: Jörg Vollmer, *Imaginäre Schlachtfelder. Kriegsliteratur in der Weimarer Republik* (Diss., Freie Universität Berlin, 2003, pp. 18–23, <http://www.diss.fu-berlin.de/2003/232/indexe.html> [accessed 20 March 2008].
23. Astrid Unverricht, "Zwischen Propaganda und Heimatgefühlen: Deutsch-Südwestafrika in der Kolonialliteratur," in *Afrika—Kultur und Gewalt. Hintergründe und Aktualität des Kolonialkriegs in Deutsch-Südwestafrika. Seine Rezeption in Literatur, Wissenschaft und Populärkultur (1904–2004)*, ed. by Christof Hamann (Iserlohn: Institut für Kirche und Gesellschaft, 2005), pp. 105–26 (pp. 118–21).
24. Karl Angebauer, *Kameraden in Südwest. Ein Tatsachenroman* (Berlin: Bong, 1936), p. 87.
25. Angebauer, *Kameraden in Südwest*, p. 118f.
26. Carl W.H. Koch, *Im Tropenhelm. Kriegstagebuch eines Kamerunkämpfers. Bearbeitet von Carl W.H. Koch* (Düsseldorf: Floeder, 1931), p. 9.
27. Ibid., p. 29f.
28. Ibid., p. 56.
29. Ibid., p. 203.

30. Ibid., p. 205.
31. This notion has been further analyzed, though in another context, by Arjun Appadurai, "Dead Certainty: Ethnic Violence in the Era of Globalization," *Public Culture*, 10.2 (1998), 225–47.
32. Mihran Dabag, "Genozidforschung: Leitfragen, Kontroversen, Überlieferung," *Zeitschrift für Genozidforschung*, 1.1 (1999), 6–35 (p. 28).
33. See Brehl, *Vernichtung der Herero*, pp. 52–8.
34. A more exhaustive examination of this question has been offered by Benjamin Madley, "From Africa to Auschwitz: How German South West Africa Incubated Ideas and Methods Adopted and Developed by the Nazis in Eastern Europe," *European History Quarterly*, 35 (2005), 429–64.

# 10 Colonial Heroes
## German Colonial Identities in Wartime, 1914–18

*Michael Pesek*

Following the defeat of the German Empire in World War One, very few parades were held in honor of the returning troops: most Germans could see no reason to celebrate the military that had waged and lost the war for European supremacy. However, in 1919, some hundred colonial officers and soldiers under the command of Colonel Paul von Lettow-Vorbeck paraded through the Brandenburg Gate and were welcomed enthusiastically by the waiting Berliners. Few facts about events in faraway East Africa had reached Germany during the war years, but this information gap had been filled by press stories of daring deeds by German troops, surprising victories over a numerically superior enemy and adventures in the jungles of eastern Africa. These narratives continued to shape memories of the German colonial project throughout the time of the Weimar Republic, when the former German colonies—which had once been notorious for scandals and mismanagement—gained immense popularity and the loss of the colonies came to be seen as part of the national post-war trauma. This essay reflects upon the making of heroic wartime narratives on the battlefields of the East African campaign and on the pages of colonial literature written after the battles had been fought and the colonies lost.

## WAR, MODERNITY AND THE HERO

According to Walter Benjamin, the hero is a true figure of modernity.[1] He represents individuality in a world where the individual risks being absorbed into the faceless mass, and he embodies the promise of individual agency in the making of history. Yet Benjamin also notes that the modern hero is merely the performer of a heroic role, and that modernity is a tragedy which offers the role of the hero, but not a genuinely heroic life.[2] As the French historian and philosopher Michel Foucault points out, it was at precisely the time in eighteenth- and nineteenth-century Europe when societies were steadily being purged of internal warlike relationships, and war itself was becoming a professional and technological monopoly of the state, that war came to be seen as the prime force of history, a history driven by brute power. As Foucault observes, the new historical understanding neglected the much less manifest but more fundamental forces by which, in reality, European society was being transformed: industrialization, urbanization, and emerging bourgeois culture.[3]

These mundane historical forces also had their impact on the way in which wars were fought from at least the latter part of the nineteenth century onward: armies became bureaucratic organizations, and modern technologies both redefined war and military craft and reduced the role of the individual soldier. The hero remained a prominent topic in narratives of the war,[4] and World War One was in some respects a prime example of this. But, while newspapers and public ceremonies created powerful imageries of heroism, these were increasingly undermined by the harsh realities of modern modes of warfare experienced on the battlefields of Europe. For Hemingway and many of his contemporaries, World War One brought the end of heroism and chivalry.[5]

The East African campaign, however, provided more space for heroic narratives. Unlike the battles fought on European soil, this campaign did not develop into a stalemate of trench warfare. The campaign was characterized by high troop mobility, and few major battles took place; these lasted no more than a few days and involved only limited use of the artillery, armored vehicles and aircraft which, in Europe, had turned the war into the modern world's first industrialized human slaughter. Of course, the East African campaign had its own hardships and cruelties, but it also clearly offered greater potential for individual initiative and therefore more space for narratives of heroism. My main argument will be that the East African campaign offered an ideal opportunity to construct the kind of heroic narrative that was scarcely possible for German post-war discourse in connection with other theaters of war. While Germany was defeated in the murderous battles of technology and mass murder, she remained victorious in the medieval fight of man against man. As we will see, the wartime hero was in many respects rooted in a discourse that had evolved long before the war, in the period of colonial conquest.

## THE RETURN OF THE COLONIAL HERO

When news reached the colony that the Emperor had ordered a General Mobilization, most Germans in German East Africa were not surprised, but few feared that the menacing storm of war would reach the colonies.[6] On 13 August 1914, British warships bombarded the port of Sphinxhafen on Lake Nyassa, and, in the days that followed, German troops entered the territory of British East Africa. There was little enthusiasm for war in the colony in the ensuing weeks. Governor Heinrich Schnee saw little hope of victory against the Allied forces, as the colony was more or less surrounded by Germany's enemies. Yet, while Schnee wished to maintain peace at any cost, Lettow-Vorbeck was determined to contribute to the Imperial war effort by tying as many Allied troops as possible to the region. These differing views quickly led to an open conflict between the civilian and the military leaderships, and consequently to a military coup d'état. In defiance of Schnee's orders, Lettow-Vorbeck amassed his troops at the northern frontier, from where he not only repelled British attacks but also made incursions into British territory. At the end of 1914, the debate between Schnee and Lettow-Vorbeck was abruptly decided following the battles at Tanga and the Longido mountains, where German troops won decisive victories over numerically superior British forces. The Germans not only captured a huge amount of modern military equipment, which was then used to arm their own troops, but, more importantly, the victory was an enormous boost to German morale. The war's opponents were silenced, and the civil administration was pushed out and subordinated to the war effort; Lettow-Vorbeck took over the command of the troops from Schnee.

The surprising victories in the two battles led to the transfiguration of Lettow-Vorbeck, who was elevated into a reincarnation of the colony's mythical founder, Hermann von Wissmann.[7] Contemporary comparisons of Lettow-Vorbeck with Wissmann were informed by the long-running pre-war conflict between the civilian administration and the military. For, although Lettow-Vorbeck was undoubtedly an able colonial officer, he had, unlike his civilian counterpart, Governor Schnee, little interest in the paradigms of colonial rule. In this respect, he followed in the footsteps of Wissmann, although he was even more willing than the colony's founder had been to sacrifice even the most basic elements of colonial order for the sake of success on the battlefield. Many of the conflicts between Lettow-Vorbeck and Schnee during the war arose from the pragmatism of the commander-in-chief. When, for instance, in the summer of 1915, the British Navy sank the German vessel *Konigsberg*, the surviving crew was integrated into the *Schutztruppe*. The sailors were ranked as ordinary soldiers, and Lettow-Vorbeck ordered that they should wear the same uniforms and be paid the same salary as the Askari, and that they should even be equipped with older rifles than their indigenous counterparts. According to Hauer, these soldiers were called *askari ulaya* (European Askari) by the Africans. He believed that the Africans paid close attention to this new system of uniforms and commented ironically upon it. Governor Schnee, who had always been far more committed to the vanishing colonial order, revoked Lettow-Vorbeck's order, only to be brought to heel immediately by the latter, who insisted that his command be implemented.[8] The making of Lettow-Vorbeck into a hero represented and was accompanied by a suspension of basic features of colonial order and discourse.

Another pre-war officer who came to inhabit the pantheon of German wartime heroes was the last Resident of Rwanda, Max Wintgens. He was perhaps the last such official who genuinely viewed the implementation of colonial policies as enacting a politics of conquest. In comparison with his predecessor, Richard Kandt, Wintgens was more favorably disposed toward the use of military methods in colonial politics. When he began a punitive expedition against a rebellious chief in northern Rwanda, he did so in more or less open defiance of orders from his superiors in Dar es Salaam. Wintgens, like so many other members of the colonial military, was convinced that one of the most important qualities of a colonial officer was the ability to make decisions independently of plans and orders conceived in the distant offices of the colonial bureaucracy. The very attitude that brought him sharp criticism in times of peace made him into a wartime hero. In spring 1917, Wintgens, who had become cut off from the main body of Lettow-Vorbeck's forces, started his own campaign in the enemy's territory; it lasted over eight months and became a nightmare for both British and Belgian troops, who chased the elusive Germans over several thousands of miles. In his memoirs, Lettow-Vorbeck expresses both criticism and admiration of Wintgens's actions.[9] For the missionary Roehl, who accompanied Wintgens during his retreat from Rwanda to Tabora, matters were simpler: *bwana tembahassi* (as Wintgens was nicknamed by Rwandans) became a "Horned Siegfried," a symbol of the power and force of the German Empire.[10]

Wintgens's trek through the hinterland generated only a low level of fighting: it was essentially a race between Allied and German troops with only few open battles. What made it suitable material for heroic narratives, however, was not its strategic value, but the backdrop it provided for individual initiative and daring actions. Following Wintgens's greatest military triumph—the capture of the island of Idjiwi, which had been occupied by a garrison of 20 Belgian troops—Roehl noted the great impression that the victory had apparently made on the Rwandans. For Roehl, the victory had raised the prestige of the Germans to new heights.[11] Triumphs on the battlefields were celebrated not only for their military importance but also for their supposed meaning for Africans, whom the Europeans had believed ever since the period of colonial conquest to be impressed only by the demonstration of military power. Carl Peters's plea at the very inception of German colonial rule in East Africa that the reputation of the Germans as the most warlike nation must be maintained still haunted the minds of the German military; and analogous concerns preoccupied the British and the Belgians to a similar extent. The African thereby served as a mirror for the fantasies of Europeans, in which the latter negotiated their identities. At their core, these identities were still based on those that had emerged during the colonial conquest, and they continued to be determined by notions of a male warrior cult. World War One seemed to provide Europeans with the possibility of staging the agonistic drama that Peters had suggested in the 1880s; the only difference was that the audience now also included European enemies.

The construction of the wartime colonial hero by the Germans had, as the Swahili name of Wintgens indicates, an African slant. Amazingly, references to the Swahili names of Germans in the colony had a long-running tradition within the Empire's colonial literature, even though many of these names (like the nickname *bwana sakarani*, given by Africans to the notoriously brutal and daring Tom von Prince) had rather ambiguous, if not pejorative, connotations. This hints at the importance of the Askaris within the German heroic narrative, in which the Africans themselves became, in a more or less idealized and depersonalized way, heroes, but where one of their most important functions was that of *claqueurs* for the heroic German officers. Askari songs of praise for the German officers can be found in several German accounts. For example, one German officer described Askaris singing songs of praise for Lettow-Vorbeck during an Askari dance at the prisoner-of-war (POW) camp at Abercorn. According to the officer, the lyrics of the song proclaimed, "Even if he wears ragged cloth and a long beard in the jungle, he is young, as was revealed after he was given back his uniform, he was always courageous and he is a wise man, we are not defeated."[12] The issue of Lettow-Vorbeck's proverbially unpretentious demeanor features in many German accounts of the Colonel. Its importance owes more to European patterns of heroic narrative than to those of East Africa, in which the hero is generally constructed as a generous self-made man rather than a puritanical ascetic.

It may not be surprising that the Askari were called into service as witnesses to the heroism of German officers; after all, there were few other candidates for this role. However, the Askari in this function had to be constructed, and this was achieved using established patterns of colonial discourse: in particular, by referring to the notion of the "savage" mind of the African as being simultaneously simple yet sensitive to certain aspects of personality. The result was the emergence of a symbiotic relationship in which the heroism of the German officer was dependent upon the witnessing Askari. In battle, the non-commissioned officer Hofmeister noted, the "personality of each German officer was revealed; he had to be frank, and . . . the *Shenzi* [savage] was sensitive to his capacities."[13] The battlefield therefore became a stage for colonial heroes, and it was the African, with his supposedly primitive and child-like mind, who was called upon to make sense of this theater.

Many Germans freely acknowledged that they owed much of their military success to the loyalty and skill of their black soldiers. In the popular colonial literature of the Weimar Republic, the figure of the Askari became a much-lauded hero, perhaps second only to Lettow-Vorbeck himself. However, the construction of the Askari as colonial hero reflected the conceptions of European officers rather than the capabilities of the African soldiers themselves. The prevailing assumption was that the Askari only acquired military value under the guidance of a capable officer. This was the other side of the symbiotic relationship: only the German colonial hero engendered the African colonial hero.

Despite this praise for the loyalty of the Askari in German colonial literature, the reality on the battlefields was much more ambiguous. Desertions among Askari were much more frequent than was acknowledged by German officers in their memoirs. This was particularly true of new recruits. The German volunteer Decher reported that, after the first battle of a company consisting mainly of young recruits, more than 70 per cent of the Askari deserted. Others were shot by their own officers to prevent them from absconding.[14] Such desertions became especially frequent in the last two years of the campaign, when German troops were on the retreat.

Europeans, too, were seldom the heroic figures they were portrayed to be. Only a few German voices chipped away at the heroic image of Lettow-Vorbeck and his officers after the war. One of these was that of Decher, who, in a remarkable account of his wartime experiences, sharply criticized the senselessness and what he saw as the selfishness of the campaign. Why, he wondered, was the war in the colony being waged, if not to allow the officers to win fame and honor and to decorate their uniforms with military medals?[15] In his account, the officers are portrayed as choleric and hysterical bureaucrats with a liking for floggings and excessive drinking.[16] Despite his reservations, Decher fought on until the end of the campaign. Many other German soldiers did not, although references to such desertions barely feature in the overall picture of the heroic struggle of the Empire's colonial military in East Africa. One German account, however, describes how many officers and soldiers ended their participation in the war en masse, following the capture of Tabora, by stating that they were sick and admitting themselves to the hospital, where they were captured by advancing Allied troops.[17] Hauer, describing a scene on the battlefield of Tanga, complains about the disastrous impression probably made on African witnesses by the escaping Europeans.[18] Later in his book, Hauer refers to the case of two officers whose death from malaria was interpreted by their Askari as God's punishment for their previous failures in battle.[19] Similar complaints were made by the British officer C. W. Hobley:

> In a campaign of this character, where troops of mixed races are employed, the close contact between black and white is an undesirable and unavoidable feature. The black troops soon came to realise the physical disabilities of the Europeans and their vulnerability. They saw Europeans shot down and even bayoneted by enemy black soldiers, they realised that very few Europeans were crack shots, they noted the inferior marching capacity of the white man, his inability to find his way about in the bush unaccompanied by a native guide, and in some cases they even saw that the courage of the white was not greater than that of the black. After all this can it be wondered that the prestige of the white race has suffered in the war![20]

## RITUALS OF THE COLONIAL HERO

As many contemporaries noted, the war posed a serious challenge to the
legitimacy of colonial rule as a European project of bringing peace and
civilization to Africans. Schnee, for example, feared that the war would
destroy the image of Europe as a force for peace. "It is hardly comprehensible to the Africans," he wrote, "that Whites now kill each another
despite having always preached peace and order to Africans and suppressed
their native wars."[21] His wife, Ada Schnee, echoed this assessment when
she noted that she was ashamed of the European war, and particularly so
when she thought of African Christians, "to whom we, whether as British,
German or French missionaries, taught the lesson of peace and brotherly
love, and now the Whites slaughter each another."[22] The impact of the
war on the image of Europeans as bringers of what Germans called *Kultur*
was feared by another German author. He compared the campaign to the
Thirty Years' War in Europe, an event that had played a long-standing and
important role in the Empire's colonial discourse as a means of marking the
difference between Africa and Europe:

> Behind us we leave destroyed fields, looted food stores and, for the
> weeks that follow, famine. We are no longer heralds of culture, our
> trace is marked by death, looting and deserted villages. This is quite
> similar to the Thirty Years' War, when the troops and their baggage
> train marching through the country did not leave behind them flourish-
> ing villages and fields.[23]

There had rarely before been a time when members of the colonial military
had reflected with such clarity and candor on the consequences of European violence on African soil. For many years, German colonial troops had
relied upon scorched earth policies against Africans. In the first years of
colonial rule, German officers had answered the criticisms that this aroused
among the German public at home with terse references to the African style
of warfare and to the African mercenaries' lack of humanity and civilization. They used the same metaphorical comparison with the Thirty Years'
War in Europe to refer to the peculiarities of the African situation. The
term *Landsknecht* (lansquenet) was used to describe the professional culture and habits of the Askari mercenaries, who had been recruited en masse
from remnants of the Egyptian army in the Sudan.[24] What made the Askari
different from Prussian soldiers was their habit of traveling with their families, the Spartan circumstances with which they contented themselves, and
the fact that they fought for money rather than a higher cause such as their
nation. Moreover, the lansquenet metaphor hinted at the supposedly lower
moral standards of an African military tradition that was held to involve
plundering, robbery, the merciless killing of the enemy, and the kidnapping
of women and children.

Despite the horrors and destruction for which World War One became known in history books and public memories, it was also the first war in which questions of war crimes played a major role in public debates. Even in the faraway African theater of war, this topic gained prominence and became linked with the civilizing mission of European colonialism. The war itself, as well as the manner in which it was fought, came to seen by many as an expression of European civilization. Unlike the tribal warfare generally associated with Africans, the European style of fighting was held to be characterized by the humanity and chivalry with which the combatants treated each another. Remarks by Ludwig Deppe, an officer in Lettow-Vorbeck's General Staff, exemplify this attitude:

> Sometimes it is not easy to eliminate the remnants of older times from the thinking and feeling of the Askari. They do not understand that, after the battle is over, the whites treat their enemies with the utmost dedication. The blacks are accustomed to hating their enemy, killing all men and women and smashing the heads of the children against the nearest tree-trunk. After a while, however, the Askari are prepared to accept the need to treat prisoners well and to respect the Geneva Cross.[25]

The Geneva Cross became a new symbol of European civilization in Africa, and the treatment of POWs was Europe's new lesson of civilization for Africans.[26] For the Germans, the target of this civilizing mission was predominately the Askari. In German accounts, we repeatedly find the African style of warfare being connected with the metaphor of the lansquenets. The German volunteer Otto Pentzel compares the behavior of his Askari after the capture of a Portuguese outpost to that of lansquenets of the Thirty Years' War: it was only with great difficulty that he was able to prevent them from killing the Portuguese captives.[27] The new scenes acted out by the colonial hero now involved preventing the Askari from committing war crimes—or, to be more precise, war crimes against European combatants. Even after Askaris had undergone the harsh disciplinary regime of Prussian barrack squares, they were still regarded as having only superficially learnt the lessons of European civilization.[28]

If the Geneva Cross became the new symbol of European civilization, then chivalry became its ritual. Both for their own benefit and for that of their African audience, the Europeans were determined to stage the European slaughter on African soil as a civilized and honorable affair. The "chivalrous" rituals involved in this performance included regular meetings of British and German officers for lunch during breaks in the fighting as well as the development of friendships across enemy lines, as one British source indicates.[29] Another important ritual of chivalry was the release of European POWs in exchange for their word of honor not to participate further in the campaign.[30] The Germans were particularly keen on this ritual, as they had few resources for maintaining POW camps. Yet this practice only ever involved the release of European prisoners; Indian and Asian soldiers, by contrast, were often forced to serve as porters for German troops—a serious violation of the Geneva and Hague conventions. Such differences in the treatment of prisoners hint at the underlying meaning of such rituals of chivalry, which not only celebrated a military code of honor but also served to reinforce racial differences in a campaign in which such distinctions were difficult to sustain.

For the war undoubtedly had negative effects on the visibility of racial differences; this was particularly the case for German troops during the *safari ya bwana Lettow*, as the Askari termed the German retreat of the years between 1916 and 1918. Never before in colonial history had the body of the European been exposed to such a high danger of being killed or wounded at the hands of Africans. During the colonial conquest, the killing of Europeans had been so rare that the number of whites slaughtered served as a measure of a battle's severity. On the East African battlefields of World War One, on the other hand, the death of Europeans became a daily occurrence. Indeed, some German and British sources report that secret orders were given to concentrate fire on Europeans because it was commonly believed that their death was decisive for the outcome of the battle.[31] For many Europeans, including the colonial military, the death of a European at the hands of an African was seen as a danger to colonial rule and the prestige of the White Man in Africa.[32] Through the rituals of chivalry discussed earlier, the officers hoped to weaken the impact of the battlefield killings of Europeans on the colonial order. Indeed, some sources indicate that agreements were made between German and British officers after the battle of Kondoa-Irangi to avoid close combat situations.[33] If such agreements existed, however, they had little impact on the fighting, in which close-combat situations were the rule rather than the exception.

Rituals of chivalry were the product of metropolitan debates about war crimes and rules of engagement, but were adapted to colonial paradigms once transferred to Africa. The East African theater of war thus became the stage upon which the colonial powers enacted their identities and compared performances, looking to the chivalrous behavior of their officers and their Askari for assurances about the condition of their respective national *Kultur*. For Hauer, who observed how thoughtfully German Askari treated wounded Indian soldiers in the battle of Tanga, this behavior was a sign of German success in colonial subject building. In his view, it represented the victory of a male German warrior culture over the tearful and weak Indian, the product of the imperial culture of the British.[34] The officer Deppe describes a similar scene during the German invasion of Portuguese East Africa:

> An Askari brings a captured Portuguese sergeant: trembling, tearful, and later even sobbing, the Portugese approaches. Then the Askari strokes his cheek to calm and comfort him. This is touching, a gesture

of pure humanity: the victor is kind to the enemy. And it is interesting from a pedagogical point of view, if one considers that the same African had recently been happy to kill his enemy, but now cares for prisoners like a mother. He has learned the lesson of our humanity. It is strange to see the blacks in this situation. But it is also shameful from the point of view of racial pride [*Rassenstolz*].[35]

The ambiguous nature of this scene arises for Deppe from the fact that Europe had allowed the war to encroach upon Africa, thereby delegitimizing both the core message of European colonialism and conceptions of the supposed primitiveness of Africans. For Deppe, it seems, Europe had lost its monopoly on civilization.

## THE DEATH OF THE COLONIAL HERO

In most German accounts, the image of the war in the colonies changes dramatically following the beginning of the Allied offensive of 1916. What had begun as a series of skirmishes along the frontier became increasingly brutal. One volunteer remembers that the war now became "more functional," or "more European," in contrast to the "childish gunfights" he had fought with Portuguese troops on the southern frontier in the first month of the war.[36] Hofmeister recollects the war becoming increasingly characterized by savage fighting methods. The illusion of the war as a chivalrous conflict soon faded away. Where casualties of different races had previously been cremated separately, such practices were no longer performed at all— another manifestation of the vanishing distinctions between Africans and Europeans in wartime.

Colonial order relied upon maintaining differences between Africans and Europeans. It was not only the color of the colonial master's skin that served as a sign of difference, but also his clothes, his possession of servants and luxury goods, and, as the historian Albert Wirz notes, what he ate and how he ate it. The consequences of the war for the material circumstances of both civilian and military Europeans posed a significant danger to the colonial order, and these consequences are described in many German accounts. After the Germans lost their colonial infrastructure due to the Allied offensive of 1916, conditions for the troops became increasingly harsh. More and more, the Germans were forced to lived from hand to mouth; and under these circumstances, the differences in diet that had existed between Europeans and Africans in peacetime became virtually impossible to sustain. Before the war, the Germans had imported most of their daily food from India or Europe and had lived mainly from canned or preserved products. In the first year of war, Germans were forced to begin altering their eating habits as their stocks of such foodstuffs rapidly ran out. They changed to fresh meat and locally grown vegetables, and moved increasingly toward local cuisine. According to Ludwig Boell, who had been an officer in Lettow-Vorbeck's general staff, the German army ceased to distinguish between food for Europeans and Africans in September of 1916.[37] When later recalling the situation during that period, Lettow-Vorbeck noted that it had caused him to abandon his belief that bread was an indispensable component of the European diet. If the Germans ate any bread at all at that time, it was made of *mtama* (millet), *muhogo* (cassava) or cooked rice.[38]

During the first two years of the war and the initial months of the *safari ya bwana Lettow*, the status of the European had also been visible in his greater access to luxury goods and servants. It had been normal for five or more porters to carry the personal equipment and belongings of a single officer, and for several servants and cooks to ensure his comfort. In contrast, Askari were allowed only one porter and possibly one other servant. When desertions by porters became frequent during the later stages of the campaign, the Germans lost not only the means to transport their belongings, but in many cases also the belongings themselves, which were often simply thrown away by the escaping porters. When the Germans crossed the border into Portuguese East Africa at the end of 1917, Lettow-Vorbeck ordered a reduction in the size of his force. Officers were now allowed only one porter, which meant that they lost much of their equipment.[39] The diaries of Governor Schnee illustrate the loss of comfort—and, consequently, of status—that resulted from this. After the crossing of the river which marked the border, the Rovuma, Schnee lost his porters, servants and cooks in quick succession. Stripped of his entourage and deprived of power by Lettow-Vorbeck, the colony's most senior official became just another member of the train of the German army on its long march. The aura of lavish sovereignty which had surrounded him before the war must have seemed like a distant memory. He observed the desertions of his personnel with increasing fatalism. Most of his orders were ignored.[40] He was already a political irrelevance by the time he became a POW in 1918.

Schnee's decline as a political figure was an extreme example of a loss of comfort being connected with the disappearance of a colonial master's aura. Looking back on this phenomenon, one officer interpreted it as a loss of his own civilization: "After all, life in the *pori* [bush] becomes a habit. Even the Central European, who regards himself as civilized, descends to the state of a nomad. It remains an open question whether this is a real loss or not."[41] As a consequence, the heroic narrative was forced to grapple with experiences that provoked a crisis of self for the colonizer. Food shortages, tropical illnesses, the death of comrades, desertions by porters and the resulting loss of personal belongings and comfort became daily occurrences for German soldiers. As in the expeditions of the mid and late nineteenth century, the European was exposed to the frightening world of the "dark continent"; and, once again, the language of adventurism and of weariness with modern civilization supplied the tools with which these experiences could be adapted to the colonial discourses of the metropolitan self. In a way which is at once unsurprising and paradoxical, the metaphor of the lansquenet came to be employed to describe the wartime experiences of Germans. Perhaps most significantly, this metaphor reflects the lowering of barriers between German officers and soldiers, on the one hand, and African Askari, on the other. The colonial hero became the last lansquenet of German history. What had once been used to mark the differences between German and African military cultures now stood for the specific identity of the German soldier at war. The following description of a camp scene by the officer Deppe—who compares it to Schiller's drama cycle of the Thirty Years' War, *Wallenstein*—is typical:

> As soon as the troops arrived at the camp a true idyll of peace emerged. The Askari erected the hut for his family within an hour, his children played nearby or raced through the camp. Women did their housework. It is a scene which reminds me of Wallenstein.[42]

In addition to the (idealized) comparison with the world of seventeenth-century lansquenets, the peaceful idyll of the camp suggests that the military order of German troops in the campaign was not entirely dominated by the officers, but also included patterns of African military tradition. The *safari ya bwana Lettow* became a distinctive society which included the fighting troops, the families of the officers and Askari, the servants, cooks and porters. At the end of German colonial rule, colonial society had become nomadic. According to the historian of the Eastern European campaign of World War One Vejas Gabriel Liulevicius, the medieval and post-medieval world of the lansquenet was a prominent topic in the German popular historical imagination at the period, and particularly during World War One itself. The Thirty Years' War came to represent a world of war, a society born in and existing only by war; and the lansquenet was seen as a new kind of human being who transcended old social identities and gave birth to a new people or race of war.[43] What Liulevicius describes for the Eastern Front is very similar to the experiences of Germans in the East African campaign. It was common for accounts of the *safari ya bwana Lettow* to describe it not so much as a colonial society at war, but as a war society in the colony—a society in which colonial relationships between Germans and Africans had been replaced by something different. While heroic wartime narratives contributed to a resurgence of colonial mythology back in Germany, wartime experiences also led to a refashioning of the very identities upon which these mythologies were based.

## NOTES

1. Walter Benjamin, *Gesammelte Schriften*, vol. 1 (Frankfurt/M.: Suhrkamp, 1991), p. 577.
2. Ibid., vol. 1, p. 600.

3. Michel Foucault, *Vom Licht des Krieges zur Geburt der Geschichte* (Berlin: Merve, 1986).
4. Bruno Preisendörfer, *Staatsbildung als Königskunst: Ästhetik und Herrschaft im preußischen Absolutismus* (Berlin: Akademie, 2000), p. 17.
5. Bernd Hüppauf, "Modernity and Violence: Observations Concerning a Contradictory Relationship," in *War, Violence and the Modern Condition*, ed. by Bernd Hüppauf (Berlin: de Gruyter, 1997), pp. 1–27; Douglas Mackaman and Michael Mays, "The Quickening of Modernity, 1914–1918," in *World War I and the Cultures of Modernity*, ed. by Douglas Mackaman and Michael Mays (Jackson: University Press of Mississippi, 2000), p. xxi.
6. Heinrich Schnee, *Deutsch-Ostafrika im Weltkriege—wie wir lebten und kämpften* (Leipzig: Quelle & Meyer, 1919), pp. 28 and 69.
7. Christen P. Christensen, *Nordschleswiger verteidigen Deutsch-Ostafrika: Bericht über die Fahrt des Blockadebrechers "Kronborg" und das Schicksal seiner Mannschaft in Deutsch-Ostafrika 1914–1918* (Essen: Essener Verlagsanstalt, 1938), p. 116.
8. Bundesarchiv (BA) Militärarchiv Freiburg, N 103/91, Marineabteilung: Kriegsakten betreffend SMS Königsberg; August Hauer, *Kumbuke: Erlebnisse eines Arztes in Deutsch-Ostafrika* (Berlin: Deutsch-Literarisches Institut J. Schneider, 1923), p. 49.
9. Paul von Lettow-Vorbeck, *Heia Safari! Erinnerungen aus Ostafrika* (Leipzig: Hase & Koehler, 1920; Biberach: Koehler, 1952), p. 155.
10. Karl Roehl, *Ostafrikas Heldenkampf: Nach eigenen Erlebnissen dargestellt* (Berlin: Warneck, 1918), p. 67.
11. Ibid., p. 33.
12. BA-Militärarchiv, N 103/91: Rudolf Wieland, in: "Schutztruppe für Deutsch-Ostafrika. Erlebnisse und Eindrücke vom Bekanntwerden des Waffenstillstandes bis zur Heimkehr der letzten 25 Lettow-Krieger." Note: translations from German throughout this essay are my own.
13. Record by Vizewachtmeister der Reserve Dr. Hofmeister, in *Kämpfer an vergessenen Fronten: Feldzugsbriefe, Kriegstagebücher und Berichte*, ed. by Wolfgang Foerster, Helmuth Greiner and Hans Witte (Berlin: Neufeld & Henius, 1931), p. 66.
14. Maximilian Decher, *Afrikanisches und Allzu-Afrikanisches: Erlebtes und Erlauschtes in Deutsch-Ostafrika* (Leipzig: Hillmann, 1932), p. 57.
15. Ibid., p. 175.
16. Ibid., pp. 118–20.
17. Record by Vizefeldwebel der Reserve Pfeiffer der 8. Feldkompagnie, *Kämpfer and vergessenen Fronten*, p. 82.
18. Hauer, *Kumbuke*, p. 63.
19. Ibid., p. 225.
20. C.W. Hobley, *Bantu Beliefs and Magic* (London: Witherby, 1922), p. 288.
21. Heinrich Schnee, *Deutsch-Ostafrika im Weltkriege*, p. 121.
22. Ada Adeline Schnee, *Meine Erlebnisse während der Kriegszeit in Deutsch-Ostafrika* (Leipzig: Quelle & Meyer, 1918), p. 41.
23. Ludwig Deppe, *Mit Lettow-Vorbeck durch Afrika* (Berlin: Scherl, 1919), p. 205.
24. Hermann von Bengerstorf, *Unter der Tropensonne Afrikas* (Hamburg, 1914), p. 5; Wilhelm Föllmer, "Die Schutz- und Polizeitruppe in Deutsch-Ostafrika," *Die Deutschen Kolonien*, 9.13 (1913), p. 71; Theodor Tafel, "Von der Schutztruppe in Ostafrika," *Deutsche Kolonialzeitung*, 31.28 (1914), p. 467; C. Waldemar Werther, *Zum Victoria Nyanza: Eine Anti-Sklaverei-Expedition und Forschungsreise* (Berlin: Paetel, 1894), p. 114.
25. Deppe, *Lettow-Vorbeck*, p. 57.

26. See, for example, remarks by the German missionary and nurse Agnes von Lewinski in her memoirs, *Unter Kriegswettern in Ostafrika* (Leipzig: Frankenstein & Wagner, n.d.), p. 12.
27. Otto Pentzel, *Buschkampf in Ostafrika* (Stuttgart: Thienemann, 1935), p. 44.
28. Artur Heye, *Vitani: Kriegs- und Jagderlebnisse in Ostafrika, 1914–1916* (Leipzig: Grunow, 1922), p. 16.
29. Wynn E. Wynn, *Ambush* (London: Hutchinson 1937), p. 40; Public Record Office, London (PRO), War Office Records, WO 106/273: "Record of the 3rd Battalion the King's African Rifles during the Great Campaign in East Africa 1914–18."
30. Richard Wenig, *Kriegs-Safari: Erlebnisse und Eindrücke auf den Zügen Lettow-Vorbecks durch das östliche Afrika* (Berlin: Scherl, 1920), p. 28.
31. See, for example, Kaiserliches Gouvernement von Deutsch-Ostafrika, *Zusammenstellung der Berichte über die in den August, September, Oktober 1914 stattgefundene Gefechte der Kaiserlichen Schutztruppe für Deutsch-Ostafrika* (Morogoro: Regierungsdruckerei, n.d. [1914]), p. 84: "Bericht Baumstarks über das am 7. Oktober 1914 stattgehabte Gefecht bei Gazi in Deutsch-Ostafrika."
32. Heye, *Vitani.*
33. Christensen, *Nordschleswiger*, p. 123.
34. Hauer, *Kumbuke*, p. 69.
35. Deppe, *Lettow-Vorbeck*, p. 172.
36. Otto Pentzel, *Buschkampf in Ostafrika* (Stuttgart: Thienemann, 1942), p. 45.
37. Roehl, *Ostafrikas Heldenkampf*, p. 105f.
38. Lettow-Vorbeck, *Erinnerungen*, p. 170; Roehl, *Ostafrikas Heldenkampf*, p. 105.
39. Decher, *Afrikanisches und Allzu-Afrikanisches*, p. 247.
40. PRO WO 106/1460: "East Africa Diary of Dr. Schnee, Governor of German East Africa."
41. Deppe, *Lettow-Vorbeck*, p. 74.
42. Ibid.
43. Vejas Gabriel Liulevicius, *War Land on the Eastern Front: Culture, National Identity, and German Occupation in World War I* (Cambridge: Cambridge University Press, 2000), p. 40.

# 11 Crossing Boundaries
## German Women in Africa, 1919–33

*Britta Schilling*

## INTRODUCTION: CROSSING BOUNDARIES

In 1919, Article 119 of the Treaty of Versailles deprived Germany of its overseas possessions. Compared with other European imperial powers of the time, Germany's overseas land holdings were relatively small, yet the fact that they had been confiscated magnified their importance for many Germans.[1] Most political parties apart from the *Kommunistische Partei Deutschlands* (KPD) supported colonial revisionism, which called for a return of the colonies and public revocation of what was known as the "colonial guilt lie." German women's actions in regard to the debate on colonial revisionism were vital to the project as a whole, but have often been overlooked, despite the fact that they traveled in increasing numbers to and around Africa as migrants, tourists, missionaries and professionals in the 1920s and 1930s.

Recent research that has focused on German women's roles in colonialism, empire and "colonial fantasies" has usually been weighted toward the colonial period,[2] and when German women's roles following the loss of the colonies are considered, the period of the Weimar Republic is often fused with the period of National Socialism.[3] Existing literature, furthermore, tends to generalize women's experiences in Africa or reduce them to the experiences of settler women and farmers.[4] Although a *Farmersfrau*-focused approach may be appropriate for the colonial period, it is not an entirely accurate depiction of women's involvement in the former colonies in the 1920s and 1930s. In fact, it ignores the changing views of femininity and the emerging ideal of the *Neue Frau*, or "New Woman," at home and abroad. By looking at German women's descriptions of themselves and African "Others" during the Weimar Republic, I show how they formed national, racial and gendered identities abroad and participated in discourses of colonial revisionism and women's emancipation at home. Using the experiences of three women as examples, I indicate that, for German women who challenged the boundaries of time (or history) and space (or geography), the discourses of colonial revisionism and women's emancipation went hand in hand. During the inter-war period, then, German women traveling between former colony and metropole, and vice versa, actively negotiated different gender identities in this "in-between" space and generated an image of a New Woman that was particular to the German postwar and post-colonial situation.

## LYDIA HÖPKER: A NEW WOMAN IN THE MAKING

There has in the past decade been much historical debate about whether or not the *Neue Frau* really existed in Weimar Germany or whether the idea of a New Woman was only constructed by the contemporary media. Popular magazines such as *Uhu* and *Die Dame* were filled with representations of lively, assertive, independent young women—women who broke the rules, had their own jobs in urban centers, smoked, drank, danced the "Charleston" and drove fast cars. They defined a post-World War One feminine ideal championing youth, beauty, athleticism and a slender physique. An older generation of bourgeois women feared that these young "promiscuous girls" and *garçonnes* would subvert long-established norms of sexual propriety and wreak havoc on the nineteenth-century equation of bourgeois "womanhood" with "motherhood."[5] Cornelie Usborne argues that these fears were based upon profound changes in female sexual norms caused by demographic developments following the war.[6] If women's mentality altered during the inter-war period, however, their status in German society did not necessarily undergo such profound changes.

As many women adopted the New Woman's *Bubikopf* (pageboy haircut) and more androgynous fashions, their bodies were still controlled by the government, which reflected growing fears about abortion and declining birth rates.[7] Some new types of white-collar jobs as secretaries, retail clerks, photographers, news reporters and doctors were available to women after the war, yet the majority continued performing unskilled labor in typical "women's" sectors, working in the most undesirable occupations and receiving markedly lower wages than men.[8] Meanwhile, bourgeois women's groups promoted women's place inside, rather than outside, the home.[9] Women were allowed to study in universities, but not allowed to acquire degrees, let alone hold professorships in the sciences and social sciences, until the late 1930s.[10] Although they were enfranchised by the Weimar constitution in 1919 and formed the majority of the electorate, women constituted only a small proportion, or 9.6 per cent, of the members elected to the Reichstag.[11] The real New Woman of the Weimar Republic was a woman caught within a mélange of competing ideals of femininity in public and private life posited by medical experts, bourgeois society, popular media and radical feminists.

Similar tensions about the construction of a German New Woman prototype raged in the former colonies in Africa. On the one hand, government organizations such as the *Frauenbund der Deutschen Kolonialgesellschaft* and the *Frauenverein vom Roten Kreuz für Deutsche Übersee* promoted women's maternal characteristics. At the same time, Germany's former colonies continued to be a testing ground for a range of female identities, accommodating the needs of maternal, domestically and familially oriented women as well as financially independent, adventurous, tomboyish and publicly active ones. Following, to a degree, the lead of some German women in Africa in the nineteenth century, those women who traveled to the former colonies in the inter-war period could continue to give vent to the very energies that were considered "masculine" at home.[12] They participated in what were usually seen as "men's" activities, such as hunting, driving and shooting, and now many of them worked in typically "male" occupations that were slowly opening up for women following World War One. A number of pioneering New Women participating in fields such as anthropology, economics, photojournalism and paleontology made their name in the former African colonies.[13]

Although it may appear that the colonies already presented a unique space for more social freedom in the nineteenth century, women did not always seize this space for themselves. Indeed, those who did, like Frieda von Bülow, were often shunned by German society abroad as much as they were in the metropole.[14] During the 1920s and 1930s, however, women farmers and plantation owners' wives writing about their pre-war experiences in Africa adopted a more self-consciously independent and feminist voice, actively engaging with the new ideals of womanhood being promoted by the media at home. The beginnings of the emergence of the New Woman abroad may already be seen in the emancipatory rhetoric used by those women who had been employed in more traditional feminine occupations in Africa before World War One. According to the memoirs of women like Lydia Höpker, Agnes von Lewinski, Charlotte Deppe and Thea de Haas, World War One was a watershed for the development of independence, courage and toughness in German women abroad.[15] Most of these memoirs were written by women who had lived in German East Africa, and their stories became especially poignant during the inter-war period, since this was one of the colonies from which both German men and women had been deported and which they were banned from re-entering until 1925. Women's memories of empire were thus crucial in motivating New Women to rediscover and emotionally and intellectually "reclaim" the former colonies.

*Um Scholle und Leben*, an autobiographical work published in 1927, describes the pre- and post-war experiences of the farmer Lydia Höpker (1884–1957) in a way that emphasizes tendencies of independence, confidence, authority and even a certain aggressiveness ascribed to New Women. Höpker arrived in South-West Africa in order to run the household at Kayas Farm: she was to look after the 19-year-old farmer's son and his young assistant, while the farmer himself temporarily returned to Germany.[16] While at Kayas, Höpker went on safaris, learned to navigate the South-West African landscape and shoot small game, and survived a serious bout of malaria. At the outset of World War One, she alone was in charge of the farm, able to rely solely on her own determination and, from time to time, the help of a neighbor. She wrote of "a hard life," but that she "was very happy that I could deliver my own tribute to the beloved fatherland."[17] Höpker thus adhered to the strong sense of hard work and nationalism that also pervaded the rhetoric of publications for and by women involved in the *Frauenbund der Deutschen Kolonialgesellschaft*. At the same time—in contrast to the *Frauenbund* ideals—Höpker went out of her way to reject any sort of maternal identity until the very end of her account.

Throughout her narrative, Höpker asserts her independence and authority, both in her interaction with German men who try to court her and over black employees. She frequently hit black men and women and complained about their lack of initiative to work without a white overseer present. As the war progressed, Höpker wrote, "the natives were ever harder to control. Only my energy and the threat of my beatings were able to keep them in check."[18] Given this capacity for violence, it is no surprise that the author asserted several times that she "could get along perfectly well without any help, especially without any men's protection."[19] Indeed, Höpker eventually started her own farm.[20] To readers, the life of a new kind of independent woman in what was seen as a "second homeland" in Africa was made palpable by her account.

Illustrations of Höpker on her horse Wotan and various other scenes taken from the narrative are scattered throughout the first edition of the book (see Figure 11.1). Interestingly, in these artist's renditions, the author is often depicted as a New Woman, with short hair, legs visible below a knee-length skirt, feet clad in fashionable heels. It is unlikely that Höpker walked through the African bush in the early 1910s with all the trappings of a fashionable lady of the 1920s. Her image as a woman was adapted in order to be palatable to a contemporary audience, blurring the lines between colony and homeland and presenting her femininity as an important issue to the publisher, readers and herself. Given this attention to the contemporary audience, it is all the more important that Höpker ultimately decided to marry her friend Rolf Witte. Although she drinks, smokes, beats African workers and can run a farm on her own, Höpker ultimately reverted to the maternal, domestic feminine ideal appropriated by so many white women in Africa before her. After an abrupt change of direction, the final scene of the book shows Höpker, content in her *Heimat* abroad, cradling her newborn "golden" son.[21]

## LOTTE ERRELL: A NEW WOMAN IN SEARCH OF "REALITY"

While the *Farmersfrau* in the 1920s and 1930s ultimately conformed to nineteenth-century norms of femininity, other women who were less concerned with their roles as mothers and wives also traveled to Africa. These

Schreckerstarrt blieb ich stehen, denn ein mächtiger Leopard stand nahe vor uns am Berghang.

*Figure 11.1*    L. Höpker, *Um Scholle und Leben*, 1927.

women were a small group of self-supporting professionals who—like Höpker—displayed characteristics of the New Woman, such as independence and adventure, but—unlike Höpker—eventually discarded maternal paradigms completely. Certainly many women writing about or traveling to Africa in the inter-war period were motivated by a search for romantic ideals such as independence and "freedom." At the same time, more typical New Women adopted a new, matter-of-fact approach to describing their experiences abroad, with a great deal of emphasis placed on the "reality" of their experiences.[22]

Lotte Errell (1903–91) was a photographic autodidact who entered the field of photojournalism—which, in the 1920s, had become flooded with practitioners keen to participate in the burgeoning visual culture of the Weimar Republic. Although she certainly acquired some technical knowledge from the studio of her husband, Richard Levy, Errell developed her own style during independent journeys abroad in the late 1920s and the 1930s. Traveling across the globe alone as a photojournalist, Errell was—like other New Women—determinedly independent. She made her first journey to Africa in 1928, accompanying the ethnologist Gulla Pfeffer and the film-maker Friedrich Dahlsheim on an expedition to the Gold Coast (now Ghana) and Togo. Errell's journey to Africa launched her career as a professional photographer, establishing a reputation for high-quality work that recommended her for later assignments for the Ullstein publishing house, Associated Press and *Life* magazine.[23]

Central to Errell's work was an adherence to the *Neue Sachlichkeit*, or "New Sobriety," style, a term that entered popular discourse shortly after it was coined in 1923 and soon gained a range of meanings, including the exact representation of the "everyday," rejection of all emotional bias and a "deliberately cultivated unsentimentality."[24] This style is visible in Errell's photographs in the form of focused close-ups, de-contextualized images, attention to detail and dramatic lighting. In her book documenting her trip to West Africa, *Kleine Reise zu schwarzen Menschen* (published in 1931), Errell included close-up portraits of members of the Ewe community in Helekpe as well as detailed, sharply focused documentation of ethnographic objects (see Figure 11.2).

Her work was influenced by contemporary photographic innovations such as smaller cameras and faster film, as well as a type of visual cataloguing used by ethnographers to gauge the shipping costs and value of "native" objects for European museums, ultimately turning art or ritual objects into commodities.[25] Errell's accompanying text also highlights a pseudo-scientific, de-romanticized approach to the subject matter. In her introduction, she wrote,

> I would like to warn you that you are mistaken if you expect from this book the myriad adventures which an *Afrikabuch* is seemingly obliged to tell . . . I would like to relate a journey which you and I and anyone

Tanz- und Nachrichtentrommel aus einem Baumstamm geschnitzt

64

*Figure 11.2*   L. Errell, *Kleine Reise zu schwarzen Menschen*, 1931.

else may undertake, if he believes he can forego the comforts of European civilization.[26]

In this text, Errell thus tries to set herself apart from traditional, "heroic" travel accounts, or *Afrikabücher*, which usually offered highly embellished tales of the adventures of virile German men in the African bush.

Also in contrast to the male-centered *Afrikabücher*, Errell included a large number of portraits of Ewe women in her account. Among these photographs is the intimate portrait of a young woman, Abra, referred to in Errell's narrative (see Figure 11.3). In this photograph, Errell chose the angle of the shot from below, creating a view that muddles the traditional power relationship between white photographers and black subjects that is typical for visual representations of racial "Others" in a colonial context. Errell's point of view literally elevates the young black woman, glorifying her body, which is smoothed out with the effect of soft light. Although a side view of the subject visually references the by then well-established genre of the ethnographic portrait, viewers regard Abra's profile in a completely different manner from that of an impartial observer. Indeed, by magnifying the details of Abra's face and body and also by including her name in the caption, Errell also magnifies Abra's importance as an individual in the viewer's consciousness. Placing the image in the context of her writing, one can argue that she is attempting to portray her as what she would call a "primitive" role model for an "over-civilized" European culture, and for European women in particular. Visually, in any case, the photographer complicated the traditional paradigms for portraying "natives," suggesting that Europeans could look up to or learn from Africans, rather than the other way around.

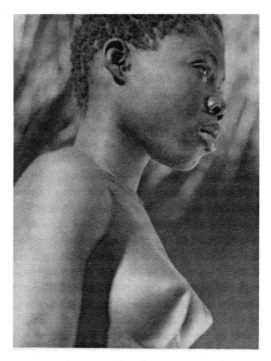

*Figure 11.3*   L. Errell, *Kleine Reise zu schwarzen Menschen*, 1931.

Although her photographs already hint at some ambiguity toward the colonial question, Errell's textual comments in her book show that, unlike most *Farmersfrauen*, she was not necessarily in favor of colonial revisionism. She wrote,

> After a while in the bush, the city and its people become unbearable. Unbearable because one finds oneself suddenly responsible for that which we, as whites, have done and are continuing to do to the natives … [T]here must be means and ways of preserving the individuality, the cultural and human value of the "savages." European states leach the wealth from their land and introduce in return their prized Civilization and Culture. Whereas one must say that the Negro has a culture very well fitted to his nature, even though he almost always loses it under our influence, and that, ultimately, he has very little to gain from Civilization.[27]

This was the "reality" that Errell found, and it did not fit in at all with the ideals of colonial revisionism, which posited that German masters must return to the former colonies in order to continue—in the rhetoric of the time—"civilizing" African "children." At the same time, Errell's statement reveals a viewpoint that kept Africans in a permanent discursive state of "primitive" otherness, rather than placing them on the same level as Europeans.

Yet it must be kept in mind that the "reality" Errell saw was not necessarily that which was presented to the public at large when her book was published. In the advertisement for *Kleine Reise zu schwarzen Menschen*, the designers highlighted Errell's contributions to photography by featuring her picture of Abra (see Figure 11.4). The publisher's decision to use a photograph rather than a drawing for the advertisement emphasized the message that the author herself tried to convey in her introduction to the book: that hers was a "real" rather than an imagined or embellished account of life in West Africa. Yet that is where the similarity of intent ends. In the commercial context, the picture of the young woman may still be read as a symbol of pride and natural or so-called "primitive" beauty, yet she appears more of an inanimate art object, her torso cropped and her figure cut out from its original surroundings. She no longer has a name. Fading into the background of the advertisement, the woman's body is covered partially by the bold letters of the book title. As advertisers altered Errell's photograph to fit the tastes of potential consumers, they erased the markers of Abra's individual identity and turned her into a symbol. Yet this is what consumers wanted: the advertisement was deemed so successful that it was included in a collection of the best examples of international advertising art in April 1932.[28]

Reviewed by one of the many colonial journals that proliferated during the Weimar Republic, Errell's volume was termed "a lovely book by a young European who relates in a fresh and lively way her little adventures on her trip through the Gold Coast and into the southern regions of

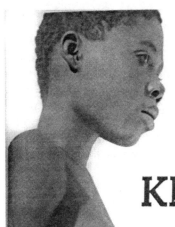

LOTTE ERRELL

# Kleine Reise zu schwarzen Menschen

Dieses Buch einer jungen modernen Frau ist das erste große Afrikaerlebnis eines Menschen, der mit offenen Augen in die Welt sieht, im Menschen überall den Menschen sucht und findet. Das Buch einer Lichtbildkünstlerin, die wie noch niemand vor ihr das Gesicht des Negers, des schwarzen Menschenbruders, im Bild festgehalten hat. Die Reise führt zur Goldküste durch die ehemalige deutsche Kolonie Südtogo. Mit jungenhaftem Sportgeist werden Gefahren und Strapazen überwunden. Dabei gelingen auf der Streife durch den Busch und die Lagunen auch ethnographisch höchst bedeutungsvolle Aufnahmen von Kultgebräuchen.

## BREHM VERLAG · BERLIN

*Figure 11.4*   *Gebrauchsgraphik*, vol. 9, no. 4, 1932.

*our* [my emphasis] Togoland. The nicest thing about this book is the 48 wonderful photographs."[29] Although this may well be true, the reviewer chose to ignore Errell's text with its anti-colonial messages. German New Women, praised for their "realistic" depictions of everyday life in Africa, were ignored when these depictions became too critical for a nation that was trying to reclaim its former colonies.

## ELLY BEINHORN: A NATIONAL NEW WOMAN

The aviatrix Elly Beinhorn was another woman self-consciously treading on male territory during the inter-war period. Beinhorn, born in 1907 in Hannover, received her first pilot's license in Berlin at the age of 18. In 1931 she made her first solo flight to Africa, joining the expedition of the Swiss anthropologist Hugo Adolf Bernatzik in Guinea-Bissau. By 1930, only 21 women in Germany held a pilot's license; as Beinhorn claimed, "[P]eople in Germany do not yet have enough trust in the capabilities of women flyers."[30] After having crossed French Senegal and entered French Sudan on the way back, Beinhorn had to make an emergency landing due to a broken oil pipe and spent four days walking 30 miles across desert and swampland to Timbuktu in a caravan of black bearers. She was supposedly the first white woman in Timbuktu, which, to her, "was logical enough, since the climate was difficult for female Europeans."[31] New adventures followed, taking her to India, Australia and New Zealand, as well as the east coast of South America. In 1933 she was awarded the Hindenburg Cup, the highest honor for an amateur aviator, for her solo flight around the world. Beinhorn thus joined an elite of aviators whose symbolic and cultural value for the German nation grew steadily throughout the Weimar Republic and into the period of National Socialism.[32]

Gender identity is constantly present in Beinhorn's accounts, including that of her 180-hour flight around Africa, from Tunis to Cairo. Beinhorn thought that she had a "manly" sense of freedom, yearning for adventure and appreciation of what she called "a feeling of limitless solitude."[33] On her journeys, Beinhorn was determined to succeed on her own without men's help, much like Höpker. She described her fellow male aviators' concerns about her safety in a tone of sarcasm. At the same time as she realized the limitations placed on her because of her gender (for she was not officially allowed to cross British territory in Africa without male accompaniment), Beinhorn also valued its advantages. In an emergency situation as she approached Keetmanshoop, she used her compact mirror to survey the outside of her plane, spot the problem and fix it. By contrast, a "real man," she says, "would never fly around with a mirror in his pocket."[34] In official photographs, Beinhorn is often seen next to her plane wearing a smart suit and skirt, unlike the usual aviators' jumpsuit, thus self-consciously playing with the New Woman ideal she embodied (see Figure 11.5).

On the other hand, Beinhorn's published travel accounts are also filled with pictures showing her hunting, wearing trousers and holding a rifle. Such photographs recall traditional portraits of European men in Africa, men who sought to dominate the wilderness and lusted for adventure (see Figures 11.6 and 11.7). Beinhorn's confidence in pursuing similar adventures as these men placed her in the same realm as the epic heroes of Germany's colonial past. Moreover, she also adopted these heroes' disparaging attitude toward blacks, remarking,

> These pretty African towns with the quaint Negro huts look much better from the air than they do from the ground. There, they are horribly

*Figure 11.5*     E. Beinhorn, *Ein Mädchen Fliegt um die Welt*, 1932.

dirty and run down. And I had imagined that the Negroes, at least in Africa, would to a large extent be walking around more or less na- ked—I had to correct this perception; they were all more clothed than the Europeans—only much worse.[36]

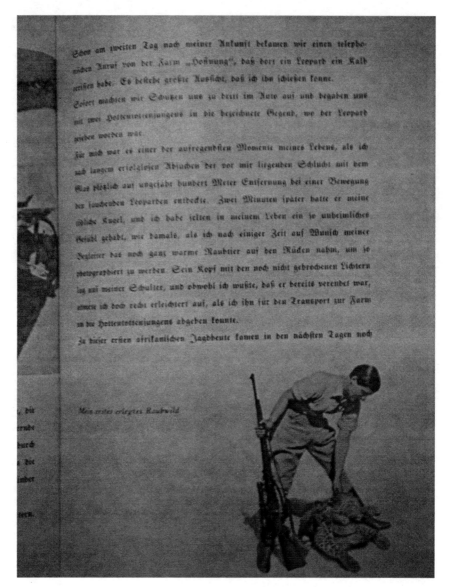

*Figure 11.6*    E. Beinhorn, *180 Stunden über Afrika*, 1933.

This statement, of course, fitted perfectly with colonial and colonial-revi-
sionist rhetoric which claimed that African "natives" must be taught to
conform to a German sense of hygiene and order. Indeed, during her journey from Tunis to Cairo, Beinhorn also made a point of flying over former
German South-West Africa and devoted an entire section of her *180 Stunden über Afrika* to the theme "Black-white-red once more over Africa."

*Figure 11.7*    Woeckner, German East Africa, c. 1910–12.[35]

She remarks that, while staying in South-West Africa, she had "completely forgotten that I was no longer at home in Germany."[37] Like colonial revisionists, she thus equated the former *Kolonie* with a second *Heimat*.

In her account of this journey, it becomes clear that Beinhorn's stress on her gender identity, and thus her participation in the debate on German femininity, is intimately linked with her views on colonial revisionism. Flying over "our former" Dar es Salaam, she remarks, "[H]ad I been born a boy and had the war not happened, I could be sitting here in some backwater as a German colonial officer."[38] Indeed, as most men were barred from the former German colonies after World War One, their authority over Africa had slipped; in the 1920s and 1930s, this authority was taken up by eager and adventurous women such as Beinhorn. Capable of handling the newest technology and traveling to "remote" lands while still self-consciously retaining a feminine identity, Beinhorn ultimately portrayed herself as a quintessentially "modern" or "new" woman. Like Höpker, Beinhorn eventually married and had a child, but not before she had achieved her own fame and success by traveling across the former colonies.

If Beinhorn's identity as a New Woman was in part based on her articulation of a supposed racial superiority over blacks, another dimension to this identity was her allegedly positive reception among former colonial subjects. According to the *Übersee- und Kolonialzeitung*, when Beinhorn touched down in Bissau in Portuguese Guinea, she was greeted by swarms of blacks and whites. A "loyal" Togolese in the audience supposedly wrote a letter to the paper, claiming that "we are proud of the courage and skill of our German white women, who show themselves as the equals of men."[39] Regardless of whether this letter was real or fabricated, the article shows how Beinhorn's image was used by colonial revisionists invoking the popular image of the "loyal subject" (who in other cases appeared as the *treuer Askari*) in order to legitimate the German presence in Africa and refute what was known as the "colonial guilt lie." During the Versailles negotiations, the Allies, headed by Great Britain, had accused Germany of "cruel methods of repression . . . arbitrary requisitions and . . . various forms of forced labour, which had resulted in the depopulation of vast expanses of territory in German East Africa and the Cameroons, not to mention the tragic fate of the Hereros in South-West Africa,"[40] and Germany's past mistakes as a colonial power were taken as a basis for claims that the nation could not again be trusted with responsibility for overseas territories. German colonial revisionists attempted to combat this largely male-induced negative image by utilizing the icon of the New Woman as a racialized but (generally) non-violent, feminine-rational symbol of an (unfairly) decolonized Germany.

## CONCLUSION: MAINSTREAMING INTO THE 1930S

Although each of the women mentioned here who traveled to Africa had their own unique experiences abroad, they exhibited a number of common characteristics that defined them as New Women. Whether presenting themselves as tough, independent women on the farm or describing their accomplishment of active professional roles in photo-reportage and aviation, these women and others like them legitimated their experiences by equating them with the supposedly rational and scientific approach of men of their generation. They self-consciously set themselves apart from bourgeois ideals of femininity, embracing what were considered male characteristics—the longing for adventure, looser dress, and mobility—while at the same time continually reasserting their identities as women. Most New Women abroad rejected maternal identities, as few of them had children at the time of their travels and many were divorced from their husbands. Their fierce yearning for independence often found expression in their sharp comments and acerbic humor. Such social transgressions, shunned in the metropole, seemed to be more acceptable in Africa, where white women had a history of exerting "masculine" authority over the native population. Much of the authority and self-worth of many, though not all, New Women in Africa was, indeed, derived from a sense of racial superiority.

Another source of authority was the New Women's sense of Germanness, perhaps a different sort of allegiance from that felt by *Farmersfrauen* or household helps sent abroad by the *Frauenbund*, but nevertheless an allegiance that included a strong desire to participate in public debates about the future of the nation. New Women's destinations in Africa were overwhelmingly sites in the former German colonies. They were thus following traces of Germany's history of dominance over African territory, reclaiming this space symbolically with their very presence and bringing it into the national consciousness by publishing their accounts and photographs. Although the former colonies in Africa had already for years been "laboratories"[41] for a New Woman prototype in terms of generating a sense of female independence and sportsmanship, the professionalizing impetus of women in new types of job, together with the commercialized image of New Women, referencing the latest fashions and technology, were exports from metropole to (former) colony. As women from the ex-colonies, such as Höpker, began to be influenced by the feminine ideals of the German metropole, women from the metropole, like Errell and Beinhorn, used the former colonies as sites for advancing their own careers.

Beinhorn, Errell and New Women like them did not comprise the majority of women who traveled to the former German colonies in Africa in the inter-war period. Nevertheless, their experiences are important because they allow us to trace the development of a New Woman prototype abroad as well as at home and show how intimately the two issues of women's emancipation and colonial revisionism were linked. Women during the Weimar Republic held varied views on both debates; as the National Socialists gained power, however, the space for a multiplicity of views became increasingly narrow. Women who spoke the "language" of colonial revisionism and racism were allowed to continue their independent and emancipated activities throughout the 1930s. The threat their non-maternalist tendencies presented to the feminine ideals of the Nazi party was of less weight than their representation of a healthy, energetic German race. Lydia

Höpker's book was in fact published in a second edition in 1936, under the title *Als Farmerin in Deutsch-Südwest*, with few changes, apart from the fact that the illustrations depicting the author and her adventures were replaced with more conventional photographs of life in Africa—including of indigenous people and vast landscapes dotted with German farms—probably taken from photographic archives of the *Reichskolonialbund* or similar NSDAP-run propaganda organizations. In *180 Stunden über Afrika*, Beinhorn is shown in a photograph giving the Nazi salute and, by 1939, the author's *Ein Mädchen fliegt um die Welt* had already reached its eighth edition. Moreover, as the case of Lotte Errell shows, women who held anti-colonialist sentiments during the Weimar Republic were tolerated, but their opinions were mainstreamed by the modern media into more marketable packages for the German public at large. In the mid-1930s, Errell, who was Jewish, left Germany entirely. She settled in the United States and never truly regained the reputation she had enjoyed in Germany as a remarkable photographer and journalist.

## NOTES

1. For more detailed discussions of the continued importance of the former colonies during the Weimar Republic, see Hartmut Pogge von Strandmann, "Imperialism and Revisionism in Interwar Germany," in *Imperialism and After: Continuities and Discontinuities*, ed. by Wolfgang J. Mommsen and Jürgen Osterhammel (London: Allen and Unwin, 1986), pp. 90–119; Dirk van Laak, *Imperiale Infrastruktur: deutsche Planungen für eine Erschliessung Afrikas 1880 bis 1960* (Paderborn: Schöningh, 2004); Jared Poley, *Decolonization in Germany: Weimar Narratives of Colonial Loss and Foreign Occupation* (Oxford: P. Lang, 2005); Klaus Hildebrand, *Vom Reich zum Weltreich: Hitler, NSDAP und koloniale Frage 1919–1945* (Munich: Fink, 1969); Tina Campt, "Converging Spectres of an Other Within: Race and Gender in Prewar Afro-German History," *Callaloo*, 26.2 (2003), 322–41.
2. See, for example, Krista M. O'Donnell, "Poisonous Women: Danger, Illicit Violence and Domestic Work in German Southwest Africa 1904–1915," *Journal of Women's History*, 11.3 (1999), 31–54; O'Donnell, "The Colonial Woman Question: Gender, National Identity and Empire in the Colonial Society Female Emigration Program 1896–1914" (unpublished PhD diss., State University of New York, Binghampton, 1996); Katharina Walgenbach, "*Die weiße Frau als Trägerin deutscher Kultur*": *koloniale Diskurse über Geschlecht, "Rasse" und Klasse im Kaiserreich* (Frankfurt/M.: Campus 2005); Nancy Reagin, "The imagined Hausfrau: National Identity, Domesticity and Colonialism in Imperial Germany," *Journal of Modern History*, 73.1 (2001), 54–86; Roger Chickering, "'Casting their gaze more broadly': Women's Patriotic Activism in Imperial Germany," *Past and Present*, February 1988, pp. 156–85; for the pre-colonial period, see Susanne Zantop, *Colonial Fantasies: Conquest, Family, and Nation in Precolonial Germany 1770–1870* (Durham, NC: Duke University Press, 1997).
3. See, for example, Amadou Booker Sadji, "African Nature and German Culture: Colonial Women Writers on Africa," in *Blacks and German Culture*, ed. by Reinhold Grimm and Jost Hermand (Madison: University of Wisconsin

Press, 1986), pp. 22–34; Horst Gründer, *Geschichte der deutschen Kolonien*, 4th edn (Paderborn: Schöningh, 2000); Marcia Klotz, *White Women and the Dark Continent: Gender and Sexuality in German Colonial Discourse from the Sentimental Novel to the Fascist Film* (unpublished PhD diss., Stanford University, 1994).

4. Lora Wildenthal, *German Women for Empire 1884–1945* (Durham, NC: Duke University Press, 2001); Martha Mamozai, *Schwarze Frau, weisse Herrin* (Hamburg: Rowohlt, 1989); Daniel Walther, *Creating Germans Abroad: Cultural Policies and National Identity in Namibia* (Athens: Ohio University Press, 2002); B. Kundrus, *Moderne Imperialisten: Das Kaiserreich im Spiegel seiner Kolonien* (Cologne: Böhlau, 2003); Rosa B. Schneider, *"Um Scholle und Leben." Zur Konstruktion von Rasse und Geschlecht in der kolonialen Afrikaliteratur um 1900* (Frankfurt/M.: Brandes & Apsel, 2003).

5. Lynne Frame, "Gretchen, Girl, Garçonne?" in *Women in the Metropolis: Gender and Modernity in Weimar Culture*, ed. by Katharina von Ankum (Berkeley: University of California Press, 1997), pp. 12–40; Cornelie Usborne, "The New Woman and Generational Conflict," in *Generations in Conflict: Youth Revolt and Generation Formation in Germany 1770–1968*, ed. by Mark Roseman (Cambridge: Cambridge University Press, 1995), pp. 137–63; see also Elizabeth Harvey, "The Failure of Feminism? Young Women and the Bourgeois Feminist Movement in Weimar Germany 1918–1933," *Central European History*, 28.3 (1995), 1–28.

6. Usborne, "The New Woman," pp. 137–63.

7. Atina Grossman, *Reforming Sex: The German Movement for Birth Control and Abortion Reform 1920–1950* (New York: Oxford University Press, 1995); Grossman, "Abortion and Economic Crisis: the 1931 Campaign against Paragraph 218 in Germany," *New German Critique*, 14 (Spring 1978), 119–38; Grossman, "The New Woman and the Rationalisation of Sexuality in Weimar Germany," in *Powers of Desire: the Politics of Sexuality*, ed. by Ann Barr Sitow, Christine Stansell and Sharon Thomson (New York: Monthly Review Press, 1983), pp. 153–71.

8. Renate Pore, *A Conflict of Interest: Women in German Social Democracy 1919–1933* (Westport, CT: Greenwood Press, 1981), p. 96f.

9. Mary Nolan, "'Housework made Easy': the Taylorized Housewife in Weimar Germany's Rationalised Economy," in Nolan, *Visions of Modernity: American Business and the Modernization of Germany* (New York: Oxford University Press, 1994), pp. 206–17.

10. Rosemarie Kullik, *Frauen "gehen fremd." Eine Wissenschaftsgeschichte der Wegbereiterinnen der deutschen Ethnologie* (Bonn: Holos, 1990), p. 39.

11. Pore, *A Conflict of Interest*, p. 96f.

12. See, for example, Wildenthal's work on Frieda von Bülow in the nineteenth century, in *German Women for Empire*, pp. 54–79.

13. For example, the ethnologist Gulla Pfeffer, the paleontologist Ina Reck or the economist Charlotte Leubuscher.

14. Wildenthal, "'When men are weak': The imperial feminism of Frieda von Bülow," *Gender and History*, 10.1 (Apr. 1998), 53–77.

15. Agnes von Lewinski, *Unter Kriegswettern in Ostafrika* (Leipzig: Frankenstein & Wagner, 1919); Charlotte and Ludwig Deppe, *Um Ostafrika. Erinnerungen von Charlotte und Ludwig Deppe* (Dresden: Beutelspacher, 1925); Thea de Haas, *Urwaldhaus und Steppenzelt* (Leipzig: Reclam, 1926).

16. For more detailed information on Höpker's biography, see Schneider, *"Um Scholle und Leben,"* pp. 212–14.

17. Lydia Höpker, *Um Scholle und Leben* (Minden: Köhler, 1927), p. 84.

18. Ibid., p. 99.
19. Ibid., p. 87.
20. Ibid., p. 145f.
21. Ibid., p. 219.
22. This is in sharp contrast to pre-war authors of colonial literature, most of whom had never been to the colonies themselves. See Sybille Benninghoff-Lühl, "Kolonialromane um die Jahrhundertwende," in *Afrika und der deutsche Kolonialismus. Zivilisierung zwischen Schnapshandel und Bibel-stunde*, ed. by Renate Nestvogel and Rainer Tetzlaff (Hamburg: Reimer, 1987), p. 84.
23. For more on Errell's wider work, see Ute Eskildsen and Dorothee Wiethoff, *Lotte Errell: Reporterin der 30er Jahre* (Essen: Museum Folkwang, 1997).
24. Fritz Schmalenbach, "The Term *Neue Sachlichkeit*," *Art Bulletin*, 22.3 (September 1940), 163; see also John Willett, *The New Sobriety: Art and Politics in the Weimar Period, 1917–33* (London: Thames & Hudson, 1978); Jost Hermand, "Unity within Diversity? The History of the Concept 'Neue Sachlichkeit'," in *Culture and Society in the Weimar Republic*, ed. by Keith Bullivant and R. Hinton Thomas (Manchester: Manchester University Press, 1977), pp. 166–82; for an analysis of an exemplary *Neue Sachlichkeit* photographer, see George Baker, "Photography between Narrativity and Stasis: August Sander, Degeneration and the Decay of the Portrait," *October*, 76 (Spring 1996), 72–113.
25. Christraud Geary, *Images from Bamum: German Colonial Photography at the Court of King Njoya, Cameroon, West Africa 1902–15* (Washington: Smithsonian, 1988), p. 85f.
26. Lotte Errell, *Kleine Reise zu schwarzen Menschen* (Berlin: Brehm, 1931), p. 5f.
27. Ibid., p. 17.
28. *Gebrauchsgraphik*, 9.4 (1932).
29. *Übersee und Kolonialzeitung*, 43.10 (Oct 1931), 238.
30. Elly Beinhorn, *Ein Mädchen fliegt um die Welt* (Berlin: Hobbing, 1932), p. 7; "Frauenwege in Böblingen," <http://frauenbeauftragte.boeblingen.de/archivinhalt/frauenwege/elli.htm> [accessed 5 January 2008].
31. Beinhorn, *Mädchen*, p. 49.
32. For more on the geo-political consequences of the globalization of air travel during the Weimar era, see Peter Fritzsche, *A Nation of Flyers. German Aviation and the Popular Imagination* (Cambridge, MA: Harvard University Press, 1992), esp. pp. 173–84; Fritzsche, "Machine Dreams: Airmindedness and the Reinvention of Germany," *American Historical Review*, 98.3 (June 1993), 685–709.
33. Beinhorn, *Mädchen*, p. 51.
34. Ibid., p. 34.
35. This photo by courtesy of Bildarchiv der Deutschen Kolonialgesellschaft, Universitätsbibliothek Johann Christian Senckenberg, Frankfurt.
36. Beinhorn, *Mädchen*, p. 19.
37. Ibid., p. 37.
38. Beinhorn, *180 Stunden über Afrika* (Berlin: Scherl, 1933), p. 26.
39. "Togoneger begrüssen Elli Beinhorn," *Übersee und Kolonialzeitung*, 43.3 (1931), 109.
40. Heinrich Schnee, *German Colonization Past and Future* (London: Allen & Unwin 1926), p. 68. This is Schnee's response to the British government's Blue Book (Cd. 9416), "A Report on the Natives of South-West Africa and their Treatment by Germany," published in 1918.

41. On the idea of colonies as "laboratories for modernity," see, for example, Ann Laura Stoler, "Sexual Affronts and Racial Frontiers: European Identities and the Cultural Politics of Exclusion in Colonial Southeast Asia," in *Tensions of Empire: Colonial Cultures in a Bourgeois World*, ed. by Frederick Cooper and Ann Laura Stoler (Berkeley: University of California Press, 1997), pp. 198–237; van Laak, *Imperiale Infrastruktur*.

# 12 Abuses of German Colonial History

## The Character of Carl Peters as a Weapon for *völkisch* and National Socialist Discourses: Anglophobia, Anti-Semitism, Aryanism

*Constant Kpao Sarè*

Carl Peters (1856–1918) can be seen as the German equivalent of Cecil Rhodes. In 1884, this young doctor of philosophy, who had lived in London from 1881 to 1883, founded the "Society for German Colonization" and traveled as a simple civilian to Zanzibar, where he acquired many of the territories which were subsequently to become the colony of German East Africa. In spite of his entirely unacceptable colonial administration and policies, which included burning down several native villages and ordering the hanging of his African concubine, Peters came to be regarded, particularly in the Third Reich, as the greatest pioneer of German colonialism. His life was even made the subject of a film, starring the famous actor Hans Albers.

Peters is the subject of two new studies, one by Arne Perras and the other by the present author. Whereas Perras's work concentrates on Peters's biography,[1] my own book pays greater attention to the myth of Peters's life, ideas and activities and the propagandistic uses to which that myth has been put.[2] In this chapter, I examine the function of the character of Carl Peters in the cultural propaganda of German colonialism, that is, in German novels, film and drama. The questions I pose here are, how did German literature use this character in colonial discourse directed against England and in the propagation of Aryan ideology and anti-Semitism? And what kinds of ideological interest did the different propagandists of the Wilhelminian era, the Weimar Republic and the Third Reich pursue?

### CARL PETERS AND HIS SIGNIFICANCE FOR GERMAN COLONIAL PROPAGANDA BETWEEN 1885 AND 1945

Born on 27 September 1856 as the son of a Pastor in Lower Saxony, Carl Peters attended school in his place of birth, Neuhaus, a village situated at the mouth of the Elb, and then in Lüneburg. After obtaining his *Abitur* in 1876, which qualified him for entry to university, he studied history, geography and philosophy, finishing his studies with a thesis on Schopenhauer and a doctoral thesis on the 1177 Peace of Venice. In 1881, Peters was invited to London by his maternal uncle Karl Engel, who had been naturalized as a British citizen after marrying an Englishwoman. Peters returned to Berlin in 1883, and in 1884, together with fellow members of the so-called *Konservativer Klub* such as Felix Behr-Bandelin and Friedrich Lange, founded the *Gesellschaft für deutsche Kolonisation* (Society for German Colonization). On behalf of this Society, Peters and three further friends—Karl Jühlke, Joachim Pfeil and August Otto—traveled to Zanzibar and there acquired many of the territories that formed the basis of the later colony of German East Africa. Although Bismarck was initially unenthusiastic about these colonial adventures in East Africa, Peters received an imperial letter on 27 February 1885, the day following the end of the Berlin Conference on Africa, guaranteeing him safe conduct in the areas he had acquired and also in the others to which he was attempting to extend his influence.[3] That effectively gave him a free hand, on the strength of which, in autumn 1885, Peters founded the *Deutsch-Ostafrikanische Gesellschaft* (German East Africa Company). Lacking diplomatic skills, Peters was finally compelled to resign as head of this company on 25 February 1889. The same year saw him mount his expedition to attempt the rescue of Emin Pasha, which, however, he failed to achieve.[4]

On 18 March 1891, Peters was sent to East Africa as an "Imperial Commissioner for Kilimanjaro." In his new post, he subsequently caused a major colonial scandal by ordering the hanging of both a young native man (Mabruk), who had slept with one of Peters's African concubines (Jagodja), and of the concubine herself. When the hangings were discussed in the *Reichstag* in March 1896, the Social Democratic leader, August Bebel, launched an attack on Peters. First, Bebel read parts of the book *New Light on Dark Africa Being the Narrative of the German Emin Pasha Expedition*, which Peters had published in 1895, to show that German colonial history was "written in blood."[5] Bebel claimed that Peters himself had stated in a letter to an English bishop, Alfred Tucker, that he had married the girl in accordance with local tradition. The *Reichstag* took these accusations (namely, the killing of Mabruk and Jagodja) seriously, and Peters was dismissed from government service on 15 November 1897.[6]

He subsequently moved to London, where he pursued his "Ophir" theory by establishing a society for the exploitation of Rhodesian gold.[7] Although Wilhelm II restored the title of Imperial Commissioner to Peters in 1905, Peters continued to live in London until the Kaiser reinstated his entitlement to a pension in March 1914. At the outbreak of World War One, Peters returned home, where he eventually died on 10 September 1918, in Woltorf.

After his death, the figure of Peters developed into a kind of national monument, as his friends and partisans continued their efforts to bring about his total rehabilitation. Ignoring the wish of Peters's widow, Thea Peters (née Herbers), for her husband to be buried in Neuhaus, the municipality of Hannover decided to inter him in a memorial garden in Engesohden.[8] Among Peters's sympathizers, both before and after his death, were militant adherents of several colonial groupings, such as the German Colonial Society and the *Alldeutscher Verband* (Pan-German League).[9] Without the official support of the German Colonial Office, these associations had, in 1914, built the first memorial to Peters with the following motto: "To the pioneer of German colonial policy—the founder of German East Africa—Dr Carl Peters. Thanks to his achievements, Heligoland in 1890 became part of the German Empire."[10] They planned to erect this memorial in Dar es Salaam, but were prevented by the outbreak of World War One.

After 1918, the supporters of Carl Peters and the leaders of German colonial revisionism combined to attack what they considered to be the *koloniale Schuldlüge* (colonial guilt lie).[11] Former colonial officers such as Ritter von Epp (1868–1946) and governors like Heinrich Schnee (1871–1949) joined the friends of Peters around Otto Arendt (1854–1936) and Fritz Bley (1853–1931) in continuing to press for the rehabilitation of the late Imperial Commissioner.[12] The monument mentioned previously was finally erected on 3 June 1931 on Heligoland. A memorial stone to Peters was also inaugurated on 27 September 1931 at his father's house in Neuhaus, bearing the following message: "To our own Dr Carl Peters, the founder of German East Africa, born on 27.9.1856." A third monument to Peters was erected on 27 October 1935 in Hannover in the presence of eminent personalities of the National Socialist Party with the text, "To the great Lower-Saxon Carl Peters, who acquired German East Africa for us." The same members of the Nazi Party who took part in the inauguration of the memorial were also instrumental in persuading Adolf Hitler in 1937 to grant Peters a full posthumous pardon.[13]

Efforts to rehabilitate the person of Carl Peters were, however, not limited to memorials. He also emerged as the perfect hero of colonial novels—in a tradition of colonial literature which began in the imperial era itself but continued through Weimar and reached its peak during the Third Reich.[14] As regards the authors of German colonial literature published during the era of Wilhelm II, we can observe that they cite Carl Peters repeatedly in their writings. Their novels, memoirs, songs, and so on, contributed greatly to contemporary apologies for his character. The novels of Frieda von Bülow, the writer described by the *Kolonialzeitung* as "the founder of the German colonial novel,"[15] present Carl Peters as a role model. In *Der Konsul* (The Consul) (1891), he appears in the guise of Baron Max von Sylffa, the consul of a town named U., who is called back to Berlin for showing disrespect to his superiors. In *Tropenkoller* (Tropical Fever) (1896), Peters's incarnation is Udo Biron, a German who executes by hanging a slave trader in Satuta. In *Im Lande der Verheißung* (In the Promised Land) (1899), the German government refuses to appoint Ralf Krome—another rendering of Carl Peters—as Governor.

The writers of the Weimar Republic were less prolific than those of the Wilhelminian era but none the less forceful in their support of colonial revisionism.[16] The authors shared in the resentment felt among sections of the population toward the accusations in the Versailles Treaty that Germany had failed in its colonialism. Thus Edith von Salburg, for example, argued in her book *Carl Peters and his People* of 1929[17] that Peters had been a friend of Africans and that his colonial methods were superior to those employed by the British and French colonialists.

Finally, the character of Peters was also an important source of inspiration for Nazi colonial writers who sought to honor him as a great German. For instance, Paul Baecker's essay about Peters was published in a collection of books written to glorify the greatest Germans, such as Arminius, Fichte, Kant, and so on.[18] Especially noteworthy are the novel *Maria in Petersland* (1937) by Josef Viera—the pseudonym of Josef Sebastian Vierasegerer—and the drama *Weg in die Welt* (Way to the World) (1940) by Josef Buchhorn;[19] both works are designed to alert the Germans to the need for *Lebensraum* (living space). The same intention can be identified in a sketch written for the Hitler Youth by the *Reichsjugendführung der NSDAP* (Nazi Party Reich Youth Directorate).[20] Among other materials used by the propagandists of the Third Reich to rehabilitate Carl Peters were a stamp and a post card with the portrait of Peters (1934),[21] as well as schools, the names of streets[22] and even a naval fleet tender.[23] The biography of Peters was also the subject of a film in 1941 with Hans Albers in the leading role. The film *Carl Peters* was not just highly popular among the German public during the Hitler era,[24] but was also a pet project of the *Reichspropagandaminister*, Goebbels, himself.[25]

In short, the factual and fictive biographers of Peters tried continually to glorify his character. One of the particularities of German colonial literature is its connection to so-called *völkische Literatur*, a genre of writing produced from the end of the nineteenth century up to the end of the Third Reich and designed to propagate "typical" German values. In accordance with their affinity with and frequent affiliation to nationalist movements, the authors of German colonial literature developed ideas similar to those seen in *völkisch* literature. As Kay Dohnke puts it, "Even the relatively short lived genre of the colonial novel with its exotic scenes and the conflicts among different ethnic groups was suitable for the realization of völkisch-racist ideology."[26] More broadly, the philosopher Hannah Arendt (1906–75) even identified a causal link between imperialism and National Socialist racism. In her voluminous book *The Origins of Totalitarianism* (1951),[27] she claims that the racist ideologies and mentalities of the Nazis were first experimented with at the colonial level, especially in Africa. Concerning Carl Peters, she writes,

> The impact of the African experience was first realized by leaders of the mob, like Carl Peters, who decided that they too had to belong to a master race. African colonial possessions became the most fertile soil for the flowering of what later was to become the Nazi elite. Here they had seen with their eyes how peoples could be converted into races and

how, simply by taking the initiative in this process, one might push one's own people into the position of the master race.[28]

There is an ongoing discussion of Hannah Arendt and the link between colonialism and National Socialism, which we need not repeat here.[29] However, even if her critics have succeeded in casting doubt on the relationship between imperialism and totalitarianism, no one can seriously dispute that the racist conceptions of *völkisch* ideology and (subsequently) the National Socialist movement were explored experimentally in the colonial sphere. In the remainder of this paper, I accordingly attempt to show how German colonial literature exploited the character of Carl Peters in propagating three favorite doctrines of this movement: Anglophobia, anti-Semitism, and Aryanism.

## ANGLOPHOBIA

Any investigation of the way in which Carl Peters's character was employed to promote Anglophobia must take the discourses of the German nationalist movements very seriously. A clear example is an article written in 1914 by Admiral Breusing and published in the *Alldeutsche Blätter* (Pan-German Journal) under the provocative title, "By the Way, I Am of the Opinion That British World Supremacy Must Be Destroyed!"[30] Although Carl Peters spent part of his life in London, he considered British imperialism more as a rival than as a model to emulate. In his articles and memoirs written from the time of his first journey to London up to the end of his life, he invested much energy and time in justifying the view that the Germans had to attack British colonial interests in order to ensure the emergence of "Greater Germany." The most emphatic expression of this conception was an article he wrote on the eve of his death, "England, Our Arch Enemy."[31]

The fictionalization of Peters's life history and his rehabilitation in colonial literature did not wait for his death: specifically, the use of his character for furthering Anglophobia began well before the end of his life. Wilhelminian colonial literature regarded Carl Peters as the role model whose biography could best be used in support of the Germans' "Platz an der Sonne" (place in the sun) against the Britons' "empire on which the sun never sets." The authors of colonial novels largely tried to show that enmity against Great Britain was the best way for the German Empire to become a global power. In her most popular novel, *Im Lande der Verheißung* (1899)—mentioned previously—Frieda von Bülow depicts British attempts to thwart all of Peters's initiatives in East Africa. In a letter written to her brother, Rainer, a character in this novel, Maleen, exposes the Heligoland-Zanzibar Treaty of 1890 as a simple British machination aimed at obstructing the activities of the Peters figure (alias Ralf Krome). The author therefore suggests that the Germans must do the same in order to break the world domination of Great Britain.[32]

Such extreme hatred against the British was even more directly formulated in the Weimar era. After 1918, the biography of Peters as an Anglophobe was seen as a motivation for colonial revisionism. In order to require the return of German former colonies, colonial literature again focused its aversion on the British. The best example of this tendency is the novel entitled *Carl Peters und sein Volk* (1929), written by Edith Salburg. The story begins with a (fictional) letter[33] supposedly signed in London by "your German son Carl" and sent by the youthful Peters to his mother in Hannover. The letter reeks of Salburg's anti-British sentiments:

> Really! I look such a fine gentleman now, Mother, that you wouldn't recognize me if you passed me in the street—you'd even be revolted at the sight of me. My head's as smooth as an eel. That's the way they are here, smooth and slippery so you can't catch hold of them. If you heard me speaking English you'd immediately feel sick. I'm already doing it perfectly.

The writer of the letter not only makes fun of the English language but also laughs at the appearance of the British: "What I dislike most here in London are the expressions on the faces." He also compares the habits of study at British and German universities. In his view, the British are far lazier than Germans: "What they learn here does not even amount to a tenth of what we learn; that's for certain." These allegations are not just the effects of colonial fantasies. As the historian Klaus Hildebrand has noted, these prejudices and verbal insults belonged to the propaganda of World War One and were reproduced in the literature of the Weimar Republic.[34]

Much the same is true of World War Two. The film *Carl Peters* (1941) was principally produced to encourage antipathy against England at a time when Hitler's popularity was beginning to wane. In the eyes of the promoters of the film, British imperialism was the main obstacle to the colonial ambitions of the Third Reich. To show how far the British were willing to go to destroy German interests, the film's director, Herbert Selpin, included a sequence in which the British Secret Service attempts to poison Peters. In reaction to these British machinations, the film hero Peters opposes extreme brutality. However, the film-maker avoids showing the cruelty against Africans of the real Peters. In all instances, his aggression manifests itself toward the British alone. In London, Selpin's version of Peters angrily boxes the ears of an Englishman who dares to insult the Germans. In the view of the nationalist movement, such violence by the film's hero was the clearest illustration of how the Germans must respond to British arrogance. The Nazi journal the *Völkischer Beobachter* commented, "We see him in England manfully asserting his Germanness."[35] To summarize, the literature of German imperialism had, from Wilhelminian times through the years of the Weimar Republic to the end of the Hitler era, consistently used the character of Peters as a device to propagate anti-British discourses.

## ANTI-SEMITISM

A close analysis of Carl Peters's life shows that he himself may not have hated Jews.[36] However, his biography was employed by the propagandists of *völkisch* and National Socialist discourses to disseminate ideas justifying the persecution of the Jews. It is known that the *völkisch* movement considered official German colonial policy as a repository of Jewish trickery, "powerful Jewish influence" ("starke[r] jüdische[r] Einfluß"),[37] the final intention of which was to prevent Germany from developing into a world power. As they failed to find aspects of Peters's life to support their propaganda, the writers of colonial books looked for people of Jewish origin who were actively involved in German colonial policy. According to their arguments, all Germans who opposed Peters's colonial ideology were Jews.

Those whose Jewish origin is documented in anti-Semitic propaganda include Paul Kayser (1845–98). It is known that this Director of the Colonial Affairs Bureau, the precursor of the German Colonial Office, was only opposed to the colonial adventures of Peters at the beginning.[38] The authors studied spread the idea that Kayser showed solidarity with other Jews in order to fight the patriotic efforts of Peters. Erich zu Klampen, an author of the Third Reich, claims that it was not the Social Democrats who rejected the German colonial policy and brought about Peters's disgrace; in his view, the Jews were the culprits. In his novel *Ein deutsches Schicksal im Kampf um Ostafrika* (1938), Klampen argues as follows:

> Is the Under-Secretary of State [Paul Kayser], an official loyal to the Emperor, acting in agreement with the revolutionary leader and Social Democrat August Bebel? Impossible? Are there not men in the Empire who will stand up and affirm the existence of an international power dedicated to world domination, namely the Jews? They ask: who was Marx? The answer: a Jew. It was he who gave Social Democracy its program. Who are the leaders of Social Democracy? They have names: Lasalle and many others—Jews! Why do you people not ask: who are the opponents of Peters? August Bebel, Jewish Social Democracy and the Foreign Office. You may object that the Foreign Office is not Jewish. Men of the oldest and purest aristocratic lineages rule in the Wilhelmstrasse. Yet who is it that fights and intrigues against Peters? Ministerial Director Kayser. He may present himself as a conservative, loyal to the Emperor, he may even strive for fame and honors for himself in the German Empire, but in the end he must obey the same inner voice which commands him to hate and destroy everything German. Ministerial Director Kayser, who heedlessly surrendered our colonial

possessions in East Africa to England and destroyed the conqueror of German East Africa, is a Jew.[39]

Thus, according to Klampen, the threat to the German Empire came not from the Social Democrats but from the Jews. The arch rival of Peters was not August Bebel but Paul Kayser.

To understand why those colonial texts were interested in opposing Peters to colonial officials and activists of Jewish origin, we must examine the discourses propagated by the *völkisch* movement during the Empire and thereafter. In fact, one must be acquainted with the term *Gegenrasse* ("anti-race"),[40] formulated by one of the leading ideologues of Nazism, Alfred Rosenberg (1893–1946), a term which proclaimed that Jews and Germans were natural enemies. Such allegations are explicit or implicit in the studied texts. In the works of the Weimar era, the reader gains an insight into other conceptions of this so-called inherent antagonism between Jews and Germans. The writers affirm that attempts at harmonious coexistence with Jews are fatal for the "German race." Edith Salburg, for example, writes about the social contacts between Bismarck and Kayser: "He [Bismarck] knew nothing of the terrible dangers of miscegenation for his race. [But] First Secretary Kayser was no stranger to Peters."[41]

What about the texts written during the Third Reich? Here, the term "anti-race" is clearly formulated. The writers try to explain that the exclusion of Peters from colonial service was not a consequence of the Kilimanjaro killings but the logical result of an innate aversion between Germans and Jews. The following portrait of Kayser as a member of the *Gegenrasse* to the Germans is to be found in Alfred Funke's book *Der Mann, der Deutschland ein Imperium schaffen wollte* (The Man Who Sought to Build Germany an Imperium), published in 1937:

> Kayser and Peters incarnate unconsciously the contrasts of the blood, of the inward view of life and the purposeful sense of duty, which must necessarily lead to conflict and thence to enmity and hatred. Dr. Kayser, of Jewish origin . . . only became Christian upon his entry into Imperial Service . . . Capital was at all times Jewish in its orientation; in Kayser, too, racial feeling was stronger than his devotion to a colonial policy which was not a matter of "business" but rather—as it was for Peters—of the worldwide greatness, standing, self-confidence of the German people.[42]

With the last sentence, the author essentially told his reader that Peters was working for Germany and Kayser for the Jewish race. Jewish business acumen had thus proved more powerful than the patriotic colonial policy of Carl Peters. If the great hero Peters had failed in his mission, so, Funke implied, the reader must recognize that the Jewish threat to German society must not be considered a banality. Furthermore, the author does not hesitate to explain why Peters failed in the struggle with Kayser. In his view, the reason was Peters's refusal to hate the Jews. He writes, "Despite all his German consciousness Peters would have never attacked a person because of his Jewish origin."[43] For Funke, Peters's disgrace was rooted in his refusal to fight the Jews effectively. Thus, in order to win where Peters had failed, the Nazis must act ruthlessly and resist sentimentality.

We can see, in short, that the whole biography of Peters, his success and his failure, either fitted or were made to fit into the anti-Semitic propaganda of the *völkisch* and National Socialist movement from the times of Wilhelm II to the end of World War Two. The authors of the German colonial literature examined here continually fuelled the alarms that a Jewish conspiracy was working against the world power of Germany.

## ARYANISM

We have seen how these authors sought to present other peoples, specifically the British and the Jews, as immoral and decadent "races" which had to be fought with great vigor. Next, I examine how they presented the Germans. With the central concept of Aryanism,[44] I analyze the function accorded to the figure of Peters in connection with the abolition of mixed marriages (miscegenation) and the complex of *Herrenrasse* (master-race, Aryan race) versus *Zigeuner* (Romany). Since the *völkisch* and National Socialist movement believed that Aryans were the superior race, I first take a closer look at the image of the "blond-haired Aryan" and compare it with the descriptions of Carl Peters in German colonial texts.

In the books analyzed, Peters is portrayed as the authentic German as Nietzsche described him: an Aryan superman, a "blond beast" (*blonde Herrenbestie*). It was therefore hardly a coincidence that the promoter of the film *Carl Peters* (1941) chose a blond actor of striking appearance, Hans Albers, to play the main role. However, this image of Peters already existed in the texts of the Wilhelminian era. In her novel *Tropenkoller* (1896), Frieda von Bülow described Udo Biron (alias Carl Peters) as follows:

> He [Udo Biron] looked far more Germanic than his sister, whose appearance verged on the Romany type; he was tall and broad-shouldered with a deep chest, a small head posed upright on his strong neck, blue eyes, a blunt nose and blond curly hair—all in all, the image of Nietzsche's "blond beast", born to rule.[45]

Thus, in this passage, the author presents Peters physically as an ideal German, and reinforces the portrayal with the contrast between Biron and his half-sister Eva: he and his sister are in every respect opposites. His allure is attractive because he is a pure German. She, with her Hungarian mother, represents the genus of *Zigeuner*; and, in the racial thinking of the time, *Zigeuner* are white primitives.

The authors of the different periods consistently sought to demonstrate that Peters belonged to the Aryan *Herrenrasse*, which meant that he was superior to members of all other races. In his novel *Maria in Petersland*, Josef Viera affirms that the Africans of *Petersland*, the imaginary country founded by Peters, noticed the difference between the quality of German "blood" and that of other Europeans:

> The black soldier was a British Askari, and it was wholly appropriate for him to view Günter, of whom he knew nothing except that he was to be kept imprisoned behind the barbed wire, as an enemy of the nation which he served as a mercenary. Nevertheless, the Askari lowered his gaze respectfully whenever the German looked at him. The reason was very simple: the blood to which Günter belonged cannot be humiliated. Even if members of that race are placed behind barbed wire and in the guard of Negroes, yet theirs is the blood of the master-race—indeed, those in whose veins such blood flows bear an obligation to it.[46]

As regards miscegenation, Peters is presented as a role model in the struggle against racial mixing—where the notion of *Mischrasse* (mixed race) applies not only to Africans, but also to other Europeans. The authors and the film-maker attempt to demonstrate that it was a threat to the Germans if they allowed their superior race to be adulterated with other, "lower" races. The novel *Tropenkoller* (1896), by Frieda von Bülow, in which Eva, Peters's half-sister, is depicted as a *Zigeuner*, has already been mentioned. In another novel, *Der Konsul* (1891), Bülow portrays Josepha, a German Catholic woman, as *Zigeuner*-like because she gets married to Nathanael Lindenlaub, a Jewish businessman. She is "as lovely as sin";[47] this is the telling characterization. To demonstrate her "Romany" tendencies, the author describes her first meeting with Sylffa (alias Peters) as follows: Sylffa visits the Lindenlaubs' shop, Mr Lindenlaub is not present, and Josepha attempts to kiss Sylffa on the mouth. Thus, the reader is invited to observe how a German girl has been shamelessly perverted by her marriage to a Jew. As for Sylffa, he is a member of a superior race and cannot behave like his racial inferiors; accordingly, he refuses to kiss her. The narrator poses two questions: "Why did he feel nothing but aversion and disgust where so many others would simply be glad to enjoy the pleasure offered? Was he inherently superior [*besserer Art*] to the others and for that reason so choosy?"[48] The narrator does not answer these questions directly, but his terminology reveals his answer: in the language of social Darwinism, the term *besserer Art* means "of better race."

The leitmotiv of miscegenation is even stronger in the texts written after 1933. They ignore Peters's obvious penchant for African women. Of course, they omit to mention that the true reason for the Kilimanjaro hangings was almost certainly Peters's jealousy, the result of his attraction to his African concubine. Their hero's way of life disappears mysteriously in almost all narratives of the Third Reich. In the film *Carl Peters* (1941), for instance, Selpin's version of Peters show no interest in African women. It is to be presumed that, at this period—in which sexual contact between Aryan and non-Aryan was viewed as *Rassenschande* (racial dishonor) and was officially a crime—any allusions in such a direction would have been intolerable.

We should conclude by returning to the thesis of Hannah Arendt that all racial discourses of the Nazis were first explored and exploited in the colonial sphere. The present essay has sought to examine how three such ideologies—Anglophobia, anti-Semitism and Aryanism—were propagated in colonial literature at the time of Wilhelm II, during the Weimar Republic and in the Hitler era. We saw how the authors persistently attempted to paint a new portrait of the character of Peters (often diverging greatly from what appears to have been the historical Peters), in order to fit him into *völkisch* and National Socialist discourses. Finally, it must be acknowledged that they did this with some success—so well, indeed, that Walter Frank (1905–45), the Nazi historian who edited Peters's collected works (and later committed suicide at the end of Hitler's regime), could praise Carl Peters as "one of the great educators of the German nation."[49]

## NOTES

1. See Arne Perras, *Carl Peters and German Imperialism 1856–1918: A Political Biography* (Oxford: Clarendon Press, 2004).
2. See Constant Kpao Sarè, *Carl Peters et l'Afrique: un mythe dans l'opinion publique, la littérature et la propagande politique en Allemagne* (Hamburg: Dr. Covac, 2006), p. 440.
3. See Kurt Büttner, *Die Anfänge der deutschen Kolonialpolitik in Ostafrika* (Berlin: Akademie, 1959), pp. 45–7; Fritz F. Müller, *Deutschland, Sansibar, Ostafrika. Geschichte einer deutschen Kolonialeroberung 1884–1890* (Berlin: Rütten & Loening, 1959), pp. 43–5.
4. See Martin Baer and Olaf Schröter, *Eine Kopfjagd. Deutsche in Ostafrika. Spuren kolonialer Herrschaft* (Berlin: Links, 2001), pp. 34–6. See also Mary E. Townsend, *Macht und Ende des deutschen Kolonialreiches* (Münster: Lit, 1988), pp. 134–6.
5. See August Bebel, "Die Kolonialpolitik ist mit Blut geschrieben," in *Ausgewählte Reden und Schriften*, vol. 4 (Munich: Saur, 1995), pp. 92–53.
6. See Martin Reuss, "The Disgrace and Fall of Carl Peters: Morality, Politics and *Staatsräson* in the Time of Wilhelm II," *Central European History*, 14 (1981), 110–41.
7. "Dr. Carl Peters Estates and Exploration Co." (later South East Africa Ltd.). See "Mein zweiter Aufenthalt in England," in *Gesammelte Schriften*, vol. 3, ed. by Walter Frank (Berlin: Beck, 1944), pp. 95–107. On the "Ophir" theory, see Cornelia Essner, *Deutsche Afrikareisende im 19. Jahrhundert* (Stuttgart: Steiner, 1985), p. 170.

8. Mentioned by Uwe Wieben, *Carl Peters. Das Leben eines deutschen Kolonialisten* (Rostock: Neuer Hochschulschriftenverlag, 2000), p. 65.
9. See the article by Michael Salewski, "Pathologischer Ehrgeiz. Carl Peters war eine Galionsfigur des Alldeutschen Verbands," *Frankfurter Allgemeine Zeitung*, 8 August 2005, p. 6.
10. On the monuments to Peters, see also Joachim Zeller, "' . . . Sein Wirken und der Gedenkstein sind umstritten.' Die Denkmäler für Carl Peters im Geschichtsunterricht," *Geschichte, Erziehung, Politik*, 6 (1997), p. 365f.
11. See the book by Heinrich Schnee, *Die koloniale Schuldlüge* (1924), 12th edn (Munich: Knorr & Hirth, 1940).
12. See Wieben, *Carl Peters*, pp. 83–90.
13. *NS-Reichsspiegel*, vol. 6, 1937. Quoted by Walter Frank, in Carl Peters, *Gesammelte Schriften*, vol. 1, p. 92.
14. On German colonial literature concerning Africa, see Joachim Warmbold, *"Ein Stückchen neudeutsche Erd . . ." Deutsche Kolonial-Literatur* (Frankfurt/M.: Haag & Herchen, 1982).
15. "Die Begründerin des deutschen Kolonialromans. Zum 75. Geburtstage von Frieda Freiin von Bülow," *Deutsche Kolonialzeitung*, 44 (1932), p. 272.
16. See "Wie schön war die Zeit. Kolonialschuldlüge und Kolonialnostalgie in der Weimarer Republik," in Martin Baer and Olaf Schröter, *Eine Kopfjagd. Deutsche in Ostafrika*, pp. 145–55.
17. Edith Salburg, *Carl Peters und sein Volk* (Weimar: Duncker, 1929).
18. Paul Baecker, "Carl Peters 1856–1918," in *Die großen Deutschen. Neue deutsche Biographie*, ed. by Willy Andreas, vol. 4 (Berlin: Propyläen, 1936), pp. 228–43.
19. Josef Viera, *Maria in Petersland. Roman* (Breslau: Bergstadt, 1937); Josef Buchhorn, *Weg in die Welt. Ein Schauspiel um den deutschen Mann Carl Peters* (Schöneberg: Schwabe, 1940).
20. *Carl Peters gewinnt Deutsch-Ostafrika*, ed. by Reichsjugendführung der NSDAP (Berlin, 1939).
21. See an image of the stamp in G.L. Steer, *Judgment on German Africa* (London: Hodder & Stoughton, 1939), title page.
22. There are more than 22 streets named after Carl Peters in Germany, according to Arne Perras, *Carl Peters and German Imperialism*, p. 253.
23. In 1939, a fleet tender of the *Kriegsmarine* was given the name "Carl Peters." See <http://www.german-navy.de/kriegsmarine/ships/fleettender/carlpeters/history.html> [accessed 1 September 2008].
24. Mentioned by Klaus Hildebrand, *Vom Reich zum Weltreich. Hitler, NSDAP und koloniale Fragen 1919–1945* (Munich: Fink, 1969), p. 435.
25. See Dorothea Hollstein, *Antisemitische Filmpropaganda* (Berlin: Verlag Dokumentation, 1971), p. 334.
26. Kay Dohnke, "Völkische Literatur und Heimatliteratur 1870–1918," in *Handbuch zur "Völkischen Bewegung" 1871–1918*, ed. by Uwe Puschner (Munich: Saur, 1999), p. 668.
27. Hannah Arendt, *The Origins of Totalitarianism* (New York: Harcourt, Brace, 1951).
28. Ibid., p. 206.
29. For an overview, see Jürgen Zimmerer, *Von Windhuk nach Auschwitz? Studien zum Verhältnis von Kolonialismus und Nationalsozialismus* (Münster: Lit, 2008).
30. Admiral z. D. Breusing, "Im übrigen meine ich, dass Englands Weltherrschaft zu zerstören sei!" in *Alldeutsche Blätter*, 24 (1914), p. 333f.
31. Carl Peters, "England, unser eigentlichster Feind" (1918), in *Gesammelte Schriften*, vol. 3, p. 506.

32. Frieda von Bülow, *Im Lande der Verheißung. Ein deutscher Kolonial-Roman* (1899) (Dresden: Reißner, 1914), p. 306.

33. Edith Salburg, *Carl Peters und sein Volk* (Carl Peters and his People), pp. 3–7.

34. Klaus Hildebrand, *Vom Reich zum Weltreich*, p. 421.

35. Otto Küster, in *Völkischer Beobachter*, 23 March 1941, p. 6.

36. See Arne Perras, *Carl Peters*, p. 183.

37. Phrase cited from Max Robert Gerstenhauer, *Der völkische Gedanke in Vergangenheit und Zukunft* (Leipzig: Armanen, 1933), p. 25.

38. In the discussion of the Kilimanjaro killings, Kayser in fact tried his best to protect Peters. See Martin Reuss, "The Disgrace and Fall of Carl Peters," p. 128f.

39. Erich zu Klampen, *Carl Peters. Ein deutsches Schicksal im Kampf um Ostafrika* (A German Fate in the Struggle for East Africa) (Berlin: Siep, 1938), p. 193f.

40. See Alfred Rosenberg, *Der Mythus des 20. Jahrhunderts*, 9th edn (Munich: Hoheneichen, 1937), pp. 304–6.

41. Edith Salburg, *Carl Peters und sein Volk*, p. 170.

42. Alfred Funke, *Carl Peters. Der Mann, der Deutschland ein Imperium schaffen wollte* (Berlin: Metten, 1937), p. 46–8.

43. Ibid., p. 48.

44. Houston Stewart Chamberlain (1855–1927) was one of the initiators of the concept of Aryanism. See, for instance, Chamberlain, *Arische Weltanschauung*, 7th edn (Munich: Bruckmann, 1934).

45. Frieda von Bülow, *Tropenkoller. Episode aus dem deutschen Kolonialleben* (Berlin: Fontane, 1905), p. 11f.

46. Josef Viera, *Maria in Petersland*, p. 331f.

47. Frieda von Bülow, *Der Konsul. Vaterländischer Roman aus unseren Tagen* (Berlin: Fontane, 1891), p. 61.

48. Ibid., p. 64.

49. Walter Frank, "Einleitung: Carl Peters," in Peters, *Gesammelte Schriften*, vol. 1, p. vi.

# 13 "Loyal Askari" and "Black Rapist"

## Two Images in the German Discourse on National Identity and Their Impact on the Lives of Black People in Germany, 1918–45[1]

*Susann Lewerenz*

In December 1933, the *Deutsche Kolonialzeitung* published an article under the title "Rassenreinheit oder Rassenmischung? Frankreichs Kolonialarmee und unsere Schutztruppe."[2] This contrasted French and German colonial policies by comparing two discursive figures of colonial soldiers: the German *Schutztruppen-Askari* and the French *Tirailleurs Sénégalais*. The essay's author, Erich Duems, began by referring to two articles in French colonial magazines. According to Duems, a piece in *L'Afrique Française* from October 1933 had pointed out that images of French and German colonial soldiers in German public discourse were contradictory. It argued that a newspaper article in the *Hamburger Fremdenblatt* had appealed to the German population to treat African migrants from the former colonies with respect because they had fought for the Germans in the colonies in the Great War. Referring to this, the article in *L'Afrique Français* concluded that, in German public discourse, German colonial soldiers were presented as comrades in arms, whereas French colonial soldiers were depicted as wild beasts. The other article, published in *Quinzaine Coloniale*, reported on violence against Africans from the former German colonies in Germany, and made reference to an announcement by the Police President of Hamburg, telling the population to treat migrants from the former colonies with respect. It claimed that, through this racist violence, the Germans had proved themselves unfit as colonizers, and should thus not regain their former colonies.

After paraphrasing the two French articles, Duems struck back. According to him, it was not the German attitude toward French and German colonial soldiers that was contradictory, but rather the arguments in the French press. How could one article state that the Germans turned former Askari soldiers into heroes, while the other claimed that they brutally attacked them? After all, Duems summarized, the announcement of the Police President of Hamburg proved that Germany did care for its former colonial subjects in the German Reich. Duems then argued that the Germans had no problems with French colonial soldiers as such, but with the French colonial policy they represented. Arming colonial subjects and letting them fight against whites on European soil was, according to Duems, an act of treason and a serious threat to the "white race," as was the French practice of racial mixing. In Germany, he argued, racial mixing was not accepted, and relationships between blacks and whites would of course be punished.

In contrast to the French colonial army, Duems continued, the German *Schutztruppe* had been established merely to protect the German colonies, and was never intended for use in Europe to fight against whites. According to Duems, it was especially this regard for racial order that proved the superiority of German colonialism over French colonial rule. Following the principle of racial segregation, he claimed, not only guaranteed the safety of the "white race," but was also appreciated by the colonized. This, Duems concluded, was demonstrated by the continued loyalty of former colonized subjects to their former German rulers:

> It is thus not disdain for alien races, but on the contrary our high esteem for the principle of racial purity, that prompts us to ensure that the naturally given borders between the races are not blurred; especially the native from the African colonies understands this, because he *despises* those whites who deny the prerogative of their blood and color. The high *esteem* that the Germans have among the natives of our colonies and their inextinguishable *loyalty* to us is based not least on this racial consciousness, which preserves the distinctive ethnic character [*völkische Eigenart*] of both the colonizing nation *and* the natives.[3]

This article from the *Deutsche Kolonialzeitung* exemplifies the way in which two complementary images of black soldiers circulated in the German colonial discourse of the 1930s: that of the "loyal Askari," that is, an African soldier who had loyally fought for the Germans in Africa in World War One, and that of the French colonial soldier as "wild beast"—as a threat to the "white race." As I show in the following pages, these two images not only played a part in the construction of German national identity after 1918, but also affected black people's lives in Germany. They were personifications of two poles of a frame of reference through which the authorities and the white German majority perceived and dealt with black people. These two poles, embodied by the "loyal Askari" and the "black rapist," were, to refer to the title of Duems's article, racial purity versus miscegenation, or in other words, racial order versus racial chaos. In this chapter, I trace where these two images originated, discuss what they tell us about German national identity between 1918 and 1945, and examine how they shaped circumstances of life, working conditions, and interaction with the authorities, for black people in Germany.

The image of the loyal Askari became most popular when Germany was forced to relinquish its colonies after its defeat in World War One. At the end of the war, colonial revisionists in Germany labeled the Allied claim that the Germans had demonstrated their inability to colonize by the mistreatment of their colonized subjects the *koloniale Schuldlüge* (colonial guilt lie).[4] As a reaction to the Allied accusations, colonial revisionist propaganda spread stories about the alleged devotion of the formerly colonized subjects of Germany: these were supposed to demonstrate the "accomplishments" of German colonialism and thus disprove Allied arguments against German colonial rule. The myth of the loyal Askari soldier, which referred to the campaign of the East African *Schutztruppe* under Paul von Lettow-Vorbeck[5] in World War One, was one of the most popular of these revisionist narratives. It was structured around two mutually dependent male characters: the loyal black soldier was the result and living proof of the achievements of the German male colonizer. Without the heroic character, the military abilities, and the disciplinary power of the latter, there would be no devoted colonial male subject.

The counterpart or antithesis of the loyal Askari was the French colonial soldier, depicted as a wild beast or, more specifically, as a rapist of white women. The former version of this stereotype had already been mobilized in the course of World War One, but it became most prominent in its latter version during the so-called *Kampagne gegen die Schwarze Schmach* (campaign against the black disgrace) in the early post-war years. When colonial troops of the *Entente* occupied parts of western Germany, the campaigners claimed that French colonial soldiers raped German women and children in the most brutal manner, thereby spreading venereal disease and leaving behind half-caste children. According to the campaign, this would not merely weaken the health of the German people. The campaigners argued that it also meant a direct threat to the German people as well as to the "white race" as a whole, because "white blood" would be "polluted" by "black blood."[6] While the protesters primarily appealed to the Western world with these accusations in order to force France to withdraw its colonial troops, the gendered tale spread in this campaign was also one about national morale. In the narrative of the *Schwarze Schmach*, the colonial order of the pre-war period was turned upside down. Not only had the Germans been forced to give up their colonies, but they were additionally humiliated by the fact that blacks now ruled over whites on German soil. The German nation—and especially German men as protectors of German women—had become powerless in the face of a crime against the "white race," symbolized by the rape of a white woman by a black man.[7] It can thus be claimed that the campaign against the *Schwarze Schmach* spread a narrative of white male powerlessness in the present, whereas the myth of the "loyal Askari" re-affirmed white male power in the past.

The effect of these complementary myths reached well beyond an appeal to the international public or a contribution to German discourses on national identity. Both of these discursive figures also had an impact on the lives of black people within Germany. On the one hand, the white German population as well as the authorities often expected black men living in Germany to be loyal former colonial subjects. In 1919, for example, the German Colonial Office tried to convince migrants from the former colonies to support its colonial revisionist aims by publicly demanding that the Germans should return to their native countries as colonial rulers. It should be added, though, that the authorities did not necessarily receive the answer they hoped for. For example, a group of migrants from Cameroon, led by Martin Dibobe, used the opportunity to speak out in public to demand equal rights instead.[8]

After 1918, African migrants from the former colonies were also often supplied with identity cards that labeled them as *former* subjects of the German colonies (*ehemalige deutsche Schutzgebietsangehörige* or *Schutzbefohlene*).[9] This indicates that they occupied an exceptional position in post-war German society. With these identity cards, they were formally caught in a now imaginary colonial power relation. The intentionally unclear legal status of colonial migrants reflected the unacceptability of the *status quo* in the eyes of the colonial revisionist officials of the Foreign Ministry and their aim of re-establishing the *status quo ante*. The latter not only included the retrieval of the colonies, but also the return of the African migrants to their native countries. For the—predominantly male—migrants, this meant a precarious dependence on the benevolence of the German authorities without a proper legal basis to which they could refer. They were not accepted as German citizens, but in many cases were also unable to return to their home countries, especially if they were married to white women and had children with them.[10]

In the course of the 1920s, the state's attitude toward this small minority was ambivalent. On the one hand, the authorities aimed at deporting colonial migrants from Germany, especially those who were known to be communist activists or were considered unruly—for example, because they demanded equal rights. On the other hand, the Colonial Department of the Foreign Ministry supported former colonial subjects in cases of economic hardship because it regarded them as potentially useful for its colonial revisionist plans.[11] The authorities' focus in this was on black men, not only because most of the migrants were male, but also because men were ascribed the position of political agents. However, in some cases the authorities also supported the children of colonial migrants.[12]

Especially in the course of the campaign against the *Schwarze Schmach*, there was an increase in racist violence against black people in Germany. This violence was mainly directed at men and children. While attackers often assumed that the black men they assaulted were French soldiers, they tended to regard black children as so-called Rhineland bastards (*Rheinlandbastarde*)—a derogatory term for children of white German women and French colonial soldiers born in the occupied territories of western Germany.[13] Against the backdrop of this increase in racist attacks in Germany, black people increasingly drew on colonial revisionist tropes to protect themselves and their families. For example, when, in 1921, a black man was beaten up on the streets because he had been mistaken for a French colonial soldier, the *Afrikanischer Hilfsverein*, an association of black people in Germany, published an open letter in a newspaper.[14] This letter pointed out that African migrants from the former colonies had the same political status as Germans—referring to the authorities' colonial revisionist instrumentalization of migrants from the former colonies mentioned above. The letter also appealed to the German public to remember that the migrants had risked their lives for Germany when they had fought under Lettow-Vorbeck in the past World War. The German population ought thus to differentiate between them and the Allied colonial soldiers in the Rhineland. This argument is interesting insofar as the *Hilfsverein* in fact explicitly accepted any black person as a member, not just people from the former German colonies or former Askari soldiers, as the letter suggests. Evoking the situation of the former—and still loyal—colonial subject was apparently regarded as the most effective strategy in the fight against racist violence in post–World War One Germany.[15]

In 1934, one year after the establishment of the National Socialist regime, the Afro-German Kwassi Bruce from Togo sent a letter to the Nazi government. In this letter, he asked for justice for the African migrants from the former colonies, most of whom had lost their jobs, due to racist discrimination. Bruce pointed out that he had volunteered for the *Schutztruppe* in the past war and had fought as bravely as the German soldiers on the European battlefields. In addition, he demanded that the Germans should differentiate between African migrants from the former German colonies and the Allied colonial soldiers in the Rhineland. He also remarked that speakers at colonial gatherings in Germany frequently emphasized how loyal the colonial subjects had been in the war, whereas, in everyday life, the Germans showed no respect for the African migrants.[16]

Bruce's appeal did not go unheard. Officials in the Colonial Department of the Foreign Ministry were open to such arguments, because they still aimed to recover the former German colonies. In their opinion, discriminating against migrants from these parts of Africa could have negative side effects on their project. They argued that this might lead to an anti-German stance in the mandated territories. Besides, the Germans would receive a bad press from the mandatory powers, Britain and France, which might reduce their chances of retrieving the former overseas territories from them.[17] Apart from this pragmatic reasoning, the myth of the loyal Askari also turned out to be quite powerful on a more symbolic level. In the second half of the 1930s, its popularity rose again[18] because, as a narrative of military as well as of white masculine power, it was well suited to a time of factual as well as "moral" rearmament and of claims of white German supremacy.[19]

Against this background, Nazi policies on African migrants and their families in the course of the 1930s oscillated between racist discrimination and colonial political instrumentalizing. On the one hand, black people were affected by racist laws as well as by everyday racism on the streets. Some—especially left-wing activists—were deported or even murdered.[20]

In 1934, on the other hand, the Colonial Department reached a compromise with the Ministry of the Interior. This implied that individuals could be exempted from racist legislation if foreign or colonial political advantage outweighed racial political disadvantage.[21] No such exceptions seem to have been made with regard to the Nuremberg Laws of 1935. However, the Colonial Department of the Foreign Ministry nevertheless tried to find employment for people from the former colonies, wrote letters of support to employers or landlords and helped individuals financially during the second half of the 1930s.[22]

At the end of 1935, the Colonial Office decided to support a privately run fun-fair show that employed black people. This show later became known as the *Deutsche Afrika-Schau*.[23] The authorities considered their support to be a means of achieving a compromise between the needs of racial and colonial politics. Black people who were deemed to be worthy of support for colonial-political reasons could be separated from the white majority and put under the racial control of the state. At the same time, they would be able to support their families. Besides this, the authorities apparently thought that a show which resembled a *Völkerschau* (ethnographic exhibition) was a suitable place for black people, because it promised to establish a clear racial difference and hierarchy between the people on display and the audience, thereby positioning the black employees outside the German *Volksgemeinschaft* and inside a "provisional Africa."[24]

However, the *Deutsche Afrika-Schau* turned out to be more difficult to handle than at first expected. One of the weaknesses of the show leads back to the Askari myth. The main argument the authorities used to legitimate the existence of the enterprise was to claim that it employed former Askari soldiers who were unable to return to their native countries because they had fought on the German side in World War One and were still loyal to the Germans. The authorities' eagerness to spread this myth stands in curious contrast to the actual line-up of the ensemble. Many of the show members did not come from the former German colonies at all, and certainly were not former Askari.

In the late 1930s, a number of white Germans wrote protest letters to the authorities. They complained that male members of the ensemble had presented themselves on stage as former soldiers who had been decorated for their service in the past war. They also pointed out that show members had worn swastika badges of the *Deutsche Arbeitsfront* and had addressed the audience as *Volksgenossen*.[25] In other words, male members of the show appropriated and transformed certain elements of the colonial revisionist imagination that had been ascribed to them. They did not perform as the submissive Askari soldiers the authorities expected them to be—as the embodiment of the "accomplishments" of the German male colonizer. Instead, they presented themselves as World War One veterans. In doing so, they suggested a relationship not of hierarchy, but of equality between themselves and white German veterans.[26]

With the beginning of the German military campaign in the west in the spring of 1940, this already controversial figure of the "loyal Askari" further collided with that of the French *tirailleur* as "black beast." In connection with the offensive in the west, the National Socialists started a major propaganda campaign against the deployment of colonial soldiers in the French army. This took up images from the so-called campaign against the *Schwarze Schmach*. French colonial soldiers were once again depicted as brutal rapists and bestial murderers. In the National Socialist version, however, it was the Jews rather than the French who were made responsible.[27]

The negative images of black soldiers spread by Nazi war propaganda clashed with the "positive" image of the Askari soldier as it was supposed to be presented in the *Afrika-Schau*—and even more with that of the worthy veteran staged by some of the male show members. The authorities, especially the Propaganda Ministry, feared that the population would become confused or even refuse to believe in the Nazi war propaganda directed against French colonial soldiers. In addition, the protests against the show became increasingly strong from 1939 onward. The reason for this may lie partly in the escalating racism of war-time, but also has to do with the fact that the show toured in the *Ostmark* from October 1939. Apparently, the "positive" colonial revisionist figure of the loyal Askari was not as familiar in Austria as it was in the "old part" of the *Reich*. In contrast to this, the Austrians proved receptive to the propaganda against French colonial soldiers.[28] Thus, in the *Ostmark*, the conflict between the image of loyal Askari and black rapist became even more severe.[29] Accordingly, the *Reichspropagandaleitung* closed the show in June 1940,

> because of the fact that negros perform here, some of them wearing the Iron Cross, Second Class, and present themselves as members of the folk [*Volksgenossen*]. At a time in which we are pointing out to the German people how reprehensible the French enlistment of negros is, we cannot simultaneously allow negros to appear in Germany as former allies or even "members of the folk".[30]

Over the course of the war, the myth of the loyal Askari increasingly lost its significance. One important development was the attack on the Soviet Union and the focusing of Nazi colonial plans on Eastern Europe rather than on Africa; another was the defeat of the German army at Stalingrad. In conjunction with these events, the situation of black people in Germany deteriorated radically. A growing number of sons and daughters of Africans from the former German colonies were sterilized by force; and some black people had to work as forced laborers, while others were incarcerated in concentration camps. Former Askari soldiers were now ruthlessly punished, if they had—or were believed to have had—sexual relationships with white women.[31]

One of the members of the *Deutsche Afrika-Schau* who became a victim of Nazi racial policy was Bajume Mohammed Hussein,[32] the son of an East

African Askari soldier who had himself been a child soldier in World War One. He had come to Germany in the Weimar Republic to claim his and his father's outstanding pay. By the middle of the 1930s, he had applied twice—unsuccessfully—for an Iron Cross, Second Class, probably not least because he wished to protect himself from escalating racist discrimination.[33] In 1941, Bajume Mohammed Hussein was incarcerated in the concentration camp at Sachsenhausen on account of an extra-marital relationship with a white woman. He died in Sachsenhausen in 1944. As Marianne Bechhaus-Gerst has argued, Bajume Mohammed Hussein had always insisted on his rights and fought against discrimination and injustice. In this connection, he had consistently referred to his status as former Askari.[34] However, under the rapidly changing conditions of the early 1940s, the frame of reference within which Nazi policies on African migrants in Germany had developed shifted from colonial revisionist instrumentalization to racist persecution. In other words, the discursive figure of the loyal Askari retreated, while that of the black beast moved to the forefront.

## NOTES

1. I should like to thank Michelle Moyd for her helpful comments and suggestions.
2. Erich Duems, "Rassenreinheit oder Rassenmischung? Frankreichs Kolonialarmee und unsere Schutztruppe," *DKZ*, 12.45 (1933), 242, 244. See also Susann Lewerenz, *Die "Deutsche Afrika-Schau": Rassismus, Kolonialrevisionismus und postkoloniale Auseinandersetzungen im nationalsozialistischen Deutschland* (Frankfurt/M.: Lang, 2006), p. 58f.
3. Duems, "Rassenreinheit," p. 244. This and subsequent translated passages are my own.
4. Heinrich Schnee, *Die koloniale Schuldlüge* (Munich: Süddeutsche Monatshefte, 1924). On colonial revisionism, see, for example, Wolfe W. Schmokel, *Dream of Empire: German Colonialism, 1919–1945* (New Haven, CT: Yale University Press, 1964); Hartmut Pogge von Strandmann, "Imperialism and Revisionism in Interwar Germany," in *Imperialism and After: Continuities and Discontinuities*, ed. by Wolfgang Mommsen and Jürgen Osterhammel (London: Allen & Unwin, 1986), pp. 90–119; Jan Esche, *Koloniales Anpruchsdenken in Deutschland im Ersten Weltkrieg, während der Versailler Friedensverhandlungen und in der Weimarer Republik (1914 bis 1933)* (PhD diss., University of Hamburg, 1989); Michael Schubert, *Der schwarze Fremde: Das Bild des Schwarzafrikaners in der parlamentarischen und publizistischen Kolonialdiskussion in Deutschland von den 1870er bis in die 1930er Jahre* (Stuttgart: Steiner, 2003), pp. 309f. On Nazi colonial plans, see, for example, Klaus Hildebrand, *Vom Reich zum Weltreich: Hitler, NSDAP und koloniale Frage 1919–1945* (Munich: Fink, 1969); Karsten Linne, *"Weiße Arbeitsführer" im "Kolonialen Ergänzungsraum": Afrika als Ziel sozial- und wirtschaftspolitischer Planungen in der NS-Zeit* (Münster: Monsenstein & Vannerdat, 2002).
5. On Lettow-Vorbeck, see Uwe Schulte-Varendorff, *Kolonialheld für Kaiser und Führer: General Lettow-Vorbeck—Mythos und Wirklichkeit* (Berlin: Links, 2006).

6. Christian Koller, *"Von Wilden aller Rassen niedergemetzelt":* Die Diskussion um die Verwendung von Kolonialtruppen in Europa zwischen Rassismus, Militär- und Kolonialpolitik (1914–1930) (Stuttgart: Steiner, 2001). See also Gisela Lebzelter, "Die 'schwarze Schmach,'" *Geschichte und Gesellschaft,* 11 (1985), 37–58; Sally Marks, "Black Watch on the Rhine: A Study in Propaganda, Prejudice and Prurience," *European Studies Review,* 13 (1983), 297–334; Peter Martin, "Die Kampagne gegen die 'Schwarze Schmach' als Ausdruck konservativer Visionen vom Untergang des Abendlandes," in *Fremde Erfahrungen: Asiaten und Afrikaner in Deutschland, Österreich und in der Schweiz bis 1945,* ed. by Gerhard Höpp (Berlin: Das Arabische Buch, 1996), pp. 211–24; Keith S. Nelson, "Black Horror on the Rhine: Race as a Factor in Post-World War I Diplomacy," *Journal of Modern History,* 42 (1970), 606–27. See also Iris Wigger's recent book, *Die "Schwarze Schmach am Rhein:" Rassistische Diskriminierung zwischen Geschlecht, Klasse, Nation und Rasse* (Münster: Westfälisches Dampfboot, 2006).

7. See Tina Campt, Pascal Grosse and Yara-Colette Lemke-Muniz de Faria, "Blacks, Germans and the Politics of Colonial Imagination, 1920–1960," in *The Imperialist Imagination: German Colonialism and its Legacy,* ed. by Sara Friedrichsmeyer, Sara Lennox and Susanne Zantop (Ann Arbor: University of Michigan Press, 1998), pp. 205–29 (p. 207).

8. Adolf Rüger, "Imperialismus, Sozialreformismus und antikoloniale demokratische Alternative: Zielvorstellungen von Afrikanern in Deutschland im Jahre 1919," *Zeitschrift für Geschichtswissenschaft,* 23 (1975), 1293–1308 (p. 1294f.). On Dibobe, see Peter Martin, "Anfänge politischer Selbstorganisation der deutschen Schwarzen bis 1933," in *Die (koloniale) Begegnung: AfrikanerInnen in Deutschland 1880–1945: Deutsche in Afrika 1880–1918,* ed. by Marianne Bechhaus-Gerst and Reinhard Klein-Arendt (Frankfurt/M.: Lang, 2003), pp. 193–206 (pp. 195–8).

9. Katharina Oguntoye, *Eine afro-deutsche Geschichte: Zur Lebenssituation von Afrikanern und Afro-Deutschen in Deutschland von 1884 bis 1950* (Berlin: Hoffmann, 1997), p. 23.

10. Oguntoye, *Eine afro-deutsche Geschichte,* p. 47f.

11. See, for example, Heiko Möhle, "Betreuung, Erfassung, Kontrolle: Afrikaner aus den deutschen Kolonien und die 'Deutsche Gesellschaft für Eingeborenenkunde'," in *Die (koloniale) Begegnung,* ed. by Bechhaus-Gerst and Klein-Ardent, pp. 225–36.

12. For more details, see Lewerenz, *"Deutsche Afrika-Schau,"* p. 55f.

13. On attacks on black children, see Fatima El-Tayeb, *Schwarze Deutsche: der Diskurs um "Rasse" und nationale Identität 1890–1933* (Frankfurt/M.: Campus, 2001), p. 162; see also Bundesarchiv (BArch) Berlin, R 1001/7562, pp. 91–100 (p. 97). Letter from Kwassi Bruce to the National Socialist Government (n.d.); printed in *Zwischen Charleston und Stechschritt. Schwarze im Nationalsozialismus,* ed. by Peter Martin and Christine Alonzo (Munich: Dölling & Galitz, 2004), pp. 411–16. On the "Rhineland bastards," see Reiner Pommerin, *Sterilisierung der Rheinlandbastarde: Das Schicksal einer farbigen deutschen Minderheit 1918–1937* (Düsseldorf: Droste, 1979).

14. Printed in Tobias Nagl, "Kolonien des Blicks: Louis Brody und die schwarze Präsenz im deutschsprachigen Kino vor 1945," *jungle world,* 20 (2002), <http://www.nadir.org/nadir/periodika/jungle_world/_2002/20/15a.htm> [accessed 18 August 2007], para. 21 of 40.

15. Eve Rosenhaft, "Afrikaner und 'Afrikaner' im Deutschland der Weimarer Republik. Antikolonialismus und Antirassismus zwischen Doppelbewusstsein und Selbsterfindung," in *Phantasiereiche: Zur Kulturgeschichte des*

*deutschen Kolonialismus*, ed. by Birthe Kundrus (Frankfurt/M: Campus, 2003), pp. 282–301 (p. 286f.).

16. BArch Berlin, R 1001/7562, pp. 91–100. See also, on this letter, Elisa von Joeden-Forgey, *Nobody's People: Colonial Subjects, Race Power, and the German State, 1884–1945* (PhD diss., University of Pennsylvania, 2004), p. 513f.; and Lewerenz, *"Deutsche Afrika-Schau,"* pp. 23 and 50f.

17. For more details, see, for example, Lewerenz, *"Deutsche Afrika-Schau,"* p. 50f.

18. See, for example, Schmokel, *Dream of Empire*, p. 42.

19. Stefanie Michels, "Deutsch-ostafrikanische Mythen: General Lettow-Vorbeck und die 'treuen Askari'" (paper presented at the Neue Gesellschaft, Hamburg, 6 December 2005).

20. *Farbe bekennen: Afro-deutsche Frauen auf den Spuren ihrer Geschichte*, ed. by Katharina Oguntoye, May Opitz and Dagmar Schultz (Berlin: Orlanda, 1986), p. 69f.; Oguntoye, *Eine afro-deutsche Geschichte*, p. 134f. See also Paulette Reed-Anderson, *Rewriting the Footnotes: Berlin und die afrikanische Diaspora—Berlin and the African Diaspora* (Berlin: Ausländerbeauftragte des Berliner Senats, 2000), p. 55f.; Clarence Lusane, *Hitler's Black Victims: The Historical Experiences of Afro-Germans, European Blacks, Africans, and African Americans in the Nazi Era* (New York: Routledge, 2002); *Zwischen Charleston und Stechschritt: Schwarze im Nationalsozialismus*, ed. by Peter Martin and Christine Alonzo (Munich: Dölling & Galitz, 2004).

21. Pommerin, *Sterilisierung der Rheinlandbastarde*, p. 67f.

22. Oguntoye, *Eine afro-deutsche Geschichte*, pp. 113–26.

23. On the *Deutsche Afrika-Schau*, see Elisa Forgey, "'Die große Negertrommel der kolonialen Werbung:' Die Deutsche Afrika-Schau 1935–1943," *WerkstattGeschichte*, 3.9 (1994), 25–33; Elisa von Joeden-Forgey, "Race Power in Postcolonial Germany: The German Africa Show and the National Socialist State, 1935–1940," in *Germany's Colonial Pasts*, ed. by Eric Ames, Marcia Klotz and Lora Wildenthal (Lincoln: University Nebraska Press, 2005), pp. 167–88; Campt and others, "Blacks, Germans and the Politics of Colonial Imagination," pp. 218–22; Lewerenz, *"Deutsche Afrika-Schau."*

24. Forgey, "'Die große Negertrommel'," p. 30f.

25. For examples, see BArch Berlin, R 1001/6383, p. 338f.: Auswärtiges Amt, note on meeting of 3 August 1939; BArch Berlin, R 1001/6383, p. 374: note by Auswärtiges Amt, Pol X, Költzsch, 11 June 1940; BArch Berlin, NS 18/519, p. 42: cover letter to statement by KdF-Dienststelle Tulln to Gauleitung Niederdonau, 29 July 1940; BArch Berlin, NS 18/519, p. 5f.: letter from Rassenpolitisches Amt, Gauleitung Niederdonau, to Gauleiter of Niederdonau, 13 May 1940.

26. Lewerenz, *"Deutsche Afrika-Schau,"* p. 118f.

27. Koller, *"Von Wilden,"* p. 352f.

28. According to secret evaluations by the Nazis, printed in *Meldungen aus dem Reich: Auswahl aus den geheimen Lageberichten des Sicherheitsdienstes der SS 1938–1944*, vol. 4: *Meldungen aus dem Reich, Nr. 66 vom 15. März 1940–Nr. 101 vom 1. Juli 1940*, ed. by Heinz Boberach (Herrsching: Pawlak, 1984), p. 1238.

29. Lewerenz, *"Deutsche Afrika-Schau,"* p. 36f.

30. BArch Berlin, NS 18/519, p. 7: presentation by Tießler, 24 June 1940.

31. *Farbe bekennen*, pp. 75ff.; Bechhaus-Gerst, "Afrikaner in Deutschland," pp. 26 and 30; Oguntoye, *Eine afro-deutsche Geschichte*, p. 134f.; Marianne Bechhaus-Gerst, "'Hinrichtung 6.18 Uhr durch das Fallbeilgerät'—ein

Askari vor dem Sondergericht Hamburg," in *Die (koloniale) Begegnung*, ed. by Bechhaus-Gerst and Klein-Arendt, pp. 41–9.

32. On Bayume Mohammed Hussein, see Bechhaus-Gerst, "Afrikaner in Deutschland," p. 22f.; Bastian Breiter, "Der Weg des 'treuen Askari' ins Konzentrationslager—Die Lebensgeschichte des Mohamed Husen," in *Kolonialmetropole Berlin: eine Spurensuche*, ed. by Ulrich van der Heyden and Joachim Zeller (Berlin: Berlin Edition, 2002), pp. 215–20. A new publication on Hussein by Marianne Bechhaus-Gerst is *Treu bis in den Tod: Von Deutsch-Ostafrika nach Sachsenhausen—Eine Lebensgeschichte* (Berlin: Links, 2007).

33. Bechhaus-Gerst, "Afrikaner in Deutschland," p. 24.

34. Ibid., p. 25.

## Part IV

# German Colonialism in the Era of Decolonization

# 14 (Post-) Colonial Amnesia?

## German Debates on Colonialism and Decolonization in the Post-War Era[1]

*Monika Albrecht*

In an article entitled "Race, Gender, and Postcolonial Amnesia," Susanne Zantop made a passing remark about "the processes of forgetting that affected the cultural memory of the second post-colonial phase, which began after World War Two and lasted well into the 1960s."[2] The article itself dealt with a film from the Nazi era, and it is unknown how Zantop would have further developed this idea in her planned study *Postcolonial Amnesia*. My suggestion is that, by looking more closely at this period of time and by studying items such as journals and magazines, she would have discovered that in the two decades after the end of World War Two there was, in fact, no "post-colonial amnesia" in Germany.[3]

For most of this period, a large part of the surface of the globe still consisted of colonies. In the early 1950s, the weekly news magazine *Der Spiegel* reported that, of the then "162 million people of Africa, 52 million [lived] under the British Union Jack and 43 under the French Tricolor."[4] Other parts of the globe were ruled by the colonial powers of Holland, Belgium, Portugal and Spain, and were on the brink of independence. Consequently, much German media coverage, concerning both Germany's European neighbors and their colonies or former colonies, dealt with the colonial and post-colonial situation. In the post-war years, *Der Spiegel*, for instance, contained special sections entitled "Colonies" or "Colonial Politics," which appeared almost every other week, and in times of the many colonial crises even on a weekly basis. In this context, journalists dealing with countries like Togo, Cameroon, South-West and South-East Africa, or Samoa and the Caroline Islands, seldom failed to mention the former German "owners" of these colonies, often reminding their readers in great detail about the territories' German colonial history. Leading German opinion-formers in the post-1945 era were therefore very well aware of the history of colonialism and its legacies, and these subjects were discussed in high-circulation news magazines and intellectual journals.[5]

A cover story in the news magazine *Der Spiegel* from March 1960, for instance, deals with the president of the then newly founded Republic of Guinea, Sekou Touré, and quotes the German president of the time, Heinrich Lübke, who claimed that "for us, for the Germans, the relationship

to the African continent has never been merely a matter of calculation."
Rather, Lübke adds, this issue was "also to be solved as a matter of the
heart."[6] Decades after its official end, therefore, politicians still strove to
sell German colonialism as a philanthropic enterprise and an alleged economic loss. Lübke's statement reveals how, even at the beginning of the
1960s, politicians could count on the Germans' understanding of such
vague allusions to German colonial history.

In the magazines I have examined, however, these former German colonies were not the prime focus of the colonial coverage. In the case of *Der
Spiegel*, at least, the reasons for this are fairly obvious. First and foremost,
such magazines tend to prioritize contemporary events over the issue of
coming to terms with the past. For example, coverage of the former German colonies in Africa was primarily focused on British, French, or South
African colonies or mandates, and although the fact that these territories
had once belonged to the German empire was certainly of interest, it was
naturally of secondary importance to a news magazine. In the post-war
era, moreover, there was simply more to report about the older British and
French colonies than about the younger ones, that is, the former colonies
of Germany. In the early post-war years, for instance, the main colonial
issues were the French war in Vietnam and the struggles for independence
in Kenya, and in the later 1950s the focus was on the war in Algeria.[7]

In the case of the magazines *Frankfurter Hefte* and *Merkur*, the situation
is somewhat different. As journals "of culture and politics" and "of European thought," respectively, their main focus was likewise not historical,
but their remits certainly allowed them to deal with themes like German
colonialism. However, while both these magazines often deal with colonialism in general terms, they very rarely mention German colonialism specifically. Given the fact that, in the 1950s, German colonialism was definitely
a topic covered by major journals like *Der Spiegel*, *Stern*, and so on, it is
hard to explain why this should be so. It is of interest, however, that articles
in the *Frankfurter Hefte* usually talk about a European colonialism—a
generalized view which includes all of Europe. In an article from August
1950, for instance, one of the editors of the journal, Eugen Kogon, speaks
of the "current aftermath of the colonial sins of *our* capitalist-imperialist
past,"[8] while an article from December 1952 on India explicitly refers to a
collective European responsibility: "It is not important whether England or
another nation [committed the] crimes of colonialism: it was a European
crime, a European abuse, and it was our common injustice which gave us
the idea."[9] It would thus seem that, even in the early 1950s, the prevailing
view of the importance of the colonies for Europe in the *Frankfurter Hefte*
very much resembled today's critical perspectives. Most contributors were
very well aware that the colonial territories were first and foremost places
of exploitation, from which, according to an article from December 1952,
most of "our material wealth of the last two centuries was drawn, even
if we did not directly take part in colonialism"; rather, we participated

indirectly—in the case of India, for instance, through economic relations with England.[10] An article from May 1952 on North Africa also maintained: "We all know that Europe's prosperity depends on this African expansion."[11]

Events in the German colonies were covered by *Der Spiegel* throughout the post-war era in diverse ways—from brief references to in-depth descriptions. The latter usually included detailed discussion of the historical context of German colonialism. In almost every case, *Der Spiegel*'s coverage of the former German colonies stated—at least briefly—that the countries used to be part of the German empire. For instance, the reports talk of "the situation in Tanganyika (the former German East Africa)"[12] or, with the terms reversed, "the former German colony of East Africa, modern-day Tanganyika."[13] A footnote informs the reader that the "districts of Rwanda and Burundi," now under Belgian administrative authority, formerly belonged to German East Africa,[14] and that the "former German colony of Togo" is now considered an African trouble spot.[15] A map of the Dutch overseas territories explicitly marks the "former German colony of Kaiser-Wilhelm-Land,"[16] and an article about the unification of Tanganyika and Zanzibar into Tanzania in 1964 repeats the legend[17] that "in 1890 the German protectorate ceded [the island of Zanzibar] to England" in exchange for Heligoland.[18] In each case, reports on the current situation of former German colonies mention their affiliation with the German empire—so much so that, in one instance, *Der Spiegel* meticulously points out former borders, marking with dotted lines where in Eastern Nigeria the "border of the German colony of Cameroon [lay] until 1920."[19]

In a context where German colonialism was a given for the readers, articles frequently contained brief allusions to Germany's colonial past. An article from July 1953 on the Mau-Mau uprising, for instance, claimed that the "partisans" in Kenya "wear big hats with the brim turned up on one side like Lettow-Vorbeck's Askaris."[20] Although seriously lacking in historical accuracy, such an article simultaneously evokes two topoi from colonial discourse.[21] While in this case it is safe to assume that this allusion was written in a pro-colonial spirit, it is important to read articles from *Der Spiegel* from this time with care.[22] For instance, when a report on the loss and redistribution of the Italian colonies after World War Two mentions the "former Italian Askaris, wistfully remembering their terms of service in the Italian colonial army,"[23] it is hardly possible that readers in post-war Germany would miss the allusion to the allegedly "devoted Askaris" of former German East Africa. Yet in this case the author had no intention of idealizing the German colonial past—on the contrary, immediately after this allusion, he informs his readers that the black soldiers in Eritrea are still waiting for "their outstanding pay" and "hard-earned pensions."[24] Such factual references counteract the legend of the "devoted Askaris" and their supposed hope for the return of their colonial masters, and the article reminds the readers that, after the end of German colonialism, the Askaris in East Africa, too, had only practical rather than sentimental reasons for emphasizing their affiliation with the colonial army.

When considering the news magazine *Der Spiegel* in the post-war era, then, we must distinguish between different ways of dealing with German colonial history, from the critical to the affirmative. It is noticeable, however, that criticism of German colonialism is distinctly more lenient than that directed at other European colonizers. Altogether, we can observe a wide diversity of positions, from censorious allusions to the colonial past (as exemplified by the last example) to occasional cases in which genocide is denied—a point on which I expand in the last section of this chapter. Between these two positions, there is a broad center in which the details of German colonialism are discussed. Since articles usually confined themselves to reporting facts, their attitude toward German colonialism is mostly hard to judge—as the following example shows. A long article about World War One includes a map of "Germany's goals for the 1914–18 war" and shows both the already existing colonies on the African continent and a number of planned "annexations and acquisitions"[25]—that is, the huge area of "German Central Africa," from Guinea to Madagascar, which the German empire intended to "acquire" from the other colonial powers.[26] Although the writer's view of the question of colonialism in this and other articles does not become clear, it seems all in all that historical information in this as in other articles is derived from older stances which focus on the competition between the then great powers and on the conflicts among European states, neglecting the "other side" of the issue—namely, real life in the colonies.[27]

Aside from scattered allusions to German colonial history in *Der Spiegel*, there are also large numbers of articles which deal with the contemporary situation in the former German colonies. Former German South-West Africa was indirectly in the news via the South African Union, but Togo, Cameroon and the former German East Africa were also reported on quite frequently; and, in the very early post-war years, this was also the case for the former German colonial territories in the Pacific. The former German South-West Africa was then the fifth province of the South-African Union. After the reform of the Union's constitution in 1949,[28] *Der Spiegel* began to follow the further development of the area closely. Titles such as "Rotten Fruit in South Africa" or "Bullock-Cart Fascism" indicate the general tenor of such articles. *Der Spiegel*'s articles were highly critical of the racial policy of the apartheid state, especially the policy of the Germans in South-West Africa—a context in which they also usually addressed South Africa's collaboration with German fascism.[29] An article from February 1949 about Prime Minister Malan's "misguided racial policy," for example, stresses how "[i]ts kinship with other ideas of race dates back a long way. In the anti-British sector of the South-African Union, ideas of race 'made in Germany' found a fertile breeding ground."[30] Due to the elections of summer 1950, South-West Africa, which was formerly considered the "South-African Union's backyard," "hit the headlines of the world press overnight."[31] An article on these elections in *Der Spiegel* also refers to the German past when it reports, "From the beer halls and restaurants of Windhoek's Kaiserstraße you could hear 'Sieg Heil!' The Germans of South-West Africa drank to the health of Pretoria's Prime Minister Dr. Malan. They did what they could to help him win the elections of 30 August."[32] Although a scholarly analysis from the 1980s of other German magazines like *Quick, Bunte, Neue Revue,* and so on, came to the conclusion that articles on South Africa usually expressed a "feeling of solidarity with the white Africans,"[33] no such solidarity is to be found in *Der Spiegel.* On the contrary, the article just mentioned endorses the way the critical world press saw the situation and quotes, for example, the London *Daily Express,* which was concerned about the mixture of apartheid and fascism in South Africa. The *Daily Express,* said *Der Spiegel,* had reported that it was "only the Germans in 'the Emperor's former colony' to whom Dr. Malan owes his election victory. 'Some of them belong to the very SS sabotage troops which were brought secretly into the country in 1939 in order to build up a German naval base.'"[34] In the context of this coverage of former German South-West Africa, but also in other contexts, the Germans of the post-war era were repeatedly subjected to the admonishment of the international press—obligingly requoted by *Der Spiegel*—which saw connections between colonialism, fascism and racism.

While *Der Spiegel* usually deals very critically with the South African apartheid state, including its German inhabitants, other articles from the magazine deviate from this critical perspective. Two articles in particular repeat the idea of the *koloniale Schuldlüge* (denial of colonial guilt) in the post-war era. According to these articles, it is evident that the "moral reproach of colonial mismanagement and misguided politics towards the natives,"[35] which had justified the partitioning of the former German colonies among the allied powers at the Treaty of Versailles after World War One, has not been forgotten after World War Two. The two *Der Spiegel* articles also reveal the kind of coalition the idea of the *koloniale Schuldlüge* could generate at this time. The first article, on the "former West-African model colony of Togo,"[36] draws a series of rather arbitrary comparisons, in which an African country at that time divided into a British and a French mandate is seen from the perspective of the contemporary West German/ East German division. Neologisms such as "Togo's British-occupied Western Zone" (*Westzone*) and "French Eastern Zone" (*Ostzone*) were obviously intended to stimulate the ideal of and desire for German reunification, but also a desire for colonial revisionism. Against this backdrop, the *Der Spiegel* article quite openly rejects the very accusation "with which the peacemakers of Versailles propagandistically justified the expropriation of the German colonies"—that is, the claim "of German incompetence in colonial politics."[37]

The second *Der Spiegel* article comes even closer to a denial of colonial genocide, and appears additionally problematic in that it deals with South-West Africa—that is, with a part of the former German territories in Africa which was particularly affected by colonial genocide. The article in question, from 1960, reports in detail on the former German colony on the occasion of South Africa's pending resignation from the Commonwealth. In this critical world situation, several new African states had asked the United Nations to support South-West Africa's struggle for independence. The title of the article, "Like the Germans," refers to the argument introduced by the new African states, namely, that "the Union of South Africa perpetuated German colonial policy in its mandate territory of South-West Africa." The *Der Spiegel* reporter saw things differently, and he began his article with the following polemic: "The Pan-African diplomats of Ghana intend to surprise the fall session of the United Nations with an anti-German propaganda play from World War One."[38] According to the *Der Spiegel* reporter, the real motive behind the demands of the "Pan-African diplomats" was an economic one. In the three columns of his article, the word "diamonds" appears five times, and in this way he manages to divert attention away from German colonial policies and toward the new African states' desire for material wealth. In addition, he repeatedly calls South-West Africa the "spoils of war" for the South Africans, leaving no doubt as to the rightful owner of these diamonds. Moreover, such arguments go hand in hand with a vision of the German colonial past which is an evident distortion of history. This begins directly after the author's assertion about the "anti-German propaganda play" performed by the new state of Ghana:

> For this propaganda, the Ghanaians use a yellowed White Paper drawn up in 1918 by the British government with the sole purpose of blackening the then German rulers of South-West Africa . . . as incompetent colonizers. The Germans—so the British authors of the White Paper claimed in those days—administered South-West Africa without taking care of the Negros' well-being and right to exist. The Herero peoples were (supposedly) decimated—from 80,000 to 15,000.[39]

Throughout the article, whenever the position of the Allies after World War One is mentioned or alluded to, the author adds restrictive parentheses or other reservations.[40] Thus the article from *Der Spiegel* of 24 August 1960 clearly denies the genocide committed in the former German colony of South-West Africa.

I can only speculate about why it was possible at this time for the magazine *Der Spiegel* so directly to deny the culpability of the Germans within the context of the colonial system, especially since, in the earlier 1950s, many politically involved journalists had striven for a highly critical representation of other European powers' colonialism, occasionally and cautiously including German colonialism too. One possible reason is the prevailing attitude of the time toward the African continent. After journalists had commented for several years and from many different angles—from sympathetic to critical—on the process of decolonization and on the various attempts at a new start in Africa, at the beginning of the 1960s, and in the context of the Congo crisis, public sentiment clearly changed. We can see here the beginnings of the "catastrophe coverage" of Africa that we are used to today. Those who had warned during the phase of decolonization that the colonized were not yet mature enough for independence saw their assumptions seemingly confirmed after the declarations of independence[41] and maintained that whatever the colonial powers had achieved was now falling apart, as the former colonies sank into chaos. However, there were also critical reporters who did not join in the general lament of other journalists, as can be seen in the following report from August 1960 on the situation in the Congo. This was written by a journalist who had clearly taken a closer look at what was happening, and had looked beyond the acts of violence to the reasons why the already chaotic image of Africa after decolonization had become even more distorted:

> The fact is, before the arrival of the United Nations troops in Léopoldville, two white women were raped, several others molested. Beyond that, a Negro had been shot by a Belgian, but there were no other deaths. Otherwise the usual lootings, smashed windowpanes, damaged cars, but everything to a relatively modest extent. The white men, however, ran like rabbits and escaped across the River Congo to Brazzaville, where they now are, guns in their holsters and dogs at their heels, drinking beer and spreading rumors.[42]

However, this article is an exception for the period, and in general another point of view was dominant in *Der Spiegel*: "Together with freedom," the conclusion of a *Spiegel* article early in 1964 read, "murder and terror came to Africa."[43] The prevailing "catastrophe coverage" of Africa shows how the political climate at this time had changed, providing a favorable context for those who were interested in a revival of the *koloniale Schuldlüge*.

## NOTES

1. This chapter, which concerns publications of the period from the aftermath of World War Two until the early 1960s, briefly summarizes one of the chapters of my monograph *"Europa ist nicht die Welt": (Post) Kolonialismus in Literatur und Geschichte der westdeutschen Nachkriegszeit* (Bielefeld: Aisthesis, 2008). I should like to thank Ben Schofield for his splendid editing of my English.
2. Susanne Zantop, "Race, Gender, and Postcolonial Amnesia," *Women in German Yearbook, 17: Feminist Studies in German Literature & Culture*, ed. by Patricia Herminghouse and Susanne Zantop (Lincoln: University of Nebraska Press, 2001), pp. 1–13 (p. 4). Zantop's claim is consistent with

those made by many other scholars during the last two decades. In the mid-1980s, for instance, a frequently quoted study on the "History of the Third-World Movement in the German Federal Republic" maintained that there were "no media" that could have "picked up the anti-colonial struggles in Africa, Asia and South America"; according to this study, "until late in the 1950s there is not much to say about 'internationalism' in the Federal Republic." *Hoch die internationale Solidarität: Zur Geschichte der Dritte-Welt-Bewegung in der Bundesrepublik*, ed. by Werner Balsen and Karl Rössel (Cologne: Kölner Volksblatt-Verlag, 1986), pp. 44 and 50. In the mid-1990s, a similar statement was made within the context of a sociological study, namely, that "until very late in the postwar era, the Germans did not take part in debates on decolonization like those conducted in other European countries." See Birgit Rommelspacher, *Dominanzkultur: Texte zu Fremdheit und Macht* (Berlin: Orlanda, 1995), p. 50. This opinion is still heard frequently today.

3. The terms colonial or post-colonial amnesia imply different meanings for different scholars. Some refer to the colonial system as such, some just think of German colonialism, and for others it is the genocide of the Nama and Herero people in the former colony of German South-West Africa that fell prey to a process of amnesia. My investigations indicate there was no post-colonial amnesia in post-war Germany in the sense that the entire colonial system fell from mind—for it did not. Nor was the specific phenomenon of German colonialism forgotten, as the present chapter shows. Beyond that, one can hardly speak of post-colonial amnesia when journalists in the post-war media denied the genocide in former German South-West Africa, since they remind their readers that the "denial of colonial guilt" and the reasons for this were once a debated topic in Germany. However, in the volumes of journals and magazines I investigated for my monograph (the volumes of *Frankfurter Hefte* from 1946 to 1965, of *Merkur* from 1947 to 1965, of *Akzente* from 1954 to 1965, of *Das Argument* from 1959 to 1965 and of *Der Spiegel* from 1947 to 1965), this issue was seldom addressed.

4. "Kolonialpolitik: Schlechte Verständigung," *Der Spiegel*, 10 September 1952, p. 9. Articles cited here from *Der Spiegel* are anonymous unless otherwise indicated.

5. See also Rosemarie K. Lester, *"Trivialneger": Das Bild des Schwarzen im westdeutschen Illustriertenroman* (Stuttgart: Heinz, 1982), pp. 191–200.

6. "Der Elefant," *Der Spiegel*, 16 March 1960, pp. 15–23.

7. Beyond that, the aftermath of historical colonialism is not as interesting from a newsroom's point of view as the present-day effects of the still existing colonial system—in this case, the situation in France in the late 1950s after the beginning of the Algerian war, which was widely discussed in the media. See "Algerien-Krieg: Demoralisierende Auswirkungen," *Der Spiegel*, 2 May 1956, p. 41f. (p. 42).

8. Eugen Kogon, "Die koreanische Demarkation," *Frankfurter Hefte: Zeitschrift für Kultur und Politik*, 5.8 (August 1950), 793f. (p. 793).

9. Albert Béguin, "Die indische Tragödie," *Frankfurter Hefte: Zeitschrift für Kultur und Politik*, 7.12 (December 1952), 925–37 (p. 935).

10. Ibid., p. 935.

11. Antoine Wiss-Verdier, "Nordafrikanische Hintergründe," *Frankfurter Hefte: Zeitschrift für Kultur und Politik*, 6.5 (May 1951), 354–7 (p. 355).

12. "Afrika: Gürtet eure Lenden," *Der Spiegel*, 30 April 1952, pp. 17–19 (p. 19). See also "Misch-Ehen: Die verkaufte Braut," *Der Spiegel*, 28 April 1954, p. 21f. (p. 21), and "Terror: Tote am See," *Der Spiegel*, 29 January 1964, pp. 74–6 (p. 74).

13. "Kolonien: Mau-Mau," *Der Spiegel*, 17 September 1952, p. 18. See also "König Mutesa: Englands Huld und Sühne," *Der Spiegel*, 23 December 1953, pp. 21–4 (p. 23).
14. "König Baudouin: Ein Lächeln," *Der Spiegel*, 22 June 1955, p. 30.
15. "Terror: Tote am See," pp. 74 and 76.
16. "Kolonialismus: Messer auf dem Tisch," *Der Spiegel*, 29 August 1962, pp. 34–6 (p. 35).
17. Cf. Martin Baer and Olaf Schröter, "Das Helgoland-Sansibar-Abkommen," in *Eine Kopfjagd: Deutsche in Ostafrika: Spuren kolonialer Herrschaft*, ed. by Martin Baer and Olaf Schröter (Berlin: Links, 2001), pp. 34–6. See also Horst Gründer, *Geschichte der deutschen Kolonien*, 5th edn (Paderborn: Schöningh, 2004), pp. 57 and 88f.
18. "Umsturz: Nelken für China," *Der Spiegel*, 22 January 1964, p. 53.
19. Herbert John, "'Westerwald, zack, zack!' *Spiegel*-Redakteur Herbert John bei den deutschen Luftwaffen-Instrukteuren in Nigeria," *Der Spiegel*, 11 November 1964, pp. 124–7 (p. 124; map on p. 127).
20. "Mau-Mau: Die große Medizin," *Der Spiegel*, 15 July 1953, pp. 17–21 (p. 17).
21. At the time of this article, Paul von Lettow-Vorbeck's memoirs from 1920, *Heia Safari!*, had just appeared in a new edition: Paul von Lettow-Vorbeck, *Heia Safari! Erinnerungen aus Ostafrika* (Leipzig: Hase & Koehler, 1920; Biberach: Koehler, 1952); and two new books by Lettow-Vorbeck, the former colonial guard general, were published in 1955 and 1957: Paul von Lettow-Vorbeck, *Afrika, wie ich es wiedersah* (Munich: Lehmann, 1955), and *Mein Leben* (Biberach: Koehler, 1957).
22. An article from November 1952, for instance, cleverly implies criticism by slipping in allusions to the black African soldiers in the Anglo-German battles in East Africa in World War One. See "Kenia: Sieben Schluck Blut," *Der Spiegel*, 19 November 1952, pp. 17–20 (p. 19).
23. "Heimweh nach Italien: Höhere Mathematik in Eritrea," *Der Spiegel*, 29 November 1947, p. 11.
24. Ibid.
25. "Wie es zum Ersten Weltkrieg kam," *Der Spiegel*, 11 March 1964, pp. 41–8 (p. 42).
26. See Baer and Schröter, "Rückzug in die Legende: Paul von Lettow-Vorbeck und der Erste Weltkrieg," pp. 127–40 (p. 133); also Gründer, *Geschichte der deutschen Kolonien*, pp. 102–5. Apart from these expansionist tendencies, other topics of historical reviews were the Empire's involvement in the "Scramble for Africa" and its influence even in places where no future German colonies were at stake. A *Spiegel* cover story of September 1955, for instance, which deals with the background of the French conflicts in Morocco, depicts the German involvement in this history. See "Französisch-Marokko: Die Gazelle," *Der Spiegel*, 14 September 1955, pp. 23–32. In the context of the Congo crisis in the early 1960s, to mention another focus of this magazine, articles often deal with Bismarck's role in the recognition of the Congo as an independent territory under the sovereignty of Leopold II. See, for example, "Patrice Emergy Lumumba," *Der Spiegel*, 22 June 1960, pp. 34–9; see also "Anarchie: Die Rache des Häuptlings," *Der Spiegel*, 20 July 1960, pp. 31–4.
27. One example among many is "Kolonialismus: Messer auf dem Tisch," *Der Spiegel*, 29 August 1962, pp. 34–6. From the end of the 1950s onward, however, in both magazines, *Spiegel* and *Frankfurter Hefte*, colonized peoples presented their own points of view, for instance, in an article from June 1959 in *Frankfurter Hefte*, which summarizes the position of the independence movements from the perspective of the people involved. See Mon'a Mundu,

"Belgisch-Kongo und Angola: Zwei Kolonien—ein Problem," *Frankfurter Hefte: Zeitschrift für Kultur und Politik*, June 1959, pp. 397–400.

28. See Georgios Chatzoudis, "Von der Kolonie Südwestafrika zum National-staat Namibia—das politische System seit 1949," *Namibia—Deutschland: Eine geteilte Geschichte. Widerstand—Gewalt—Erinnerung. Publikation zur gleichnamigen Ausstellung im Rautenstrauch-Joest-Museum für Völkerkunde der Stadt Köln und im Deutschen Historischen Museum*, ed. by Larissa Förster, Dag Henrichsen and Michael Bollig (Berlin: Minerva, 2004), pp. 258–73 (p. 260).

29. See, for example, "Ohm Krüger redivivus: Faule Früchte in Südafrika," *Der Spiegel*, 5 June 1948, p. 8. The title "Ohm Krüger redivivus" refers, of course, to the connection between Malan's politics and that of German fascism, in that it is an allusion to both the South African Boer leader and politician (1825–1904) and to the Nazi propaganda film of 1941. The article describes Malan's career, including his relationship with Nazi Germany.

30. "Ochsenkarren-Faschismus: Mit gefährlicher Sprengwirkung," *Der Spiegel*, 19 February 1949, p. 12f. (p. 12).

31. "Südwest: In Afrikas Hinterhof," *Der Spiegel*, 13 September 1950, p. 15f. (p. 15).

32. Ibid., p. 15. A later article also emphasizes the fact that the Germans in the Union were on Malan's side: "Malan: Angst vorm schwarzen Mann," *Der Spiegel*, 2 April 1952, pp. 18–21 (p. 19).

33. Lester, *"Trivialneger,"* p. 193.

34. "Südwest: In Afrikas Hinterhof," p. 15.

35. Gründer, *Geschichte der deutschen Kolonien*, p. 217.

36. An article of February 1963 on the assassination of the president of Togo also uses this set phrase ("ehemalige deutsche Musterkolonie"): "Togo: Drei Kugeln," *Der Spiegel*, 6 February 1963, p. 56.

37. "Togo: Das deutsche Schicksal," *Der Spiegel*, 27 June 1956, p. 30f. (p. 30).

38. "Südwestafrika: Wie die Deutschen," *Der Spiegel*, 24 August 1960, p. 28f. (p. 28).

39. Ibid., p. 28.

40. See also in the same article ("Südwestafrika: Wie die Deutschen"): "With this White Paper, however, the UNO diplomats of Ghana seek to prove that the South African mandate power ignores the same rights of the black people of South-West Africa as *allegedly* did their German predecessor" (p. 28); and, "Moreover, a secret memorandum by the foreign ministry of Ghana for its country's propagandists dictates that 'the South African slave system' has to be compared to the—*allegedly*—dubious colonial methods of the Germans" (p. 29; my emphasis in both cases).

41. For an example of a critical voice from this period, see the editorial foreword to an article on Sri Lanka (then Ceylon) by Melanie Bieri: "Zwei Religionen, zwei Rassen und zwei Sprachen: Ein Bericht aus Ceylon," *Frankfurter Hefte: Zeitschrift für Kultur und Politik*, 15.4 (April 1960), p. 270.

42. Otto von Loewenstern, "Die eingemauerten Nonnen: Ein Bericht aus dem Kongo (Der Münchener Journalist berichtet von einer Reise durch die wichtigsten Unruhegebiete der Kongo-Republik)," *Der Spiegel*, 3 August 1960, p. 38f. (p. 38).

43. "Terror: Tote am See," p. 74. Early in 2006, in the weekly newspaper *Die Zeit*, the Swedish writer Henning Mankell criticized the ongoing journalistic tendency to depict Africa as a "continent torn by civil wars." See Henning Mankell, "Zeigt das wahre Afrika! Nur Elend und Sterben—warum die westlichen Medien ein falsches Bild vom schwarzen Kontinent zeichnen," *Die Zeit*, 12 January 2006, p. 45.

# 15 *Denkmalsturz*

## The German Student Movement and German Colonialism

*Ingo Cornils*

Toppling monuments and statues is a highly symbolic and political act.[1] We remember the elation of the crowds in Moscow, Warsaw and East Berlin when statues of Lenin were pulled down after the fall of Communism, and of course the globally televised fall of Saddam Hussein's statue in Baghdad in 2003. *Denkmalsturz* (toppling memorials), both a violent and a cathartic demonstrative act against official representations of former rulers, dictators and conquerors, signifies a public protest against once widely accepted (or enforced) interpretations of their influence and power, and a massive change in perception of their historical significance.

In the context of German colonialism, we can date the beginnings of such a change in perception to the late 1960s, when the German Student Movement identified the glorification of former colonial "heroes" in monuments and statues as a manifestation of German attitudes of superiority and ruthlessness against other races that had led, in their view, to the catastrophe of the Holocaust. The students believed that, by attacking this "embodiment of the Aryan master race"[2] in direct action, they could unmask the West German establishment as heirs to Nazism and contribute to a "change in consciousness" that would lead to solidarity with the struggle of liberation movements in the Third World and a revolution against a perceived deeply ingrained deference to authority at home.

In this chapter, I focus on the toppling of the statue of the colonial officer Hermann von Wissmann (1853–1905) by radical students at the University of Hamburg in 1967–8. While this event may be seen as merely a footnote in the history of protest actions during the student rebellion of the 1960s, it has become part of cultural memory through the works of Uwe Timm, one of Germany's foremost contemporary writers. Not only did Timm include the Wissmann episode in *Heißer Sommer* (Hot Summer) (1974), one of the best literary representations of the German Student Movement; as an "engaged writer," he has continued to influence the debate on Germany's militaristic past and its effect on the German psyche to the present day.

I conclude with an unexpected turn which the story of the Wissmann statue took in 2004–5: in a striking intervention, the artist Jokinen unearthed the statue from its hiding place of 30 years in the basement of the *Sternwarte* (astronomical observatory) in Hamburg Bergedorf and exhibited it in Hamburg harbor, inviting a public debate on how we should deal with our colonial history, thus fulfilling the students' demand for an open debate in the "public sphere."

## HERMANN VON WISSMANN—FROM HERO TO HATE-FIGURE

Until the late 1960s, Hermann von Wissmann was generally remembered in West Germany as a pioneering *Afrikaforscher* (African explorer),[3] on a par with Heinrich Barth (1821–65) and Gustav Nachtigal (1834–85). Streets were named after him, members of student dueling fraternities drank beer to remember him, and children read about his encounters with elephants and lions. He twice crossed the African continent from Luanda to Zanzibar, and added to the knowledge of the upper Congo River basin. He was feted for the "courageous" way in which he dealt with a rebellion of Arab slave traders, "pacified" the tribes of Eastern Africa, and set up nature reserves and game parks.

What was conveniently forgotten was the fact that, as military commander and later as imperial commissioner in German East Africa (today's Tanzania), Wissmann brutally suppressed an uprising against the new colonial power and employed a "scorched earth" tactic that caused widespread famine and disease among the indigenous population.[4] With a budget of 2 million *Reichsmark* voted for by the *Reichstag* in January 1889, he formed and commanded a *Schutztruppe* (protection force) of 1,000 Askaris. These native mercenaries were recruited mainly from Mozambique and the Sudan, the rationale being that they had little in common with the population they were "protecting" and would thus have little compunction in suppressing them.

Wissmann and his troop fought numerous battles against local tribes who resisted the theft of their land and cattle and the introduction of forced labor. On Wissmann's orders, the Askaris murdered, pillaged, and torched the villages. While the German public was fed a string of lies about what was happening on the "black continent," with descriptions of Wissmann as a gentle, civilizing factor, disturbing news about the brutality of colonial rule eventually reached the German Empire, but only the Social Democrats under August Bebel and Wilhelm Liebknecht openly protested against the systematic exploitation of the Africans.[5]

From 1895 to 1896, Wissmann was governor of German East Africa. His legacy was the introduction of a *Hüttensteuer* (hut tax), which caused serious unrest and eventually led to the Maji-Maji uprising (1905–7), during which more than 100,000 Africans lost their lives.[6] Due to ill health, Wissmann retired after a tenure of only nine months and returned to Germany, where he wrote several books, including a handbook, *Zur Behandlung des Negers* (On the Treatment of the Negro).[7] Following his death in

1905, several statues of "Germany's greatest African" were commissioned by the *Deutsche Kolonialgesellschaft* (German Colonial Company) to serve as focal points for identification with Germany's global ambitions, and to establish a myth of national success. At the consecration of the statue in Dar es Salaam in the spring of 1909 that later ended up in Hamburg, Wissmann was described as "a true leader, born to dominate men and animals."[8]

The statue portrays Wissmann as a heroic figure, at his feet a black Askari, looking up at his master and draping the imperial flag over a dead lion. The symbolism is crass: the colonial ruler, measuring 2.60 meters in height, towers over the Askari, who measures 1.70 meters. This "lion of Africa" was to command respect from his subjects, as the inscriptions on the plinth reminded the observer in German, Arabic and Swahili:

> Governor von Wissmann / our former master / he pacified the coastal region / and showed us the right path / Wissmann was our sultan / he of the forty-fold understanding / he was a man we could trust / we all loved him / he is no longer of this world / the possessor of a brave heart in battle / look upon this statue / so that you may remember him.[9]

After the end of World War One and the loss of all German colonies, the Wissmann statue in Dar es Salaam was dismantled and taken to London as a war trophy. However, in 1921 the British Government listened to the pleas of the German colonial movement, and the statue was shipped to Hamburg. Here, at the former "gateway to the German colonies," in front of the main building of the former *Hamburger Kolonialinstitut* that in 1919 had become Hamburg University, the statue was consecrated in 1922 as a reminder of "Germany's glorious colonial past" and as an admonition to all Germans to win back their former colonies.

While the cult around Wissmann served the integration of a small community of colonial revisionists who felt excluded from official politics during the Weimar Republic, with the advent of National Socialism the statue became the focus of a new movement for *Lebensraum* (living space). Indeed, Wissmann served as a popular example among conservative fraternities and National Socialist student groups, and the Nazis saw a reinvigorated colonial policy as an ideal instrument for the "awakening and encouragement of warlike instincts."[10]

After World War Two, the newly formed Federal Republic of Germany did not, in marked contrast to the GDR, pull down all colonial monuments and statues. This included the Wissmann statue in Hamburg, which had been knocked off its plinth during a bombing raid: it was put up again in 1949, but was then generally forgotten or ignored.[11] This state of affairs began to change in the 1960s. In 1961, students at Hamburg University demanded the removal of the "Conquistadors" from the campus, arguing that the statue was not likely to impress their black fellow-students from Africa. However, the rector refused. The

German writer Siegfried Lenz, a student at Hamburg University in the early 1960s, remembers his own and his fellow-students' combination of embarrassment and "ironic detachment" toward the statue in such a prominent position.[12] This refusal of identification with Germany's colonial past increased when more and more students became politicized during the protests against the Vietnam War and began to support the various liberation movements in the Third World. Wissmann was not only seen as outmoded, but as a representative of an authoritarian tradition that had become intolerable.[13]

## DENKMALSTURZ IN DEN KÖPFEN (TOPPLING MEMORIALS IN THE MIND)

Several aspects came together to make the Wissmann statue the focus of attention. First, students at Hamburg University were taught by a number of historians who had radically broken with the established view of recent German history. Second, the ideologists of the *Sozialistischer Deutscher Studentenbund* (SDS) (Socialist German Student Federation) quickly recognized that, in the context of the debate about liberation movements in the Third World, Germany's colonial past was an excellent example to demonstrate the "evil machinations" of capitalism. Third, the fact that Hamburg University as an institution stood by this "symbol of oppression," thus allowing a comparison between institutional heavy-handedness on campus and Wissmann's heavy-handed rule in Africa, made it the perfect target for direct action.

The "Hamburg School"[14] of historians around Fritz Fischer taught that National Socialism had not just been a "historical accident," brought about by the radical Hitler movement, but was in fact a direct consequence of Germany's imperialistic ambitions in the nineteenth century. In *Griff nach der Weltmacht* (1961), which was published in English as *Germany's Aims in the First World War* in 1967, Fischer had argued that the rush for colonies had been motivated by the imperial government's wish to turn attention away from internal social problems, and that its ambition to gain "a place in the sun" had created a complex web of forces—"not least material factors"[15]—that had led to the outbreak of World War One.

Such straight talking electrified the students, who had generally grown up with the myth that the national state and the army had been blameless in the catastrophe of the Third Reich. At the end of the 1960s, the historians around Fischer focused on Germany's colonial past from a number of socio-economic perspectives and explored the relationship of economic interests, social structures and administrative systems in the colonies.[16] Their findings, according to Karl Heinz Roth, one of the instigators of the *Wissmann-Denkmalsturz*, were "devoured" by the students.[17]

The SDS's analysis of the colonial/imperial tradition has to be seen against the events in Third World countries in the 1960s that, in its view, heralded the rapid decline of capitalism. From the Cuban revolution to the Vietnam War and the Cultural Revolution in China, the Third World appeared to be breaking its chains and emancipating itself from the rule of its former colonial masters. Rudi Dutschke, the charismatic leader of the SDS and figurehead of the German student movement, argued in February 1968 that any radical opposition had to be understood in global terms, that it was the mass movement of the underprivileged around the world that would define the character of the revolution they were working toward. Citing Frantz Fanon's *Les Damnés de la Terre* (The Wretched of the Earth) (1961), which was published in German in 1966, he warned that the hoped-for independence of former colonies would merely turn into new dependence and exploitation unless the existing capitalist system was overthrown.[18]

## WISSMANN FALLS

On 8 August 1967, the Hamburg SDS announced that they would pull down the "memorial of shame." In a flyer distributed widely on campus and in the city, the student group drew a link between colonial "pacification" in Wissmann's days, the Indian wars in North America, and the Vietnam War that was escalating at the time.[19]

A different flyer, entitled "Ein Wissmann stürzt selten allein!" (A Wissmann seldom falls alone), by an *Aktionskomitee* called "Die Köpfe rollen" (Heads roll), announced a celebration that evening at the *Amerikahaus* which would celebrate "the eighteenth anniversary of the founding of the People's Republic of China, the fall of the Wissmann statue, the victory of the Vietcong, the struggle of the liberation movements in Latin America and the social revolution in Africa."[20]

Thus the scene was set and maximum media attention guaranteed (two camera crews were on hand to record the event),[21] but when the students attempted to pull down the statue that had already been sprayed with red paint, the police intervened and arrested five "ringleaders." A second attempt on the night of 26–27 September 1967 was successful,[22] but the statue was put back on its plinth by the Hamburg Department for Higher Education. The students did not give up, though, and, following a vote organized by the student union, Wissmann was pulled down in the night of 31 October. The next day students carried the statue to the refectory in triumph. This time, the University administration decided to avoid any further damaging confrontations, and removed the statue to the observatory in Hamburg-Bergedorf for storage.

For the instigators of the "action," the *Denkmalsturz* was a defining moment in their lives. Not only was the "breaking of a taboo" experienced as an exhilarating moment of emancipation and fun,[23] but the subsequent trial brought new opportunities to rail against "the system" and challenge authoritarian institutions. Peter Schütt, who lost his job as a research assistant at the University because of his involvement, recalls the tumultuous scenes at the Auditorium Maximum, to which the trial had been transferred due to great public interest. When the presiding judge asked the defendants' expert witness, Helmut Bley, "Do you really wish to condemn the entire colonial period?", Bley, to great applause, responded ironically that it was not yet judgment day and neither the colonial epoch nor the *Denkmalstürzer* should be dismissed out of hand.[24]

The trial turned into a complete farce when an art historian, asked whether the portrayal of the Askari was really as discriminatory as the students claimed, stated that, in colonial times, Africans tended to be portrayed "in a pre-civilized state of innocence and nakedness." This was the cue for four female comrades to strip off in front of the judge and sing, "We are the natives of Trizonia," earning them a night in jail.[25]

The media, particularly the newspapers of the Springer publishing house, which was engaged in a bitter war of words with the students, were up in arms, criticizing the "vandals" for besmirching the memory of a "great German," who had brought "peace and civilization" to the Africans. Letters from enraged citizens lambasted the action against the statues of Wissmann and Hans Dominik (1870–1910, another officer of the *Schutztruppe*) as the "childish lynching of two German Africans."[26] One particular flyer distributed at Hamburg University at the end of October 1968 by the *Aktion zur Rettung des Deutschtums* (Action for the preservation of Germanness), entitled "Ostafrika ist deutsch," is indicative of the strong feelings awakened by the *Denkmalsturz* among conservative Germans.[27] With the headline "Radical Far-Left Elements Strike Yet Again," the text rails against the defendants, "who attempted to desecrate our conquerors and now have to face just punishment," and attacks their lack of patriotism: "Like an epidemic the brood of evil seems to be spreading. Decades of German honor and tradition have been dragged through the dirt." The students are characterized as "slit-eyed University Chinamen," "muck-rakers," "scum of society," and "long-haired vagrants." The flyer concludes, "Landgraf, be tough! God lives, Dominik lives, Wissmann lives, Che is dead!"

Both the student flyers and the "Ostafrika ist deutsch" flyer reflect the entrenched positions and combative language in this confrontation. Part of the SDS tactic was to provoke and taunt their opponents into unmasking themselves as the unreformed Nazis they believed them to be.[28] The *Aktion zur Rettung des Deutschtums* obliged, but it is the official reaction to the *Denkmalsturz*, the heavy-handedness of the police, the unsympathetic attitude of the judge and the harsh sentences that reveal the extent to which Germany's colonial past was still perceived as a positive achievement.

Partly as an attempt to explain their action, and partly to drive home further the message that the University of Hamburg was controlled by a "faction of former Nazis," a number of students collaborated to write a book about the many links the city and the University had had with the colonial movement in the past, and the extent to which research at the University was integrated into "neocolonial conditions of exploitation" in the present. *Das permanente Kolonialinstitut*, published in 1969 to coincide with the official celebrations on the occasion of the 50th anniversary of the University, argues that Wissmann had served "the interests of imperialist capital," and that as long as the statue was allowed to stand it would be seen as a "symbol of Germany's striving to become a world power." The University's history as a "Kolonialinstitut," with the brief to prepare German officials for their tour of duty in the colonies, and the scientific support it gave to business to make optimum use of colonial goods, were seen as a collusion of notionally independent thinkers with the dark forces of imperialism. While the authors base their polemic on "forgotten" facts (some of them deeply disturbing, for example the continued employment of former Nazis after 1949), it is obvious that their investigation into the University's role in the colonial "system" served their own political agenda. They saw themselves as an avant-garde and "progressive force" in the fight against capitalism, and "spun" the events to fit their particular view.

## *DENKMALSTURZ* REMEMBERED

In reality, the students' action was soon forgotten. With the Wissmann statue safely stored out of harm's way, the fragmentation and ultimate demise of the German Student Movement in 1969, and a new Social-Liberal coalition government in place, this is where the story would have ended, had it not been for the writer Uwe Timm, who in 1974 included the Wissmann episode in his novel *Heißer Sommer*. The protagonist, the student Ullrich Krause, moves from Munich to Hamburg and becomes involved in the protests organized by the SDS. Krause is an "average" alienated young man, initially merely seeking a good time but, like many others, politicized by the death of the student Benno Ohnesorg on 2 June 1967. He comes to the realization that his claustrophobic childhood, under the shadow of a father who still adores Hitler, and the authoritarian atmosphere in the universities he has attended both have their roots in his country's past. Timm places Krause right in the middle of the *Denkmalsturz*: it is through his eyes that we witness the "exemplarische Aktion."[29] Krause takes part in distributing flyers, and is instrumental in pulling the statue down. While he is tightening the rope around Wissmann's head, he remembers how he used to imagine being a colonial explorer as a child:

> As a boy he had once been given a book as a birthday present. His father had found it, after much searching, as he stressed, in a second hand book shop: *Haia Safari*. By Lettow-Vorbeck. Ullrich had devoured it in

a few days and imagined himself with a troop of devoted Askari, send-
ing the English packing. For some weeks he and some other boys had
played Haia Safari amongst the weeds growing on the bomb sites. But
they kept arguing, because no one wanted to take on the role of the
Askari. (HS 148)

Krause is psychologically torn between the elation of the collective action,
his hatred and his fear. He follows the student slogan, "destroy what
destroys you," and relishes the thought of "tearing down all this rubbish,
the crashing, the whacking," thinking that afterward everything would be
different. But there is also intense fear as he realizes both the significance
of the transgression they are committing right in front of the police and the
potential consequences (HS 149).

Timm's text allows the reader to experience the *Denkmalsturz* from the
perspective of the students, with a physical immediacy that no documentary or historical account can supply: "the metal had been cold," "everyone
clapped, shouted, and ran about" (HS 150). But he also interprets the event:
when Wissmann has fallen to the ground, the narrator comments, "the
Askari now looked up at a sky that had been liberated from Wissmann."
Timm expertly conveys the dialectic of the Utopian moment of emancipation: on the one hand, Krause is deeply afraid when he hears the sirens and
sees the flashing blue lights of the police cars (HS 150), a reaction that parallels exactly what was intended by the statue in Dar es Salaam in the first
place. On the other hand, the narrator suggests that the act of toppling this
representation of colonial power and authority has made a difference: "He
felt he had taken part in an event of decisive significance" (HS 152). What
the significance was is left for the reader to decide.

Twenty-seven years later, Uwe Timm included the Wissmann episode in
another novel, *Rot* (Red) (2001).[30] This time, though, the event is remembered
with much less enthusiasm. The protagonist, Thomas Linde, a former "'68er"
who works as a funeral orator, has inherited a pack of explosives from his
deceased former comrade, Aschenberger, and is tasked with blowing up the
*Siegessäule* (victory column) in Berlin on the day of the move of the German
government from Bonn to Berlin, as a sign of protest against, as Aschenberger
interprets it, the continuation of the country's imperialistic and militaristic
tradition. Just like the Wissmann statue, the *Siegessäule* is described as a
"lump"[31] that needs to come down. Visiting the *Siegessäule*, Linde reflects on
the apparent failure of his generation to effect any lasting change.

Linde realizes that Aschenberger has chosen him to carry out his plan
because they had both taken part in the Wissmann *Denkmalsturz* back in
1968. He visits Krause, now an upright citizen and himself a "colonist" in
the *Neue Länder* (New Provinces) of former East Germany. As a mixture
of penance for his bourgeois existence and lingering loyalty to the cause,
he maintains an archive of socialist literature of the *außerparlamentarische
Opposition* (APO) (Extra-Parliamentary Opposition) in his spare time. As

the former revolutionaries walk down memory lane, they realize how much perceptions have changed: "We were ahead of our time. Today, nobody wants to be reminded of the glorious colonial period. Today, the authorities themselves would remove the statue, quietly and in secret. Times change, and so do our moral judgments" (R 329). If this assessment is correct, and given the manifest failure of the German Student Movement to change "the system" through protest in the streets, we need to ask ourselves what process has changed moral perceptions in the intervening years. In Timm's case, I would argue that his own commitment to the "long march through the institutions" had a lot to do with it. He followed up his interest in Germany's colonial past with a solid piece of research culminating in his description of the genocide perpetrated by German soldiers in German South-West Africa in his novel *Morenga* (1978) and his volume of photographs from German colonial times, *Deutsche Kolonien* (1981).

## THE IDEAS OF '68

*Morenga* not only reflects the break by the '68ers with the traditions of their fathers, but also the escalation of the confrontation that had occurred after the demise of the student movement. While the majority of students had "moved on," many, like Timm himself, had joined communist groups, and a small minority had turned to guerrilla warfare against the state. Thus we find both the "ideas of '68" and the new vocabulary of the "armed struggle" of the Red Army Faction reflected in the narrative of the veterinarian Gottschalk who is intrigued and fascinated by the culture of the Herero, but realizes that with his colonial mindset it will be impossible for him ever to identify fully with them.

Timm summed up his own conclusions from his *Morenga* project in the preface to *Deutsche Kolonien* in 1981. He notes that the Africans had tended to live in classless societies, and this had been a constant challenge to their colonial masters, who realized that, unless there was greater competition for resources among the Africans, very little profit would be made. Timm comments,

> This . . . is typical of the ideology of the colonizers. It stems from economic thinking and is determined by an unquestioning sense of superiority, which in turn is based on a belief in technological progress. In this way, any life form that is different becomes the Other in the eyes of the colonizer; it becomes something alien, primitive, without his ever reaching a position where he would be able to see this other culture as rich and complex in its own right.[32]

There is a clear link between the moral outrage of the students against the Wissmann statue and the outrage Timm himself feels against the treatment

of the colonized as children who need to learn the German virtues of punc-
tuality, order and diligence. In fact, it was against these "German virtues"
that the generation of 1968 rebelled.


## NEW PERCEPTIONS

By writing about German colonialism in a sustained way, Timm has contributed to the change in perception that the '68ers had set out to achieve.
In tune with many other intellectuals, writers, broadcasters, educators
and activists, he is still involved in the "long march" of his generation to
put their ideas on the political and cultural agenda in modern Germany.
Indeed, during the era of the Red–Green coalition government from 1998
to 2005, former '68ers had gained political power and dominated, argu-
ably, the *Kulturkampf* about the interpretation of Germany's past.

Thus, the public apology to the Nama and Herero given by the German
minister for economic aid and development in 2004 can be interpreted as
a consequence of the student protest of the late 1960s, and a reflection
of changed attitudes in Germany.[33] Heidemarie Wieczoreck-Zeul, born in
1942, is a '68er herself and was known as "Red Heidi" in the 1970s. Not
only was she the first German politician who openly acknowledged her
country's guilt for the genocide, but she also talked about the "colonial
madness" which had opened the door to violence, discrimination, racism
and destruction in Germany's name.[34]

One highly visible consequence of the renewed interest in Germany's
colonial past was a controversial three-part documentary, "Die Deutschen
Kolonien," shown on the *Zweites Deutsches Fernsehen* (ZDF), Germany's
second public broadcasting channel.[35] This high-profile production, broadcast at prime time in November 2005, included mention both of the profits
the German companies hoped to make and of the suffering and misery of
the colonized: "this is the beginning of a nightmare for many natives"; "the
German culture of corporal punishment"; "Wilhelm II puts forward a new,
saber-rattling policy"; and so on. Gisela Graichen, one of the authors of
the series, claims that it was her intention to narrate "typical stories of real
people," and to "observe closely." She concludes,

> Perhaps we can achieve one thing by revisiting our colonial history:
> the habit of looking closely, of looking beneath the surface of legends,
> whatever direction they may come from, of understanding, too, that
> it is always about meeting and interaction, that no culture is "better"
> than the other, only different.[36]

One could go on: the recent spate of books on Germany's colonial past, the
continued interest in post-colonial studies (in spite of occasional criticism
that "banging the colonial drum" prevents us from looking toward the

future), the plethora of exhibitions,[37] lectures and conferences,[38] all confirm the impression that the debate about Germany's colonial past has entered a new phase. My final example brings us back to the *Wissmanndenkmal*, and an unexpected new chapter in its history.

## THE "AFRIKA-HAMBURG" PROJECT

From October 2004 to November 2005, the citizens of Hamburg had the opportunity to come face to face with the Wissmann statue once again. As part of a series of events called "Vom Togokai zum Tanzaniapark [from Togo quayside to Tanzania park]—Hamburg postcolonial,"[39] the artist Jokinen exhibited the statue on the *Überseebrücke* in Hamburg. Her aim was to create a "Nachdenkmal-Raum" (play on words: a space for a statue, but also a place provoking thought), to explore the "(post-) koloniale Mentalitätsgeschichte" of this *artefact trouvé*, to engage with and break up the "persistent myths" surrounding Wissmann in particular and the city's involvement in colonialism in general, and to give the citizens of Hamburg a forum to debate how they wished to deal with this aspect of their past.

Intended as a participatory event, the "artistic deconstruction"[40] of the statue in an unfamiliar and yet fitting environment right on the harbor that had handled most of Germany's colonial trade was just one element of the project. Thus the installation of the statue in a public space that invited passers-by to stop, to view a selection of photographs of the statue's history and perhaps to engage in a debate on public representations of power was complemented by a large copper plaque on the plinth that referred viewers to the project website.[41]

Here, visitors could express their opinions and pick up threads from previous discussions. About 800 contributions are preserved in the archive, which reflect a broad spectrum of opinions. Provoked by articles in newspapers that described Wissmann as a "colonial criminal,"[42] numerous messages argue that Wissmann's actions have to be seen in the context of his time and that the organizers are part of a left-wing conspiracy bent on destroying German identity. This section of the contributors clearly feels provoked by what they see as an *Instrumentalisierung der Geschichte* (instrumentalization of history) by the "current elites."[43]

In a section titled "Abstimmung" (vote), visitors were encouraged to express a view on what should happen to the Wissmann statue in future. More than 5,600 votes were cast, with 95 per cent indicating that it should not be returned to storage but publicly exhibited in some form. Opinions differ, though, as to how this vote should be interpreted. Jokinen herself believes that she has the mandate to continue with her plan to gather all existing colonial statues and create a "Park Postkolonial" in Hamburg-Harburg that would allow viewers to remember the past and seek reconciliation with the descendants of the colonized.[44] Revisionists, on the other hand, believe that the vote indicates that we have reached a "state of normality": "Wissmann belongs back where left-wing radicals had toppled him: in Hamburg University gardens."[45]

In any case, the time does not seem ripe for either option. The Wissmann statue was returned to storage in November 2005 and, on 23 February 2006, the Hamburg Senate decided against Jokinen's plan, for the time being.

## CONCLUSION

Joachim Zeller believes that the debates about historico-political interpretation described in this chapter may contribute to a permanent shift in perception of our past.[46] I am skeptical whether we have yet reached that stage. The current dominant view of colonialism as "a tale of slavery, plunder, war, corruption, land-grabbing, famines, exploitation, indentured labor, impoverishment, massacres, genocide and forced resettlement"[47] is challenged by neo-conservative historians, who argue that colonialism was not such a bad thing after all.

A much greater challenge to serious engagement with our colonial past appears to lie in the general apathy surrounding the debate outside academic circles. Five thousand votes over 14 months in a city of 2 million inhabitants do not really indicate a deep involvement. Perhaps people tire of endlessly looking backward and apologizing for the crimes of their forefathers;[48] perhaps Winfried Speitkamp is right when he observes that the memory of our colonial past, in spite of all the recent activity, is still marginal at best.[49] Similarly, Uwe Timm has begun to doubt the effectiveness of literature for social change, at least in the short term.[50] If this is the case, then we will have to wait for Wissmann's next return. An alternative is for us to laugh at his representation as *Herrenmensch* on a pedestal, and think of him at a rave in the Congo, sharing a pipe of cannabis with the natives.[51]

## NOTES

1. Cf. *Denkmalsturz: Zur Konfliktgeschichte politischer Symbolik*, ed. by Winfried Speitkamp (Göttingen: Vandenhoeck & Ruprecht, 1997).
2. Peter Schütt, "Der Denkmalssturz," *die tageszeitung*, 7 August 1992, <http://www.taz.de/pt/1992/09/07/a0223.1/textdruck> [accessed 4 January 2008].
3. The standard Wissmann biography is Alexander Becker et al., *Hermann von Wissmann: Deutschlands größter Afrikaner. Sein Leben und Wirken unter Benutzung des Nachlasses* (Berlin: Schall, 1911). For a short introduction from a modern perspective, see Thomas Morlang, "Finde ich keinen Weg, so bahne ich mir einen," in " . . . *Macht und Anteil an der Weltherrschaft": Berlin und der deutsche Kolonialismus*, ed. by Ulrich van der Heyden and Joachim Zeller (Münster: UNRAST-Verlag, 2005), pp. 37–43.

4. Jürgen Herzog, *Geschichte Tansanias* (Berlin: Deutscher Verlag der Wissenschaften, 1986), p. 44f.
5. Winfried Speitkamp, *Deutsche Kolonialgeschichte* (Stuttgart: Reclam, 2005), p. 139.
6. Cf. Bartholomäus Grill, "Eine deutsche Hölle," *Die Zeit*, 30 June 2005 (no. 27); Claus Kristen, "Die Taktik der 'verbrannten Erde': Die Folgen der deutschen Kolonialherrschaft in Ostafrika," *analyse & kritik—Zeitung für linke Debatte und Praxis*, 17 February 2006 (no. 503), <www.akweb.de/ak_s/ak503/15.htm> [accessed 4 January 2008]. See also *Der Maji-Maji-Krieg in Deutsch-Ostafrika. 1905–1907*, ed. by Felicitas Becker and Jigal Beez (Berlin: Ch. Links, 2005).
7. In Hermann von Wissmann, *Afrika: Schilderungen und Rathschläge für den Aufenthalt und den Dienst in den deutschen Schutzgebieten* (Berlin, 1895).
8. Winfried Speitkamp, "Der Totenkult um die Kolonialheroen des Deutschen Kaiserreiches," *zeitenblicke*, 3.1 (June 2004), p. 1.
9. Speitkamp, *Deutsche Kolonialgeschichte*, p. 120f.
10. Autorenkollektiv Allgemeiner Studentenausschuss (ASTA) an der Universität Hamburg, *Das permanente Kolonialinstitut: 50 Jahre Hamburger Universität* (Hamburg, 1969), p. 25.
11. Speitkamp, *Deutsche Kolonialgeschichte*, p. 173f.
12. Joachim Zeller, *Kolonialdenkmäler und Geschichtsbewußtsein: Eine Untersuchung der kolonialdeutschen Erinnerungskultur* (Frankfurt: IKO—Verlag für Interkulturelle Kommunikation, 2000), p. 207.
13. In a letter to the author, Karl Heinz Roth, a medical student and member of the Hamburg SDS at the time, declared, "Wir haben das Denkmal damals als junge Studierende gestürzt, weil wir in seinem Schatten nicht atmen und studieren konnten. Wir wollten eine Welt ohne faschistische und kolonialistische Kontinuitäten, auch und gerade im Bereich der Hochschule und der Wissenschaft." ("We toppled the statue in those days as young students because we felt that in its shadow we could not breathe or study. We wanted a world without fascist and colonial continuities, also and especially in the areas of university and science.")
14. Cf. Volker Berghahn, "Ostimperium und Weltpolitik—Gedanken zur Langzeitwirkung der 'Hamburger Schule,'" *geschichte.transnational*, 13 April 2006, <http://hsozkult.geschichte.hu-berlin.de/forum/2006-04-001.pdf> [accessed 1 February 2008].
15. Fritz Fischer, *Griff nach der Weltmacht* (Düsseldorf: Droste, 1961), p. 11.
16. For example, Helmut Böhme, *Deutschlands Weg zur Großmacht: Studien zum Verhältnis von Wirtschaft und Staat während der Reichsgründungszeit 1848–1881* (Cologne: Kiepenheuer & Witsch, 1966); Helmut Bley, *Kolonialherrschaft und Sozialstruktur in Deutsch-Südwest-Afrika, 1894–1914* (Hamburg: Leibniz, 1968). The students also had access to an early study from the GDR which used the "genocide" accusation for obvious ideological reasons: Horst Drechsler, *Südwestafrika unter deutscher Kolonialherrschaft: Der Kampf der Hereros und Namas gegen den deutschen Imperialismus* (Berlin: Akademie-Verlag, 1966).
17. In a letter to the author, Roth writes, "Die Wissmann-Aktion stand selbstverständlich im Vietnam-Kontext, aber zur selben Zeit erschienen auch schon die ersten kritischen historischen Studien zur deutschen Kolonialherrschaft aus dem Umfeld Fritz Fischers, und die haben wir verschlungen." ("It goes without saying that the Wissmann action was part of the Vietnam context, but at the same time we already had the first critical historical studies on German colonial rule by historians associated with Fritz Fischer, and those we devoured.")

18. Rudi Dutschke, "Die geschichtlichen Bedingungen für den internationalen Emanzipationskampf" (Speech at the International Vietnam Congress in West Berlin, February 1968), in Dutschke, *Geschichte ist machbar* (Berlin: Wagenbach, 1980), pp. 105–21.
19. Zeller, *Kolonialdenkmäler und Geschichtsbewußtsein*, p. 208.
20. *Das Leben ändern, die Welt verändern!* ed. by Lutz Schulenburg (Hamburg: Edition Nautilus, 1998), p. 79.
21. The film-maker Theo Gallehr had followed the preceding debates and caught the happening on celluloid. His documentary film "Landfriedensbruch" was produced by the *Norddeutscher Rundfunk* (NDR), but not broadcast. It stayed in the archives until 1988, when it was shown on NDR3 to mark the twentieth anniversary of the student revolt.
22. In a letter to the author, Karl Heinz Roth recalls how a group of students had "prepared" the scene to ensure that the statue would definitely fall this time: "Wissmann wurde 1967 zweimal angegangen, zuerst als Happening, was zu Festnahmen und Strafverfolgung führte. Wir haben uns dann dadurch 'gerächt', dass wir ein zweites 'Happening' ankündigten, bei dem wie beim erstenmal Wissmann symbolisch eine Leine um den Hals geworfen werden sollte. In der Nacht zuvor haben wir aber die Beine angesägt und die zentrale Stellschraube gelockert, sodass das Denkmal zur Verblüffung aller beim ersten Zug am Seil umstürzte. Die Verwirrung war so groß, dass die Polizeieinheiten 'vergaßen', die Seilzieher wie beim erstenmal festzunehmen. Die 'Happening'-Leute wussten natürlich nichts von unserer kleinen Aktionsgruppe." ("In 1967 we had two attempts to topple Wissmann: the first one was a 'happening' which led to arrests and prosecutions. We took our 'revenge' by announcing a second 'happening' when we would once again, symbolically, put a rope around his neck. However, in the night before we had sawed away at the legs and loosened the central screw that connected the statue to the plinth, so that the statue, to the great astonishment of all, fell over as soon as we tugged the rope. The confusion was so great that the police 'forgot' to arrest those who had pulled the rope. The 'happening' people had had no knowledge of our little action group.")
23. Zeller, *Kolonialdenkmäler und Geschichtsbewußtsein*, p. 212.
24. Peter Schütt, "Der Denkmalssturz." Helmut Bley, currently Professor of African History in Hannover, has continued to influence the debate to the present day. See also Jürgen Zimmerer, *Von Windhuk nach Auschwitz. Beiträge zum Verhältnis von Kolonialismus und Holocaust* (Münster: LIT, 2008).
25. The five defendants were found guilty and sentenced to prison, but the amnesty for minor offences during the student revolt declared by Willy Brandt's new government in 1969 came into force before they had to start their terms.
26. *Die Welt*, 2 November 1968.
27. Reprinted in: Autorenkollektiv Allgemeiner Studentenausschuss (ASTA) an der Universität Hamburg, *Das permanente Kolonialinstitut*, p. 239.
28. A famous example is the incident at the *Rektoratsfeier* (inauguration of University President) in Hamburg in November 1967, when neatly dressed students unfurled a banner in front of the procession that read "Unter den Talaren der Muff von 1000 Jahren" (Beneath the robes, the stench of a thousand years). One of the professors was so incensed that he shouted: "Sie gehören alle ins KZ!" ("You should all be sent into a concentration camp"). Cf. Autorenkollektiv Allgemeiner Studentenausschuss (ASTA) an der Universität Hamburg, *Das permanente Kolonialinstitut*, p. 29.
29. Uwe Timm, *Heißer Sommer* (1974) (Munich: DTV, 1998), p. 143 (hereafter referred to as HS).

30. See my "Long Memories. The German Student Movement in Recent Fiction," *German Life and Letters*, 56.1 (January 2003), 89–101.
31. Uwe Timm, *Rot* (Cologne: Kiepenheuer & Witsch, 2001), p. 103 (hereafter referred to as R).
32. Uwe Timm, *Deutsche Kolonien*, Autorenedition (1981) (Cologne: Kiepenheuer & Witsch, 2001), p. 10. The book mostly contains images of the colonized, and challenges the viewer to see German occupation through their eyes.
33. "Deutschland entschuldigt sich für Kolonialverbrechen", *Der Spiegel* online, 15 August 2004, <http://www.spiegel.de/politik/ausland/0,1518,druck-313373,00.html> [accessed 4 January 2008].
34. See also an interview with Wieczoreck-Zeul: "Ich fand, es war an der Zeit", *Weserkurier*, 26 September 2004, <http://www.bmz.de/de/presse/reden/ministerin/rede20040926.html> [accessed 4 January 2008].
35. See <http://www.zdf.de/ZDFde/inhalt/26/0,1872,2372506,00.html> [accessed 4 January 2008].
36. Gisela Graichen, "Deutsche Kolonien—Traum und Trauma," <http://www.zdf.de/ZDFde/inhalt/22/0,1872,2383862,00.html> [accessed 4 January 2008]. Graichen backs up her rather sanctimonious statement by citing the passage from Uwe Timm's *Deutsche Kolonien* (p. 10).
37. For example, "Namibia—Deutschland. Eine geteilte Geschichte", at the German Historical Museum in Berlin (November 2004 to April 2005), <http://www.dhm.de/ausstellungen/namibia/index.html> [accessed 4 January 2008].
38. Cf. "Deutschland postcolonial," <http://www.deutschland-postkolonial.de> [accessed 1 February 2008].
39. See <http://www.hamburg-postkolonial.de> [accessed 4 January 2008].
40. Gernot Knödler, "Denkmäler am Pranger," *die tageszeitung*, 21 February 2006, <http://www.taz.de/pt/2006/02/21/a0268.1/textdruck> [accessed 4 January 2008].
41. See <www.afrika-hamburg.de> [accessed 4 January 2008]. A critical review of the website by Larissa Förster can be found at <http://hsozkult.geschichte.hu-berlin.de/rezensionen/id=127&type=rezwww> [accessed 4 January 2008].
42. Jonas Berhe, "Geschichte dekodieren," *die tageszeitung*, 29 September 2004.
43. Hans-Joachim von Leesen, "Kampf gegen die Vergangenheit," *Junge Freiheit*, 21 May 2004.
44. See <http://www.afrika-hamburg.de/parkd.k.html> [accessed 4 January 2008].
45. Jochen Arp, "'Schmelzt ihn ein.' Linke Gruppen möchten Wissmann-Denkmal entfernen," *Preußische Allgemeine Zeitung* 11 March 2006, <http://www.webarchiv-server.de/pin/archiv06/1020060311paz12.htm> [accessed 4 January 2008].
46. Joachim Zeller, "(Post-)Koloniale Monumente: Denkmalinitiativen erinnern an die imperiale Übersee-Expansion Deutschlands," <http://www.afrika-hamburg.de/denkmal5.html> [accessed 4 January 2008].
47. Priyamvada Gopal, "The story peddled by imperial apologists is a poisonous fairytale," *The Guardian*, 28 June 2006, p. 30.
48. Cf. Sidney Tarrow, "Banging the Post-Colonial Drum: George Steinmetz's Imagined European Studies," <http://www.columbia.edu/cu/ces/pub/Tarrow_june03.html> [accessed 4 January 2008], and, in response, George Steinmetz, "Drums in the Postcolonial Night," <http://www.columbia.edu/cu/ces/pub/Steinmetz_june03.html> [accessed 4 January 2008].
49. Speitkamp, *Deutsche Kolonialgeschichte*, p. 186.
50. Uwe Timm, *Erzählen und kein Ende* (Cologne: Kiepenheuer & Witsch, 1993), p. 106f.

51. Hermann von Wissmann, *African Highlife 1888: Bei den bekifften Bena Riamba in Lubuku. Breit unter deutscher Flagge im Namen des Kaisers Wilhelm durchs Haschischparadies* (Löhrbach: Pieper und die Grüne Kraft, 2000).

# 16 *Vergangenheitsbewältigung à la française*
## Post-Colonial Memories of the Herero Genocide and 17 October 1961

*Kathryn Jones*

In 2004, the centenary year of the Herero genocide in Namibia, an unprecedented level of attention was paid to the German colonial past. Debates were given a new dynamic, and the longstanding veil of amnesia covering German colonial legacies seemed to have been partly lifted, even if perhaps only temporarily. Demonstrating the influence of a new wave of historical research on media debates, most journalists accepted and frequently employed the term "genocide" to refer to the colonial violence perpetrated by the German army in 1904. Alongside a series of newspaper articles and numerous radio and television contributions, seven exhibitions played an important part in raising public awareness of the anniversary. A number of disparate civil initiatives and ceremonies took place on a non-official level in several different cities across Germany in 2004. These were organized by human rights and international solidarity groups such as the *Gesellschaft für bedrohte Völker*, the Global African Congress, the specially formed umbrella group *Erinnern—Deutsche Kolonialgeschichte aufarbeiten*, and church organizations.[1] Many of these small-scale ceremonies and commemorative actions focused on memorial landscapes and visual memory, engaging with existing colonial monuments in Bremen and Hamburg and street names in Munich and Berlin. However, the event perceived as the real milestone of the centenary occurred not in Germany but in Namibia, during the ceremony held in Okakarara on August 14 2004 to commemorative the decisive Waterberg battle of the Herero war.[2] In the course of her speech, the socialist German development minister, Heidemarie Wieczorek-Zeul, expressly characterized the colonial atrocities as a *Völkermord* and recognized Germany's historico-political and moral-ethical responsibility. Although the minister asked for forgiveness for Germany's guilt, her statement of repentance was also carefully worded in order to avoid any commitment to the payment of reparations, as demanded by Herero campaigners. None the less, following previous refusals by German state representatives to recognize Germany's responsibility for the genocide, the semi-official apology indicated a significant change in policy.

This chapter offers a comparative perspective on these recent attempts at coming to terms with the German colonial past by reference to parallel debates in France. The semi-official apology by Wieczorek-Zeul for the 1904 genocide of the Herero, Nama, Damara and San peoples and the commemorative activities held in Germany during 2004 is contrasted with a long-term campaign by pressure groups for a similar act of contrition by the French authorities regarding the brutal repression of an Algerian war protest in Paris on 17 October 1961, which is now referred to as a massacre. The commemoration of both these atrocities has played a vital role in recent discussions on French and German colonial legacies as perpetrator nations. The final few years of the twentieth century witnessed a gradual change in the emphasis of French memory debates regarding the Algerian War, from official amnesia and silence to private testimony, public commemoration and multi-faceted representation. France's famed memorial obsession is now focused to a greater extent on its colonial heritage, which has moved from the periphery to the centre of memory debates. The chapter highlights the interplay between official and civil agents of memory and the changing hierarchies of memory, and thereby analyzes important commonalities and differences in the re-emergence of French and German colonial memories with reference to two emblematic events. Such an approach provides new perspectives and illuminates common patterns of remembrance, indicating how studies which move beyond a narrow national framework allow for a more nuanced view of responses toward colonial legacies. The need for a transnational approach becomes particularly apparent in the context of a "globalization" of concepts of memory.[3]

At the same time, it is also imperative to underline key differences between the German and French colonial memory contexts. Algeria and France were engaged in a lengthy and bloody war of decolonization, which only ended in 1962, and the fact that some of the war's historical actors are still alive (and are also voters) leads to a very different dynamic for memory debates. The longer duration of French colonial rule and the greater proximity of the Algerian War in time and place, together with the presence of competing memory groups in French society, contribute toward the difficulty of achieving a cohesive national memory of the event. These groups include former soldiers, *harkis* (Algerian auxiliary soldiers in the French army and police), the Algerian independence movements *Front de Libération National* (FLN) (National Liberation Front) and *Mouvement National Algérien* (Algerian National Movement), the 1 million French settlers who were repatriated to France after Algerian independence and, most significantly, Algerian immigrants in France and their descendants. Their conflicting experiences mean that Algerian war memories are characterized by division. These factors signified that, unlike in the case of Germany, there was not a widespread perception that France was morally unencumbered (*unbelastet* is the German term) as a colonial power.

The brutal repression of a pacifist protest by 30,000 Algerian men, women and children in the heart of Paris on 17 October 1961 has by now become emblematic, due to the light it sheds on state-sponsored cover-ups and amnesia about French colonial history.[4] In the context of a period of intensified attacks and reprisals between the police, the FLN and the anti-independence terrorist group *Organisation de l'Armée Secrète* (OAS) (Secret Army Organization) toward the end of the Algerian war, the protest had been organized by the FLN in favor of independence and in defiance of a curfew recently imposed on Algerians in Paris. Headed by Maurice Papon, the Paris police were authorized to use all available means to stop this perceived threat to the French capital and nation. The unarmed demonstrators were beaten and shot by the police, and many were thrown into the Seine and left to drown. A further 11,538 Algerian men were rounded up and held in sports stadia, and hundreds of arrested Algerians were deported to prison camps in Algeria until the end of the war. According to the official version of events, only 3 protesters were killed and 64 injured, but the exact number of those who died that night and the extent of government responsibility remain matters of considerable dispute among historians to this day, with recent estimates ranging from 30 to 200 dead. The true extent of the police brutality was hidden by official state silence, all judicial investigations were blocked, a series of amnesties concerning the Algerian War were passed, and the event disappeared from public discussion very quickly. This was the most public of France's colonial atrocities, as it was the only one to be carried out in the heart of the French capital, and as such the government felt it was imperative to cover up the massacre in the name of national cohesion.

It was not until the early 1980s that the event resurfaced, due to the work of memory activists and a series of written and film narratives. In the absence of official commemoration of the atrocity, it was left to oppositional forms of memory and civil initiatives to ensure that the event would be brought back into the consciousness of the French public, and a parallel can be seen here with the civil initiatives that took place in Germany in 2004. A number of anti-racist and immigrant associations functioned as key agents of memory in initiating a long-term campaign for official recognition of the massacre, and they were joined by left-wing groups and minor political parties during the course of the 1980s. The campaign has therefore been a broader-based and a longer-scale enterprise in comparison to the calls for an apology in 2004 by human-rights and church organizations in Germany. In the latter instance, calls for an official apology were strongest in the former colony itself, and came mainly from Herero representatives rather than the Namibian government. As would be the case with the Herero genocide, larger-scale commemoration and public awareness of France's colonial legacy would only come with advances in the field of historiography, that is, with a marked increase in studies on the French colonial past from the beginning of the 1990s: the first major commemoration of the 17 October massacre, on its 30th anniversary in 1991, was accompanied by the publication of several full-length historical studies dealing with the repression of the protest.

In recent years, campaigners have joined forces to form the 17 October 1961 Collective, a broad-based umbrella group encompassing around 20 organizations, which include immigrant associations, human-rights and anti-racist organizations such as *Mouvement contre le racisme et pour l'amitié entre les peuples* (MRAP) (Movement Against Racism and for Friendship Between Peoples) and *La Ligue des droits de l'homme* (Human Rights League), trade unions, and several left-wing political parties, as well as a number of memory groups with a specific focus on the legacy of colonialism, such as *Au nom de la mémoire* (In the Name of Memory), and *Devoirs de mémoires* (Duties of Remembrance).[5] For campaigning groups, the 17 October massacre has a wider contemporary symbolism, as they maintain that it links previous forms of racism to present hostility toward Maghrebi migrants and their descendants. The demand for official recognition is therefore connected to issues of equality, political representation and citizenship. As the historians Jim House and Neil MacMaster have noted, the memory of October 17 1961 is, for activists, a "strategic resource in the contestation of racism in France."[6] Calls by campaigners have included the official condemnation of the true extent of the massacre and its recognition as a crime against humanity committed by the French state. They have also called for the creation of a memorial site for the victims, and for changes to the 1979 archive law in order to allow historians access to key documents relating to the Algerian war, as well as its inclusion in school syllabuses.

Precedents do exist in France for the official recognition and condemnation of state atrocities, most notably in the case of World War Two, with President Jacques Chirac's official acceptance in 1995 of state responsibility for the role played by the Vichy regime in the deportation of Jews from France;[7] activists have been highly critical of this disparity between the acceptance of France's complicity in the Holocaust and its continuing reluctance to face up to its colonial past. Similarly, the issue of slavery was deemed sufficiently remote and uncontroversial to allow for a law to be passed in May 2001 condemning slavery as a crime against humanity. Moreover, when the French government made the denial of the Armenian genocide a criminal offence in 2006 and urged Turkey formally to recognize the genocide, campaigners were quick to highlight official French eagerness to pass memorial laws condemning some crimes against humanity, but not those committed in the French colonial context.

As in the case of Germany, where many of the debates regarding the Herero genocide have focused on the issue of the singularity of the Holocaust and possible continuities between the two German genocides, the filter of the Vichy regime and the Holocaust was needed for the French state to break its silence on the events of 17 October 1961. This state action has come from political and judicial officials, though not from the very highest representatives of the state, and a clear parallel can be seen here with the apology made by Wieczorek-Zeul. French reluctance officially to recognize 17 October 1961 as a massacre and accept state responsibility continues to be common to both left- and right-wing governments at the highest level. As with the Herero compensation claim in 2001, judicial proceedings were instrumental in initiating a state response, in spite of the fact that, due to France's comprehensive amnesty legislation, no direct legal recourse regarding 17 October 1961 is possible. Even though his actions as the Paris prefect of police were not the formal focus of the 1997–8 trial of the high-ranking government and civil service figure Maurice Papon for the deportation of Jews from Bordeaux during World War Two, the trial did bring a new spotlight on the 17 October demonstration, and some commentators even spoke of a trial within a trial. Although Papon had effectively stifled any judicial investigation in 1961, ironically his decision to sue the historian Jean-Luc Einaudi for libel, disputing his claim that Algerians had been killed by the police "under the orders of M. Papon," had the effect of drawing renewed attention to the events of October 17. The libel case in February 1999 marked a significant step in terms of official recognition, as, for the first time, the state, through the deputy public prosecutor and the judge, accepted the use of the term "massacre" to describe the repression of the protest in October 1961. In the light of these judicial proceedings, Lionel Jospin's government was forced to acknowledge that the official narrative could no longer stand unchallenged. The Mandelkern and Geronimi reports of 1998 and 1999, which were based on documents available in the interior and justice ministry archives, revised the number of dead to 32 and 48, respectively, though several historians continue to dispute these figures. More archives were opened up to researchers when a law was passed in May 1999 to facilitate historical research, but access is still restricted in some cases.[8]

These developments paved the way for the unprecedented media attention given to the massacre on its 40th anniversary in 2001. The anniversary provided the impetus for a new wave of publications, including six historical works and several novels, and there were exhibitions, theater productions, writers' workshops, film screenings and debates.[9] Yet in contrast to Germany in 2004, when eleven conferences and symposia were held as well as a series of lectures, discussions and seminars, there was comparatively little focus on academic activity in France. It is estimated that between 5,000 and 8,000 people participated in a commemorative march along one of the routes taken by the 1961 protestors. The socialist mayor, Bertrand Delanoë, broke the silence of the Paris municipal government when he unveiled a commemorative plaque on the Pont St Michel opposite the Paris police headquarters, bearing the inscription: "A la mémoire des nombreux Algériens tués lors de la sanglante répression de la manifestation pacifique du 17 octobre 1961" (In memory of the numerous Algerians killed during the bloody repression of the peaceful demonstration of 17 October 1961). Campaigners hailed it as a major step forward which they hoped would lead to the event becoming a part of French collective memory. Yet, while attesting to the increased visibility of the massacre in the public sphere, this ceremony also demonstrated the extent to which memories of the Algerian war and their moral associations continue to be divided along political lines. The ceremony took place in a tense atmosphere, having been boycotted by the right-wing municipal opposition, who called the plaque "selective" and a provocation; and the extreme right staged a counter-demonstration on the other side of the bridge.[10] Moreover, the inscription itself elided both the role of the Parisian police in the repression of the protest and the number of dead, as the council had failed to agree on a less ambiguous wording.

The Paris memorial continues to be controversial, as the plaque has been repeatedly defaced and damaged, and has had to be replaced several times since its inauguration. The frequency of media references to the role played by Delanoë implied that this was a one-man crusade by a politician who had included the inauguration of the plaque in his list of election pledges. Similarly, the impression that the German development minister had acted as an individual was reinforced by the lack of national official ceremonies or memorials in the Federal Republic itself in 2004. The German parliament confined its action to a resolution passed on 17 January 2004 that commemorated all victims of the colonial war in German South-West Africa but avoided the term genocide, and expressed regret without offering an apology.

In comparison to France, official responses to Germany's colonial past have not created real divisions along political lines. Although a few dissenting viewpoints were heard from right-wing politicians who feared that Wieczorek-Zeul's apology would facilitate expensive compensation payouts, the gesture was generally accepted as appropriate and timely, and did not trigger further widespread debate. In spite of the unprecedented media attention given to the 100th anniversary of the Herero war in 2004, concerns have been raised that its impact on German memory discourses may prove to be rather short-lived, and that a broad public consciousness and acceptance of Germany's colonial guilt has not yet materialized. Just over a year after the development minister's words of national repentance in Namibia, the historian Jürgen Zimmerer, in an article published by the *tageszeitung* newspaper, offered a strong critique of the continuity of colonial amnesia and the absence of the colonial past in current memory debates in Germany.[11] He maintained that the government had failed to involve German civil society in the process of dealing with legacies of colonialism, and he emphasized the need for broad discussion about the effects of German colonialism in order to make up for the lack of effect of the apology, which had remained solely an act of state.

In the case of France, although campaigners had hoped that the inauguration of the first commemorative plaque in 2001 would pave the way toward official recognition and condemnation of the massacre on a national level, now—almost a decade on—initiatives remain mainly on a local footing. Even so, the unveiling of plaques similar to that on the Pont St Michel in several Parisian suburbs, together with the naming of a street, square and *métro* station in the suburbs of La Courneuve, Saint-Denis and Genn-evilliers after the massacre, may be indicative of a new emphasis on visual memory, as campaigners attempt to inscribe the date of the massacre into the French landscape. Despite the continuing state silence regarding the events of 17 October 1961, the massacre has not retreated into the background, and to some extent its commemoration has taken on a new life.

The final part of this chapter examines some of the reasons why the memorial process has not ground to a halt since the 40th anniversary in 2001, and explores how the French situation offers both a positive model and a cautionary tale for Germany. Unlike the case of Germany after 2004, the annual commemoration of 17 October 1961 in France was well established, with structures in place to allow annual rituals of remembrance to carry on. The annual ceremonies on October 17, with several hundred participants on average, have provided a forum for repeated calls for the official recognition of the massacre by the highest authorities of the Republic, and this is the only one of the campaigners' main demands that has yet to be realized. House and MacMaster maintain that such memory activism focuses on the "politics of symbolic reparation" in the absence of the possibility of direct judicial proceedings.[12] The prolonged state silence should be contrasted with a growing public awareness of the event. Its annual commemoration continues to receive media coverage, and a series of literary and filmic narratives thematizing the massacre have appeared, including a major feature film, *Nuit Noire* (Dark Night), which was released in 2005. It is now part of the baccalaureate history syllabus, and is included in some school textbooks of modern French history, although not all.

The range of commemorative activities and agents of memory has therefore been broader in France than in Germany. The differing dynamics of commemoration in France and Germany result predominantly from the presence or absence in the metropole of victim groups and their descendants, which has led to a French focus on oppositional memory activism rather than to reconciliatory initiatives, as in Germany. The key role played in the campaigns by second- and third-generation descendants of Algerian immigrants, for whom the massacre has become a foundational event for familial memory and identity formation, has been a crucial factor in ensuring the continuity of its commemoration within French society. So, too, has the location of the 17 October 1961 massacre, in the heart of the French capital rather than in the former colony. By contrast, the absence of a Namibian immigrant community within Germany has meant that, with the exception of a few small-scale human-rights groups, demands for official recognition of colonial atrocities have come from elsewhere.

There are clear signs that 17 October 1961 has become part of the memorial fabric of French society within a changing context of wider debates. This historical event is now used as a contemporary point of reference, as France addresses issues concerning immigration, integration and social justice. During civil unrest in France's suburbs in November

2005, commentators were quick to point out that the government had re-introduced a curfew law last deployed during the Algerian war in Paris, and several references were made to painful continuities with the events of 17 October 1961. The commemoration of this massacre has provided the impetus for calls for the official recognition of other marginalized colonial atrocities, such as the massacres by the French army and colonial police of several thousand Algerians demonstrating in favor of independence at Sétif and Guelma on 8 May 1945.[13] In February 2005, the French ambassador to Algeria paid homage to the memory of the victims by laying a wreath at the Sétif memorial, and he explicitly condemned the massacres, calling them "an inexcusable tragedy." In a further reconciliatory move, in July 2005, during a state visit to Madagascar, the French President, Jacques Chirac, recognized the "unacceptable character" and "tragic events" of the repression by French colonial forces of a pro-liberation uprising in March 1947, which resulted in the deaths of many thousands of Madagascans, although he refrained from using the term "massacre."[14]

It is instructive to note that both these gestures took place on foreign soil in the former colonies, and were not repeated in metropolitan France, and a comparison can be drawn here with the German apology in Namibia. In any case, there is a clear divide between these reconciliatory gestures abroad and the more hard-line stance of the right-wing government regarding the colonial past that has inflamed political and public memory debates. A law was passed on 23 February 2005 officially to honor and compensate those responsible for administering and controlling France's former colonies, including French settlers in Algeria, the *harkis* and members of the OAS terrorist group. A last-minute amendment to the law proved particularly controversial. Article 4 proclaimed, "School curricula recognize in particular the positive role of the French presence overseas, notably in North Africa." Such political discourses advocating the benefits of colonization seemed a decisive move away from the possibility of official recognition of colonial atrocities such as the 17 October massacre, and the state was accused of perpetuating colonial amnesia, of glorifying French colonial history and suppressing its darker episodes. However, the discussions that followed have ensured that France's colonial past is being debated as never before. Campaigners against the law repeatedly drew on the example of 17 October and its subsequent cover-up, and the commemorative ceremony in 2005 provided a focal point for protests against the law. The massacre was now being evoked in the context of wide-ranging debates on French engagement with its colonial past, the question of official history, and also the role of historians and teachers. Article 4 was eventually repealed in February 2006 after months of acrimonious parliamentary and public debates, which demonstrated the extent to which the wounds of the Algerian war remain open.[15]

Criticism of the law also came from abroad, and this international context increased the temperature of already heated memory debates. The law's strongest critic was Algeria, which in 2005 had been in the process of negotiations to sign a friendship treaty with France. The negotiations became a platform for discussions of the shared colonial past rather than of future cooperation, as the Algerian president Abdelaziz Bouteflika became increasingly vocal in his calls for France to sign a statement of repentance for crimes committed during its colonial rule in Algeria. It was reported that France had accepted the principle of apologizing to the former colony, but President Chirac needed to be seen to avoid what was termed "unilateral repentance," and had hoped to include a reference in the treaty to the murders of 15–20,000 *harkis* after Algerian independence. The issue proved to be insurmountable, and the repeated accusations of colonial genocide by the Algerian president contributed to a diplomatic crisis and ultimately to the failure to sign the friendship treaty.

It could be suggested that the discussion of the French colonial past as part of both internal and foreign political debates is one important factor in the new prominence now given to colonial legacies in France. By contrast, German official memory has externalized the colonial past by perceiving it primarily as a question of foreign policy, and the government's continued inability to change the terms of debates away from the donation of development aid could be seen as contributing toward the marginalization of colonial legacies in Germany. None the less, the unwillingness of the French state to ask forgiveness for its colonial past emphasizes how unusual and remarkable the apology by the German development minister in August 2004 was, despite concerns regarding its longer-term impact on German (though not Namibian) memory cultures, and despite the postponement of the German–Namibian state-level reconciliation initiative. It could almost be said that the German government's apology came too early, and, due to the lack of a broad social consensus behind it in Germany, it may have served, intentionally or otherwise, to draw a kind of line under Germany's colonial past.

In France, paradoxically, it is precisely the lack of official recognition that has led to the continued high-profile presence of October 17 in memory debates. French civil society has been instrumental in taking the memorial initiative, and has subsequently reacted strongly to state-led actions such as laws and treaties. Both October 17 and the Herero genocide are now used as yardsticks for measuring the recognition and commemoration of other colonial atrocities or their absence, such as the Sétif and Guelma massacres and the Maji-Maji war, for which no comparable official apology has been forthcoming.[16] It could be argued that the process started by the commemoration and discussion of October 17 has contributed toward the re-emergence of other memory groups, such as repatriates and the *harkis*, and other issues such as the use of torture by the French army and the unequal treatment of foreign conscripts.

French colonial memory is now coming to the forefront of memory discourses, and there are repeated signs of a new critical engagement with the

French colonial past and a new memorial militancy, with the actions of radical movements such as *Les Indigènes de la République* (The Indigenous People of the Republic) hitting the headlines. In a speech made on France's first slavery remembrance day, held on 10 May 2006, Jacques Chirac maintained that "facing up to France's colonial past is key to national cohesion." 2011 will mark the 50th anniversary of 17 October 1961, and it can be anticipated that calls for its official recognition as a crime against humanity will increase substantially in the run-up to this anniversary. By contrast, it is difficult to see ways in which the Herero genocide will return to German public consciousness to a similar extent unless or until it can be linked to wider debates regarding the legacies of Germany's colonial past.

## NOTES

1. For an overview of these commemorative activities, see Joachim Zeller, "Genozid und Gedenken. Ein dokumentarischer Überblick," in *Genozid und Gedenken*, ed. by Henning Melber (Frankfurt/M.: Brandes & Apsel, 2005), pp. 163–88.
2. See Reinhart Kössler, "La fin d'une amnésie? L'Allemagne et son passé colonial depuis 2004," *Politique Africaine*, 1.102 (2006), 50–66, for an analysis of Wieczorek-Zeul's apology.
3. Christine Deslaurier and Aurélie Roger, "Mémoires grises. Pratiques politiques du passé colonial entre Europe et Afrique," *Politique Africaine*, 1.102 (2006), 5–27 (p. 18). The journal provides an instructive example of the benefits of a trans-national approach.
4. For detailed accounts of the events of October 17 1961, see Jean-Luc Einaudi, *La Bataille de Paris: 17 octobre 1961* (Paris: Seuil, 1991), and his *Octobre 1961: un massacre à Paris* (Paris: Fayard, 2001); Joshua Cole, "Remembering the Battle of Paris: 17 October 1961 in French and Algerian Memory," *French Politics, Culture and Society*, 21.3 (2003), 21–50; and the excellent analysis of the events and afterlives of 17 October 1961 by Jim House and Neil MacMaster, *Paris 1961: Algerians, State Terror, and Memory* (Oxford: Oxford University Press, 2006).
5. Like the *Deutschland postkolonial* forum and the *afrika-hamburg.de* network, which are indicative of a new focus on internet sites for debating German colonial history, these recently formed campaigning groups maintain an important web presence.
6. Jim House and Neil MacMaster, "'Une journée portée disparue': The Paris Massacre of 1961 and Memory," in *Crisis and Renewal in France 1918–1962*, ed. by Kenneth Mouré and Martin S. Alexander (Oxford: Berghahn, 2002), pp. 267–90 (p. 280).
7. See Sandrine Lefranc, *Politiques du pardon* (Paris: Presses universitaires de France, 2002).
8. See House and MacMaster, *Paris 1961*, pp. 8–13.
9. See Cole, "Remembering the Battle of Paris," pp. 44 and 49.
10. See Brigitte Jelen, "17 octobre 1961—17 octobre 2001: Une commémoration ambiguë," *French Politics, Culture & Society*, 20.1 (2002), 30–43.
11. Jürgen Zimmerer, "Die verordnete Versöhnung," *die tageszeitung*, 19 September 2005, p. 12.
12. House and MacMaster, *Paris 1961*, p. 314.

13. Historians have discredited both the initial official death toll of 1,500 issued by the French interior ministry in 1945 and the Algerian government's claims of 45,000 dead, but as yet, due to the slow emergence of impartial historical research and a lack of documentation, no consensus has been reached regarding more accurate figures.

14. Until recently the Madagascan authorities estimated the number of dead to be 100,000, and their revised figure of 89,000 dead was accepted by Jacques Chirac during his 2005 visit. Based on the few documents in existence, historians such as Jean Fremigacci have argued that the true death toll was, rather, between 20,000 and 30,000.

15. See Peter Dunwoodie, "Postface: History, Memory and Identity—Today's Crisis, Yesterday's Issue," *French History*, 20.3 (2006), 318–32.

16. As well as a *Gedenkveranstaltung*, three conferences dealing with the Maji-Maji war were held in Germany in 2005. See Rafael Binkowski, "Erinnerung an ein deutsches Massaker," *die tageszeitung*, 27 August 2005, p. 27.

# 17 The Persistence of Fantasies
## Colonialism as Melodrama on German Television

*Wolfgang Struck*

In January 2000, one of the leading public TV channels in Germany, the ZDF, broadcast a film that was rather unusual at that time: *Die Wüstenrose* (The Desert Rose), a feature-length, prime-time historical melodrama set in colonial South-West Africa, is the first fictional film explicitly depicting a German colony since the adaptation of Uwe Timm's novel *Morenga* shown by the WDR, another major public channel, in 1985. But, unlike this rather elitist piece of art, *Die Wüstenrose* was successfully aimed at a mass audience. Its first screening, in January 2000, was viewed by 12 million people, and it has since been repeated several times in both Germany and Austria.

As an introduction to the first screening, the ZDF magazine program *Hallo Deutschland* announced an interview with one of the leading actors as follows:

> There are women who've only ever watched [the series] *Girlfriends* for one reason: not for the girls—women always think they're better themselves than the ones they see on TV. No, it's for [the actor] Walter Sittler. He plays a character called Ronaldo, and seeing him gives them suggestive thoughts by the dozen. And if that's the case just with a 45-minute series, how will these viewers cope with the two parts of *Die Wüstenrose*—3 hours in all? Here, there's no end of Walter Sittler, and in a colonial uniform, too.[1]

Why, was my first reaction to this announcement (and still is my question), why should we (or at least the female Walter Sittler fan—admittedly, an alien species to me) view a colonial uniform as enhancing a womanizer's attractiveness? Even though uniforms currently seem a little more fashionable than, say, 20 years ago, Germany still does not appear to be a particularly militarized and uniform-loving country. Also, colonialism does not generally conjure proud memories. The 2005 ZDF documentary *Deutsche Kolonien*, for example, may be dubious in its racial stereotyping, but it does not (at least not openly or intentionally) promote a positive memory of colonialism. And this is also true of *Die Wüstenrose*. Of course, the

ZDF does not propose the re-establishment of a colonial empire, even if its popular productions do not seriously criticize colonialism. But what else can explain the attraction attributed to the colonial uniform?

The aforementioned interview with Walter Sittler gives a first hint, by emphasizing the beauty and loneliness of the Namibian landscape, thus promising a journey into a more elementary world of male adventure, with horse riding, hunting and the overcoming of dangers. But that explains neither why this world is linked to colonialism, nor why there has to be a uniform that seems to highlight the setting's aggressive aspects. Indeed, in the film, Sittler plays a civilian farmer, so he does not in fact wear a uniform at all. Why announce it, then?

I wish to propose an answer that can be partially found in *Die Wüstenrose* itself. I therefore offer a brief reading of the film and outline a specific concept of fantasy on which my argumentation is based, a concept I find useful not only for an analysis of the film, but also for the discussion of national identity.

The atmosphere of the film owes much to the Namibian landscape, depicted as a territory of wide expanses, nature and wildlife, and as providing the setting for a story of romance and adventure. The story begins with the arrival of the two female protagonists in Swakopmund in 1908. Henriette Laroche (played by Mariella Ahrens) is to marry a wealthy farmer; Klara von Sellin (Birge Schade) becomes an assistant doctor at the local hospital. Soon, both young women are confronted with unexpected racism on the part of colonial society. Klara loses her job because she ignores the hospital director's strict order and treats a seriously wounded African boy. Henriette is shocked by the sadistic brutality her new husband exercises against his African workers, particularly by the cruel whipping of a man (shown in full detail), which she herself has unintentionally caused. In the end, however, the heroines will not only find personal happiness in the colony, but also succeed in establishing a new, more humane order.

At that point, the two characters who represent colonial violence are both dead. The first, a young lieutenant of the *Schutztruppe*, veteran and hardliner of the military campaign against the Herero and Nama, shoots himself; this is after Klara, who is initially attracted by his masculine charm, rejects him once he has raped her. The other, Henriette's husband, who turns out to be the story's real villain, dies during a severe attack of tropical disease (*Tropenkoller*). He climbs the tower of his would-be castle, declares himself master of the world, and falls, when trying to unfold the entangled national flag. Thus, the over-excited nationalist is brought down to earth; this is an exorcism, in which the death and consequent absence of the single figure in whom all the colonial evil seems to be concentrated opens up opportunities for new relationships between Africans and Germans. Henriette comes to lead the farm as a fair employer, partner and friend to her African workers. And Klara will overcome the racial prejudices of her old superior and build up a hospital for Africans. The Germans stay, but they change their role from imperialist aggressor to *Entwicklungshelfer* (voluntary foreign aid worker), who brings money and know-how to the poor, undeveloped country.

This, of course, does not affect the hierarchy between colonizers and colonized: the film shows the African population as completely controlled by German rule. But this rule is also highly individualized. Its negative, cruel aspects are shown as isolated acts of violence. The paradigmatic victim, the whipped man, for example, finds himself forced into an almost ritualistic, sado-masochistically inspired scenario, caused by—what else could it be?—trouble with women, and providing a good look at his naked, bleeding body. What we do not see are the more systematic forms of oppression, such as identification marks, forced labor in chains, or the concentration camp in Swakopmund, which was still being utilized in 1908 to hold the victims of the Herero war[2]—a conflict that, in the world of *Die Wüstenrose*, is merely a remote, almost faded memory. What we see instead, the individual suffering, can also be overcome by individuals, in the same way that Klara treated and healed the wounds which had been inflicted by the whipping.

In the end, all conflicts are resolved. In 2000, German television had apparently already found an answer to the question of compensation which was raised one year later by the lawsuit filed by the Herero against some German companies and the German state: everything has already been done to heal the wounds of this war, so *Die Wüstenrose* suggests by leaving its protagonists in an optimistic and affirmative situation.

Of course, this interpretation is polemical. Worse, it also misses the point, because it is in a way too abstract. The film is not intended as a political statement, or any other kind of statement. Its sole intention is entertainment. Thus, the colony primarily serves as an interesting location for a melodramatic plot in which the aim for the heroine, Klara, is neither to reach an understanding of the political situation, nor to achieve professional success and independence, but to find true love, marriage and family. Following the rules of popular narration, however, the happy ending has to be delayed, and so the heroine must first of all overcome difficulties and obstacles. These are provided by the colonial setting, which, as far as this function is concerned, has been chosen more or less randomly.

An equivalent production of the 1950s would probably have been set in the Alps or the Lüneburg Heath. Here, trouble could have been supplied by a gypsy girl or—even more exotic for the cinema of the 1950s—by an urban businesswoman. It could also, however, have been Africa, as, for example, in *Liane—Das Mädchen aus dem Urwald* (Liane—Jungle Girl) (1956), which adapts themes of colonial exoticism for the male fantasies of the 1950s and presents an African jungle in which German traders, scientists and adventurers also feel comfortably at home. A decade later, *Unser Haus in Kamerun* (Our Cameroon Home) featured a very young Götz George as a farmer in Cameroon, demonstrating that colonialism was not yet completely forgotten. A common feature shared by settings like the Alps, the heath and also the jungle is a supposed remoteness from urban modernity, which offers the notion of origin—an origin which German culture since the nineteenth century has called *Heimat* (Home/Homeland).[3] Here, as the standard plot of the most popular genre of German cinema in the 1950s and 1960s, the *Heimat* film, tells us, an endangered or even completely lost identity can be resecured by returning to this origin. *Unser Haus in Kamerun* demonstrates that this could even be found in Africa; but why Cameroon can be a home for Germans is something that the film does not explain. This is only possible on the basis of a colonial past which is not completely forgotten, but is remembered in a way that neglects the further historical context of decolonization. And precisely this characterizes *Heimat* in the sense of the *Heimat*-film: it seems to be untouched by time and history. It can thus provide the source of a more authentic identity, for which the *Heimat*-film searches. The search for identity is, however, never a direct process, and the danger of loss is always there. Thus, *Heimat* is an ambivalent territory, a source of fear as well as of desire.

*Die Wüstenrose* shows the colony in this way: as something that is past, but is not history, a territory of the past created precisely by eliminating or simply neglecting history. At this point, the initial question recurs: why does the film use the colonial setting at all? What kind of identity is to be found there? Not very surprisingly, it is (as often in matters of origin) an "uncanny" identity, at least when viewed from the perspective of postcolonial criticism. It bears a strong resemblance to the fantasies which previously fuelled Wilhelminian colonialism itself, and which, in a broader context, Homi K. Bhabha has described as being aimed at an "'otherness' that is at once an object of desire and of derision, an articulation of difference contained within the fantasy of origin and identity."[4]

This can be observed quite clearly in the sequence of processes of displacement and disfigurement that takes place in *Die Wüstenrose*. First, the colonial topic is transposed into a sexual one. Instead of using military conflict as the source of danger required by the plot, potential risks come from a seductive, daemonic and threatening sexuality which, at the same time, is a general metaphor employed to describe "Africa." Additionally, this sexuality is identical with the fantasy of colonialism. This narrative is a (sexualized) rewriting of history which also distracts from the fact that the real issue in the setting and period in question was genocide and oppression. This is acted out in the story of the male protagonist, Richard von Salomon (Walter Sittler), who engages Klara as a housekeeper after she has lost her job at Swakopmund. In return, he offers her his help in building up her own hospital. This supposed economic agreement, supported by an equivalent view of the colonial situation as a relationship that should be based on partnership rather than on military aggression, soon turns into true love. The two protagonists are, however, unsure about their feelings and struggle with them. Only the rape and other negative experiences lead

Klara to believe that she needs male protection against the dangers the foreign country presents. She therefore finally accepts von Salomon's marriage proposal. For a modern melodrama, however, this is a somewhat problematic reason for marriage. Matters then become even more complicated when Klara finds out that she is pregnant from the rape. She does not know how to explain the situation to her husband, with whom she has, due to the trauma of the rape, not yet had sex.

At precisely the moment when von Salomon articulates his sexual frustration and is rejected by his wife, "Africa" seems to intervene to suggest that it might provide better resources for (male) desire than the civilized, academic European woman: once the argument is over and Klara has left the room, von Salomon's African housemaid enters, not only to pick up pieces of broken china, but also to give von Salomon a telling look, implying he would be better off with her. And, indeed, the housemaid was previously von Salomon's lover and has not yet been completely supplanted by his new wife. Her unfathomable but all the more seductive look, the added music and, particularly, her name, Luna, seem clearly to ascribe her to a twilight zone of unarticulated desires.[5]

This, however, is a dead end. Only a few minutes' running-time later, Luna has assumed the role of the loyal housemaid, has accepted the superiority of the farm's new mistress and is even assisting her in her fight for von Salomon's love. Such domestication of a potential source of seduction is soon followed by a scene that demonstrates remarkably explicitly the polarity of the African setting and an exclusively German narrative. Von Salomon takes Klara on a hunting safari, where the terrific landscape forms the stage for an iconography of colonial fantasies. White hunters on horseback are accompanied by a caravan of African "boys," who are not only responsible for the comfort of the white masters but also supply a romantic atmosphere to the evening desert camp. The film even uses the motif of the brave white hunter doing the Africans a great kindness by liberating them from the bloodthirsty lion—the beast that represents wildness and danger. "Lions are the kings of the country," von Salomon explains; but the sequence first of all shows the strict limitations and confines of this kingdom. Lions, African "boys" and the entire landscape are completely forgotten when the film returns to its narrative—which reaches a climax when Klara finally tells her husband about her pregnancy. How German gender trouble completely pushes aside the African setting is brought out explicitly by the use of camera effects and music. While the focus shifts from panoramic views to close-ups, the camera circles the protagonists in an ever-decreasing radius, almost literally cutting them out of the landscape. At this point, the music has also completely changed. Gone, now, is the percussion motif, which was used during the safari scene from the moment when von Salomon aimed his gun at a springbok. Here, in the way von Salomon points his gun, in a gesture that can quite clearly be seen as both aggressive and phallic, his relation to the African wilderness is once more defined as one of desire and fear, danger and joy. All this is underlined by the percussion, the same motif that has already been established in association with Luna, the African maid/lover. And all this is forgotten when the film returns to German gender trouble.

So what we have here is, *first*, an association of sexualized nature with naturalized sex (that of the African female), both of which disfigure the political reality of the colony by transforming violence into sex, sex into nature. And *second*, this nature is domesticated by the narration—domesticated, but not completely subjugated. In this distorted way, real violence is still present, but it is precisely through these processes of disfigurement that even the atrocities of colonial violence can function, or can be redefined as a source of seduction.

This is, I think, a figure already at work in the "original" colonial situation of the late nineteenth and early twentieth centuries.[6] I would like to elucidate this by taking a brief look at one of the most ambivalent characters on the German colonial stage, Carl Peters. In a recent study, Arne Perras uses Peters as a medium for "an inquiry into the link between a young activist and his political patrons. This approach may improve our understanding of how public enthusiasm came to influence governmental action in the colonial field."[7] Indeed, Perras provides a deep insight into this topic, which he finally summarizes in the following way: "In fact, there is no other figure within the German colonial movement who combined at least three important functions to promote the imperial cause: colonial theory, public agitation, and colonial pioneering."[8]

As a conclusion to an otherwise brilliant analysis, this strikes me as somewhat unsatisfactory. At least, I find one capacity of Peters to be missing that seems to me almost more important than the three mentioned: the ability to fuel fantasies. Was Peters in the view of his contemporaries (or at least the colonial enthusiasts among them) really the leading theorist? Was he really perceived as somebody with a brilliant, rational and coherent understanding of the situation and a clear vision of a bright future—and who, as an activist, could work out realistic plans? And could he appear to be all this in spite of the ugly stains his reputation had acquired from the scandals that drove him out of his position in the colonial administration of German East Africa? I doubt this. Rather, I would argue that precisely the dark region, the precarious moments of his past, the never-clarified details of his acts of violence, sex (perhaps), and certainly unreliability, were the elements that fuelled his popularity in the Wilhelminian Empire and also in the Weimar Republic.

What Peters colonizes is not so much the political map of Africa (others have been much more efficient in that field), but the landscape of fantasy. This can be shown in texts about Peters as well as in his own writings, which contain very little useful advice for colonial practice.[9] Instead, they match a structure of fantasy which Freud conceptualized in the same period by studying "cases" not so different from that of Peters. This very concept has been adapted in post-colonial theory (Bhabha) and recent film theory. Having studied genres such as the melodrama, the film scholar Linda Williams argues that "fantasies are not . . . wish-fulfilling linear narratives of mastery and control leading to closure and the attainment of desire. They are marked, rather, by the prolongation of desire and by the lack of a fixed position with respect to the objects and events fantasized."[10] Or, in other words, they build up "a setting for desire," where a drama is staged which, as Steven Shaviro puts it, "displays a logic of contamination and repetition, rather than one of linear, psychological causality."[11]

What we find in this genre is a conflict between fantasy and narration: while the narration leads to problem-solving, conquest and final solutions, fantasy has a tendency to—and relies on—the prolongation of the unsolved situation ("give me more of this"). Fantasies set the stage on which ambivalent desires, moments of destruction, loss and impotence, as well as omnipotence, are acted out. But in spite of this, they fit into and sometimes even inspire narrations that channel them into the construction of more stable identities.

Here, the uniform, which was my starting point, may come into play. It connotes not so much the aspect of military power as the ability to move through a foreign space without being affected by it, even though the mover may be powerless. This is precisely what *Die Wüstenrose* does: it leads into a highly precarious setting which even bears the marks of genocide, marks that may have been transfigured but are still visible. This, however, does not affect the narration. And that is what makes *Die Wüstenrose* so intolerable.

## NOTES

1. *Hallo Deutschland*, ZDF Television, 6 January 2000, introduction to interview with Walter Sittler. On colonialism and German television, see, for example, *Strategien der Annäherung. Darstellungen des Fremden im deutschen Fernsehen*, ed. by Julia Bayer, Andrea Engl and Melanie Liebheit (Bad Honnef: Horlemann, 2004).
2. On the history of the Namibian war, see *Völkermord in Deutsch-Südwestafrika. Der Kolonialkrieg 1904–1908 in Namibia und seine Folgen*, ed. by Jürgen Zimmerer and Joachim Zeller (Berlin: Links, 2003).
3. See, for example, *Bayern und Film*, ed. by Hans Krah (Passau: Karl Stutz, 2007).
4. Homi K. Bhabha, *The Location of Culture* (London: Routledge, 1994), p. 67.
5. If one likes to play with names: Luna's counterpart, Richard von Salomon, may be held to resemble Ernst von Salomon, a prominent writer from the 1920s to the 1960s, who, as the scriptwriter of the Nazi propaganda film *Carl Peters*, as well as for *Liane—Das Mädchen aus dem Urwald*, is closely associated with African fantasies. In his script, Liane is named Luna. Thus, Luna in *Die Wüstenrose* could be read as a secret tribute to the forefather of this particular fantasy.

6. The connection between German popular culture and colonialism has been the subject of a number of studies. See, for example, John K. Noyes, *Colonial Space: Spatiality in the Discourse of German South West Africa 1884–1915* (Philadelphia: Harwood, 1992); *The Imperialist Imagination. German Colonialism and its Legacy*, ed. by Sara Friedrichsmeyer, Sara Lennox and Susanne Zantop (Ann Arbor: Univ. Michigan Press, 1998); and my *Die Eroberung der Phantasie. Kolonialismus, Literatur und Film zwischen deutschem Kaiserreich und Weimarer Republik* (Göttingen: Vandenhoek & Ruprecht, 2010).

7. Arne Perras, *Carl Peters and German Imperialism 1856–1918. A Political Biography* (Oxford: Oxford University Press, 2004), p. 11.

8. Ibid.

9. See for example Carl Peters, *Im Goldland des Altertums. Forschungen zwischen Zambesi und Sabi* (Munich: Lehmann, 1902).

10. Linda Williams, *Film Bodies: Gender, Genre, and Excess*, in *Film Genre Reader*, vol. 2, ed. by Barry Keith Grant (Austin: University of Texas Press, 1995), pp. 140–58 (p. 153). See also Kristin Thompson, "The Concept of Cinematic Excess," in *Film Theory and Criticism*, ed. by Leo Braudy and Marshall Cohen, 5th edn (Oxford: Oxford University Press, 1999), pp. 487–98. The Freudian concept of fantasy has been outlined by Jean Laplanche and Jean Bertrand Pontalis, "Fantasy and the Origins of Sexuality," in *Formations of Fantasy*, ed. by Victor Burgin, James Donald and Cora Kaplan (London: Methuen, 1986), pp. 5–34.

11. Steven Shaviro, *The Cinematic Body* (Minneapolis: University of Minnesota Press, 1994), p. 5.

Part V

# Local Histories, Memories, Legacies

# 18 Communal Memory Events and the Heritage of the Victims

## The Persistence of the Theme of Genocide in Namibia[1]

*Reinhart Kössler*

Can it be that the children, grandchildren and great-grandchildren of victims still feel and perceive themselves as victims? In Namibia, many descendants of those who survived the genocide perpetrated by the German *Schutztruppe* in the early twentieth century certainly make such claims. These expressions are heard especially from Ovaherero, but are dismissed by many, probably too readily, as merely an instrumental argument to back up the claim for reparation pursued by leading Herero vis-à-vis the German state. Such dismissals miss the point of a deeply entangled and intersecting history, as well as ignoring memorial practice.[2]

In the following, I try to show the basis of such sentiments, and how they are reproduced through communal practices. In order to do this, I address one significant practice with a rather high public profile, namely, communal memory events as observed by various traditional communities in central and southern Namibia, usually in annual celebrations. After giving some essential general background, I focus on two such events, one set in a Nama and one in a Herero context. This focus highlights significant differences between the two events, even though they both take their historical reference from events and personages intimately connected with the wars of 1904–8.

Although it utilizes existing literature and some archival study to contextualize the events, my account draws mainly on participant observation. It is an attempt to expose commemoration practice as performance by—above all—the communities themselves, which are both the subjects of such practices and their vital contexts of reference. In this sense, the resuscitation and re-enactment of memory of historical events is primarily a performance of community, a central factor in the reproduction of the communal nexus. This does not preclude direct as well as more indirect interventions in the national political arena. Heroes' Day in Gibeon and Herero Day in Okahandja emerge, in this way, as complex and multi-layered events that testify to communal resilience and to a deep concern with "history" and commemoration. At the same time, these events relate to current politics and strategies and, not least and in very diverse ways, cater to participants' wishes and needs for fellowship and enjoyment.

## LONG-TERM EFFECTS OF GENOCIDE

Even a century after the event, it is hard to ignore how the wars of 1904–8 form the key historical event in the identity constructions of various ethnic groups in the former "Police Zone" of Namibia, the area where the white settler farming system was established by colonial rule—crucially, in the aftermath of these wars.[3] This is true in terms of social structure, as the wholesale expropriation of most indigenous communities from their land created the prerequisites for the settlement of almost the entire region by white farmers; it is also true for the constructions of history prevalent among people living in this area.[4] The very act by which German colonialism cleared the way for what would become apartheid has also had a persistent impact upon peoples' visions of the past and upon their conceptions of history.

This central concern with the long-term effects of colonial wars and genocide can be observed among the Ovaherero and Nama as well as among German-speaking Namibians, even if perspectives differ sharply. This is particularly true when it comes to designating the strategy pursued and the deeds perpetrated by the German military as "genocide." The ongoing controversy does not concern us here. There can be little doubt that the masses of orphaned children,[5] victims of deportation, survivors of concentration camps or those who made their way out of the waterless Omaheke steppe emerged deeply traumatized by their experiences.[6] Communal life was shattered, family and kinship ties were broken and the rules imposed by German native ordinances and policy made it extremely difficult for communities ever to re-assemble. For an illustrative source document, one may refer to a petition which was addressed by leaders of the Witbooi group to the South African authorities after the colony had been wrested from German rule in 1915. This account tells of the group's fate after their surrender in 1905–6. It is a tale of betrayal, of thousands of deaths in the concentration camp on Shark Island,[7] and of deportation to places as far away as Cameroon. The group had suffered pain and bereavement not only in the face of death, but also by being continuously uprooted and, for more than a decade, forced into a life of permanent movement.[8] This had been the fate of the surviving members of most groups that resisted German colonial rule during the wars of 1904–8, as well as of those who had rebelled against colonial rule during the preceding decade.

Today in Namibia, this experience, together with the resilience shown in resuscitating communal life against heavy odds in the aftermath of genocide and during the first decades of South African rule, forms a core part of collective identity for many Herero and Nama groups. This is one main reason why conceptions of history diverge widely in Namibia,[9] and also why "history," in the rather positivistic sense of facts, dates and important figures, plays such an important role in the construction of communal identities.[10] This has become evident at specific events, such as at the centenary of the battle of Ohamakari on 14 August 2004, when throngs of Ovaherero wore placards with the names of their "German grandfathers" on them to underline Germany's responsibilities. More regularly, "history" is rehearsed in the communal memory events that are staged, generally on an annual basis, by Herero and Nama groups.

## VISITING THE DEAD

In what follows, I take a closer look at two such events, Herero Day at Okahandja and Heroes' Day at Gibeon, both of which are deeply enmeshed in the memory of the genocide of 1904–8. Despite some marked differences, which are revealed in what follows, there are important elements common to both events. The central theme is the "visit to the ancestors," in the phrasing of Ovaherero, the celebration of the memory of one important chief, frequently also referred to as *ons ou Kaptein* (our old chief), who is treated as a lynchpin of collective memory and identification. Significantly, these personages are linked in the two cases under discussion to the colonial wars. At Okahandja, the reference is to Samuel Maharero, who, after achieving recognition of his claim for paramountcy by the German authorities,[11] headed the Ovaherero during the war and died in exile in Bechuanaland (now Botswana) in 1923. After this, he was interred in the burial-ground of the chiefs at Okahandja. At Gibeon, the reference is to Hendrik Witbooi, an icon of anti-colonial resistance who surrendered to colonial rule only after years of dogged resistance, to rise up once more against that rule 10 years later, in late 1904, and be killed in action by the German forces in late 1905.

Besides ritual forms of remembrance, the commemoration of the revered dead is linked to a rehearsal of their deeds and accomplishments, the "history" of the group, but also to concerns of the present. In that way, the festival serves as a venue for meeting friends and relatives, as a medium for the reproduction of the community concerned, as a locus for the experience of togetherness and belonging, and also to a greater or lesser extent for common enjoyment. Polar attitudes to the last of these are represented by the admonitory instructions issued during the run-up to the great centennial commemoration of the battle of the Waterberg and ensuing genocide against the Herero in 2004. And at Heroes' Day 2005, on the centenary of Hendrik Witbooi's death, participants were ordered, on the one hand, to behave properly for a funeral,[12] but were, at the same time, encouraged to adopt a festive and even joyous mood, since people should also "celebrate that he lived."[13]

An important way of recalling the past in all these events consists in allusions to the military past of the groups involved, mainly through performances of warlike display: for example, military costume, the ritual appearance of riders on horseback who circle the graveyard,[14] or, since independence, the firing of gunshot salutes, as well as the recital and re-enactment of historical events.

The sites at which these celebrations regularly take place are of vital importance for the communities. In many cases, including at Okahandja and Gibeon, the sites have previously been included within the jurisdiction of "white" municipalities. The appearance of Herero or Witbooi in force at these sites therefore implied claims to the sites and amounted, at least temporarily, to re-appropriation. Finally, the festivals have manifest links to current politics—expressed either in explicit speeches at the event itself, or in more oblique demonstrations of existing or potential alliances, to be inferred by the guests present.

## THE PAST IN THE PRESENT: HEROES' DAY AS A COLORFUL PAGEANT[15]

As far as can be ascertained, the celebration of Heroes' Day, which refers to the death of *Kaptein* Hendrik Witbooi on 29 October 1905, goes back to 1930. Its initial form was a solemn church service at the cemetery containing the tombstone of *Kaptein* Isaak Witbooi. This also commemorated his father, Hendrik, whose grave is unknown. The service was preceded by a procession from what was then the Witbooi site. At the time, this was presented as having been sponsored by the resident magistrate and the local missionary.[16] By the mid-1970s, the service was accompanied by a song of praise played on a tape recorder, by recitations of historical accounts, and by the commemoration of all Witbooi *Kapteins* who had lived at Gibeon since 1863, as well as by salutes from horse riders at the cemetery.[17]

In its present form, stretching from Friday evening until Sunday at noon, the festival is a result of transformations stretching over decades. In their decisive stages, the changes to the event resulted from conscious political action by Hendrik Witbooi, great-grandson of the old *Kaptein* and incumbent in the position of *Kaptein* since 1978. Having joined Swapo in 1976,[18] after which he soon became Vice President and turned Gibeon into a hub of activity in the south of the country,[19] Hendrik Witbooi gave the festival a distinctly national flavor, without relinquishing any of its communal or spiritual roots. This involved, in particular, endowing the event with a public political profile.[20] The most obvious step consisted of renaming *Witbooi Fees* as Heroes' Day in 1980, turning the event into an annual manifestation of the desire for genuine independence. This was linked with the involvement of important personages from outside the Witbooi group, in order to strengthen the intended national impact. Again, the inclusion of spectacular show elements, in particular the use of large groups of horse riders to enact episodes from the Witbooi history of anti-colonial resistance in the natural arena of the Fish River bed adjacent to Gibeon, added attraction and underscored the specific Witbooi contribution to national history and heritage (see Figure 18.1).[21]

A further element, placed at the opening of the sequence on Friday at sunset, presents a theme of territorial appropriation. In an elaborate

*Figure 18.1* Enactment of *Kaptein* Hendrik Witbooi's last battle at Heroes' Day, Gibeon, 2005.

ceremony, the fountain discovered by *Kaptein* Kido Witbooi in 1863 is opened, and all participants are invited to share some water drawn from the old source. Clearly, this also asserts Witbooi's claims to exclusive jurisdiction in Gibeon, which has been contested ever since the arrival in the area of a considerable number of *Bondelswarts*, members of another Nama group, who had been evicted from their homes in southernmost Namibia during the implementation of the Namibian homeland dispensation in the late 1960s.[22] A different dimension of re-appropriation is represented in the choice of venues outside Gibeon, such as that, in 1997, of the old Hendrik Witbooi's mountain stronghold at Hornkranz, near the Gamsberg Pass, and, in 2004, of the farm Goamus to the south east of Gibeon, "where the late Captain Dawid Moses Witbooi found a spring."[23]

The whole event is organized like a pageant, exhibiting both cultural syncretism and the quest for a national culture within a situation of diversity and gross inequality.[24] This was enhanced after Namibia reached its independence in 1990, and the Witbooi were symbolically acknowledged as protagonists in anti-colonial struggles, including visually, with the image of the old *Kaptein* Hendrik Witbooi printed on the back of every bank note. One of the salient features of later events is the inclusion of elements involving specifically "white" groups, such as majorettes from De Villiers

Secondary School, Keetmanshoop, performing in 1995, or obviously urban school-children singing Nama songs on the same occasion. Such acts can be understood as paying homage to a hero of anti-colonial resistance, and thus as a form of reconciliation that differs markedly from the Swapo government's approach, which focuses on blanket amnesty and on silencing both past conflicts and present ambiguities.[25] The emphatic appeal to "history," and to the need, particularly, for youth to be conversant with and grounded in it, underpins this approach. At the same time, such "history" is deployed to motivate the persistent aspirations of the Witbooi leaders, which may be summarized as the recovery of lost communal life and its basis, adequate and suitable ancestral land.[26]

A further feature is the way the occasion is transformed into a full-scale festival, with a deft combination of solemn ritual and opportunities for enjoyment and togetherness. It is true that much of this will be lost on those invited spectators who arrive from Windhoek on Saturday morning and leave in the late afternoon, in time to cover the 350-odd kilometers back. They miss out on the music, *langarm* dance and *Nama stap*, interspersed at the centenary occasion in 2005 with speeches by guests who had waited hours for their turn in an overcrowded program, but also with sketches commenting satirically on everyday problems, such as conflicts between youth and their elders (see Figure 18.2).

*Figure 18.2*   Dance performance at Heroes' Day, Gibeon, 2005.

Together with the riders' performance, such elements evidently add color and variety to an everyday life all too often marked by want and monotony, and a situation of rampant unemployment and considerable destitution, as well as conflicts of various kinds.

Since independence, the official guests present at the occasion have clearly documented the high status of the Witbooi leadership in independent Namibia. Thus, in 1995, the *Kaptein*, a Cabinet member during the first three legislative periods, was able to attract personages such as the Chinese Ambassador and the United Nations Development Program representative in Namibia. A further feature is the regular appearance of a detachment of the Namibia Defence Force, performing military drill in honor of the national hero, Hendrik Witbooi Sr. At the centenary event in 2005, the presence of guests representing important relationships was even more in evidence than usual. They included a great number of Nama chiefs, who were presented to the participants at the opening ceremony at the fountain; the German Ambassador; and the Speaker of the National Assembly, Theo-Ben Gurirab, who delivered the keynote speech, having donned a typical Witbooi hat. Finally, an array of Herero chiefs and representatives documented the willingness to overcome historical schisms stretching back to pre-colonial times (see Figure 18.3). The event can therefore also be

*Figure 18.3*  Heroes' Day, Gibeon, 2005. The German Ambassador, Dr. Wolfgang Massing, handing over to *Kaptein* Hendrik Witbooi a ledger of letters by the latter's great-grandfather, which had been captured by German troops in 1904–5. The late Herero Chief Tuvahi Kambazembi (Watersberg) is on the right.

understood as a public open stage for alliance building among traditional leaders in southern and central Namibia.

The new historical situation following independence can also be gauged from the changed form of conveyance used when moving between the festival sites. Up to the late 1980s, participants moved on foot in a solemn procession to the cemetery, where a church service, the central ceremony on Sunday, is held (see Figure 18.4). They were led by the *Kaptein*. Clearly, this procession was not greatly different from that documented in 1930. More recently, the procession has been replaced by a motorcade, including the *Kaptein*'s gold-colored Mercedes, with riders and pedestrian participants arriving in informal order, to assemble at the graveside where the service is held. However, the creative momentum of the whole affair is maintained even when the staging of the event runs into difficulties. Thus, *Kaptein* Witbooi, when asked for reasons why the festival had not been observed in 2006, argued that this was partly due to the lack of an innovative new idea which could also be part of the event every year thereafter.[27]

## HERERO DAY AT OKAHANDJA[28]

Herero Day, observed in late August at Okahandja, forms a contrast to Heroes' Day in Gibeon in a number of ways. Yet there are also parallels, certainly in terms of the reference to ancestors, but also in the central role of

*Figure 18.4*   Heroes' Day, Gibeon, 1995, ceremony at the cemetery. The white gravestone is *Kaptein* Isaak Witbooi's, also commemorating his father, *Kaptein* Hendrik Witbooi, whose grave site is unknown.

the event for the reproduction of community, in this case for the Red Band, based in Okahandja, as well as Ovaherero in general. The event takes its cue not from the genocide itself, but from the first spectacular demonstration of Herero resilience, which indeed might be understood as a successful feat of nation building.

The burial of Samuel Maharero on 26 October 1923, at the burial-ground of his ancestors, the chiefs, in Okahandja, was highly significant for three main reasons. First, it signified the symbolic return of the exiled (though controversial) paramount chief, after he had died in Bechuana-land. Furthermore, it testified to the visible re-emergence of Ovaherero as a more or less coherent community—a community displaying clear ethnic markers and with an identity and organizational structure recognized, at least informally, by the government, but independent both of the mission church and of the then influential Marcus Garvey movement.[29] Finally, it marked something like a first phase in an ongoing struggle to safeguard the burial sites of Ovaherero chiefs and other important personages which are situated in the center of what was then the "white" municipality of Okahandja.

In Ovaherero culture, such graves have been associated first and foremost with the marking of territorial claims, and the fight to secure the graves against the claims of the municipality was therefore of strategic importance.[30] At the burial itself, "through the ceremonial occupation of Okahandja, the uniformed troops symbolized and demonstrated the vision of a united people, reinforcing their claim to ancestral land." [31] One main feature of this was the appearance *en masse* of uniformed men, the *otruppa*, one of the central symbols of Herero collective identity that evolved after the catastrophe of 1904. Even though other events are observed by Ovaherero groups in similar fashion, such as Zeraua Day at Omaruru or the Mbanderu event at Okaseta, the annual observance of the date of Samuel Maharero's burial quickly emerged as the main regular meeting, with significance for the local "Red Band" as well as the other local groups. In fact, oral tradition claims that the annual observance of this event stems from the admonishment of one of the *Otruppe* "generals" at Samuel Maharero's funeral.[32]

However, the re-appropriation or even "re-occupation" of central sites in Okahandja for a long time remained precarious, at best. It was contested by the municipality, which erected a public park and a swimming pool right next to the graves of the chiefs and claimed Herero visitors to the graves might spoil the park[33] or cause "molestation etc. of the ladies using the swimming bath near the graves."[34] In this way, desecration of the graves was set off symbolically against the purity of white women. The solution reached after lengthy consultations between the central administration, the municipality and leading Ovaherero not only restricted access to the graves for Ovaherero to "a single day" every year,[35] but also entailed further restrictions. Permission had to be sought for every single occasion, and for years was granted only on condition "that no uniforms or red tabs are worn and . . . that no drilling is indulged in."[36] These were severe infringements of central symbols of Herero identity as they had evolved since 1904. Eventually, a Herero spokesman was able to insist on adherence to "the request of Samuel Maharero personally, he said those who belong to him shall be those who will bury him in uniforms in the form of troop"; and this rule is now followed.[37]

From today's perspective, such a show of ethnic symbols has not been contested for a long time. After being welcomed on the morning of the festive day by the paramount chief at the Herero *Kommando* in the former township, a solemn procession, complete with flags and horse riders, men in the front and women at the back, arrives in the vicinity of the graves in what, today, is named Heroes' Street (see Figure 18.5). Riders dismount, and the crowd moves to the chiefs' graves, some hundred meters from the road. A senior representative of the Maharero family announces the visitors to the ancestors, and the participants then file past the graves, symbolically touching the encircling wall (see Figure 18.6).

The same procedure is repeated at a further group of graves, most prominently those of Hosea Kutako and Clemens Kapuuo, as well as the immediately adjacent one of Jonker Afrikaner, the Orlam chieftain who, in the mid-nineteenth century, ruled his incipient state from Okahandja. The procession finally reaches the graveyard at the back of the old mission church,

*Figure 18.5*   Herero Day, Okahandja, 2005. Horse riders arriving at Heroes' Street.

*Figure 18.6* Herero Day, Okahandja, 2005. Women who have just visited the graves of the chiefs.

where further eminent Ovaherero are buried. Some people also touch crosses at the adjacent German war cemetery when leaving the churchyard. The event is regularly observed by tourists arriving in a few buses from Windhoek, and it is also presented as a tourist attraction.[38]

Back at the *Kommando* site, which is adorned with national and ethnic flags as well as the holy fire so central to Herero ritual, the afternoon is taken up mainly by speeches, with interspersed choir performances. This rather unspectacular arrangement, in comparison to Heroes' Day at Gibeon, may be seen as underlining the high political profile the event has commanded, particularly in recent years. It makes a twofold reference to current national politics. On the one hand, Herero Day regularly clashes with the national Heroes' Day on 26 August, which commemorates the first armed engagement of the liberation war in 1966. The official celebrations, for which on several occasions the entire cabinet has traveled to the north of the country, do not leave much room for official recognition of Herero Day. Moreover, this clash has been linked in recent times to the second dimension of the politics of the latter event, where speeches have been marked to a large extent by references to the ongoing campaign by the Herero Paramount Chief, Kuaima Riruako, for adequate German compensation for the genocide. As long as the Namibian government has tended to shun this issue,[39] attendance has seemed ill advised from their point of view. The reparation issue came to the fore, for example, in 2005, with the appearance of the South African attorney Jeremy Sarkin, who briefed listeners on the position of pending lawsuits in the United States. It was even more prominent a year later with the speech by the Left Party Deputy in the German Bundestag, Hüseyin Aydin. These interventions pointed to the controversial linkage between Herero identity and the question of genocide, which had been especially highlighted on the occasion of the centenary in 2004. At that time, the commemoration of the battle of Ohamakari served as an occasion to give the issue high public profile, and included an apology by the German Minister of Economic Cooperation and Development.[40]

The underlying sentiments, certainly, of many participants, were articulated at Herero Day 2005 by a picture display summarizing key events from Herero history and, in particular, those of the year 1904. The tent in which the display was housed bore a huge banner with the inscription:

> We resisted German occupation for the sake of freedom
> Those who resisted lost cattle and land
> We survived extermination
> The torch we bore and handed down we now share in reconciliation

This text highlights the persistence of bereavement and trauma in the wake of genocide, while at the same time pointing clearly to the resilience of the Ovaherero community from which Herero Day takes its central cue (see Figure 18.7).

Finally, these two motifs are linked to the overarching watchword of reconciliation, which, however ill defined, has shaped Namibian politics since independence in decisive ways. These motifs also point back to the obligation that the German state still bears as a consequence of the genocide. Herero Day is one of the important public contexts in Namibia where this concern is articulated. The tension that exists in relation to the reparations issue can be gauged from Hüseyin Aydin's speech at Herero Day in 2006, when he stated, "Genocide does not lapse, either morally or legally . . . To recognize the demand for reparation for the genocide in German Southwest Africa is an integral element of coming to terms with the past. And it is a precondition for the struggle for a better world."[41] Seen from this perspective, both Heroes' Day in Gibeon and Herero Day in Okahandja carry a common message: reconciliation, both among the various groups

*Figure 18.7* Herero Day, Okahandja, 2005. Banner outside tent housing memorial exhibition.

and tendencies in Namibia and between the posterity of the survivors of genocide and the German state as the official representative of the German nation, is predicated on a clear recognition of what has happened, and on the sincere determination to seek whatever redress is possible for the atrocities and injustices of the past.

## NOTES

1. The following text forms part of ongoing research on communal memory events in Namibia, in the context of the composite research- and capacity-building project "Reconciliation and Social Conflict in the Aftermath of Large-Scale Violence in Southern Africa: The Cases of Angola and Namibia,"

which is based at the Arnold Bergstraesser Institute, Freiburg, and funded by the Volkswagen Foundation's "Knowledge for Tomorrow" program. Thanks to Tara Elyssa, Windhoek, for checking my English.

2. Cf. Reinhart Kössler, "Genocide, Apology and Reparation—the Linkage Between Images of the Past in Namibia and Germany," paper presented at the AEGIS European Conference on African Studies, 11–14 July 2007, Leiden, Netherlands.

3. Jürgen Zimmerer, *Deutsche Herrschaft über Afrikaner: Staatlicher Machtanspruch und Wirklichkeit im kolonialen Namibia* (Münster: Lit, 2001).

4. Cf. Reinhart Kössler, "Facing a Fragmented Past: Memory, Culture and Politics in Namibia," *Journal of Southern African Studies*, 33 (2007), 361–82.

5. See the lists in Gordon McGregor, *The Prisoner of War Tokens of German South-West Africa* (Windhoek: Namibia Scientific Society, 2003).

6. Generally on long-term trauma after genocide, including the "survivor syndrome," see Boris Barth, *Genozid: Völkermord im 20. Jahrhundert: Geschichte—Theorien—Kontroversen* (Munich: Beck, 2006), p. 55f.; for Namibia in particular, this is examined in Gesine Krüger, *Kriegsbewältigung und Geschichtsbewusstsein: Realität, Deutung und Verarbeitung des deutschen Kolonialkrieges in Namibia 1904 bis 1907* (Göttingen: Vandenhoek & Ruprecht, 1999); see also Kirsten Alnaes, "Living with the Past: The Songs of the Herero in Botswana," *Africa*, 59.3 (1989), 267–99.

7. On the concentration camps and Shark Island in particular, see Casper Erichsen, *"The Angel of Death Has Descended Violently Among Them": Concentration Camps and Prisoners-of-War in Namibia, 1904–08* (Leiden: African Studies Centre 2005).

8. See Reinhart Kössler, "From Hailing the 'English Flag' to Asking for UN Control: Witbooi Petitions and Appeals under South African Rule, 1919–1956," *Journal. Namibia Scientific Society*, 47 (1999), 41–65 (pp. 50–2 and 61f.).

9. Cf. Kössler, "Facing a Fragmented Past."

10. See ibid. and Jonathan Friedman, "Making Politics, Making History: Chiefship and the Post-Apartheid State in Namibia," *Journal of Southern African Studies*, 31.1 (2005), 23–52 (p. 35).

11. See Gerhard Pool, *Samuel Maharero* (Windhoek: Gamsberg Macmillan, 1991), pp. 77–84 and 100–24.

12. Arnold Tjihuiko in a speech at the Herero Commando, Katutura (Windhoek), 12 August 2004 (personal observation).

13. *Kaptein* Hendrik Witbooi, Jr., in a speech on 29 October 2005 (personal observation).

14. This is physically impossible in Okahandja, but happens, besides at Gibeon, at Omaruru and Vaalgras.

15. Observation of Heroes' Day 1995 was conducted in the context of a research project under the auspices of the German Research Foundation (DFG), covered in Reinhart Kössler, *In Search of Survival and Dignity: Two Traditional Communities in Southern Namibia under South African Rule* (Frankfurt/M.: IKO, 2006); participation in 2005 was made possible by the friendship and cooperation particularly of André du Pisani (Windhoek), Talita !Ui≠nuses (Windhoek) and Cynthia !Ui≠nuses (Gibeon), as well as by the hospitality of their family.

16. Cf. Johannes Olpp, "Eindrücke einer Reise über die sieben Rh. Missionsstationen des Namalandes (II)," *Berichte der Rheinischen Missionsgesellschaft*, 87 (1930), p. 141.

17. Etienne Du Pisani, "The Annual Witbooi Festival," *SWA annual*, 32 (1976), 132–53; Pisiani, "Die Nama van Gibeon. 'n Etnografiese studie met besondere verwysing na sosiaal-ekonomiese aspekte" (unpublished MA thesis, Stellenbosch, 1976).
18. Peter H. Katjavivi, *A History of Resistance in Namibia* (London: Currey; Addis Ababa: Inter-African Cultural Fund; Paris: UNESCO, 1988), p. 100.
19. Colin Leys and John Saul, *Namibia's Liberation Struggle: The Two-Edged Sword* (London: Currey; Athens: Ohio University Press, 1995), pp. 69 and 75–8.
20. Interview with *Kaptein* Hendrik Witbooi, Windhoek, June 1995; Reinhart Kössler, "'A Luta Continua': Strategische Orientierung und Erinnerungspolitik am Beispiel des 'Heroes' Day' der Witbooi in Gibeon," in *Völkermord in Südwestafrika: Der Kolonialkrieg (1904–1908) in Namibia und seine Folgen*, ed. by Jürgen Zimmerer and Joachim Zeller (Berlin: Links, 2003), pp. 184–91.
21. All photographs in the present article are by Reinhart Kössler.
22. Cf. Kössler, *In Search*, pp. 102–5, 238–41 and 253f.
23. *The Namibian*, 9 November 2004; see also the remarkable Web site <http://www.goamus.com/> via <http://www.kmosbach.de/index.html> [accessed 15 January 2008]; for 1997, see Kössler, *In Search*, p. 252f.
24. On the latter point, see Reinhart Kössler, "Im Schatten des Genozids: Erinnerungspolitik in einer extrem ungleichen Gesellschaft," in *Genozid und Gedenken: Namibisch-deutsche Geschichte und Gegenwart*, ed. by Henning Melber (Frankfurt/M.: Brandes & Apsel, 2005), pp. 65–8.
25. Cf. Andre du Pisani, "Liberation and tolerance," in *Re-Examining Liberation in Namibia. Political Culture since Independence*, ed. by Henning Melber (Uppsala: Nordiska Afrikainstitutet, 2003), pp. 129–36; also, Kössler, *In Search*, p. 251.
26. Cf. Kössler, *In Search*, p. 251; Kössler, "'A Luta Continua'," p. 190f.
27. Interview with *Kaptein* Hendrik Witbooi, Windhoek, November 2006.
28. The following cannot present a full exposition of the event, but merely provides some background and highlights.
29. Cf. Jan-Bart Gewald, *"We Thought We Would be Free . . .": Socio-Cultural Aspects of Herero History in Namibia 1915–1940* (Cologne: Köppe, 2000), pp. 149–56.
30. Cf. Krüger, *Kriegsbewältigung*, pp. 271–90.
31. Gesine Krüger and Dag Henrichsen, "'We have been Captives Long Enough: We Want to be Free': Land, Uniforms & Politics in the History of the Herero in the Interwar Period," in *Namibia Under South African Rule: Mobility & Containment 1915–1946*, ed. by Patricia Hayes and others (Oxford: James Currey; Windhoek: Out of Africa; Athens: Ohio University Press, 1998), pp. 149–74 (p. 159).
32. Cf. ibid., p. 158.
33. Cf. Krüger, *Kriegsbewältigung*, pp. 274–82.
34. Town Clerk (Okahandja) to Senior Officer Lands Branch, Windhoek, 12 July 1934; National Archives of Namibia (henceforth: NAN), SWAA A 50/51, vol. 1.
35. Krüger, *Kriegsbewältigung*, p. 281.
36. Administrator/Chief Native Commissioner to Magistrate/Native Commissioner Okahandja, 29 July 1941; NAN, SWAA A 50/51, vol.1; this file contains numerous similar regulations for other years.
37. Translation of letter "A," dated Windhoek, 15 August 1938, transl. by Fritz Kasuto, Interpreter Native Languages; NAN, SWAA A 50/59.

38. For instance, in the in-flight magazine of Air Namibia, *Flamingo*, December 2001.
39. To a certain extent this has changed since late 2006; see Kössler, "Genocide, Apology and Reparation."
40. On these issues, see Reinhart Kössler, "La fin d'une amnésie? L'Allemagne et son passé colonial depuis 2004," *Politique africaine*, 102 (2006), 50–66.
41. Hüseyin Aydin, MdB, Speech on Herero Day in Okahandja, Namibia, 27 August 2006, <http://www.hueseyinaydin.de/article/87.die_herero_und_nama_haben_ein_anrecht_auf_reparationen.html> [accessed 30 July 2007].

# 19 The Genocide in "German South-West Africa" and the Politics of Commemoration

## How (Not) to Come to Terms with the Past

*Henning Melber*

In January 1904, large sections of the Herero people rose up against German colonial rule. In October of the same year, a number of Nama communities followed their example, taking up arms against the German colonial army. A century later, these colonial wars and their aftermath have become the subject of intense public and academic debate. The present chapter reflects on visible discourses, political cultures and ideologies currently existing as a result of these two wars in the two republics of Namibia and Germany. The centenary of the wars' outbreak in 2004 provided a particular focus for a program of public events and statements about the war. In the following, the selectivity of remembrance by various actors in both states will be critically analyzed and commented upon. The chapter does not claim to provide conclusive answers, but instead intends to offer reflections that might challenge, or at least influence, these discourses.[1]

## THE GENOCIDE AS A CONTESTED NOTION

During the late 1960s, two German historians—one from each of the then separate German republics—provided different yet complementary evidence and analysis of the totalitarian practices and subsequent methods of mass destruction applied by colonial forces in German South-West Africa, now the Republic of Namibia.[2] Their seminal contributions to Namibian historiography were strengthened further by a more theoretically based work combining the theoretical approaches guiding the other two historians, namely Hannah Arendt's Marxist theory of totalitarian rule.[3] These pioneering studies have been reinforced and substantiated (though again with minor differences in the analytical focus and particular argumentation) in a series of academic monographs—published PhD theses—since the late 1990s.[4] On the basis of these contributions as well as widely established contemporary definitions, we can describe the historical events that took place at the beginning of the twentieth century in eastern, central and southern parts of the German colonial territory called South-West Africa, with confidence, as being tantamount to genocide. The United Nations-commissioned "Whitaker Report" substantiated this conclusion in the mid-1980s by describing the events in German South-West Africa between 1904 and 1908 as the first genocide of the twentieth century.[5]

The most striking phenomenon one encounters when dealing with these historical events a century later is the fact that analyses and conclusions still vary fundamentally in public perception as well as in scholarly and political discourse—in so far as the genocide, its understanding and classification are considered or cared about at all. An impulse actively to glorify Imperial Germany's "civilizing mission" is still sporadically in evidence, especially among coteries of dreamers descended from the colonizers themselves. For the most part, however, this chapter in German history has been forgotten—if, in fact, it ever existed at all. The tendency has been to consider it as, at most, a mere footnote, with no wider significance for German collective memory: a century after the genocide in the German colony, there is widespread amnesia or indifference, with little effort made to address the injustices that were committed.

In contrast to this ignorance and lack of interest in Germany, the trauma lives on among parts of the Namibian population, most notably the Herero and the Nama, but also increasingly the Damara communities, who all bore the brunt of the colonial onslaught. Often neglected and overlooked, the various San or Bushmen communities suffered to a very similar degree over an extended period of time and were exposed to genocidal practices. Despite the selectivity of historical memory and political commitment, their strong collective memory has resulted in the demand by sections of Namibian society for recognition of and compensation for the crimes committed in the former colony. This trend, which has been emerging for the last few years, has also forced the descendants of German colonial settlers, the so-called *Südwester*, who still own a disproportionately large segment of commercial land in Namibia, to respond to the historical record (or in many cases to deny it). The legacy and its treatment remain a battlefield on which there are often uncompromising exchanges about how the past is to be dealt with in the present.

Notwithstanding some uncomfortable observations which it produced about the various forms of denial, the centenary also resulted in a remarkable body of new literature, which has reinforced the need to seek common ground with regard to established knowledge and shared insights. As matters currently stand, we are still far away from such common ground. This refers not only to ideologically reactionary attempts to defend the so-called "civilizing role" of German colonialism, which wholly reject the charge of genocide against German colonial troops, but even to differences within the ranks of scholars who concerned themselves with this historical issue from a professional standpoint.[6]

This chapter does not examine the many colliding arguments in detail; nor does it engage with those who seek to cast doubt on the scale and intention of mass destruction and, in some cases, seek to ridicule the arguments of the proponents of the genocide description.[7] I share the position of those they criticize, who identify the events as genocide.[8] One argument that might offer some common ground in this schism, however, is the recently proposed notion that considerable settler pressure in the colony provoked a transformation from the original—and officially sanctioned—measures carried out by the German colonial army to the eventual genocidal domination.[9] According to this understanding, the concept of total war was applied and developed to its full extent in the German settler colony of South-West Africa and eventually resulted in an act of genocide.[10] The following does not provide further evidence to support this conclusion, but relies on previous efforts undertaken elsewhere. Instead, the subject of this chapter is the different modes of remembrance cultivated (if at all) in the two countries.

## REMEMBRANCE IN NAMIBIA: MONOPOLIZATION VERSUS IGNORANCE

Almost two decades after Independence, many of those holding high-ranking posts within the Namibian government still have a track-record as "comrades in the struggle," dating back to the years of the formation and consolidation of the liberation movement Swapo in the late 1950s and early 1960s. A militant rhetoric with its origins in that period is still widely used as a tool for inclusion or exclusion within post-colonial national identity, and it also tends to promotes a somewhat exclusive approach to national history, claiming Swapo as the country's sole liberator. At the same time, the specific blend of physical remnants from the colonial past and newly emerging symbols of the anti-colonial struggle, which are celebrated in the dominant post-colonial nation-building process, create a rather peculiar public sphere and memory "landscape" in the country's physical environment.[11] This tendency has emerged notwithstanding earlier acknowledgments from within the party leadership that various stages of the country's liberation history were in reality not directly connected to Swapo. In contrast to the myth of continuity from the first to the third *chimurenga*, as cultivated (with devastating consequences) by ZANU-PF in neighboring Zimbabwe, Swapo has not been able to establish such a tradition for itself. The liberation movement's official history summarizes matters as follows:

> Out of the country's pre-colonial population, only the Ovambo escaped the full rigour of German rule . . . the Germans, preoccupied with their subjugation of the Herero and Nama and deterred by Ovambo numbers and military power, left them alone. Even when, after the genocidal suppression of the 1904–7 national uprising, the colonial economy became heavily dependent on Ovambo migrant labour for its mines

and railways, the colonial regime limited its contacts with the Ovambo kings strictly to "protection" treaties and diplomatic "persuasion."[12]

What is interesting here is not only the acknowledgment that Ovambo communities (which nowadays represent more than half of Namibia's population and form the backbone of Swapo) were not involved in the anti-colonial resistance against the Germans, but also the surprising and contradictory reference to this anti-colonial resistance as a "national uprising." Such an appropriation and generalization ironically echoes the equally dubious monopolization of primary resistance history by some members of the Herero communities.

At Herero Day in Okahandja in 2002, the Herero Paramount Chief, Kuaima Riruako, attempted to justify the private claims for reparations from the German government and certain German companies that had been presented to a U.S. court on his instructions during late 2001. Riruako became so carried away that he declared the question of land redistribution in Namibia to be solely a Herero issue.[13] Even if this is consistent with the admission made in the Swapo publication quoted previously, namely, that the communities north of the then Police Zone had not been directly affected, it is still a blatant denial of the sacrifices made by other communities, such as the Nama, in particular, but also the Damara and the San. This sort of logic, which allowed the paramount Herero leadership to claim the sole authentic status of victimhood in relation to the genocide, largely dominated commemorative events during 2004. This monopoly of victimhood on the part of the Herero was not limited to the group's own commemorations, but was also in evidence during the two large conferences held on the topic, the first of which was held in August 2004 at the University of Namibia in Windhoek and the other in November 2004 in Bremen. Though the perspectives of foreign and local white speakers were also powerfully represented at both events, the articulation of Namibian views was otherwise largely confined to Herero positions, which were often claimed to represent the only valid standpoint.

The Namibian government, meanwhile, deliberately kept a low profile. No government-sponsored public events or other initiatives were organized to mark the occasion (and by so doing, uphold the commitment previously made to honor the contribution of primary resistance to early nation-building). Instead, such constructive engagement as there was was left to private initiatives organized mainly by Herero groups (and to a lesser extent by local Nama communities).[14]

When the then Minister of Information and Broadcasting, Nangolo Mbumba (who became Minister of Education in March 2005), announced on behalf of the Cabinet the decision to honor the centenary of the genocide by issuing a special commemorative stamp, he was also quick to emphasize that this would not involve singling out particular groups such as the Germans or the Herero. The stamp initiative was to be seen instead as an effort to contribute to a broader, more general reconciliation. Namibia's government, as he explained further, did not support the initiative of a group of Herero to seek reparations from Germany.[15] The Minister of Higher Education, Nahas Angula (who became Prime Minister in March 2005), supported, if from a slightly different perspective, the view that the war should be accorded inclusive national significance: in a panel debate, he expressed the opinion that the commemoration of the genocide should be a matter involving all Namibians and should also be considered part of the wider Namibian struggle for liberation.[16]

In early August 2003, the Head of State had been rather less conciliatory in his attitude toward the annual celebrations by conservative and reactionary elements among the German-speaking community in Namibia, who, like the Herero in Okahandja, had gathered every August since the 1920s to commemorate the decisive military encounters around the Waterberg.[17] This meeting was banned at short notice and by public Presidential Decree. As the President argued,

> It was the heroic struggle of our forefathers against colonialism and imperialism that provided the necessary inspiration and impetus for the Swapo-Party to carry out the modern struggle for national liberation. The Liberation Movement, under the banner of Swapo, broke and threw away the apartheid colonial yoke and oppression . . . There is no doubt in our mind that if the celebration was allowed to go ahead, there is a strong likelihood that the victims of the deliberate and calculated genocide would react against such insensitive and provocative celebration. This would undoubtedly lead to the breakdown of peace, law and order in the country . . . I need not remind the nation that if there is endangerment of peace, stability and security, no one, including this small group of German-speaking Namibians, would be spared.[18]

Given this intervention, one might have expected the government to take a more active role during the subsequent centenary commemorations in 2004. Instead, the Namibian President, Sam Nujoma, and other senior government officials declined an invitation to attend the ceremonies in Okahandja marking the 100th anniversary of the beginning of the Herero war against German colonial occupation.[19] In contrast to this offensive absence, which was tantamount to a boycott, high-ranking representatives of the Swapo party and government marked the centenary of the military encounter considered to have been the beginning of the Herero defeat. Hifikepunye Pohamba, President Nujoma's designated successor as Head of State, attended the ceremony commemorating the Waterberg battle, which was held at Okakarara in August 2004. It is possible that this was mainly a result of protocol considerations: the German government was represented on a ministerial level at this event. Be that as it may: Namibian government officials were again conspicuously absent when the Herero gathered for their annual Otjiserandu commemoration activities, held during the last weekend of August at the grave of Paramount Chief Samuel Maherero. Instead, Cabinet members and the President gathered at a monument in the North, erected in memory of the beginning of the armed struggle between Swapo and the South African regime in 1966.

## THE GERMAN GOVERNMENT'S HALF-HEARTED REMORSE

In preferring to keep a lid on the reparation issue, the Namibian government seemed almost to be in silent agreement with the German-speaking minority in Namibia and with those representing the official position of the German government. The German ambassador to Namibia used the occasion of the commemoration ceremony on 11 January 2004 in Okahandja to reiterate his government's position on the reparation issue, stating, "It would not be justified to compensate one specific ethnic group for their suffering during the colonial times, as this could reinforce ethnic tensions and thus undermine the policy of national reconciliation which we fully support."[20] In contrast to this official German inaction, a considerable number of initiatives and commemoration activities, organized mainly by non-governmental organizations, took place within Germany.[21] It could be argued that these events contributed to a clear change of tactics or conscience among high-level government officials.

Previously, successive German governments, regardless of their political hue, had consistently avoided making even a nominal apology. The idea of an apology had repeatedly been rejected on the grounds that it could encourage the descendants of the survivors to seek legal redress and compensation for damage past and present. Disreputably, state visits to independent Namibia maintained cordial relationships with German-speaking Namibians while stonewalling calls for a response to the consequences of colonial genocide. As late as 2003, the German Foreign Minister, Joschka Fischer, articulated the official government position that no apology would be offered because it could become associated with calls for compensation. In January 2004, the German Chancellor, Gerhard Schröder, during his first series of official visits to African countries, carefully avoided Namibia, and was consequently able to sidestep the historical debate surrounding German–Namibian relations and the genocide.

During the commemoration of the Waterberg Battle at Ohamakari near Okakarara in August 2004, the actions of the German Minister for Economic Cooperation, Heidemarie Wieczorek-Zeul, seemed to indicate a marked deviation from previous official denials by the German government. In an emotional speech, the Minister made what could only be interpreted as an admission of guilt as well as of heartfelt remorse. She described German conduct during the war against the Herero and Nama communities as tantamount to war crimes and genocide, as seen from a twenty-first-century perspective. Asked for an apology (the word did not appear in the text she read out), she replied that her whole speech was intended as an apology. This took the audience by surprise and wholly changed the dynamic of the event, giving it a far stronger tone of reconciliation.

The speech was not followed by direct signs of a change of policy with regard to the issue of compensation. In May 2005, however, Minister Wieczorek-Zeul announced plans to establish a Namibian-German Panel on Reconciliation as a long-term initiative to assist financially the main groups that had been affected by the colonial genocide. According to the Minister, 20 million Euros were to be earmarked in support of the initiative over a period of 10 years (2 million Euros annually). At the same time, the Minister announced an increase in bilateral development aid for Namibia. Germany had long prided itself on being Namibia's most important donor, on account of the historical connection between the two countries: Namibia receives by far the highest per capita aid allocation of Germany's development spending on African countries. The sign of goodwill suggested by the reconciliation initiative, which addressed the historical injustices at least indirectly, did not initially meet with much enthusiasm from the Namibian government. The commitments, which would essentially have resulted in ethnically targeted development and were therefore regarded as preferential treatment, were disapproved of by the Namibian gatekeepers of reconciliation and affirmative action.

This reluctance led to a somewhat ironic situation, whereby the German government's official initiatives, acknowledging, at least in part, the need for specifically targeted measures of compensation, were for several years not implemented due to the disapproval of the Namibian government. The conflict was only resolved at the end of 2006, when a tender was announced for plans to spend the money in accordance with a regional (non-ethnic) development approach in some of the areas most affected by German annihilation practices. This tension highlights once again the collision of interests which a post-colonial nation-building strategy that is based, as that of Namibia increasingly is, on "patriotic history" provokes—a strategy which, in the Namibian case, denies groups other than those shaping the hegemonic discourse any meaningful role in the creation of the state (if not nation), despite their history of primary resistance.

A parliamentary debate initiated by the Herero Paramount Chief and Member of Parliament Kuaima Riruako was surprisingly free of such limitations. During several sessions in September and October 2006, the legislators engaged in extensive discussions of the Herero claims for compensation. In the end, Riruako's motion in support of the Herero claims for compensation was adopted with the support of the Swapo party. This was considered a major breakthrough in public political discourse, as well as in the government's official position. However, it was more than a year before this motion was communicated by Namibia's foreign minister to his German counterpart, in mid-November 2007.

## THE GENOCIDE IN "GERMAN SOUTH-WEST AFRICA" AND THE HOLOCAUST

Of additional interest in the context of this chapter is the fact that the entire reparations debate, both within the official German policy arena and in most areas of wider public discourse, avoids—intentionally or otherwise—any reference to developments in Germany, following World War One and the loss of her colonies, which resulted in the Holocaust. The commemoration of genocidal atrocities such as those committed in German South-West Africa during the early twentieth century is about more than just dealing with guilt and remorse.

There are a number of further reasons why commemoration and remembrance should be important, and these can be understood more clearly if viewed along two interrelated trajectories. The first of these trajectories is connected with the development of both political society and culture in Germany, while the second concerns the overall dynamic and logic of genocide as it unfolded over the course of the twentieth century. The distinction between these two trajectories is also related to the hotly debated issue of the singularity of the Holocaust perpetrated by Nazi Germany against European Jewry and other groups, such as the Sinti and Roma.

As has been argued elsewhere,[22] the Namibian genocide contributed to the establishment of a new pattern of extermination. The inherent racism of settler colonialism worked to increase tolerance of mass killings, with similar manifestations occurring in the Americas, Australia and Southern Africa. In the Namibian case, this is connected to the specifically German trajectory, where we can observe continuities between novels and accounts read by a mass readership, military practice, the activities of specific people, and military doctrines and routines that linked strategic ideas of "decisive battles" to the concept of a "final solution" and the extinction of the enemy that culminated in the Holocaust of the 1940s. Although anti-Semitism remains virulent, even in Germany, the Holocaust has become the object of continuous official and civic remembrance. It should be noted, however, that such remembrance and repentance, along with the (inevitably inadequate) material redress associated with it, have been highly selective, neglecting and even excluding certain groups of victims.

## IDENTITY MATTERS—AND POLITICS TOO

For the *Südwester*, who, by origin and tradition, were socialized within a culture of European domination and imperialism, re-examining the colonial past may be particularly difficult. They are confronted with the—possibly very painful—challenge of decolonizing their own minds through critical introspection. They will have to accept that the basis of their rationality, which is rooted in Western expansionism and a dubious era of enlightenment, had fatal consequences for those at the receiving end of the "civilizing mission." In addition, however, a similar challenge exists for those coming from "the other side" of the same historical process. Upholding—now under the opposite premise—the divide between "them" and "us," separating the "good" from the "bad" on the basis of pigmentation or cultural roots, leads only to the creation of the opposite dichotomy, rather than to a more fundamental change in modes of perception. It maintains an essential polarity on the basis of mutually exclusive domains and entitlements. Yet originating from a group of erstwhile victims does not protect one from becoming a perpetrator oneself. Those who have experienced discrimination are also capable of resorting to discriminatory practices themselves. Nor does originating within a group of perpetrators (in a historical and collective sense) mean that individuals are unable to emancipate their own thoughts, perceptions, convictions, commitments and deeds from this legacy—despite the ambiguities that such socio-political, cultural and, indeed, psychological processes might involve.

A similar challenge exists for those who claim the legacy of the "Wretched of the Earth" to the extent of causing suffering to others. Despite the dubious character of its logic, a policy of claiming exclusive and authentic status as victims of the German genocide has been actively pursued in interventions dominated by Herero groups on various commemorative occasions. As late as August 2004, a spokesperson for the "Coordinating Committee for the First Official Commemoration of the Ovaherero Genocide" stated that, in Namibia, the term genocide would only apply to what had happened to the Herero.[23]

Since Independence, claims to genuine Herero identity have been increasingly and inseparably linked to sole victim status vis-à-vis the colonial genocide. This linkage both created and reinforced an aura of exclusivity and consequently a "them and us" divide between the Herero and the rest of the world. As Jan-Bart Gewald has noted,

> Historically, Herero speakers were divided amongst themselves. Not all sections of Herero society were equally affected by the genocide, let alone in the Apartheid years. Yet discourse on the genocide allows people to paper over these distinctions. It is thus the first truly shared experience of all Herero speakers in the present.[24]

Members of these Herero groups tend to brush aside expressions of concern about their monopolization of victim status. They abuse their "biological authenticity" as successors to the victims in a way that excludes any serious debate of dissenting views. Instead, accusations of racism and Eurocentrism are convenient tools that readily allow an off-hand dismissal of any discussion on how best to develop the issue in a way that serves the interests of more than just one group. Vezera Kandetu, a member of the Herero community, former Dean of Students at the University of Namibia and, since 2005, the Director General of the Namibian Broadcasting Corporation, has energetically rejected the argument that the Herero were not the only victims of colonial genocide, by warning that it is "important to call attention to insensitive intellectualizing about Namibia and the genocide debate."[25] According to Kandetu,

> [T]he context of historical analysis by some academics of euro-centric orientation is infested with insensitivity and masqueraded in arrogance. For they prefer to use historical events selectively . . . This parochial perception is reinforced by the belief on the part of these experts, that they as descendants of European cultures have everything to teach others and nothing to learn from them.[26]

This polemical rebuttal of what is shrugged off as unwarranted interference denies others the right to a dissenting view and prevents any meaningful dialogue or debate. The motives of those who, in such a reductive way, seek the recognition so far denied to them may be perfectly understandable. They wish to pursue and achieve what they consider to be historical justice. But this happens at the expense of others, who remain outside of the arena defined by public interest and are therefore denied recognition as victims. This phenomenon of "competition among the victims," resulting in claims for a monopoly of victim status, is certainly not confined to the Namibian case,[27] but it is illustrated in a particularly obvious way by the Namibian situation.

The claim made by sections of the Herero people that they are the only victims of genocide under German colonial rule is only one example of a selective revisiting of the past. Another (and one which fits in with the German government's policy of half-hearted remorse) is the Namibian government's tendency to deny the descendants of the main victim groups their due recognition and specific entitlement to compensation. One commentator's observation concerning the organized memorial politics of the Holocaust holds true, equally, for the different parties and their interests in the case of Namibia's colonial genocide. As Michael Fleming has said,

> An integral component of representation is simplification. Practices of memory are not only about inclusion, but also exclusion. Some facts just don't fit with the co-creation of memory groups, national myths, propaganda agendas, or sell photos. As a consequence some groups are marginalized, histories unwritten and complexities reduced.[28]

## NOTES

1. An earlier version of this text was presented in the panel on "Genocide, Memory and Identity" at the conference "Genocides: Forms, Causes and Consequences: The Namibian War (1904–08) in Historical Perspective,"

Haus der Kulturen der Welt, Berlin, 13–15 January 2005, and has been extensively revised and updated for this volume. For related and complementary analyses, see also Henning Melber, "'Namibia, Land of the Brave': Selective Memories on War and Violence within Nation Building," in *Rethinking Resistance: Revolt and Violence in African History*, ed. by Jon Abbink, Mirjam de Bruijn and Klaas van Walraven (Leiden: Brill, 2003), pp. 305–27; and Henning Melber, "How to Come to Terms with the Past: Re-visiting the German Colonial Genocide in Namibia," *Afrika Spectrum* 40.1 (2005), 139–48. I should like to thank Casper Erichsen and Jeremy Silvester, who commented on a first draft of this text and improved its language.

2. Horst Drechsler, *Südwestafrika unter deutscher Kolonialherrschaft: Der Kampf der Herero und Nama gegen den deutschen Imperialismus (1884–1915)* (Berlin: Akademie, 1966, revised 1984; English edn London: Zed, 1980); Helmut Bley, *Kolonialherrschaft und Sozialstruktur in Deutsch-Südwestafrika 1894–1914* (Hamburg: Leibniz, 1968; English edn London: Heinemann, 1971).

3. Peter Schmitt-Egner, *Kolonialismus und Faschismus: Eine Studie zur historischen und begrifflichen Genesis faschistischer Bewusstseinsformen am deutschen Beispiel* (Giessen: Achenbach, 1975); Peter Schmitt-Egner, "Wertgesetz und Rassismus: Zur begrifflichen Genesis kolonialer und faschistischer Bewusstseinsformen," in *Gesellschaft: Beiträge zur Marxschen Theorie*, 8–9 (1976), 350–404.

4. Jan-Bart Gewald, *Herero Heroes: A Socio-Political History of the Herero of Namibia, 1890–1923* (Oxford: Currey; Athens: Ohio University Press, 1999); Gesine Krüger, *Kriegsbewältigung und Geschichtsbewusstsein: Realität, Deutung und Verarbeitung des deutschen Kolonialkrieges in Namibia 1904–1907* (Göttingen: Vandenhoeck & Ruprecht, 1999); Jürgen Zimmerer, *Deutsche Herrschaft über Afrikaner: Staatlicher Machtanspruch und Wirklichkeit im kolonialen Namibia* (Münster: Lit, 2001); Andreas Heinrich Bühler, *Der Namaaufstand gegen die deutsche Kolonialherrschaft in Namibia von 1904–1913* (Frankfurt/M.: IKO, 2003).

5. Drafted by the special rapporteur Ben Whitaker for the United Nations Sub-Commission on Prevention of Discrimination and Protection of Minorities—an element of the UN Economic and Social Council (UNESCO) Commission on Human Rights—the document was adopted as *Revised and Updated Report on the Question of the Prevention and Punishment of the Crime of Genocide* (Document E/CN.4/Sub.2/1985/6, 2 July 1985)

6. For a summary of the opposing positions and an overview of the protagonists, see Janntje Böhlke-Itzen, *Kolonialschuld und Entschädigung: Der deutsche Völkermord an den Herero 1904–1907* (Frankfurt/M.: Brandes & Apsel, 2004).

7. An article by Brigitte Lau, the late director of the Namibian national archive, who died in a car accident in the mid-1990s, has been used particularly prominently to support arguments against the genocide interpretation. Her other work contrasted markedly with the political message later abused by historical revisionists to downplay the extent of the violence in the former German colony. See Brigitte Lau, "Uncertain Certainties," *Mibagus*, 2 (1989), 4–5 and 8. Since the author's untimely death, the article has gained major prominence and been widely circulated in German translation. For recent representative arguments by those who dismiss the genocide, see, in particular, Till Philipp Koltermann, "Zwischen Amnesie und Quellenfälschung: Defizite der neuesten Historiographie zum Herero-Deutschen Krieg 1904/05," *Nachrichten, Wissenschaftliche Gesellschaft Swakopmund*, 38.2 (2006), 24–42; and Jakob Zollmann, "Polemics and Other Arguments—a German Debate

Reviewed," *Journal of Namibia Studies*, 1.1 (2007), 109–30. A major contribution to the controversy surrounding the contested notion of genocide, originally presented in response to Brigitte Lau's surprising view, is Tilman Dedering, "The German-Herero War of 1904: Revisionism of Genocide or Imaginary Historiography?" *Journal of Southern African Studies*, 19.1 (1993), 80–8. For an interesting recent contextualization of the controversial article, see Werner Hillebrecht, "'Certain uncertainties': or Venturing Progressively into Colonial Apologetics?" *Journal of Namibia Studies*, 1.1 (2007), 73–95. A polemical discussion siding with those accused of being "genocidals" and attacking "revisionists" and "fence sitters" is Christoph Marx, "Entsorgen und Entseuchen: Zur Diskussionskultur in der derzeitigen namibischen Historiographie—eine Polemik," in *Genozid und Gedenken: Namibisch-deutsche Geschichte und Gegenwart*, ed. by Henning Melber (Frankfurt/M.: Brandes & Apsel, 2005), pp. 141–61.

8. I had already positioned myself along these lines more than a quarter of a century ago; see the later summary, Henning Melber, "Kontinuitäten totaler Herrschaft: Völkermord und Apartheid in 'Deutsch-Südwestafrika': Zur kolonialen Herrschaftspraxis im Deutschen Kaiserreich," in *Jahrbuch für Antisemitismusforschung*, vol. 1, ed. by Wolfgang Benz (Frankfurt/M.: Campus, 1992), pp. 91–116. For a range of related positions, see contributions to the two comprehensive volumes compiled on occasion of the centenary: *Völkermord in Deutsch-Südwestafrika: Der Kolonialkrieg (1904–1908) in Namibia und seine Folgen*, ed. by Jürgen Zimmerer and Joachim Zeller (Berlin: Links, 2003; revised and updated English version, Monmouth: Merlin, 2008); and *Namibia—Deutschland: Eine geteilte Geschichte. Widerstand—Gewalt—Erinnerung*, ed. by Larissa Förster, Dag Henrichsen and Michael Bollig (Cologne: Minerva, 2004).

9. Trutz von Trotha, "Genozidaler Pazifizierungskrieg: Soziologische Anmerkungen zum Konzept des Genozids am Beispiel des Kolonialkriegs in Deutsch-Südwestafrika, 1904–1907," *Zeitschrift für Genozidforschung*, 4.2 (2003), 31–58.

10. Hendrik Lundtofte. "'I believe that the nation as such must be annihilated . . . '—The Radicalization of the German Suppression of the Herero Rising in 1904," in *Genocide: Cases, Comparisons and Contemporary Debates*, ed. by Steven L.B. Jensen (Copenhagen: Danish Center for Holocaust and Genocide Studies, 2003), pp. 15–53.

11. Reinhart Kössler, "Public Memory, Reconciliation and the Aftermath of War: A Preliminary Framework with Special Reference to Namibia," in *Re-examining Liberation in Namibia: Political Culture since Independence*, ed. by Henning Melber (Uppsala: Nordic Africa Institute, 2003), pp. 99–112.

12. Department of Information and Publicity/SWAPO of Namibia, *To Be Born A Nation: The Liberation Struggle for Namibia* (London: Zed, 1981), p. 14f.

13. Stephanie Heise, "Herero-Häuptling greift Deutschland an," *Allgemeine Zeitung*, 27 August 2002. The Herero perspective on the colonial genocide and its consequences informs the work of Jan-Bart Gewald, as summarized in: "Herero Genocide in the Twentieth Century: Politics and Memory," in *Rethinking Resistance: Revolt and Violence in African History*, ed. by Jon Abbink, Mirjam de Bruijn and Klaas van Walraven (Leiden: Brill, 2003), pp. 279–304; see also Jan-Bart Gewald and Henning Melber, "Genozid, Herero-Identität(en) und die Befreiungsbewegung an der Macht," in Melber (ed.), *Genozid und Gedenken*, pp. 79–102.

14. It should be noted that, mainly through the initiative of the Evangelical churches as manifested in the so-called "Bishops' Committee," a few

members of the local German-speaking community were willing to participate in these activities.

15. Eberhard Hofmann, "Briefmarke zur Versöhnung," *Allgemeine Zeitung*, 27 November 2003. It is one of the numerous ironies of post-colonial Namibian reality that, in an editorial published the following day, the same journalist expressed appreciation of the conscientiousness this position would signal in relation to dealing with the past; see Eberhard Hofmann, "Sorgfalt im Engagement," *Allgemeine Zeitung*, 28 November 2003.

16. Irmgard Schreiber, "Debatte um Gedenken: 1904—nationale oder ethnische Gedenkfeier?" *Allgemeine Zeitung*, 1 December 2003.

17. The co-organising local *Pfadfinderbund*, the *Alte Kameraden* and the *Traditionsverband ehemaliger Schutz- und Überseetruppen* represent some of the most conservative and colonial-apologetic segments of the German minority in Namibia. Their history (and ideology) dates back to the anything-but-good old days. The infamous battle at Waterberg essentially marked the beginning of the genocide and the demise of the Herero.

18. Republic of Namibia, Office of the President, "Presidential Press Release," *New Era*, 8–10 August 2003.

19. Petros Kuteeue, "Nujoma to Miss 1904 Genocide Service," *The Namibian*, 9 January 2004.

20. Quoted in Petros Kuteeue, "No Apology, No Payout for Herero," *The Namibian*, 12 January 2004. I termed such complicity elsewhere a pact among elites, and was taken to task for this by Birthe Kundrus in "Grenzen der Gleichsetzung: Kolonialverbrechen und Vernichtungspolitik," *iz3w*, 275 (2004), p. 33. Kundrus emphasised that, whether one likes it or not, the distancing from the Herero initiative and any other form of compensation claim was the decision of a sovereign Namibian government. While this is undisputed, it nonetheless remains a pact among (government) elites. While governments may be formally entitled to undertake dubious initiatives, others are at liberty to criticize them for these.

21. An impressively detailed overview of relevant activities has documented six separate exhibitions and over 20 different seminars, panel debates, public lectures series and conferences from mid-2003 until mid-2005 in Germany—far more than in Namibia. In addition, several public acts of commemoration have been held in various locations. It is noteworthy, however, that none of these had an official character, in the sense of being initiated (or attended) by German state authorities. See Joachim Zeller, "Genozid und Gedenken—ein dokumentarischer Überblick," in *Genozid und Gedenken*, pp. 163–88.

22. See especially Reinhart Kössler and Henning Melber, "Völkermord und Gedenken: Der Genozid an den Herero und Nama in Deutsch-Südwestafrika 1904–1908," in *Völkermord und Kriegsverbrechen in der ersten Hälfte des 20. Jahrhunderts: Jahrbuch 2004 zur Geschichte und Wirkung des Holocaust*, ed. by Fritz Bauer Institut (Frankfurt/M.: Campus, 2004), pp. 37–75. Most prominent among those arguing along similar lines is Jürgen Zimmerer; for a summary of his approach, see "Rassenkrieg und Völkermord: Der Kolonialkrieg in Deutsch-Südwestafrika und die Globalgeschichte des Genozids," in Melber (ed.), *Genozid und Gedenken*, pp. 23–48. Medardus Brehl offers a related perspective in his recent article, "'Diese Schwarzen haben vor Gott und Menschen den Tod verdient': Der Völkermord an den Herero 1904 und seine zeitgenössische Legitimation," in *Völkermord und Kriegsverbrechen*, pp. 77–97; and *Vernichtung der Herero: Diskurse der Gewalt in der deutschen Kolonialliteratur* (Munich: Fink, 2007). Critics of these views tend to oversimplify our approaches by constructing a notion of linearity, determinism or mono-causality between the subsequent events to

which none of us subscribe. Such misleading interpretations certainly make it easier to dismiss the suggested continuities. Classic examples are Pascal Grosse, "What Does German Colonialism Have to Do with National Socialism? A Conceptual Framework," in *Germany's Colonial Pasts*, ed. by Eric Ames, Marcia Klotz and Lora Wildenthal (Lincoln: University of Nebraska Press, 2005), pp. 115–34; and Birthe Kundrus, "From the Herero to the Holocaust? Some Remarks on the Current Debate," *Africa Spectrum*, 40.2 (2005), 299–308. Interestingly enough, Kundrus after her shadow-boxing presents a range of challenging topics for further research, and these are very similar to the investigations proposed by those whose approaches she had just rejected. For a response, see Reinhart Kössler, "From Genocide to Holocaust? Structural Parallels and Discursive Continuities," *Africa Spectrum*, 40.2 (2005), 309–17.

23. Quotation taken from "Whose Genocide? Why are Only the Herero Taking the Bull by the Horns?" *Insight*, September 2004, p. 20.

24. Gewald, "Herero Genocide," p. 303.

25. Vezera Kandetu, "Namibia Cold Discourse Upon Chronic Pain," *New African*, January 2005, p. 66.

26. Ibid., p. 65.

27. One of the most prominent examples is the dominant association of the Holocaust with an exclusively Jewish victimization process and status. Other targets of annihilation, such as the Sinti and Roma, as well as homosexuals, have long been denied recognition as Holocaust victims. Even the newly erected Holocaust memorial in Berlin only commemorates Jewish victims and fails to recognize other groups which faced systematic mass murder.

28. Michael Fleming, "Holocaust and Memory," *Ethnopolitics*, 4.1 (2005), p. 122.

# 20 The Struggle for Genocidal Exclusivity

## The Perception of the Murder of the Namibian Herero (1904–8) in the Age of a New International Morality

*Dominik J. Schaller*

Each year in the last weekend in August, representatives of the Herero gather in Okahandja, a central Namibian town, to celebrate "Herero Day." The men parade in traditional military uniforms and make a procession to the graves of the old Herero chiefs. The origin of this annual ceremony of commemoration is the funeral of Samuel Maharero in August 1923. After the bloody suppression of the Hereros' resistance against German rule during the colonial war of 1904–8, Maharero had managed to escape to British Botswana, where he remained in exile until his death. The transfer of his mortal remains to Namibia and his burial in Okahandja on 26 August 1923 were a milestone in the history of the Herero: for the first time since the German colonizers' attempt to annihilate the Herero and destroy their ethnic identity, the survivors and their descendants demonstrated publicly that they had achieved social and political reorganization and were once again a self-aware and self-administering political community with a distinct national identity.[1] The German historian Gesine Krüger has noted that, before the war against the Germans, the Herero had not perceived themselves as a nation, for nationhood is in reality a concept and category of European origin. The reorganization and the identity-building of the Herero can thus be understood as an "invented tradition," and as an innovative way of dealing with the disastrous social effects of the colonial war.[2]

Although German colonial rule in Namibia had "only" lasted for 30 years, its bloody legacy is still present in Namibia and makes up a large part of the Hereros' collective memory. It can be added that the central position of victimhood in post-colonial identity is a global phenomenon: the struggle for historical justice and against annihilation unites politically and even culturally dispersed societies in regions formerly dominated by foreign colonizers. It is not surprising that "Herero Day" has become the platform upon which leaders of Herero opinion demand financial reparations from Germany. Until the end of the Cold War and Namibia's independence, these claims remained unheard and the murder of the Herero by the German *Schutztruppe* was just one of the many forgotten genocides in world history. The commemoration in August 2004, however, marked an important caesura. The German Minister of Economic Cooperation and

Development, Heidemarie Wieczorek-Zeul, visited Namibia and attended a ceremony marking the centenary of the Battle of Waterberg on 11 August 1904, and during the ceremony she apologized for the atrocities committed by the German colonizers:

> A century ago, the oppressors "blinded by colonialist fervor" became agents of violence, discrimination, racism and annihilation in Germany's name. The atrocities committed at that time would today be termed genocide and nowadays a General von Trotha would be prosecuted and convicted. We Germans accept our historical and moral responsibility and the guilt incurred by Germans at that time. And so, in the words of the Lord's Prayer that we share, I ask you to forgive us our trespasses.[3]

The official German apology was widely celebrated as a promising start to a European state's unbiased dealing with a dark and largely neglected episode of its past, as well as a potential example for other former colonial powers to follow. The Herero, however, were not at all convinced, since the German government refused to pay retrospective compensation. Kuaima Riruako, Paramount Chief of the Herero, has claimed that the German unwillingness to provide the Herero with financial reparations is because the victims of German colonialism were "only" Africans. He thus accuses Wieczorek-Zeul and her colleagues of racism.[4]

Nevertheless, the perception of Wieczorek-Zeul's speech and the related discussion of financial compensation show that the fate of the Herero is no longer forgotten. Whereas, before the turn of the millennium, only a small handful of Western historians were interested in German colonial rule in Africa, the colonial war of 1904–8 and the murder of the Herero seem finally to have entered the German collective memory.[5] The topic is now taught at German schools and universities and has been the topic of several major academic conferences. A widely noted exhibition staged by the German Historical Museum in Berlin in 2004–5, TV documentaries and the publication of popular scientific books on German rule in Namibia have all provided the public with pertinent information. However, the increased awareness of the murder of the Herero is not limited to Germany. Rather, it has become part of global memory. International genocide scholarship, for example, has adopted the case of the Herero and portrays it as the archetypal colonial genocide or even the first genocide of the twentieth century. This phenomenon can partly be explained by the fact that the murder of the Herero is often understood as a kind of precursor of the Holocaust and is viewed as the "first German genocide."[6] Thus, most genocide scholars agree that the extermination of the Herero must be accorded significant and adequate space in the global history of mass violence or the "archaeology of genocide."[7] It is no longer possible to omit the case of the Herero from genocide studies and the related textbooks.[8]

In short, the German genocide against the Herero, which was forgotten and ignored outside Namibia for almost 100 years, has gained considerable academic and public prominence in the last decade. But how did this come about? What mechanisms and factors caused the annihilation of the Herero to emerge from the shadows? And why is the fate of the Herero recognized as *the* imperial genocide, and not, for instance, the equally brutal suppression of the Mau-Mau movement in Kenya in 1952–7, the Italian atrocities in Libya in 1923–33, or the so-called Maji-Maji War in what is now Tanzania, where the German scorched-earth policy resulted in the deaths of hundreds of thousands of Africans?

An answer to these questions must take account of a phenomenon that has emerged with the end of the Cold War: a new international morality. This term was coined by the Israeli historian Elazar Barkan and is based on the observation that victims of historical injustices or their descendants have increasingly turned to restitution in order to remedy past sufferings.[9] Relative prosperity and political openness after the dissolution of the bipolar world system together with euphoric hopes that the fall of the Berlin Wall would lead to the "end of history" (Francis Fukuyama), or at least to a new peaceful and just world order, have fostered Western politicians' readiness to recognize, apologize for and probably even pay restitution for such historical injustices as genocide, expulsion or systematic dispossession. Moreover, although colonialism and genocidal mass violence were already previously central elements of memory in Africa, Asia and Latin America, European concessions of guilt have further heightened the significance of victimhood in the ex-colonies for the process of post-colonial identity-building.

However, as my earlier reference to the Mau-Mau War in Kenya or the brutal suppression of the Maji-Maji movement indicates, not all cases of past injustice are subject to reconciliation or reparation. This relates to a distinctive characteristic of the era of the new international morality: the acrimonious competition which often exists between different victim groups.[10] Whether the fate of a certain group will be internationally recognized and thus integrated into global collective memory depends not least on the power of the respective lobbies and their ability to stir the public into action and raise international pressure. Consequently, it is not coincidental that certain cases of mass murder or genocide are remembered and others are not. Collective memories are thus subject to a specific kind of politics: the politics of memory. National parliaments and international bodies like the European Council, national and international courts of justice and, above all, historiography have become the principal arenas for memory politics. In these fora, different victim groups compete for political, academic and media attention and seek recognition of their fate as genocide, which is regarded internationally as the worst possible crime, the crime of crimes. But, since the label "genocide" appears devalued if too many instances of mass murder are associated with it, victim groups and their lobbies dispute other victims' claims. The struggle for genocidal exclusivity is thus a characteristic feature of memory politics and of the age of a new international morality.

It is the intention of this chapter to describe the political struggle around global memory and discuss the motives of the participants in that struggle—in order thereby to understand the strategies adopted by representatives of the Herero and ways in which their claim has successfully competed with the demands of other victim groups for historical justice.

## THE CENTRAL POSITION OF THE HOLOCAUST IN THE AGE OF A NEW INTERNATIONAL MORALITY

Elazar Barkan's assertion that a new international morality conditions the way Western societies nowadays come to terms with the dark sides of their pasts is well founded. Recent changes in the nature of political and public exposure to the murder and dispossession of European Jewry by the National Socialists and their allies is the best example: whereas the fate of Jewish survivors was largely ignored until the 1980s, their claims were given serious consideration from the 1990s onward. As a consequence, Swiss banks, for instance, were accused of refusing to return monies deposited with them by Jews seeking a safe place for their assets in the face of persecution and extermination. For several decades, survivors and the descendants of the original owners of dormant accounts had vainly struggled to secure the return of their property. Not until international political pressure—mainly from the United States—grew significantly were Swiss financial institutions ready to cooperate with Jewish representatives and organizations. What is more, Holocaust assets litigation led to a rewriting of Swiss national history. Switzerland's carefully cultivated image as a heroic country that had resisted the German threat during World War Two and had selflessly welcomed Jewish refugees had to be drastically revised. The results presented by an official commission of historians led the Swiss government to apologize officially for the non-acceptance of Jewish refugees.

The Holocaust restitution movement that was launched in the 1990s has been rather successful: not only Switzerland and its banks were accused, but also financial institutions throughout Europe. Furthermore, German and Austrian companies were finally forced to compensate former slave laborers from Eastern Europe. Currently, courts in Central Europe and in the United States are confronted with cases concerning the restitution of looted art. As a result of the political and legal efforts of Jewish victim groups, Holocaust-era settlement payouts have so far totaled more than 8 billion U.S. dollars.[11]

As indicated previously, the Holocaust restitution movement has had a deep impact on historiography and on the public perception of this instance of genocide. The increased public and scholarly interest in the murder of the

European Jews by the Nazis has been accompanied by a de-contextualization and de-historification of the event. The Holocaust is widely perceived as an experience unparalleled in human history, since the Nazis' aim was the extermination of every single Jew in the world. The American professor of religion Steven T. Katz therefore claims that the Holocaust is the only genocide that has ever occurred.[12] Closely related to the influential uniqueness thesis is the widespread belief that it will never be possible to grasp intellectually the Nazis' policy of hatred and genocide. Accordingly, the Holocaust has assumed a kind of universal religious quality as a symbol of radical evil. As the historian Peter Novick has convincingly shown, the Holocaust has in the last 10 years become a central element of American identity.[13] Although the murder of the Jews did not happen in North America, the event has moved to the center of American intellectual, cultural, religious and political life. Thus, the Holocaust serves as a moral concept in a globalized collective memory.[14]

## RIVALS IN THE ARENA OF SUCCESSFUL MEMORY POLITICS

The new global significance of the Holocaust has altered the status of victimhood as such. This is especially true for many post-colonial societies in Africa. Whereas, during the first decades after colonization, representatives of former anti-colonial resistance movements stressed and glorified African strength and persistence in the fight against the European colonizers, the memory of suffering has increasingly become the constituent feature of modern identity building. The successes achieved by the Holocaust restitution movement have also encouraged representatives of other victim groups to ask for material compensation and symbolic justice. Among the more prominent cases are the demands by victims of Japanese slave labor during World War Two, claims by African Americans for reparation for pre–Civil War slavery, and litigation against U.S. and European companies for cooperating with the apartheid regime in South Africa.

Compared to the amounts the Holocaust restitution movement has obtained, the 37.5 million U.S. dollars secured by the descendants of survivors of the Armenian genocide through class action lawsuits against insurance companies for unpaid policies purchased by victims of the Young Turks seem rather modest.[15] Nevertheless, Armenian lobby groups have been highly successful in memory politics. Despite the Turkish government's ongoing denial, the murder of the Anatolian Armenians during World War One is far from being a "forgotten genocide." Armenian activists and human rights campaigners who sympathize with their cause have conducted a struggle against Turkish denial for the international recognition of this genocide. Both international bodies like the European Parliament and national parliaments have acknowledged the fate of the Armenians as representing genocide and have passed laws prohibiting its public denial. And these laws are no paper tigers: in Switzerland and France, for instance, the denial of the Armenian genocide has concrete legal consequences. Whereas the Swiss "anti-racism law" of 1994 prohibits the denial of genocide as such, the French National Assembly considers only the negation of the Holocaust and that of the Armenian genocide to be a punishable offence. By so doing, the French give preferential treatment to specific victim groups and attach greater importance to their fate than to that of others.

Since its establishment, genocide scholarship has been infused with activist ideals and principles. It is therefore not surprising that leading representatives of this still young discipline sympathize with the Armenians' concerns and participate in their struggle for historical justice. To achieve academic and consequent political recognition of the murder of the Armenians, scholars have resorted to the method which is commonly applied in genocide studies: comparison. Although the aim of objective scholarly comparison is the identification of similarities and differences, genocide scholars' approach is often reductive, since their ultimate aim is to place the destruction of the Armenians on the same level as the Holocaust, which is regarded as genocide in its pure form.[16] Thus, scholars struggling to gain international recognition for the Armenian genocide stress only the similarities of these two genocidal cases and neglect the differences that exist. Moreover, studies of the extermination of the Armenians claim that the event is (mono-) causally connected with the Nazi genocide against the Jews. Hitler's infamous Armenian quotation ("Who, after all, speaks today of the annihilation of the Armenians?") from August 1939, shortly before the German attack on Poland, serves as evidence for this thesis.[17] The fact that the quotation is in all likelihood inauthentic is generally ignored.[18]

The strategy of pro-Armenian activists and scholars to link the genocide by the Young Turks with the Holocaust has proved highly successful. The murder of the Armenians and the Turkish denial have become contemporary issues and are regularly covered by the media. As a result, the violent dissolution of the Ottoman Empire is solely associated with the Armenians, while the fate of other victim groups (Kurds, Greeks, and Assyrians) is truly forgotten.[19]

Since 2005, when the world commemorated the centenary of the beginning of the Young Turks' extermination program, the Armenian tragedy has commonly been regarded as the "first genocide" of the twentieth century or even the "first modern genocide." The categories of "modern" and "pre-modern" genocide can often be found in the scholarly literature. Their scientific value, however, is highly questionable, given their inherently judgmental character. Scholars who resort to them suggest a clear dividing line between modern genocides like the Armenian and Jewish cases and so-called pre-modern genocides such as, for example, colonial mass murder; and they sustain this by asserting that the motives of the Nazis and the Young Turks were racist or nationalist and thus "irrational," whereas perpetrators of "pre-modern" genocides were mainly driven by "rational" motives such as greed or revenge.[20] This approach leads inevitably to a "double uniqueness thesis," which claims that both the Holocaust and the murder of the Armenians are distinctive and are the only "real genocides." The result of such an exploitation of the comparative method is a hierarchy of suffering, which is the logical outgrowth and predominant characteristic of memory politics.

Although atrocities and campaigns of mass murder committed by former European colonial powers do not normally gain privileged status in the pantheon of genocides, these cases are not completely elided by the new international morality asserted by Elazar Barkan. In February 2008, for instance, the Australian Prime Minister Kevin Rudd declared a national apology for the state program of "breeding out the color" and the corresponding forcible removal of children from Aboriginal families, which lasted until 1940. Another example of an apology by a former imperial power is the speech by Heidemarie Wieczorek-Zeul in Okakarara/Namibia in August 2005, mentioned earlier. It is true that both Rudd and Wieczorek-Zeul were disinclined to use the word "genocide" in their apologies. Whereas the German Minister of Development at least stated that the massacre committed by General Lothar von Trotha "would today be termed genocide," the Australian Prime Minister omitted the "g-word" completely.[21] This reluctance can partly be explained by the widespread fear of diminishing the significance and supposed uniqueness of the Holocaust by calling "pre-modern" atrocities genocide; in addition, however, Western politicians are afraid that the admission of genocide would lead to an avalanche of reparation claims by formerly colonized peoples. Nevertheless, both Herero and Aborigines insist that their peoples were genocide victims. It is not the legal background alone that generates this persistence. If the status of genocide victimhood were internationally acknowledged, their fate would gain considerable significance as a crime akin to the Holocaust.

As already stated in the introductory section of this chapter, the annihilation of the Herero is probably the best-known case of colonial mass murder and the one most generally acknowledged to have been genocide. This is quite remarkable, since the Herero, as victims of a so-called "pre-modern" genocide, would normally have much greater difficulty in attracting media and scholarly attention than those of a more recent episode. Analysis of the text of the claim submitted by the Herero People's Reparation Corporation in September 2001 in New York reveals that the Herero representatives adopted a strategy similar to that of Armenian lobby groups: they stressed mono-causal links between their fate and the Holocaust.

## THE MURDER OF THE HERERO AS A
## PRECURSOR OF THE HOLOCAUST?

In September 2001, the Herero People's Reparation Corporation filed a lawsuit against three German companies at the U.S. Federal Court. The plaintiffs accused these companies of having supported the German military campaign in South-West Africa, in 1904–8, which had led to the extermination of the Herero, and they claimed reparations to the sum of 2 billion U.S. dollars. A few weeks later, the Reparation Corporation filed a separate claim for the same amount against the government of the Federal Republic of Germany in respect of the annihilation of the Herero. Since the terror attacks of 9/11 dominated the media coverage almost completely, the Hereros' claim did not attract great attention, although it was the first time an ethnic group had demanded reparations for colonial policies that fitted the definition of genocide.[22] The Herero claimants based their claim on the Alien Torts Claim Act of 1789, which grants jurisdiction to U.S. Federal Courts over "any civil action by an alien for a tort only, committed in violation of the law of nations or a treaty of the United States." Thus, American legal culture provided the Herero with convenient conditions for their cause.[23]

Nevertheless, the Hereros' claims encountered numerous political and legal obstacles. As already mentioned, Western politicians have not been at all interested in a positive outcome of this case, since they are afraid this would motivate other victim groups to follow the Herero example. Furthermore, it is a matter of dispute whether the 1948 United Nations Genocide Convention can be applied retroactively to cases of mass murder that have occurred before its ratification. Due to these legal problems and their lawsuit's minimal chances of success, the plaintiffs sought to fuel emotions and attract as much attention as possible by linking their fate to the Holocaust. In their statement of claim, the Herero People's Reparation Corporation described the murder of their people as a direct precursor of the Nazi genocide:

> Foreshadowing with chilling precision the irredeemable horror of the European Holocaust only decades later, the defendants [the three German companies] and Imperial Germany formed a German commercial enterprise which cold-bloodedly employed explicitly sanctioned extermination, the destruction of tribal culture and social organization, concentration camps, forced labor, medical experimentation and the exploitation of women and children in order to advance their common financial interests.[24]

In the Hereros' claim statement (as, quite often, in the less reflective academic writing on the colonial war in Namibia), the infamous German anthropologist Eugen Fischer serves as living proof of the causal linkage between the two genocides:

> German geneticist Eugene [sic] Fischer commenced his racial medical experiments in the concentration camps in South West Africa. He used the Herero and mulattos—the offspring of the German settlers and Herero women—as guinea pigs. Fischer tortured Herero men and

women to explore his horrific theories about race. A book he wrote about his findings, The Principle of Human Heredity and Race Hygiene, was a favourite of Adolf Hitler. Fischer later became chancellor of the University of Berlin, where he taught medicine to Nazi physicians, including Josef Mengele.[25]

From a historian's perspective, this construction of causality is too crude. It is true that Fischer conducted research among the Rehobothers in Namibia, though not during the war and not in concentration camps. The aim of this historical misrepresentation is clear: major names such as Hitler and Mengele guarantee attention, increase pressure on Germany, and thus contribute to international recognition of the Hereros' fate. In fact, ideological and even personal continuities between German colonial rule in Africa and the Nazis' policy of occupation and extermination certainly exist, as the work of Jürgen Zimmerer and others has convincingly shown;[26] but these are complex connections requiring sophisticated approaches, and are not elucidated by political polemics.

## MEMORY POLITICS AND THE STRUGGLE FOR GENOCIDAL EXCLUSIVITY IN NAMIBIA

In Namibia, the Hereros' claim for reparation led to political controversy and dispute among the country's different ethnic groups. The national government, dominated by representatives of the Ovambo, which is Namibia's largest population group, refused to support Kuaima Riruako's efforts to secure compensation. Politicians of the South West Africa People's Organization (SWAPO), the governing party, are fearful that the Hereros' demands might damage Namibia's special relationship to its former colonizer and put an end to the flow of funds from Germany. Hitherto, Namibia has been one of the major recipients of German development funding, and both German and SWAPO politicians understand this aid as a kind of reparation for the sufferings stemming from the colonial conquest.[27] The Herero, however, do not accept this view. They claim that the government misuses these monies for investments in northern Namibia, which is mainly populated by Ovambo, and that the latter were not affected by German colonial rule in the same manner as the Herero. In fact, the SWAPO government rejects the exclusive status of the Herero as victims of European imperialism and, instead of commemorating the colonial war of 1904–8 in isolation, it prefers the celebration of national Namibian anti-colonial resistance in general, which includes both the Hereros' fight against the Germans and the Ovambo-led struggle against South African apartheid. This attitude is motivated by the fear that the Herero might transform their moral capital, which stems from their self-alleged status as prime victims of German colonialism, into political

274 Dominik J. Schaller

capital and consequently challenge the dominant position of the Ovambo in Namibian politics.

Although the Namibian government seeks to protect its own and the Ovambos' interests, its accusation that the Herero leaders contribute to the promotion of tribalism through their insistence on separate German reparations cannot be dismissed completely. In a speech at the parliament in Windhoek, Kuaima Riruako made quite clear that he perceives the Herero as the sole victims of the German colonizers: "The Ovaherero was the only group singled out to be exterminated by an official legal order."[28] This quotation reveals that in Namibia, too, the competition among different victim groups and the corresponding struggle for genocidal exclusivity is in full swing: the Herero, themselves for a long time the victims of genocide denial, deliberately negate the fate of other groups. Both Nama and San (the so-called "Bushmen") were subject to genocidal violence at the time of German colonial rule: after the military defeat of the Herero in 1904, German colonial troops resorted to massacres against non-combatants, deportations, incarceration in concentration camps and slave labor in order to suppress the Namas' resistance. Until the end of German rule in South-West Africa in 1914, the *Schutztruppe* regularly hunted the nomadic San and tried to force them to settle in permanent villages, which is a clear case of cultural genocide.[29]

## CONCLUDING REMARK: THE SPIRAL OF MEMORY POLITICS

Since the end of the Cold War, the veneration of martyrdom and victim-hood has become important for the construction of collective memories and national histories. Suffering is increasingly valued and promoted. In post-colonial societies, this phenomenon must be understood as a crucial element in the nation-building process. As the charisma and unifying qualities of the old anti-colonial resistance movements fade, the artificially established nation states in Africa need new legitimizing foundations. If the nation is perceived as a community of fate, then ethnic, economic and political diversities and tensions can be overcome, so some African politicians hope. The more significant the nation's fate appears, the more successfully it can be used to unify society. Leaders in post-colonial states therefore try to stress the exclusivity of their nation's victimhood by calling it genocide and by struggling for international recognition. In fact, only the loudest voices are heard, which leads to a global competition among victim groups. As a result, some cases of colonial mass violence are nowadays well known, whereas others are still ignored.

Until the late 1990s, the murder of the Herero was forgotten outside Namibia. Most Germans did not even know that their country had once occupied considerable parts of Africa. But matters have changed: the Herero genocide has become more and more a part of global collective memory and is nowadays recognized as one of the worst crimes in history. The increased perception of this case is not least the result of clever lobbying activities and the tireless efforts of pressure groups. The other side of the coin is that the growth of memory politics generates ever more elaborate hierarchies of suffering: if the genocidal war against the Nama and the forced assimilation of the San in German South-West Africa have been neglected in historiography and public memory, the suppression of the so-called Maji-Maji movement in present-day Tanzania is completely and truly forgotten. Although the war in German East Africa, in which up to 300,000 Africans were killed or starved to death, had no less devastating consequences for the indigenous societies in that region than did the German warfare in Namibia for the Herero and Nama, the centennial commemoration of the outbreak of this war in 2005 attracted far less attention than the remembrance the previous year of the murder of the Herero.

## NOTES

1. Jan-Bart Gewald, "The Funeral of Samuel Maharero and the Reorganisation of the Herero," in *Genocide in German South-West Africa. The Colonial War of 1904–1908 and its Aftermath*, ed. by Jürgen Zimmerer and Joachim Zeller (Monmouth: Merlin, 2008), pp. 207–16.
2. Gesine Krüger, *Kriegsbewältigung und Geschichtsbewusstsein. Realität, Deutung und Verarbeitung des deutschen Kolonialkriegs in Namibia 1904 bis 1907* (Göttingen: Vandenhoeck & Ruprecht, 1999), pp. 201–3.
3. Speech by Heidemarie Wieczorek-Zeul at the commemorations of the 100th anniversary of the suppression of the Herero uprising, Okakarara, Namibia, 14 August 2004. An English version of the speech can be found on the Web site of the German embassy in Windhoek: <http://www.windhuk.diplo.de/Vertretung/windhuk/en/03/Bilaterale__Beziehungen/seite__rede__bmz__engl__okakahandja.html> [accessed 19 August 2008].
4. See Jürgen Zimmerer, 'Entschädigung für Herero und Nama,' *Blätter für deutsche und internationale Politik*, 50.6 (2005), 658–60 (p. 658).
5. The pioneering works on the German war against the Herero are Helmut Bley, *Southwest Africa Under German Rule* (Oxford: Heinemann, 1971); Horst Drechsler, *Let Us Die Fighting: Namibia Under the Germans* (London: Zed, 1984); Gesine Krüger, *Kriegsbewältigung und Geschichtsbewusstsein*; Jürgen Zimmerer, *Deutsche Herrschaft über Afrikaner* (Münster: LIT, 2001).
6. Jürgen Zimmerer, 'War, Concentration Camps and Genocide in South-West Africa: The first German Genocide,' in *Genocide in South-West Africa*, pp. 41–63.
7. Jürgen Zimmerer, 'Colonialism and the Holocaust: Towards an Archaeology of Genocide,' in *Genocide and Settler Society. Frontier Violence and Stolen Indigenous Children in Australian History*, ed. by A. Dirk Moses (New York: Berghahn, 2004), pp. 49–76.
8. On the historiography of the Herero genocide, see Jürgen Zimmerer, 'Colonial Genocide: the Herero and Nama War (1904–8) in German South West Africa and its Significance,' in *The Historiography of Genocide*, ed. by Dan Stone (Basingstoke: Palgrave Macmillan, 2008), pp. 323–43.

9. Elazar Barkan, *The Guilt of Nations. Restitution and Negotiating Historical Injustices* (New York: Norton, 2000).

10. Jean-Michel Chaumont, *La concurrence des victimes. Génocide, identité, reconnaissance* (Paris: Editions La Découverte & Syros, 1997).

11. Michael J. Bazyler, "Lex Americana: Holocaust Litigation as a Restitution Model for Other Massive Human Rights Abuses," in *Enteignet-Vertrieben-Ermordet. Beiträge zur Genozidforschung*, ed. by Dominik J. Schaller et al. (Zürich: Chronos, 2004), pp. 349–94 (p. 349).

12. Steven T. Katz, *The Holocaust and Comparative History* (New York: Leo Baeck Institute, 1993).

13. Peter Novick, *The Holocaust in American Life* (Boston: Houghton Mifflin, 2000).

14. Daniel Levy and Natan Sznaider, *Holocaust and Memory in the Global Age* (Philadelphia: Temple University Press, 2006).

15. Bazyler, *Lex Americana*, pp. 367–9.

16. For an unbiased comparison between the Holocaust and the Armenian genocide, see the contributions in *The Armenian Genocide and the Shoah*, ed. by Hans-Lukas Kieser and Dominik J. Schaller (Zürich: Chronos, 2002).

17. Vahakn N. Dadrian, *The History of the Armenian Genocide: Ethnic Conflict from the Balkans to Anatolia to the Caucasus* (New York: Berghahn, 1995), p. 403.

18. Dominik J. Schaller, "Der Völkermord an den Armeniern und der Holocaust. Grenzen und Möglichkeiten eines Vergleichs," in *Zum 90. Gedenkjahr des Völkermordes an den Armeniern 1915–2005. Stimmen aus Deutschland*, ed. by Ischchan Tschiftdschjan (Beirut: Druckerei des Armenischen Katholikosats, 2005), pp. 196–201 (p. 200).

19. Dominik J. Schaller and Jürgen Zimmerer, "Late Ottoman Genocides: the Dissolution of the Ottoman Empire and Young Turkish Population and Extermination Policies," *Journal of Genocide Research*, 10.1 (2008), 7–14.

20. Yehuda Bauer, *Die dunkle Seite der Geschichte. Die Shoah in historischer Sicht. Interpretationen und Re-Interpretationen* (Frankfurt/M.: Jüdischer Verlag Suhrkamp, 2001), pp. 71–4.

21. Tony Barta, "Sorry, and Not Sorry, in Australia: How the Apology to the Stolen Generations Buried a History of Genocide," *Journal of Genocide Research*, 10.2 (2008), 191–9.

22. Allan D. Cooper, "Reparations for the Herero Genocide: Defining the Limits of International Litigation," *African Affairs*, 106.422 (2007), 113–26 (p. 113).

23. Bazyler, *Lex Americana*, p. 374f.

24. The Hereros' statement of claim can be found on the following Web site: <http://www.ipr.uni-heidelberg.de/Mitarbeiter/Professoren/Hess/Hess-Forschung/zwang/herero.pdf> [accessed 19 August 2008]. The quotation is from p. 21.

25. Ibid., p. 57.

26. Jürgen Zimmerer, "The Birth of the Ostland out of the Spirit of Colonialism: A Postcolonial Perspective on Nazi Policy of Conquest and Extermination," *Patterns of Prejudice*, 39.2 (2005), 197–219.

27. Henning Melber, "'We never spoke about reparations': German-Namibian Relations between Amnesia, Aggression and Reconciliation," in *Genocide in German South-West Africa. The Colonial War of 1904–1908 and Its Aftermath*, ed. by Jürgen Zimmerer and Joachim Zeller (Monmouth: Merlin, 2008), pp. 259–73.

28. Motion on the Ovaherero Genocide introduced in the Namibian Parliament by the Honorable Kuaima Riruako, Paramount Chief of the Ovaherero

people, 19 September 2006. The text can be found on the Web site of the *Association of the Ovaherero Genocide in the U.S.A.*: <http://ovahererog-enocideassociationusa.org> [accessed 19 August 2008].

29. Dominik J. Schaller, "From Conquest to Genocide: Colonial Rule in German Southwest Africa and German East Africa," in *Empire, Colony, Genocide. Conquest, Occupation, and Subaltern Resistance in World History*, ed. by A. Dirk Moses (New York: Berghahn, 2008), pp. 296–324 (pp. 312–14).

# 21 Narratives of a "Model Colony"
## German Togoland in Written and Oral Histories

*Dennis Laumann*

This chapter examines how the German Togoland colony has been depicted in European and other written accounts and remembered in Ghanaian popular memory over the past century. The historiography of the colony—encompassing German and non-German colonial-era books, studies by East and West German historians, and scholarship by African and other academics—has centered on perceptions of Togoland as a so-called model colony.[1] Collective memories of the Germans, as exemplified by oral history articulated today in areas of the former Togoland, often highlight issues absent in the written literature.[2] Thus, all these various written and oral sources constitute divergent narratives of a small, short-lived colony which was considered the star of Germany's African empire.

## GERMAN TOGOLAND

The Togoland colony dates to February 1884, when a group of German soldiers kidnapped chiefs in Anécho, a town located in present-day southeastern Togo, and forced them into negotiations aboard a warship. Further west, a protectorate was proclaimed over the Lomé area in a treaty signed in July that year by Gustav Nachtigal, a German Imperial Commissioner, and Plakkoo, an official of the town of Togo, after which the new colony was named by the Germans. It was not until the early 1890s that the German regime began expanding its occupation from the coast. Through the Heligoland Treaty of July 1890 between Germany and Great Britain, part of the Peki Ewe state was transferred to German rule from the neighboring Gold Coast (present-day Ghana). Further north, German agents on so-called scientific expeditions negotiated treaties of protection, many of which were later disputed and dismissed as fraudulent by African leaders, extending German territorial claims about 250 kilometers (156 miles) inland.

During its 30-year occupation by the Germans, Togoland was held up by many European imperialists as a model colony, primarily because the German regime produced balanced budgets after a limited period of "pacification" devoid of any major wars. These imperialists also praised the colonizers for their construction of essential infrastructure, including rail, road, and telegraph systems. These achievements were realized, however, through a combination of forced labor and excessive and arbitrary taxation imposed on Togolanders. Moreover, the minimal infrastructural development which did occur was limited to the southern part of the colony. And, while those Europeans considered the German regime benevolent, Togolanders endured a governance characterized by capricious and harsh punishments inflicted by German district officers, grossly inadequate health care and education systems, and prohibition from many commercial activities. In southern Togoland, where the German occupation was most tangible, many Togolanders simply migrated to the British-ruled Gold Coast to escape German rule.

## FIRST SET OF NARRATIVES: COLONIAL-ERA WRITTEN ACCOUNTS

At the start of World War One, British and the French forces invaded the colony and the Germans capitulated, after only a few skirmishes, on 26 August 1914. When the Germans in Togoland abruptly surrendered, Togolanders had "joyously hail[ed] the arrival of [Allied] troops as presaging a return to freedom," so one British writer asserted four years later.[3] The *Gold Coast Leader* commented at the time, "The surrenders [sic] of Togoland has given rise to outbursts of joy and thankfulness among natives throughout the colony . . . The terrible doings of the Germans in Togoland . . . have become common knowledge."[4] The euphoria with which Togolanders evidently greeted the defeat of their German occupiers—according to both the European writer and the African newspaper just quoted—conflicted with the previously held contention among many European imperialists that Togoland was a model colony governed by "liberal" and "enlightened" rulers. Togoland had been extolled as an example for the other European colonizers to replicate, and German imperialists promoted their "achievements" with pride. As the *Kölnische Zeitung* stated in 1894,

> Our model colony, which has been built up almost from scratch and has prospered on the basis of its own customs revenue with almost no financial support from the Reich, has so far caused us no worries at all, unlike Cameroon, South-West Africa and East Africa. German blood has never been shed there.[5]

The model colony idea was, not surprisingly, encouraged by German writers who visited or worked in Togoland during the German occupation. Prior to World War One, numerous German-language accounts of Togoland were published, mostly by "explorers" and administrators based in the colony for various periods of time. Among the more famous of the explorers was Hugo Zöller, the reporter for the *Kölnische Zeitung* cited previously, who "discovered" the Haho River and wrote a highly influential account of his travels throughout the colony.[6] Like many of his colleagues, Zöller also involved himself in the colonization process and agitated for the expansion of German occupation to other parts of the African continent. Heinrich Klose, who authored numerous publications on Togoland, wrote a lengthy account of his participation in a "scientific" expedition to the northern areas of the colony in the late 1890s.[7] He viewed the "success" of Togoland as evidence of Germany's abilities as an imperial power. The publications by Zöller and Klose, and additional accounts by other German travelers and administrators,[8] presented the German occupation only in the best possible terms and provided ammunition for the increasingly vocal imperialist forces within Germany. Their propaganda, as well as observations by other European imperialists, served to encourage the idea that the Germans had created a model colony in Togoland.

The League of Nations, created at the end of World War One, assigned the former German colonies as mandated territories to the British, French and Belgians. Roughly one third of Togoland was attached to the neighboring British Gold Coast colony, while the remaining two thirds were mandated to the French. Soon after the defeat of the Germans, writers from the Allied nations focused on the harshness of the German regime in Togoland and its supposed unpopularity among Togolanders. These works highlighted what the authors believed to be the negative characteristics of German administration and prompted a series of responses by German imperialists, who sought to defend their record in Togoland.

The first to present a critical assessment of German rule in Africa was Albert F. Calvert, the British writer quoted previously on the German surrender. Calvert produced his works on German Africa immediately after World War One, but before the League of Nations had formally mandated areas of Togoland to both Great Britain and France. His writings must thus be interpreted within this context, for Calvert sought not only to dismiss the Germans as failed colonizers but, more importantly, to promote the British as superior in the task of ruling Africans. Indeed, this agenda appears quite clearly in Calvert's writings, as evidenced by the following assessment by him of the German record in Africa:

> The fact has, indeed, been revealed in Germany's thirty-year effort in Colonial-empire building that the Germans have no genius for the high task of colonisation. They have experimented with their policy of "pipe-clay, red-tape and finance" in Africa, and the native races, the land and the progress of the world have suffered from their intrusion . . . Germany has never really colonised at all, either in Africa or anywhere else. In order to colonise it is necessary to possess some sort of perception of the rights of humanity, and Germany has invariably committed the fatal error of misjudging humanity altogether.[9]

Calvert suggests that the British are "better" colonizers than their defeated enemy. But, in specific reference to Togoland, Calvert is less severe in his indictment of the Germans, perhaps cognizant of the earlier imperialist praise for Germany's accomplishments in the model colony. Calvert concedes that in Togoland, as a result of the German occupation,

> a stable government has been established, the hinterland has been opened up, three railways and many excellent roads have been built, slavery has been abolished and inter-tribal warfare discouraged, and a number of experimental plantations have been formed. The [German] Government, by its energetic policy, have developed the resources of the country, established trade and commerce on sound lines, and made considerable progress towards the betterment and prosperity of the people.[10]

Yet, he maintains that, in its treatment of Togolanders, the Germans were unnecessarily harsh. As a result, Calvert argues, at the onset of World War One "the natives of Togoland threw off their allegiances to the [German] Fatherland in the first moments of hostilities, and welcomed the invasion of the French and British forces with tumultuous enthusiasm."[11]

Calvert was not alone in his denunciation of German rule in Africa. A more virulent judgment was Evans Lewin's *German Colonizers in Africa*, in which the British author characterizes the German administrators as "cruel, brutal, arrogant, and utterly unsuited for intercourse with primitive peoples, lustful and malicious in their attitudes toward subject races."[12] Many French newspapers also published articles which, according to an American historian during that period, sought "to terrorize and to inflame the populace with the danger of restoring Germany's colonies."[13]

German writers quickly responded to these attacks, systematically identifying the "contributions" the German regimes had made to their former colonies. Heinrich Schnee, who was the last governor of German East Africa, rebuts many of the accusations made by the Allies against the Germans. Furthermore, he argues that there is now "confusion and retrogression"[14] in the mandated territories of the former German colonies and maintains that Africans, "satisfied, and more than satisfied, with German sovereignty, [had] desired nothing more than its continuance."[15] Schnee and the German imperialist writers who followed him emphasized the infrastructural development of their former colonies, and compared this with the record of the Allies in the mandated territories. Schnee argues that "[a]ll the colonial territories which were blossoming under German rule are now being economically ruined."[16]

The early years of Nazi Germany witnessed a steady stream of publications not only defending the German occupation of African territories, but also arguing for their return to German rule. Several German writers traveled widely in the African continent during the late 1930s, visiting the former German colonies, and published accounts conforming to the imperialist rhetoric of Nazi Germany. One of the most notable of this group of propagandists was Louise Diel, who piloted her own plane to each of the colonies and published a nationalistic tract entitled *Die Kolonien warten!* (The Colonies Await!).[17] The authors of these books all claimed to have experienced warm welcomes in the former colonies from Africans who longed for the return of the German occupation. Schnee, for example, maintains, "Wherever Germans appear in the Mandate regions they are at once greeted with every manifestation of joy, and their presence is heralded as a sign that the happier days of German rule will return."[18] A number of books in this defensive vein were published specific to Togoland. The most influential was O. F. Metzger's *Unsere alte Kolonie Togo* (Our Former Colony of Togo).[19] Metzger, who was based in Togoland from 1904 until 1914, served as a forester under the German regime. Although his book is very much representative of the political climate in which it was written, Metzger's polemic is distinctive because of what may be regarded as its scholarly thoroughness. The author not only catalogues what he argues were the accomplishments of the German occupation in Togoland, but also includes lengthy sections on the cultures of several of the ethnic groups of the former colony.

The Allied governments were clearly concerned about Nazi Germany's increasing economic and military power and its designs on Africa. Pro-mandate literature published during this period helped undermine German propaganda. In 1939, the British writer G. L. Steer visited the former German colonies in Africa, with the exception of Togoland, and wrote a pointed indictment of the German occupations.[20] By this time, of course, the British had become well entrenched in their mandates, but the Germans had largely recovered from the devastation of World War One and were assuming an expansionist policy in Europe and beyond. The British accounts of German-occupied Africa produced during the 1930s thus served to promote Britain's continued possession of the mandates and reminded readers of what the authors regarded as Germany's poor performance as colonizers in Africa.

One study published during this period, however, stands out for its self-defined "balanced" judgment of the German colonial experience. Mary Evelyn Townsend, an American professor, delivers a mixed verdict on the German occupations in Africa.[21] Townsend's work is unusual because of its (albeit selective) criticisms of colonialism, evidenced by the following excerpt, in which she discusses the "pacification" phase:

> During the first twenty years of Germany's colonial history . . . the native had been most cruelly treated and unjustly exploited. In short, he had suffered the same fate as befalls every such population throughout those stormy initial years which lay the foundations of all colonial empires. Robbed of his lands, his home, his freedom and often wantonly and cruelly of his life by the colonial adventurer, official or trading

company, his continuous and fierce revolts were the tragic witnesses to his wretchedness and helplessness.

However, Townsend fails to pursue this portrait of violent imperialism and instead searches for evidence of "enlightened" colonialism:

> Nothing, indeed, is more significant of the change for the better in Germany's colonial administration toward the native than the fact that there occurred no actual uprisings during the years 1908–1914. Peace prevailed throughout the oversea empire.[22]

Townsend supports some of the standard allegations leveled against the German regimes in Africa, arguing that many of the German administrators "tended to be exceedingly strict and in some cases unduly severe and cruel"[23] and that the "German system did lead to confusion, dissatisfaction and sometimes injustice."[24] But she defends the Germans against the charges of forced labor, claiming that they "strictly enforced" prohibitions on this illegal activity,[25] and she praises the German record on providing social services. Thus, Townsend's book assumes a middle position between the propaganda of the Germans, longing for their former colonies, and that of the British imperialists, anxious to contain the newly confident and expansionist German state and also to preserve their own, recently awarded mandated territories.

## SECOND SET OF NARRATIVES: POST-COLONIAL SCHOLARSHIP

After the defeat of Nazi Germany in World War Two, the ideological battle between the Federal Republic of Germany and the German Democratic Republic which characterized the Cold War also played out in the academic realm, as post-colonial scholarship on Togoland continued to revolve around the "model colony" thesis. The post–World War Two historical literature on Togoland may be classified into three groups: neo-imperialist, Marxist, and liberal. The neo-imperialist scholarship in many ways mimics the propaganda of the colonial-era writers, emphasizing German administration and development. Marxist historians forcefully demolish the model colony myth and focus on the issues of African labor and resistance. Lastly, scholars in the liberal group acknowledge the violence of German occupation but simultaneously draw attention to what they consider the progressive economic and social policies implemented in Togoland.

The idea that Togoland was a model colony continued to be widely embraced in West Germany. Indeed, the first general work published on Togoland after World War Two, by Josef Schramm, reiterated the model colony thesis.[26] Outside of academia, many West German politicians, though mainly those on the right, also sought to highlight what they perceived to be Germany's "positive" administration of Togoland. For example, in a 1984 publication commemorating 100 years of "Africa and the Germans," a development studies professor and former governmental official declared that Togoland was "moderately and effectively administered."[27] Popular histories produced in the Federal Republic of Germany often celebrated the German occupation of Africa and neglected to discuss its violent nature.[28] And, in general, West German scholars refrained from critically evaluating the model colony idea, but instead produced studies of specific topics from Togoland's history.[29]

In stark contrast, the main agenda of East German Marxist scholars was to dismantle the myth of the model colony. Manfred Nussbaum's study, *Togo, eine Musterkolonie?* (Togoland, a Model Colony?), was the first item in a body of literature highly critical of German imperialism.[30] His primary purpose in this work is to undermine the model colony thesis by arguing that the Germans did not deliberately attempt to produce such an example, but were merely fortunate to have occupied an especially rich area of West Africa. Furthermore, he dismisses the idea that Togoland was ruled by "enlightened" administrators.

The neo-imperialist view of German colonial history has been advanced most forcibly by historians outside the two Germanies. Peter Duignan and Lewis H. Gann, based in the 1970s at the Hoover Institution at Stanford University, produced several studies of what they term "German Africa." These historians have two main goals in their works: first, to examine economic development in the German colonies and, second, to profile the colonial officials who administered the German-occupied territories. Gann and Duignan almost reluctantly admit that the German conquest of African territories "involved violence and brutality," but consistently underscore the "positive contributions" of German occupation, which they list as follows:

> [The Germans] provided a basic infrastructure of modern transport; they encouraged new forms of economic enterprise; they promoted mining; they stimulated research; they imported new crops; to some extent they promoted peasant agriculture in export crops. They were responsible for the first feeble beginnings of secondary industry in their territories. They made a start, however slight, in providing western-type education, hospitals, and dispensaries, government research in medicine, agriculture, and veterinary problems. They built a Western-type civil administration; they laid the foundations of new states. Their colonial elite helped to force German Africa into the world economy; they introduced new skills and new occupations, and created new economic needs and new economic opportunities. German colonialism thus was an engine of modernization with far-reaching effects for the future. German rule provided African people with new alternatives and a wider range of choices.[31]

If Gann and Duignan are the "fathers" of the neo-imperialist school of scholarship on German Africa, Helmuth Stoecker is their counterpart among the East German Marxists. Based mainly at the Humboldt University in East Berlin, he and his colleagues enjoyed almost exclusive access to the archives of the *Reichskolonialamt* (Imperial Colonial Office). Among this small group of scholars, Peter Sebald specialized in the history of Togoland.[32] Sebald's classic book on Togoland not only builds upon the argument initially put forth by Nussbaum, but is also the first work on the former colony to focus mainly on the impact of the German occupation on Togolanders.[33] Cognizant of the limitations of previous studies, which viewed all initiatives during the occupation as arising solely from the German colonialists, Sebald concentrates his analysis on the lives of Togolanders, albeit through the use of European archival sources. The result is a meticulous investigation of the violence of German colonialism in Togoland and an emphasis on the "actions" and "reactions" of Togolanders.

Numerous scholars straddle the huge middle ground between the neo-imperialist and Marxist positions, sometimes emphasizing the harsh policies of the German regime while more often presenting what they perceive to be the "benefits" of the German occupation. The majority of these scholars advocating a liberal interpretation are based in the United States and West Africa.[34] Among them is the Ghanaian historian D. E. K. Amenumey, who has written widely on the history of the Ewe ethnic group, including during the period of German occupation. In his succinct overview of the German occupation of southern Togoland, Amenumey argues that the German period was

> characterized by the exaction of compulsory labour, the imposition of a host of direct taxes, restriction of the freedom of the people to trade, infringement of their right to the land and a curtailment of the power of the chiefs. Despite the provision of social services and the increased employment opportunities provided by the construction programme of the government, the people of Togo were completely disenchanted with the nature of the administration and found it unbearable. They reacted accordingly.[35]

This excerpt neatly summarizes the liberal position. First, the German administration, although not nearly as draconian as the regimes in the other German colonies on the African continent, denied Togolanders their basic freedoms and imposed an endless series of economic demands on them. Even though the Germans provided social services, including medical care and education, together with economic prospects which variously benefited Togolanders, these advantages were outweighed by the harshness of life in the colony, leading to resistance to the occupation by diverse means.

The only book-length study of Togoland written in English is Arthur J. Knoll's 1978 monograph.[36] A student of Gann and Duignan, Knoll does not entirely mimic the neo-imperialist position of his mentors. Knoll's book focuses on the administrative and economic policies of the German regime in Togoland. The result is another study largely centering around the activities of the German imperialists, with Togolanders emerging as only secondary actors during the occupation. While Knoll certainly provides ample evidence of German violence and African resistance, his book does not directly reject the model colony thesis.

Another American who has written on Togoland, Woodruff D. Smith, assumes a similar position. He argues that the abuses and atrocities committed in Togoland were less frequent than in the other German colonies and, with respect to the model colony idea, he says, "Much of this reputation was deserved." He continues, however: "[I]t should not obscure the fact that like other colonies Togo was an arena for forcible exploitation in which the European position was maintained through violence, real or threatened."[37]

The French-language literature on Togoland produced since World War Two generally fits within the liberal grouping. Togolese scholars, working with German archival materials housed in their own country, have authored numerous locally published studies emphasizing the activities and perceptions of Togolanders, rather than of the German imperialists.[38] The historical writings of Robert Cornevin, a former French colonial official, have perhaps been the most widely read works on Togo. He has published several popular histories of Togo, in which he also assumes a middle position on the German occupation.[39]

In the post–Cold War academic world, the ideological stakes involved in defending or attacking the model colony thesis certainly have become less important.[40] The most recent study of the German occupation is by Ralph Erbar,[41] the first German to produce a book-length study on Togoland since German Reunification.[42] Unlike the previous work by his fellow Germans, Erbar's analysis does not fit into either the neo-imperialist or the Marxist approaches to Togoland history. Nevertheless, it tends to follow familiar paths, as Erbar relies on archival materials to reconstruct the administrative and economic history of the former German colony. Outside of academia, the term "model colony" continues to be associated with German Togoland, as any cursory search on the Internet will confirm.

## THIRD SET OF NARRATIVES: PRESENT-DAY ORAL HISTORY

My own work examines the history of German Togoland based on oral history collected over the past decade in the central Volta Region of eastern Ghana.[43] The goal of this research is to counter the Eurocentric bias of previous studies, which almost exclusively relied on German and other European primary sources. By recording oral history in a number of towns and villages in Ghana, where memories of the Germans are vivid and comprehensive, I attempt to present African perspectives on the German occupation.

Interestingly, oral historians do not distinguish between the early German presence in the central Volta Region, beginning with the arrival of missionaries and traders in the mid-nineteenth century, and the formal colonial occupation commencing in 1884. The era as a whole is often termed "Gruner's time," in reference to Dr Hans Gruner, the local German district commissioner for most of the colonial period, who remains part of everyday discourse. For instance, older people in the area have an expression, "not in Gruner's time," to convey their dissatisfaction with aspects of today's society.[44]

The oral history describes economic and social transformations, technological and agricultural innovations, and opposition to German rule. Specific events are discussed in great detail, such as the exile to Cameroon of a local chief, Dagadu, and the cotton-growing campaign by African American scientists from the Tuskegee Institute. Some of these subjects are largely absent from colonial sources and later scholarly works based on those European materials.

Generally speaking, oral historians emphasize what they describe as the "honesty," "order," and "discipline" of the German era (especially in contrast to the British occupation which followed), while also detailing the violence, burdens, and inconveniences associated with the German regime. In a typical assessment of the so-called positive aspects of German rule, for example, one oral historian, Gilbert Joel Nyavor, claims that "honesty and truth were virtues which were practiced to the letter during the German colonial occupation" and "people were law-abiding and respectful." Yet, in recounting the broad nature of German rule, Nyavor also states that "the Germans were a very tough people and they used very tough laws in ruling the colony."[45]

Indeed, while oral historians seem to admire the work ethic they attribute to the Germans, the harshness of the German occupation is well remembered. The use of flogging, or lashing with a whip, as a form of punishment by German colonial officials features prominently in popular memory. Edward Kodzo Datsa recalls that offenders against colonial orders were given 24 strokes of the cane and a "twenty-fifth one was for the Kaiser."[46] The persistence of this particular memory is evidenced in the Ghanaian novel *The Narrow Path*, in which the narrator recalls a childhood punishment: "As he brought the cane down for the last time, my father said 'And one for the Kaiser.' Was it our German rulers who taught our people such cruelty?"[47]

Principally on the topic of German violence, the significance of oral history as a source material, in contrast to the colonial-era accounts and records on which most of the secondary literature is based, is quite apparent. Several generations after the Germans were forced to abandon the Togoland colony, oral historians still speak of the forced labor, draconian and often fatal health measures, and many other negative characteristics of the German occupation. And while the Germans did not face organized, armed rebellions like in some of their other colonies, oral historians recount various methods of resistance to German rule. The most common was for

Togolanders simply to migrate to the neighboring British Gold Coast colony in order to "avoid German high-handedness," as Nyavor explains.[48]

But, again, oral historians emphasize what they regard as the positive aspects and beneficial legacies of German rule. During the German occupation, "there was truthfulness and adherence to public order," a Ghanaian chief asserts, "There was no indiscipline."[49] Mathias Yevu Tegbe claims, "When [the Germans] left, it was considered a great loss."[50] And the traits identified with the Germans by oral historians are claimed by those who reside in this area of the former German Togoland today. As Mosis Kofi Asase explains, "We have the German spirit in us. By the German spirit, I mean honesty, humility, and godliness. These are the virtues that the Germans imparted on our parents and they in turn imparted on us."[51]

When assessing the oral history, contrasting it with the written history of German Togoland, analyzing the relevant archival materials, and interrogating my own fieldwork, two main points become clear. First, there is a direct correlation between "positive" memories of the Germans and the perceived marginalization of the former German Togoland during the British mandate/trusteeship period, an era which also witnessed the (re-) construction of local ethnic and regional identities. In the face of what was perceived as British indifference to Togoland, nostalgia for the German period, articulated in petitions to international bodies and manifested in the formation of the *Bund der Deutschen Togoländer,* a local pro-German organization also known as the *Togobund,* developed in the early years of mandate rule. This period also saw the emergence of a distinct "Togoland" identity, which was contrasted with both closely and distantly related ethnic groups in the British Gold Coast who had not experienced German rule.

Second, a male elite—composed of chiefs, elders, and so-called "German scholars"—is today responsible for the articulation and sustenance of this oral history. The role of these locally known German scholars—old men (or their sons) who are Christian, German-educated, and in many cases served as cultural brokers or "middle figures" during the German occupation—is especially crucial to understanding the oral history. In central Volta Region communities, residents defer to the expertise of German scholars for narratives and interpretations of German rule. And, in many ways, these German scholars maintain what can be termed the official oral history on this subject, especially when articulated in public settings.

By probing the broader historical context of the area, the local control of intellectual resources, and the dynamics of collective memory, my research lays out how the oral history has evolved into its present form. In relation to the written history discussed previously, the oral history may be classified as falling within the liberal group, but perhaps with a greater weight being given to German brutality and Togolander resistance, since oral historians have first-hand knowledge of both. It is also apparent that—for the oral accounts of German Togoland just as for the written ones—the contemporary agendas of the authors shape their presentation of the past. What is none the less clear is that a colony which existed for only about three decades and was insubstantial in comparison to other German colonial territories has been the subject of ardent debates in written works and lives on today in local popular memory.

## NOTES

1. For an extended version of the literature review which follows, see Dennis Laumann, "A Historiography of German Togoland, or the Rise and Fall of a 'Model Colony'," *History in Africa*, 30 (2003), 195–211.
2. This is the subject of my monograph *Remembering the Germans in Ghana* (New York: Lang, in press).
3. Albert F. Calvert, *Togoland* (London: Laurie, 1918), p. xii.
4. From the 12 September 1914 issue, as quoted in ibid., p. 83. *The Gold Coast Leader* was published in Cape Coast from 1902 to 1929 by the Ghanaian lawyer and politician J.E. Casely-Hayford.
5. Quoted from Peter Sebald, "Togo 1884–1900," in *German Imperialism in Africa: From the Beginnings Until the Second World War*, ed. by Helmuth Stoecker (London: Hurst, 1986), p. 85.
6. Hugo Zöller, *Das Togogebiet und die Sklavenküste*, vol. 3 of Zöller, *Die deutschen Besitzungen an der westafrikanischen Küste* (Berlin: Spemann, 1885).
7. Heinrich Klose, *Togo unter deutscher Flagge* (Berlin: Reimer, 1899).
8. See also, among others, Matthias Dier, *Unter den Schwarzen: Alles aus Togo über Land, Leute, Sitten und Gebräuche* (Steyl: Missionsdruckerei, 1901); Ernst Henrici, *Das deutsche Togogebiet und meine Afrikareise 1887* (Leipzig: Reissner, 1888); Ludwig Külz, *Blätter und Briefe eines Arztes aus dem tropischen Deutsch-Afrika* (Berlin: Süsserott, 1906); and Georg Trierenberg, *Togo: Die Aufrichtung der deutschen Schutzherrschaft und die Erschließung des Landes* (Berlin: Mittler, 1914).
9. Albert F. Calvert, *The German African Empire* (London: Laurie, 1916), p. xxi.
10. Ibid., p. 215.
11. Ibid., p. 276.
12. Evans Lewin is quoted from Mary Evelyn Townsend, *The Rise and Fall of Germany's Colonial Empire 1884–1914* (New York: Macmillan, 1930), p. 375. See Evans Lewin, *The Germans and Africa: Their Aims on the Dark Continent and How They Acquired Their African Colonies* (London: Cassell, 1915).
13. Townsend, *Germany's Colonial Empire*, p. 374.
14. Heinrich Schnee, *German Colonization Past and Future: The Truth About the German Colonies* (New York: Knopf, 1921), p. 32.
15. Ibid., p. 169.
16. Ibid., p. 170.
17. Louise Diel, *Die Kolonien warten!* (Leipzig: List, 1939). Other examples from this period are Genta Dinglreiter, *Wann kommen die Deutschen endlich wieder? Eine Reise durch unsere Kolonien in Afrika* (Leipzig: Koehler & Umeland, 1935), and Paul Leutwein, *Das deutsche Afrika und seine Zukunft* (Berlin: Weller, 1937).
18. Schnee, *German Colonialism*, p. 170.

19. O.F. Metzger, *Unsere alte Kolonie Togo* (Neudamm: Neumann, 1941). Several other former officials from the Togoland regime produced books defending the German record in the colony, for example, August Full, *Fünfzig Jahre Togo* (Berlin: Reimer, 1935), and Richard Küas, *Togo-Erinnerungen* (Berlin: Wegweiser, 1939).

20. G.L. Steer, *Judgment on German Africa* (London: Hodder & Stoughton, 1939).

21. See Townsend, *Germany's Colonial Empire*, cited previously.

22. Ibid., p. 273.

23. Ibid., p. 277.

24. Ibid., p. 279.

25. Ibid., p. 287.

26. Josef Schramm, *Togo* (Bonn: Schroeder, 1959).

27. Gabriele Wülker, "'Musterkolonie' an Afrikas Westküste: Togo unter deutscher Kolonialverwaltung," in *Hundert Jahre Afrika und die Deutschen*, ed. by Wolfgang Höpker (Pfullingen: Neske, 1984), p. 43: my translation.

28. See, for example, Karlheinz Graudenz, *Deutsche Kolonialgeschichte in Daten and Bildern* (Munich: Südwest, 1984).

29. These included, among others, works on trade, education, and missionary societies. See, for example, Christel Adick, *Bildung und Kolonialismus in Togo* (Weinheim: Beltz, 1981), and Karl Müller, *Geschichte der katholischen Kirche in Togo* (Kaldenkirchen: Steyl, 1958).

30. Manfred Nussbaum, *Togo, eine Musterkolonie?* (Berlin: Rutten & Loening, 1962).

31. Lewis H. Gann and Arthur J. Knoll, "Introduction," in *Germans in the Tropics: Essays in German Colonial History*, ed. by Knoll and Gann (Westport: Greenwood, 1987), pp. xi–xii.

32. For an English-language survey including work by several of these East German historians, see *German Imperialism in Africa*, ed. by Helmut Stoecker.

33. Peter Sebald, *Togo 1884–1914: Eine Geschichte der deutschen "Muster-Kolonie" auf der Grundlage amtlicher Quellen* (Berlin: Akademie, 1988).

34. The exceptions among the latter are the Ghanaians Ansa Asamoa and M.B.K. Darkoh. Asamoa's analyses are unabashedly Marxist: see, for example, his "On German Colonial Rule in Togo," in *Studien zur Geschichte des deutschen Kolonialismus in Africa: Festschrift zum 60. Geburtstag von Peter Sebald*, ed. by Peter Heine and Ulrich van der Heyden (Pfaffenweiler: Centaurus, 1995), pp. 114–25. Darkoh's work on Togoland is clearly neo-imperialist. See M.B.K. Darkoh, "Togoland under the Germans: Thirty Years of Economic Development—Part I," in *Nigerian Geographical Journal*, 10.2 (December 1967), 107–22, and "Togoland under the Germans: Thirty Years of Economic Development—Part II," in *Nigerian Geographical Journal*, 11.2 (December 1968), 153–68.

35. D.E.K. Amenumey, "German Administration in Southern Togo," in *Journal of African History*, 10.4 (1969), 636.

36. Arthur J. Knoll, *Togo Under Imperial Germany 1884–1914* (Stanford: Hoover Institution, 1978).

37. Woodruff D. Smith, *The German Colonial Empire* (Chapel Hill: University of North Carolina Press, 1978), p. 68.

38. See, for example, the following two collections, which include articles dealing with aspects of the German occupation: *Les Togolais face à la colonisation*, ed. by N.L. Gayibor (Lomé: Presses de l'Université du Bénin, 1994), and *Le Togo depuis la conférence de Berlin 1884–1984*, ed. by N.L. Gayibor (Lomé: Goethe-Institut, 1984).

39. See, for example, Robert Cornevin, *Le Togo: Des origines à nos jours* (Paris: Sciences d'Outre-Mer, 1987), and *Histoire de la colonisation allemande* (Paris: Presses Universitaires de France, 1969). The latter was translated into German by Hans Jenny as *Geschichte der deutschen Kolonisation* (Goslar: Hübener, 1974).

40. For a recent collection of articles on German colonialism in Africa, published in honor of Peter Sebald and including pieces by some of the writers discussed above, see *Studien zur Geschichte des deutschen Kolonialismus in Africa*, ed. by Heine and van der Heyden.

41. Ralph Erbar, *Ein "Platz an der Sonne"? Die Verwaltungs- und Wirtschaftsgeschichte der deutschen Kolonie Togo 1884–1914* (Stuttgart: Steiner, 1991).

42. Another German scholar, Trutz von Trotha, produced a more recent monograph on German Togoland. But von Trotha, a sociologist, merely uses the colony as a case study for a theory of state formation advanced in the book. See Trutz von Trotha, *Koloniale Herrschaft: zur soziologischen Theorie der Staatsentstehung am Beispiel des "Schutzgebietes Togo"* (Tübingen: Mohr, 1994).

43. This area of Ghana, situated in the Volta Region and including the large towns of Ho, Hohoe, and Kpandu, constituted part of the Misahöhe-*Bezirk* (District) of Togoland and later the British Togolands mandate. See Laumann, *Remembering the Germans*.

44. Edward Kodzo Datsa (Amedzofe: 17 April 1996). This reference and similar ones which follow list the name of the oral historian and, in parentheses, the location and date of the interview cited in the text. All interviews were conducted in Ghana by the author along with a team of research assistants. For a detailed explanation of research methodology, see Laumann, *Remembering the Germans*.

45. Gilbert Joel Nyavor (Kpandu: 5 March 1997).

46. Edward Kodzo Datsa (Amedzofe: 17 April 1997).

47. Francis Selormey, *The Narrow Path* (Portsmouth, NH: Heinemann, 1996), p. 58.

48. Gilbert Joel Nyavor (Kpandu: 5 March 1997).

49. Togbe Kuleke (Waya: 16 June 1997).

50. Mathias Yevu Tegbe (Hohoe: 17 June 1997).

51. Mosis Kofi Asase (Ho: 15 April 1997).

# 22 Suspended Between Worlds?

## The Discipline of *Germanistik* in Sub-Saharan Africa

*Arnd Witte*

The academic discipline of "German" in sub-Saharan Africa is a relic left behind by the colonizers when they withdrew in the 1960s. Whereas German could rely on the political determination of the colonizers before political independence, the subject has since struggled to establish an identity of its own in the various African countries: it has tried—not always successfully—to combine the inherent requirements of the discipline with the socio-educational requirements of young African students in those 39 universities in 16 sub-Saharan countries where German is presently taught—by 98 lecturers and 16 *Lektors* sent by the state-funded *Deutscher Akademischer Austauschdienst* (German Academic Exchange Service).[1]

One can safely say that in post-colonial Africa, as in post-colonial discourse at large, the academic discipline of German, or *Germanistik*, has not so far gained any significant prominence, either as a subject in itself or as an object of analysis. It thus remains one of the most pressing issues for the African version of German Studies to establish authentic research areas of its own within the complex polycentric environment of third-level institutions in sub-Saharan Africa. This is even more difficult as there is as yet, due to infrastructural and funding problems, no overarching African version of *Germanistik*; instead, there are different local, or at best regional, approaches to research in and teaching of German.[2]

Some of the current problems facing the subject German can be traced back to colonial times, because it was imported to Africa by the French and British colonizers largely by coincidence. Whereas in the short-lived German colonies no significant attempt was made to introduce German as a foreign language in schools, other than in government schools for the children of German officials, the British and French simply extended their domestic school curricula to their respective colonies without considering the implications for the local education systems. Hence, young Africans in French colonies not only learned French history under the maxim, "My ancestors the Gauls," but they also had to learn the foreign language of German from schoolbooks produced in France for a French audience, even though they would never have the opportunity of applying this linguistic knowledge outside school.

However, the subject of German was hardly ever actually taught in schools at all, even when it was part of the official school curriculum. This was particularly the case in the British colonies of West and East Africa. For example, German has been listed in the secondary school curriculum of Nigeria since 1859,[3] but in reality it had until recently never been taught in public secondary schools.[4] In some Anglophone countries, however, German was actually introduced in secondary schools after independence, albeit on a small scale, for example in Uganda in 1969, in Ghana in the 1960s (though it was not taught continuously) and in Kenya in the early 1980s. These developments indicate the existence of a certain demand for German, independent of the school curricula imposed by the colonial powers, even if the actual introduction of German relied to a large extent on financial and pedagogical support provided by the German government.

In the French colonies, where *direct rule* was practiced (as opposed to *indirect rule* in the British colonies), German was taught at school level to a greater extent. Initially, this was mainly by French citizens.[5] However, following the Franco-German treaty of 1963, all French teachers of German were in 1967 recalled from Benin, Burkina Faso, the Ivory Coast, Cameroon, Madagascar, Mali, Niger, Senegal, Togo, Chad and the Central African Republic; and they were replaced in most of these countries by Germans and indigenous teachers.[6] The Federal Republic of Germany subsequently concluded bilateral cultural agreements with some of these states in which the status of German was explicitly defined. For example, it was stipulated in the German–Senegalese cultural agreement of 1972 that German would be offered as the *first* foreign language in Senegalese schools,[7] and it was taken in the early 1980s by approximately 20 per cent of the pupils;[8] however, in 1999, there was only one secondary school left in Senegal which offered German as the first foreign language.[9] The rapid expansion of German in Francophone Africa from the 1960s to the 1980s was clearly economically motivated on the German side: they envisaged developing new and promising markets for German products. The motivation for the Senegalese government—and most other sub-Saharan African states which introduced German in their respective educational systems— was primarily political, as they wanted to reduce their cultural and economic dependency on France. In order to satisfy the subsequent demand for teachers of German, the subject was introduced in teacher training colleges in many Francophone African countries, where it was taught by educators from both German states.[10] In the 30 years since, the dependency on personnel sent from Germany has been completely eliminated, in that the vast majority of teaching staff for German at both secondary and tertiary level can now be sourced from within the respective countries.

Despite these encouraging post-colonial developments in German at secondary level in some Francophone countries, the first introduction of German as a subject at tertiary level took place in two universities in Anglophone countries, namely Ibadan (Nigeria) and Kampala (Uganda).

The foundation of universities in British colonies was a result of two parallel developments: the demands for equality and political independence, accelerated by World War Two (where African soldiers fought shoulder to shoulder with British and French soldiers), and the recognition by the British that the Empire could not be maintained militarily or politically in the long run. Consequently, the Colonial Office in London decided to educate political elites who would be able to take over the running of the respective countries after independence. Since functioning autonomous universities with adequate staff and administrations could not be set up in such a short time, the Asquith Commission recommended in their *Report on Higher Education in the Colonies* of 1945 the establishment of colleges which would be administered by British universities through an "Inter-University Council for Higher Education in the Colonies,"[11] staffed solely by British academics—all this in order to ensure an international academic "gold standard" of teaching and research, a need which seemed especially acute in view of some "dreadful spectres of comical Indian degree-factories," as one commentator put it.[12]

Consequently, the Universities of Ibadan (Nigeria), Legon (Ghana) and Makarere (Uganda) were founded in 1948 as Colleges of the University of London. This meant that the curricula and examinations were controlled by University of London academics, while educated Africans remained willingly aloof in order to ensure the patina of the academic gold standard for the colonial universities. After having been introduced as a subsidiary subject to assist scientists in reading relevant German texts in the 1950s, German became a BA discipline in its own right in 1967 in both Ibadan and Kampala. Soon, other universities followed this trend, for example, the University of Nigeria in Nsukka, together with universities in Ife (Nigeria) and Nairobi. The discipline of German was introduced in universities in Francophone countries only a little later, for instance in Dakar in 1973[13] and in Yaoundé in 1980.[14]

Namibia and South Africa constitute a special case in the development of German in sub-Saharan Africa, because Germans settled there in larger numbers. The beginnings of German as an institutionalized school subject can be traced back to the 1830s, but it was not before the end of the nineteenth century that German was taught in more than the occasional school.[15] The first Chairs in German on the African continent were established in 1918 at the universities of Cape Town and Stellenbosch. At present, in 2008, German is offered by the Namibian National University and by 16 universities in South Africa.

Despite these markedly different historical developments in the Anglophone and Francophone countries, as well as in South Africa and Namibia, there have been inherent legitimatory problems for the discipline that are common to all universities in sub-Saharan Africa at which German is offered. In the case of universities in West, East and Central Africa, political discussions about the role of universities as relics and extensions of colonialism affected many academic disciplines, including German. The definition of the university given by the prominent Kenyan historian Ali A. Mazrui is typical of the view of many African academics in the years after Independence: "The university is an analogue to a multinational corporation: born as an extension of a metropolitan university whose direction and instructions come from a European country, the African university continues to serve other than African interests."[16]

In the case of Nigeria, while many students in the 1960s were sad to see the College status of the University of Ibadan disappear (because the degree was now conferred by the indigenous African university rather than by the prestigious University of London—something which was widely regarded as a devaluation of the qualification),[17] high academic standards for research and teaching were invoked by those who reluctantly agreed to recognize the historical inevitability of establishing autonomous African universities. When the first Chancellor of the University of Ibadan was installed in 1963, the Chancellor of the University of London explicitly reminded his Nigerian counterpart in his speech at the celebrations,

> You are now free to appoint your own academic staff, you can devise your own courses and curricula and set your own examinations as all established universities can do. I was almost about to add that you can now set your own standards and while in a sense it is perfectly true that it is now open to you to do so I would qualify it by reminding you that academic standards and the degrees that represent them belong to a currency that is an international one and far transcends local and national boundaries.[18]

However, this metropolitan approach was not welcomed by all indigenous academics. Like Mazrui, many Africans suspected universities of being institutions for covertly prolonging colonialism and imperialism through the range and structure of the academic disciplines on offer. Consequently, they insisted that the African university had to develop its own distinctive profile on the international academic scene, rather than just copying the methodologies, concerns and approaches of metropolitan universities and their disciplines. In Nigeria, the chairman of the influential political party the National Council of Nigerian Citizens (NCNC) and later first President of Nigeria, Nnamdi Azikiwe, emphasized the necessity for Nigerian universities to take the specifically Nigerian political, social and cultural circumstances into consideration in their teaching and research:

> In order that the foundation of Nigerian leadership shall be securely laid, to the end that this country shall cease to imitate the excrescences of a civilization which is not rooted in African life, we recommend that a full-fledged university should be established in this [Eastern] Region [of Nigeria] without further delay. Such a higher institution of learning

should not only be cultural, according to the classic concept of universities, but it should also be vocational in its objective and Nigerian in its content.[19]

This approach was echoed by some academics in metropolitan universities:

What is needed are centers for research and training in the periphery, not carbon copies of ourselves, but healthy antibodies in the international bloodstream of discovery: centers which are capable and independent enough to create, maintain, and disseminate a more authentic knowledge base for coping with the specific needs of their country within the framework of its own intellectual and cultural traditions.[20]

The renowned Nigerian historian Ajayi concluded, "[African universities have] to evolve an identity of their own and adapt the alien form of the university to one that is recognizably part of the African social and cultural environment."[21]

These discussions about the degree of autonomy maintained by African universities from the Western-dominated academic scene had implications for many academic disciplines, including German. There were two distinct possibilities for the justification and further development of the subject: it could either follow and disseminate the developments of metropolitan *Germanistik* (*Binnengermanistik*) and thus maintain a high academic standard, as measured by international recognition, at the cost of being perceived as a relic of colonialism, or it could try to define its own distinct profile as an specifically African *Germanistik* (*Auslandsgermanistik*) with its own field of research, focusing on topics relevant for African students, for instance by researching the imagology of German colonial literature from an African point of view.

Other subjects in the humanities which seemed even more remote from the educational needs of Africans than German successfully adopted an authentic African perspective for their subject matter, with potentially revolutionary results. For example, John Ferguson, a British scholar of Classics at the University of Ibadan, emphasized the unique potential of African students to interpret classical texts dealing with oracles, rituals of sacrifice, magical charms, and so on, on the basis of social and phonetic parallels between the Ancient Greek and Yoruba cultures. These would throw new light on both Ancient Greek and the African culture forms, the latter having been devalued for too long as not being rooted in history. He argued,

My students know what it means to consult an oracle; I do not. My students understand sacrifice; in my inmost being I do not . . . My students are surrounded by *numina*; I am not. They know the amulets and charms which I scorn, and, though they would not lightly admit it, some use them . . . It follows that if we can produce [in] West African universities scholars who will see the world of Greece and Rome with their own eyes, and look beyond the prejudices of their European text-books and European teachers, we are likely to find that we in Europe are learning from Africa new truths about the ancient world which is the root of our European culture.[22]

Although German was seen in many quarters as a superfluous subject in sub-Saharan Africa, others insisted that it, too, could contribute to the cultural and political development of Africa. Discussions about the legitimacy of German and its role as a university subject were initiated in the 1980s, first of all in the Francophone countries by the Senegalese scholar of German Amadou Booker Sadji and the Cameroonian Kum'a Ndumbe III—with an argumentation which in both cases echoes the ideals of the Negritude movement. Sadji maintains that the African countries will only be able to learn from German not only technological and economic but also political and cultural development if they are able to recognize in the development of African countries in the 1980s, as Sadji himself does, a "process of similar symptoms as existed previously in the European process at the same phase of development."[23] This implies that "German Studies can become an important source for the development planners in our countries,"[24] "in order to close the parenthesis of colonialism."[25] Sadji emphasizes the invaluable paradigmatic character of the German masterpieces of literature, art and philosophy for the intellectual and moral education of Africans, that is, in order "comprehensively to educate and perfect the African human being, both intellectually and morally,"[26] as these masterpieces allegedly embody the social, political and cultural development of Germany at a time when it was on the threshold of evolving from a feudal into a bourgeois society.[27]

With this statement, Sadji suggests that the metropolitan cultures are located on a higher level than African cultures: Africans must learn from European cultures in order to develop and perfect their own subjective character and to define a collective cultural identity within national boundaries. Apart from revealing a limited and essentialized understanding of culture, such a line of argument completely ignores the socio-cultural and linguistic realities of African countries, and it implies a prolongation of neo-colonial dependency even in the very area where an auto-centric development has long since taken place, namely, on a cultural level. The argument is based on a modernizing paradigm that sees African countries as merely repeating the political and economic developments of European countries during the industrialization process. This assumption had already been discredited in the 1960s, on the basis that the industrialization process in post-colonial Africa had taken place under completely different historical, political, economic, and social conditions from those which prevailed in Europe, so the assumed parallelity of development with that of Europe in the nineteenth century was plainly wrong. Hence, Sadji's and Ndumbe's attempts to justify German in sub-Saharan Africa are based on unsustainable assumptions:

they imply that German would not be a critical-hermeneutic discipline, but an affirmative one that would legitimize a continuation of neo-colonial dependencies on cultural and economic levels. Such an approach cannot provide a viable theoretical basis for legitimizing the place of *Germanistik* in African universities: it is neither intellectually sustainable nor politically feasible under current post-colonial conditions.

In contrast to this school of justification of the discipline of German in African universities, a different approach was developed in Germany. This has become known as *Interkulturelle Germanistik*, or Intercultural German Studies, developed by Alois Wierlacher and his colleagues. It proposes a *Germanistik* among "equal partners" throughout the world, seeking to emphasize the value of contributions by *Auslandsgermanistik* to the discussions of *Binnengermanistik*. At first glance, this seems a viable concept, which takes Third World countries seriously as partners in the co-operative development of a universal *Germanistik*. But on closer inspection, it becomes evident that the concept operates on an illusory level. It ignores the situation of economic dependency that has historically developed between Europe, including Germany, and her "partners" in the Third World: one of these asymmetrical partners—the one which lacks a viable cultural identity after having endured over 100 years of colonialism—is in a state of subordination. Intercultural *Germanistik* aims to offer a form of cultural development aid in order to rectify this situation. One of the proponents of Intercultural *Germanistik*, Bernd Thum, writes,

> It is essential to point out that, with the historical differentiation of our cultures [in Europe], a great service is done to the peoples of the Third World. The definition of "Western" culture specifically as German, Austrian, Swiss—instead of universally "human"—makes it easier for intellectuals in the Third World—indeed, it *forces them*—to define their own cultures in opposition to Western culture, in which, as Frantz Fanon puts it, they "are in danger of being submerged."[28]

This concept of *Hilfe zur Selbsthilfe* (guided self-help), though well intentioned, defines Germanic cultures in a rather monolithic manner and uses this as a supposedly positive symbol of identification for other cultures. Like Sadji's concept, it ignores cultural development in African countries and implies a "higher" standard of Western culture that can only have an enriching effect on African cultures. Again, *Germanistik* here serves as an extension of colonialism by obscuring the existing state of economic dependency between the metropolitan and African countries. The materialization of the discipline of German and the motivation for supporting German as a subject abroad was spelled out by official German government circles when, for example, Barthold Witte, Head of the Cultural Section of the German Foreign Office from 1983 to 1992, openly declared the following:

Those who know our language, possibly even love it, have a better understanding of us [Germans]—und usually also like us more—than people who have no access to it . . . A person who speaks and understands German is also *more likely to buy German goods* than someone ignorant of the language.[29]

A third conception of a type of *Germanistik* appropriate to Africa has also been devised in Germany, namely by Leo Kreutzer.[30] He takes a different approach from Wierlacher in that he attempts to analyze constructively and seeks to overcome the situation of dependency. Kreutzer defines *Germanistik* in Africa explicitly as an *Entwicklungswissenschaft* (developmental science) which is emancipatory, critical of ideologies and conscious of political implications. The Cameroonian *Germanist* Alioune Sow writes in his PhD thesis, supervised by Kreutzer, "The creation of a developmental science of this kind is characterized by a continual process of reflection on political realities and their ideological backgrounds; and from such reflection constitutive themes for scholarly activity emerge." [31]

Rather than presenting the economic and cultural developments of European countries affirmatively as paradigmatic examples for the economic and cultural developments of African nations, this approach seeks to analyze the *differences* in the industrial-cultural development of Europe and Africa in their respective processes of industrialization, as reflected in the medium of literature. Such an analysis of differences between the literatures of Germany and the respective African countries in a comparative approach aims at establishing commonalities and divergences in their respective responses to processes of global industrial development. This then serves as a platform to counter the destructive effects of globalization and to maintain cultural distinctions in spite of such globalizing tendencies. In effect, the approach implies that a discipline of literary analysis must be established in each African country, because the whole project aims at analyzing how social conflicts were aesthetically concretized as communicative structures became uncommunicative, and as the indigenous African culture was suppressed by the foreign culture. It suggests, further, that the discipline of *Germanistik* has to be complemented by the cognate disciplines of history, psychology, sociology and linguistics in order to provide comprehensive analyses of the existing societies, which can then provide a kind of identificatory framework, on both individual and collective levels, to fill the identity vacuum caused by colonialism. In effect, it implies revolutionary socialist changes, prompted by the theoretical analysis of literary artifacts, but reaching into the domains of politics and cultural policy. Twenty years after they were first advocated, one can safely conclude that these potentially revolutionary developments have not yet been realized: that is to say, the approach was far too ambitious in its claims, and was thus illusory.

Common to all three of these legitimatory approaches is their location in the field of German literature and their revolutionary aspirations, detached from the field of literary studies. They have relied for too long on a fashionable vocabulary of progress, liberation and anti-colonial resistance. As a result, *Germanistik* from sub-Saharan Africa has been noticed on the international scene at best only marginally and at worst condescendingly—as the well-known *Germanist* Werner Röcke has put it.[32]

In order to overcome this situation, the time might now be ripe to incorporate the "post-colonial turn" in cultural studies into the discipline of German in sub-Saharan Africa. Although rooted in historico-political approaches, the post-colonial turn has developed in recent times into a post-structuralist, cultural-epistemological project. It has shifted its focus to a discursive level, analyzing the *discursive* construction of colonial and present African identities and interactions. By doing so, it is simultaneously initiating a self-critical de-centering of European theoretical discourses. Western knowledge about "the Others" is now being deconstructed by these "Others" themselves, albeit in terms of Western categories of knowledge. The Bakhtinian notion of intentional linguistic hybridity, taken up by Bhabha, insinuates that there is no univocal grip on meaning. Consequently, the discourse of colonial authority finds itself open to the trace of the language of the other, thus enabling the critic to trace complex movements of disarming alterity in the colonial text.[33]

I would argue that the academics of the discipline *Germanistik* in Africa are in an ideal liminal situation, since they are part of both the subaltern *and* the Western or, more specifically, German discourses, which they can access without any potentially distorting translations. They have the unique potential to operate in a hybrid "third space" between the discourses of the colonized and the West. And this third space enables African *Germanists* to apply unique analytical methods and methodological approaches, for example the crossing of perspectives in a "trans-cultural reading" of German colonial, and post-colonial, literature from an African perspective. From this distinctive hybrid space, the African *Germanist* can ask questions, addressed to both metropolitan and marginal discourses, as to the discursive construction of narratives of identity, culture, nation, and so on. Since no one else can ask these questions with such authority (an authority which is, by the way, itself open to discursive deconstruction), the intercultural discipline of *Germanistik* in Africa might succeed in finding its rightful hybrid position, located in between the inherent requirements of the discipline and the wider socio-cultural project of constructing a continental African voice, a national Nigerian, Senegalese, Cameroonian etc. voice, a regional or a local voice, from the discursive analysis of literary and linguistic artifacts. But an intercultural discipline of *Germanistik* not only has the potential to address these problems on continental, national, or regional levels. It can also significantly contribute to the construction of truly *inter*cultural spaces for the individual student of the discipline, based on intimate knowledge of and competence in the transitions between different discourses, languages and cultures, thus initiating new constructs of identity and opening up new spaces of discourse.

In conclusion, it can be said that the academic discipline of German in sub-Saharan Africa has encountered difficulties right from the moment of its inception as a mere by-product of colonialism. Its establishment was neither intentionally facilitated by the colonizers (with the exceptions of South Africa and Namibia) nor was it particularly needed by the colonized. These coincidental historical roots have contributed to a high degree of internal uncertainty about the justification for the place of *Germanistik* at universities in sub-Saharan African countries. The conceptual framework of "nation-building" impacted on early discussions in the latter half of the twentieth century about the potential tasks of Western-style universities in general and *Germanistik* in particular: the role of African *Germanistik* was primarily conceptualized as being both a contributing and a criticizing factor in construing notions of national socio-economic and political development. However, the collapse of nation-building theories and activities rang the death knell for these developmental approaches. This article has argued that, after a period of further uncertainty in the 1990s, an African version of Intercultural *Germanistik* can find its rightful role at the beginning of the twenty-first century by positioning itself firmly within the conceptual framework of post-colonial discourse. It can contribute in a potentially significant manner to the discourses of post-colonialism *and* of intercultural *Germanistik*, in that African Germanists can analyze German colonial documents and literature from the position of a hybrid "third space," trying to combine local African perspectives and German (post-) colonial constructs. This would not only diminish the often-criticized Western dominance of post-colonial discourse, but it could also develop new insights into German colonial literature and colonialism from the point of view of the subaltern in both a historical and a discursive context.

## NOTES

1. *Germanistik an Hochschulen in Afrika Subsahara: Verzeichnis der Hochschullehrerinnen und Hochschullehrer*, ed. by Deutscher Akademischer Austauschdienst (Bonn: DAAD, 2002).
2. Arnd Witte, "Germanistik und DaF in Afrika (Subsahara)—Geschichte, Bestandsaufnahme, Aussichten," *Acta Germanica*, 30–1 (2003), 169–79.
3. Michael A. Omolewa, "French and German Languages in the Nigerian Secondary School Curriculum: 1859–1959," in *Curriculum in Theory and Practice*, ed. by Pai Obanya (Ibadan: ERSC, 1984), pp. 416–38 (p. 416).
4. Michael A. Böhm, *Deutsch in Afrika: Die Stellung der deutschen Sprache in Afrika vor dem Hintergrund der bildungs- und sprachpolitischen Gegebenheiten sowie der deutschen Auswärtigen Kulturpolitik* (Frankfurt/M.: Lang, 2003), pp. 398–400.
5. Salifou Traore, "Deutschunterricht und Germanistikstudium in Mali," in *Deutsch als Fremdsprache: Ein internationales Handbuch, 2. Halbband*, ed. by Gerhard Helbig and others (Berlin: de Gruyter, 2001), pp. 1635–41 (p. 1635).

6. Barthelemy Dakouo, "Deutschunterricht in Mali," *Etudes Germano-Afric-aines*, 5 (1987), 29–32; Peter Kasprzyk, "Das Förderungsprogramm des DAAD für afrikanische Deutschlehrer aus dem frankophonen Afrika," in *Afrikanische Germanistik: Eine Dokumentation*, ed. by Peter Kasprzyk and Norbert Ndong (Bonn: DAAD, 1989), pp. 11–18.

7. Manfred Prinz, "Zur Tradition interkulturellen Sprachunterrichts in Senegal," in *"Interkulturelle Germanistik"—Dialog der Kulturen auf Deutsch?* ed. by Peter Zimmermann (Frankfurt/M.: Lang 1989), pp. 175–89 (p. 181).

8. Amadou B. Sadji, "Deutschunterricht und Germanistik in Senegal," *Jahrbuch Deutsch als Fremdsprache*, 10 (1984), 75–85 (p. 75).

9. Michael A. Böhm, *Deutsch in Afrika*, p. 81.

10. Dakouo, *Deutschunterricht in Mali*, p. 30f.; Traore, *Deutschunterricht und Germanistikstudium in Mali*, p. 1635.

11. "Asquith Commission Report 1945," p. 27, cited in Ajuji Ahmed, "The Asquith Tradition, the Ashby Reform, and the Development of Higher Education in Nigeria," *Minerva*, 27 (1989), 1–20 (p. 3).

12. John D. Hargreaves, *The End of Colonial Rule in West Africa* (London: Macmillan, 1979), p. 104.

13. Sadji, *Deutschunterricht und Germanistikstudium in Senegal*, p. 75.

14. Norbert Ndong, "Deutschunterricht und Germanistik in Afrika—Ein Überblick," *Mitteilungen des deutschen Germanistenverbandes*, 38 (1991), 11–18 (p. 14).

15. Rainer Kußler, "Deutschunterricht und Germanistikstudium in Südafrika," in *Deutsch als Fremdsprache: Ein internationales Handbuch*, pp. 1609–18.

16. Ali A. Mazrui, "The African University as a Multinational Corporation: Problems of Penetration and Dependency," *Harvard Educational Review*, 45 (1975), 191–210 (p. 191).

17. Vincent Chukwuemeka Ike, *University Development in Africa: The Nigerian Experience* (Ibadan: Oxford U.P.), p. 1; Jide Oshuntokun, untitled article, in *Our U.I.*, ed. by Bunmi Salako (Lagos: Lyntana, 1990), pp. 158–62 (p. 162).

18. P.S. Noble, "Address at the Installation of the Chancellor by Dr P.S. Noble, Vice-Chancellor of the University of London, 18 November 1963," in *Ibadan Voices: Ibadan University in Transition*, ed. by Tekena Tamuno (Ibadan: Ibadan University Press, 1981), pp. 338–9 (p. 338).

19. B. Nnamdi Azikiwe and Louis P. Ojukwu, *Economic Rehabilitation of Eastern Nigeria* (Enugu: Govt printer, 1955) p. 34, cited in Nduka Okafor, *The Development of Universities in Nigeria: A Study of the Influence of Political and Other Factors on University Development in Nigeria, 1868–1967* (London: Longman, 1971), p. 111.

20. Hans N. Weiler, "The Political Dilemmas of Foreign Study," *Comparative Education Review*, 28 (1984), 168–79 (p. 179).

21. J.F. Ade Ajayi, "Towards an African Academic Community," in *Creating the African University: Emerging Issues of the 1970s*, ed. by T.M. Yesufu (Ibadan: Oxford University Press, 1973), pp. 11–19 (p. 11).

22. James Ferguson, "Ibadan Arts and Classics," *Universities Quarterly*, 19 (1965), 396–408 (p. 404).

23. Sadji, *Deutschunterricht und Germanistikstudium in Senegal*, p. 80.

24. Amadou B. Sadji, "Ein Senegalese zur kulturellen Außenpolitik der Bundesrepublik Deutschland," in *Im Urteil des Auslands: 30 Jahre Bundesrepublik*, ed. by Johannes Haas-Heye (Munich: Beck, 1979), pp. 196–207 (p. 199).

25. Kum'a Ndumbe III, "Zur Problematik der Deutschlandstudien in der afrikanischen Germanistik," in *Deutschlandstudien international: 1. Dokumentation*

*des Wolfenbütteler DAAD-Symposiums 1988*, ed. by Hans J. Althof (Munich: iudicium, 1990), pp. 167–75 (p. 168).

26. Sadji, *Deutschunterricht und Germanistikstudium in Senegal*, p. 78.

27. Ibid., p. 80.

28. Bernd Thum, "Einleitung," in *Gegenwart als kulturelles Erbe: Ein Beitrag der Germanistik zur Kulturwissenschaft deutschsprachiger Länder*, ed. by Bernd Thum (Munich: iudicium, 1985), pp. xv–lxvii (p. xix; emphasis added).

29. Barthold C. Witte, *Dialog über Grenzen: Beiträge zur auswärtigen Kulturpolitik* (Pfullingen: Neske, 1988), p. 233f.

30. Leo Kreutzer, *Literatur und Entwicklung: Studien zu einer Literatur der Ungleichzeitigkeit* (Frankfurt/M.: Fischer, 1989).

31. Alioune Sow, *Germanistik als Entwicklungs-Wissenschaft? Überlegungen zu einer Literaturwissenschaft des Faches "Deutsch als Fremdsprache" in Afrika* (Hildesheim: Olms, 1986), p. 73.

32. Werner Röcke, "Perspektiven einer afrikanischen Germanistik," *Zeitschrift für Germanistik: Neue Folge*, 8.3 (1998), 525f. (p. 525).

33. Robert J.C. Young, *Colonial Desire: Hybridity in Theory, Culture and Race* (London: Routledge, 1995), p. 22.

# Contributors

**Monika Albrecht** received her doctorate from the University of Münster, Germany, and in 2009 completed her *Habilitation* at the University of Salzburg, Austria. At present, she lectures at the University of Limerick, Ireland, having previously taught at the University of Nottingham, at the University of Massachusetts, Amherst, and at St Olaf College in Minnesota. Her recently published book is entitled *"Europa ist nicht die Welt": (Post)Kolonialismus in Literatur und Geschichte der west-deutschen Nachkriegszeit* (Bielefeld: Aisthesis 2008), and she is a member of the DFG (German Research Council) research network "Postkoloniale Studien in der Germanistik." Her current research focuses on a project that aims to clarify how issues of post-coloniality and multiculturalism can best be interlinked in the humanities.

**Jeffrey Bowersox** is Assistant Professor in the Department of History at the University of Southern Mississippi. His research interests include the histories of modern Germany and colonialism, education and youth, popular culture, and the African diaspora. He has published numerous articles on these themes, including on Germans and Poles in Upper Silesia (*Canadian Journal of History*, August 2003), on Africans in Germany at the turn of the twentieth century (in *Unbekannte Biographien*, Kai Homilius Verlag, 2008), and on colonialism in German education (in *German Cultures of Colonialism*, Duke University Press, forthcoming). Currently he is adapting his dissertation (University of Toronto, 2008) into a book manuscript examining German youth and colonial cultures.

**David Ciarlo** is currently Assistant Professor of Modern European History at the University of Cincinnati. He received his PhD from the University of Wisconsin-Madison in 2003, and then taught at the Massachusetts Institute of Technology for a number of years. His first book, *Advertising Empire: Colonialism, Commerce, and Visual Culture in Germany 1887–1914*, will shortly be published by Harvard University Press. This detailed investigation of advertising traces the circulation of black figures through German commercial culture, and shows the transformation of these representations of blacks in relation to the colonial project. Ciarlo is currently working on a number of articles on such topics as the Deutsches Kolonialhaus, the image of King Bell, and German Orientalist cigarette advertising. He has also begun his next book project, tentatively entitled *Selling War: Empire, Nation, and the Commercial Origins of Fascist Visual Culture, 1914–1918*, which will explore the construction of whiteness in the world of militarized consumer imagery.

**Ingo Cornils** is Senior Lecturer in German and Head of the Department of German, Russian and Slavonic Studies at the University of Leeds. His research focuses on the relationship between political, utopian and fantastic thought, with a particular interest in Hermann Hesse, the German Student Movement, German science fiction, and the literary representation of German colonialism. Among his publications are the volumes *Hermann Hesse Today* (co-edited with Osman Durrani, London: University of London, 2005), *(Un-)erfüllte Wirklichkeit: Neue Studien zu Uwe Timms Werk* (co-edited with Frank Finlay, Würzburg: Königshausen & Neumann, 2006), *Baader-Meinhof Returns: History and Cultural Memory of German Left-Wing Terrorism* (co-edited with Gerrit-Jan Berendse, New York: Rodopi, 2008), and *A Companion to the Works of Hermann Hesse* (ed., Rochester: Camden House, 2009).

**Katy Heady** studied German and Italian at the University of Cambridge, took an MA at Durham University and completed her PhD in nineteenth-century German at the University of Sheffield in 2007. Publications include her book *Literature and Censorship in Restoration Germany: Repression and Rhetoric*, published by Camden House (Rochester, NY) in 2009.

**Kathryn Jones** is Lecturer in French at Swansea University. Her research interests encompass twentieth and twenty-first century French, Francophone and German literature and cultural history, including particularly the study of memory, conflict and gender in transnational contexts. Her publications include *Journeys of Remembrance: Memories of the Second World War in French and German Literature, 1960–1980* (Oxford: Legenda, 2007), and a series of articles on post-colonial memories and literary representations of the 17 October 1961 Algerian War protest. She has recently co-edited a special issue of the *Journal of Contemporary European Studies* (17.1, April 2009) on the topic of memories of conflict in "Eastern Europe." Her current research focuses on twentieth-century travel narratives by French and francophone women writers.

**Kristin Kopp** is a member of the German Studies faculty at the University of Missouri, Columbia. Her research interests include German-Polish cultural history, German colonialism, and German film, with a specific focus on the construction of Poland as German colonial space in the nineteenth and twentieth centuries. She is co-editor of *Die Großstadt und das Primitive: Text, Politik, Repräsentation* (with Klaus Müller-Richter, Stuttgart: Metzler, 2004), which investigates the use of colonial categories to map urban space in the fin-de-siècle European metropolis, and of Peter Altenberg, *"Ashantee." Afrika und Wien um 1900* (with Werner Michael Schwarz, Vienna: Löcker, 2008), the most famous German-language text to depict the colonial "people shows" that were popular at the turn of the twentieth century.

**Reinhart Kössler** is a sociologist working at the Arnold Bergstraesser Institut in Freiburg, Germany. Trained in Eastern European history, social anthropology and Chinese studies as well as sociology in Heidelberg, Leeds and Münster, he has a long-established interest in southern Africa, both as a scholar and as an activist. His interests include theory of development, theory of society, political sociology, ethnicity and memory politics, the last with a special emphasis on Namibia. He is on the editorial board of the German quarterly *Peripherie* and is Corresponding Editor of *International Review of Social History*. Recent publications include *In Search of Survival and Dignity: Two Traditional Communities in Southern Namibia under South African Rule* (Frankfurt: IKO, 2007), *Gesellschaftstheorie und die Heterogenität empirischer Sozialforschung* (co-edited, Münster: Westfälisches Dampfboot, 2006) and *The Long Aftermath of War: Reconciliation in Namibia* (co-edited, forthcoming).

**Constant Kpao Sarè** is Assistant Professor at Abomey-Calavi University in Benin. He read German Studies at Université Nationale du Bénin, at the Universität des Saarlandes, Germany, and at the Université Paul Verlaine de Metz (France), where he received his doctorate in German Literature in 2006. He also studied public administration at the Deutsche Hochschule für Verwaltungswissenschaften Speyer, Germany. Teaching and research interests include nineteenth and twentieth century German literature, especially German colonial and post-colonial literature about Africa, theory and practice of migrations, *Vergangenheitsbewältigung* in literature. His publications include *Carl Peters et l'Afrique. Un mythe dans l'opinion publique, la littérature et la propagande politique en Allemagne* (Hamburg: Dr Covac, 2006).

**Volker Langbehn** is Associate Professor of German at San Francisco State University, California. He is the author of *Arno Schmidt's Zettels Traum: An Analysis* (Columbia, SC: Camden House, 2003) and has published articles on Friedrich Nietzsche, Christa Wolf, Arno Schmidt, Fritz von Unruh, Novalis and Gert Heidenreich, as well as the visual representation of German colonialism. He is the co-editor of a forthcoming book provisionally entitled *Colonial (Dis)-Continuities: Race, Holocaust,* *and Postwar Germany* (New York: Columbia University Press, 2010). His current book project, titled *The Visual Representation of Cultural Identity in German Mass Culture around 1900*, focuses on visual representations of "otherness" in German mass culture. His research interests include theories of modernity, the history of aesthetics, German literature and culture of the nineteenth and twentieth centuries, European colonialism and post-colonialism, genocide and Holocaust studies, and visual studies.

**Dennis Laumann** is Associate Professor of African History at the University of Memphis. A specialist in West African history, his research and publications focus mostly on Ghana. His first book, *Remembering the Germans in Ghana* (Peter Lang, in press), examines the oral history on German colonialism in eastern Ghana. He is the Chair of the Ghana Studies Council and a former Fulbright Scholar at the University of Ghana.

**Jörg Lehmann** works as freelance author, lecturer and consultant. He received his doctorate (DPhil) from the Free University of Berlin. His research interests range from depictions of violence in the media to techniques of conflict resolution. He is the author of *Imaginäre Schlachtfelder. Kriegsliteratur in der Weimarer Republik* (Berlin: Diss. FU Berlin, 2003; the title was published under his birth name of Jörg Vollmer) and co-author of *Afghanistan zwischen Gestern und Heute* (Freiburg: Lambertus, 2006). His current research focuses on vigilantism in film and literature.

**Susann Lewerenz** studied history and English literature and culture at the University of Hamburg. Her master's thesis was published under the title *Die "Deutsche Afrika-Schau" (1935–1940). Rassismus, Kolonialrevisionismus und postkoloniale Auseinandersetzungen im nationalsozialistischen Deutschland* (Frankfurt: Lang, 2005). Lewerenz is currently a doctoral student at the Carl von Ossietzky University, Oldenburg, and holds a scholarship from the Heinrich Böll Stiftung. In her doctoral thesis, she is examining the presence of artists of African and African American as well as Asian and Arab descent working in German show business between 1920 and 1960. She is investigating the forms, functions, and effects of visual displays of the "exotic," as well as the living and working conditions and creative role of artists of color.

**Yixu Lü** is Senior Lecturer in Germanic Studies in the School of Languages and Cultures, University of Sydney, Australia. She has published widely on Heinrich von Kleist, Medea in German literature, and German colonial adventures in China. Some recent publications include: "German Colonial Fiction on China: The Boxer-Uprising 1900–1901," in *German Life and Letters*, 59:1, 2006; "*Das Käthchen von Heilbronn,*" in *Kleist-Handbuch. Leben—Werk—Wirking*, ed. by Ingo Breuer (Stuttgart: Metzler, 2009); and the monograph *Medea unter den Deutschen. Wandlungen einer literarischen Figur* (Medea among the Germans. Transformations of a Literary Figure) (Freiburg: Rombach, 2009).

**Henning Melber** went to Namibia in 1967, where he joined SWAPO. Exiled in 1975, he returned to Namibia in 1992, with degrees in political sciences (PhD) and sociology (*venia legendi* in development studies), to be Director of the Namibian Economic Policy Research Unit (NEPRU). He joined the Nordic Africa Institute in Uppsala in 2000 as Research Director. Since 2006 he has been Executive Director of the Dag Hammarskjöld Foundation. His work areas include Southern Africa (especially Namibia) and the history of racism. He is Vice-President of the International Network of Genocide Scholars (INoGS), co-editor of the *Africa Yearbook* and managing co-editor of *Africa Spectrum*. His latest book (with Roger Southall) is *A New Scramble for Africa?* (Scottsville: University KwaZulu-Natal Press, 2009).

**Kenneth J. Orosz** is Assistant Professor at Buffalo State College, where he teaches European, African and colonial history. He is a former Fulbright grant recipient and the author of several forthcoming articles on missionary activities in colonial Africa. His book entitled *Religious Conflict and the Evolution of Language Policy in German and French Cameroon, 1885–1939* (New York: Peter Lang, 2009) was awarded the 2009 Heggoy Prize for the best work in French colonial history. In addition to working on a biography of Flora Shaw, former Colonial Editor of the London *Times*, his current research interests include cultural exchanges in the age of imperialism, the internment of German colonial missionaries in World War One, and Cameroonian resistance movements.

**Michael Perraudin** is Professor of German at the University of Sheffield, having previously taught at Trinity College, Dublin, and the University of Birmingham. His research focus is on nineteenth-century German literature, especially that of the Biedermeier/Vormärz, and its social and political contexts. His books include *Literature, the 'Volk' and the Revolution in Mid-19th-Century Germany* (Oxford: Berghahn, 2000) and *Formen der Wirklichkeitserfassung nach 1848. Deutsche Literatur und Kultur vom Nachmärz bis zur Gründerzeit in europäischer Perspektive* (co-edited with Helmut Koopmann, Bielefeld: Aisthesis, 2003). He has also published numerous articles on nineteenth- and twentieth-century literary authors: Heine, Mörike, Wilhelm Müller, Büchner, Nestroy, Georg Weerth, Heinrich Böll, Kleist, Eichendorff, Theodor Storm, including on colonial/pre-colonial fiction by the last three of these.

Michael Pesek teaches in the African Studies program at the Humboldt University, Berlin. He has published widely on the politics and culture of German imperialism and colonialism, especially in East Africa. This has included in particular his monograph *Koloniale Herrschaft in Deutsch-Ostafrika: Expeditionen, Militär und Verwaltung seit 1880* (Frankfurt: Campus, 2005).

Tracey Reimann-Dawe completed her PhD thesis entitled *Time, Identity and Nation in German Travel Writing on Africa 1848–1914* in 2008 at Durham University, UK, where she is currently a Teaching Fellow. Her research interests include issues of German colonialism, nationalism, and national identity.

Dominik J. Schaller teaches history at Ruprecht-Karls-Universität Heidelberg, Germany. His studies focus on mass violence, colonialism, and African history. Schaller is co-editor of the *Journal of Genocide Research* (Routledge) and Executive Secretary of the International Network of Genocide Scholars (INoGS). He is contributing co-editor of the volumes *The Armenian Genocide and the Shoah* (Zürich: Chronos, 2002), *Enteignet-Vertrieben-Ermordet. Beiträge zur Genozidforschung* (Zürich: Chronos, 2004), *The Origins of Genocide: Raphael Lemkin as a Historian of Mass Violence* (London: Routledge, 2009), and *Late Ottoman Genocides* (London: Routledge, 2009). Schaller has written numerous articles on the Armenian and Rwandan genocides, the Holocaust, and German colonial rule in Africa.

Britta Schilling was born in Princeton, New Jersey, and earned a BA in history and art history from Rutgers University. She moved to Britain in 2003 to study at Oxford University, where she completed her MPhil dissertation on German women in Africa in the inter-war period. She has taught history as a Lecturer at Trinity College, Oxford, and is currently finishing her DPhil dissertation, entitled *Memory, Myth and Popular Culture: Visions of Empire in Postcolonial Germany*, at St Antony's College, Oxford. Her research interests include visual and material culture, memory studies, transnational history, and family archives.

Wolfgang Struck is a Professor of German Literature at the University of Erfurt. His research focuses on literature, film and television. His most recent publication is *Die Eroberung der Phantasie. Kolonialismus, Literatur und Film zwischen deutschem Kaiserreich und Weimarer Republik* (Göttingen: V&R unipress, 2009).

Brian Vick is Assistant Professor of History at Emory University, Atlanta. He is the author of essays on German nationalism, liberalism, historicism, and ideas of race, as well as the monograph *Defining Germany:*

*The 1848 Frankfurt Parliamentarians and National Identity* (Cambridge, MA: Harvard University Press, 2002). His current book project explores the Congress of Vienna as an event in both cultural and political history, including such questions of post-Napoleonic political culture as the political engagement of women, the development of liberal and conservative politics, and the role of religious revival. He also has a substantial article forthcoming on the campaigns for legal reform by Germanist legal scholars in the mid-nineteenth century, in which issues of gender and political culture feature centrally.

**Arnd Witte** is Senior Lecturer and Head of the Department of German at the National University of Ireland in Maynooth. In the context of his work as DAAD lecturer in Bristol (1984–6) and in Ibadan (1986–90), he developed his research interest in intercultural aspects of foreign-language teaching/learning. His present research focuses on defining and evaluating the concept of intercultural competence. His most recent book publications are *The Concept of Progression in Teaching and Learning Foreign Languages* (ed., Oxford: Lang 2005), and *Translation in Second Language Learning* (ed., Oxford: Lang, 2009). He is also co-editor of the book series *Intercultural Studies and Foreign Language Learning* (Oxford: Lang).

**Jürgen Zimmerer** is Reader in History at the University of Sheffield and Director of the Centre for the Study of Genocide and Mass Violence there. He is founding president of the International Network of Genocide Scholars and co-editor of the *Journal of Genocide Research*. His interests include the history of colonialism, comparative genocide and the Holocaust. He is the author of *Deutsche Herrschaft über Afrikaner. Staatlicher Machtanspruch und Wirklichkeit im kolonialen Namibia* (Münster: Lit, 2003) and *Von Windhuk nach Auschwitz? Beiträge zum Verhältnis von Kolonialismus und Holocaust* (Münster: Lit, 2010), as well as the editor of various essay collections.

# Bibliography

Abrams, Lynn. "From Control to Commercialization: The Triumph of Mass Entertainment in Germany, 1900–1925." *German History*, 8 (1990), 278–93.

Altehenger-Smith, Sherida. "Language Planning and Language Policy in Tanzania during the German Colonial Period." *Kiswahili: The Journal of the East African Swahili Committee*, 48.2 (1968), 73–80.

Aly, Götz. *"Final Solution": Nazi Population Policy and the Murder of the European Jews* (London: Oxford University Press, 1999).

Amenumey, D.E.K. "German Administration in Southern Togo." *Journal of African History*, 10.4 (1969), 623–39.

Ames, Eric. "Where the Wild Things Are: Locating the Exotic in German Modernity" (PhD diss., University of California, Berkeley, 2000).

Ames, Eric, Marcia Klotz, and Lora Wildenthal (eds). *Germany's Colonial Pasts* (Lincoln: University of Nebraska Press, 2005).

*Amtsblatt für das Schutzgebiet Kamerun*, 6.14 (May 1913).

Angebauer, Karl. *Kameraden in Südwest. Ein Tatsachenroman* (Berlin: Bong, 1936).

Ankum, K. von (ed.). *Women in the Metropolis: Gender and Modernity in Weimar Culture* (Berkeley: University of California Press, 1997).

Anna, Susanna. *Historische Plakate 1890–1914* (Stuttgart: Daco, 1995).

Appadurai, Arjun. "Dead Certainty: Ethnic Violence in the Era of Globalization." *Public Culture*, 10.2 (1998), 225–47.

Arata, Stephen D. "The Occidental Tourist: *Dracula* and the Anxiety of Reverse Colonization." *Victorian Studies*, 33 (1990), 621–44.

Arendt, Hannah. *The Origins of Totalitarianism* (New York: Harcourt, Brace, 1951).

Austen, Ralph, and Jonathan Derrick. *Middlemen of the Cameroons Rivers: The Duala and their Hinterland, c. 1600–c. 1960* (Cambridge: Cambridge University Press, 1999).

Autorenkollektiv Allgemeiner Studentenausschuss (ASTA) an der Universität Hamburg. *Das permanente Kolonialinstitut: 50 Jahre Hamburger Universität* (Hamburg, 1969).

Axster, Felix. "Die Angst vor dem *Verkaffern*—Politiken der Reinigung im deutschen Kolonialismus." *Werkstattgeschichte*, 39 (2005), 39–53.

Aynsley, Jeremy. *Graphic Design in Germany, 1890–1945* (Berkeley: University California Press, 2000).

Bade, Klaus J. *Friedrich Fabri und der Imperialismus in der Bismarckzeit: Revolution—Depression—Expansion* (Freiburg/Br.: Atlantis, 1975).

Baecker, Paul. *Der letzte Wiking. Carl Peters erobert Ostafrika* (Berlin: Junge Generation, 1934).

Baer, Martin, and Olaf Schröter. *Eine Kopfjagd: Deutsche in Ostafrika* (Berlin: Links, 2001).

Balsen, Werner, and Karl Rössel. *Hoch die internationale Solidarität: Zur Geschichte der Dritte-Welt-Bewegung in der Bundesrepublik* (Cologne: Kölner Volksblatt-Verlag, 1986).

Barkan, Elazar, *The Guilt of Nations: Restitution and Negotiating Historical Injustices* (New York: Norton, 2000).

Barkan, Elazar, and Ronald Bush (eds). *Prehistories of the Future: The Primitivist Project and the Culture of Modernism* (Stanford, CA: Stanford University Press, 1995).

Barta, Tony, "Sorry, and Not Sorry, in Australia: How the Apology to the Stolen Generations Buried a History of Genocide." *Journal of Genocide Research*, 10.2 (2008), 191–99.

Barthes, Roland. *Mythologies* (New York: Hill & Wang, 1972).

Bastian, Adolf. *Zwei Worte über Colonial-Weisheit von jemandem dem dieselbe versagt ist* (Berlin: Dümmler, n.d).

Bauer, Yehuda, *Die dunkle Seite der Geschichte. Die Shoah in historischer Sicht. Interpretationen und Re-Interpretationen* (Frankfurt/M.: Jüdischer Verlag Suhrkamp, 2001).

Baumann, Adalbert. *Das neue, leichte Weltdeutsch für unsere Bundesgenossen und Freunde! Seine Notwendigkeit und seine wirtschaftliche Bedeutung von Prof. Dr. Adalbert Baumann. Vortrag, geh. 1915. In laut-shrift geshriben* (Diessen: Huber, 1916).

Bazyler, Michael J., "Lex Americana. Holocaust Litigation as a Restitution Model for Other Massive Human Rights Abuses." In *Enteignet–Vertrieben–Ermordet. Beiträge zur Genozidforschung*, ed. by Dominik J. Schaller et al. (Zürich: Chronos, 2004), pp. 349–94.

Bechhaus-Gerst, Marianne. "Afrikaner in Deutschland 1933–1945." *1999*, 12.4 (1997), 10–31.

Bechhaus-Gerst, Marianne. "'Hinrichtung 6.18 Uhr durch das Fallbeilgerät'—Ein Askari vor dem Sondergericht Hamburg." In *Die (koloniale) Begegnung. AfrikanerInnen in Deutschland 1880–1945. Deutsche in Afrika 1880–1918*, ed. by Marianne Bechhaus-Gerst and Reinhard Klein-Arendt (Frankfurt/M.: Lang, 2003), pp. 41–9.

Bechhaus-Gerst, Marianne. *Treu bis in den Tod. Von Deutsch-Ostafrika nach Sachsenhausen—Eine Lebensgeschichte* (Berlin: Links, 2007).

Beinhorn, E. *180 Stunden über Afrika* (Berlin: Scherl, 1933).

Beinhorn, E. *Ein Mädchen fliegt um die Welt* (Berlin: Hobbing, 1932).

Bengerstorf, Hermann von. *Unter der Tropensonne Afrikas* (Hamburg, 1914).

Benjamin, Walter. *Gesammelte Schriften*, vol. 1 (Frankfurt/M.: Suhrkamp, 1991).

Benjamin, Walter. "Kleine Geschichte der Photographie." In *Angelus Novus. Ausgewählte Schriften*, vol. 2 (Frankfurt/M.: Suhrkamp, 1988), pp. 229–47.

Benninghoff-Lühl, Sibylle. *Deutsche Kolonialromane 1884–1914 in ihrem Entstehungs- und Wirkungszusammenhang* (Bremen: Übersee-Museum, 1983).

Berman, Russell A. *Enlightenment or Empire: Colonial Discourse in German Culture* (Lincoln: University Nebraska Press, 1998).

Bhabha, Homi K. *The Location of Culture* (London: Routledge, 1994).

Blanke, Richard. *Prussian Poland in the German Empire (1871–1900)* (New York: Columbia University Press, 1981).

Blaut, J.M. *The Colonizer's Model of the World: Geographic Diffusionism and Eurocentric History* (New York: Guilford, 1993).

Bley, Helmut. *Kolonialherrschaft und Sozialstruktur in Deutsch-Südwest-Afrika, 1894–1914* (Hamburg: Leibniz, 1968).

Bley, Helmut. *South-West Africa under German Rule, 1894–1914* (London: Heinemann, 1971).

Boa, Elizabeth, et al. (eds). *Heimat—A German Dream: Regional Loyalties and National Identity in German Culture 1890–1990* (London: Oxford University Press, 2000).

Boberach, Heinz (ed.). *Meldungen aus dem Reich: Auswahl aus den geheimen Lageberichten des Sicherheitsdienstes der SS 1938–1944*, vol. 4, *Meldungen aus dem Reich, Nr. 66 vom 15. März 1940–Nr. 101 vom 1. Juli 1940* (Herrsching: Pawlak, 1984).

Böhlke-Itzen, Janntje. *Kolonialschuld und Entschädigung: Der deutsche Völkermord an den Herero 1904–1907* (Frankfurt/M.: Brandes & Apsel 2004).

Böhm, Michael Anton. *Deutsch in Afrika: Die Stellung der deutschen Sprache in Afrika vor dem Hintergrund der bildungs- und sprachpolitischen Gegebenheiten sowie der deutschen Auswärtigen Kulturpolitik* (Frankfurt/M.: Lang, 2003).

Böhme, Helmut. *Deutschlands Weg zur Großmacht: Studien zum Verhältnis von Wirtschaft und Staat während der Reichsgründungszeit 1848–1881* (Cologne: Kiepenheuer & Witsch, 1966).

Borscheid, Peter, and Clemens Wischermann. *Bilderwelt des Alltags. Werbung in der Konsumgesellschaft des 19. und 20. Jahrhunderts* (Stuttgart: Steiner, 1995).

Brehl, Medardus. "'Das Drama spielte sich auf der dunklen Bühne des Sandfeldes ab': Die Vernichtung der Herero und Nama in der deutschen (Populär-)Literatur." In *Völkermord in Deutsch-Südwestafrika: Der Kolonialkrieg (1904–1908) in Namibia und seine Folgen*, ed. by Jürgen Zimmerer and Joachim Zeller (Berlin: Links, 2003), pp. 86–96.

Brehl, Medardus. "'Diese Schwarzen haben vor Gott und den Menschen den Tod verdient'." In *Völkermord und Kriegsverbrechen in der 1. Hälfte des 20. Jahrhunderts. Jahrbuch 2004 zur Geschichte und Wirkung des Holocaust*, ed. by Irmtrud Wojak and Susanne Meinl (Frankfurt/M.: Campus 2004), 77–97.

Brehl, Medardus. *Vernichtung der Herero. Diskurse der Gewalt in der deutschen Kolonialliteratur* (Munich: Fink, 2007).

Breiter, Bastian. "Der Weg des 'treuen Askari' ins Konzentrationslager—Die Lebensgeschichte des Mohamed Husen." In *Kolonialmetropole Berlin: eine Spurensuche*, ed. by Ulrich van der Heyden and Joachim Zeller (Berlin: Berlin Edition, 2002), pp. 215–20.

Bridenthal, Renate, Atina Grossman and Marion Kaplan. *When Biology Became Destiny: Women in Weimar and Nazi Germany* (New York: Monthly Review Press, 1984).

Brumfit, Anne. "The Rise and Development of a Language Policy in German East Africa." *Sprache und Geschichte in Afrika*, 2 (1980), 219–332.

Bryson, Norman. *Vision and Painting: The Logic of the Gaze* (New Haven, CT: Yale University Press, 1983).

Bucher, Georg. *Westfront 1914–1918. Das Buch vom Frontkameraden* (Wien: Konegen, 1930).

Buchhorn, Josef. *Weg in die Welt. Ein Schauspiel um den deutschen Mann Carl Peters* (Schöneberg: Schwabe, 1940).

Bühler, Andreas Heinrich. *Der Namaaufstand gegen die deutsche Kolonialherrschaft in Namibia von 1904–1913* (Frankfurt/M.: IKO, 2003).

Bülow, Frieda von. *Der Konsul. Vaterländischer Roman aus unseren Tagen* (Berlin: Fontane, 1891).

Bülow, Frieda von. *Im Lande der Verheißung. Ein deutscher Kolonial-Roman* (Dresden: Reißner, 1914).

Bülow, Frieda von. *Tropenkoller. Episode aus dem deutschen Kolonialleben* (Berlin: Fontane, 1905).

Büttner, Thea, and Gerhard Brehme (eds). *African Studies—Afrika-Studien* (Berlin: Akademie, 1973), 383–97.

Campt, Tina, Pascal Grosse and Yara-Colette Lemke-Muniz de Faria. "Blacks, Germans and the Politics of Colonial Imagination, 1920–1960." In *The Imperialist Imagination. German Colonialism and its Legacy*, ed. by Sara Lennox, Sara Friedrichsmeyer and Susanne Zantop (Ann Arbor: University of Michigan Press, 1998), pp. 205–29.

Chatzoudis, Georgios. "Von der Kolonie Südwestafrika zum Nationalstatt Namibia—das politische System seit 1949." In *Namibia—Deutschland: Eine geteilte Geschichte. Widerstand—Gewalt—Erinnerung. Publikation zur gleichnamigen Ausstellung im Rautenstrauch-Joest-Museum für Völkerkunde der Stadt Köln und im Deutschen Historischen Museum*, ed. by Larissa Förster, Dag Henrichsen and Michael Bollig (Berlin: Minerva, 2004), pp. 258–73.

Chaumont, Jean-Michel. *La concurrence des victimes. Génocide, identité, reconnaissance* (Paris: La Découverte & Syros, 1997).

Chickering, Roger. "'Casting Their Gaze More Broadly': Women's Patriotic Activism in Imperial Germany." *Past and Present* (February 1988), 156–85.

Chickering, Roger. "Language and the Social Foundations of Radical Nationalism in the Wilhelmine era, 1870/71–1989/90." In *1870/71–1989/90: German Unifications and the Change of Literary Discourse*, ed. by Walter Pape (Berlin: de Gruyter, 1993), pp. 61–78.

Christadler, Marieluise. "Zwischen Gartenlaube und Genozid. Kolonialistische Jugendbücher im Kaiserreich." In *Die Menschen sind arm, weil sie arm sind*, ed. by Jörg Becker and Charlotte Oberfeld (Frankfurt/M.: Haag & Herchen, 1978), pp. 61–98.

Christensen, Christen P. *Nordschleswiger verteidigen Deutsch-Ostafrika: Bericht über die Fahrt des Blockadebrechers "Kronborg" und das Schicksal seiner Mannschaft in Deutsch-Ostafrika 1914–1918* (Essen: Essener Verlagsanstalt, 1938).

Ciarlo, David. *Advertising Empire, Consuming Race: Colonialism, Commerce and Visual Culture in Germany, 1887–1914* (Cambridge, MA: Harvard University Press, forthcoming).

Ciarlo, David. *Consuming Race, Envisioning Empire: Colonialism and German Mass Culture, 1887–1914* (PhD diss., University of Wisconsin, Madison, 2003).

Ciarlo, David. "Rasse konsumieren: Von der exotischen zur kolonialen Imagination in der Bildreklame des Wilhelminischen Kaiserreichs." In *Phantasiereiche: Zur Kulturgeschichte des deutschen Kolonialismus*, ed. by Birthe Kundrus (Frankfurt/M.: Campus, 2003), pp. 135–53.

Cohen, Paul A. *History in Three Keys: The Boxers as Event, Experience and Myth* (New York: Columbia University Press, 1997).

Cole, Joshua. "Remembering the Battle of Paris: 17 October 1961 in French and Algerian Memory." *French Politics, Culture and Society*, 21.3 (2003), 21–50.

Conrad, Sebastian. *Globalisierung und Nation im deutschen Kaiserreich* (Munich: Beck, 2006).

Consten, Hermann. " . . . und ich weine um dich, Deutsch-Afrika" (Stuttgart: Strecker & Schröder, 1926).

Conze, Werner, and Wolfgang Zorn (eds). *Die Protokolle des Volkswirtschaftlichen Ausschusses der deutschen Nationalversammlung 1848/49* (Boppard am Rhein: Boldt, 1992).

Cooper, Allan D., "Reparations for the Herero Genocide: Defining the Limits of International Litigation." *African Affairs*, 106.422 (2007), 113–26.

Cooper, Frederick. *Colonialism in Question: Theory, Knowledge, History* (Berkeley: University of California Press, 2005).

Cooper, Frederick, and Ann Laura Stoler. *Tensions of Empire: Colonial Cultures in a Bourgeois World* (Berkeley: University of California Press, 1997).

Corbey, Raymond. "Alterity: the Colonial Nude." *Critique of Anthropology*, 8 (1988), 75–92.

Dabag, Mihran, Horst Gründer and Uwe-K. Ketelsen (eds). *Kolonialismus. Kolonialdiskurs und Genozid* (Munich: Fink, 2004).

Dabag, Mihran. "Genozidforschung: Leitfragen, Kontroversen, Überlieferung." *Zeitschrift für Genozidforschung*, 1.1 (1999), 6–35.

Dadrian, Vahakn N. *The History of the Armenian Genocide: Ethnic Conflict from the Balkans to Anatolia to the Caucasus* (New York: Berghahn, 1995).

Decher, Maximilian. *Afrikanisches und Allzu-Afrikanisches: Erlebtes und Erlauschtes in Deutsch-Ostafrika 1914–17* (Leipzig, 1932).

Dedering, Tilman. "The German-Herero War of 1904: Revisionism of Genocide or Imaginary Historiography?" *Journal of Southern African Studies*, 19.1 (1993), 80–8.

Department of Information and Publicity/SWAPO of Namibia. *To Be Born A Nation: The Liberation Struggle for Namibia* (London: Zed, 1981).

Deppe, Ludwig. *Mit Lettow-Vorbeck durch Afrika* (Berlin: Scherl, 1919).

Deslaurier, Christine, and Aurélie Roger. "Mémoires grises. Pratiques politiques du passé colonial entre Europe et Afrique." *Politique Africaine*, 1.102 (2006), 5–27.

Dirks, Nicholas B. *Colonialism and Culture* (Ann Arbor: University of Michigan Press, 1992).

Drechsler, Horst. *Let Us Die Fighting: Namibia under the Germans* (London: Zed, 1984).

Drechsler, Horst. *Südwestafrika unter deutscher Kolonialherrschaft: Der Kampf der Herero und Nama gegen den deutschen Imperialismus (1884–1915)* (Berlin: Akademie 1966; 2nd rev. edn, 1984).

Duems, Erich. "Rassenreinheit oder Rassenmischung? Frankreichs Kolonialarmee und unsere Schutztruppe." *DKZ*, 12 (45) (1933), 242–44.

Dunwoodie, Peter. "Postface: History, Memory and Identity—Today's Crisis, Yesterday's Issue." *French History*, 20.3 (2006), 318–32.

Eckart, Wolfgang U. *Medizin und Kolonialimperialismus* (Paderborn: Schöningh, 1997).

Einaudi, Jean-Luc. *La Bataille de Paris: 17 octobre 1961* (Paris: Seuil, 1991).

Einaudi, Jean-Luc. *Octobre 1961: un massacre à Paris* (Paris: Fayard, 2001).

Eley, Geoff. "Making a Place in the Nation: Meanings of 'Citizenship' in Wilhelmine Germany." In *Wilhelminism and Its Legacies: German Modernities, Imperialism, and the Meanings of Reform, 1890–1930*, ed. by Geoff Eley and James Retallack (New York: Berghahn, 2003), pp. 16–33.

El-Tayeb, Fatima. *Schwarze Deutsche: der Diskurs um "Rasse" und nationale Identität 1890–1933* (Frankfurt/M.: Campus, 2001).

Engelhard, Jutta, and Peter Mesenhöller. *Bilder aus dem Paradies* (Cologne: Jonas, 1995).

Erichsen, Casper. *"The Angel of Death Has Descended Violently Among Them." Concentration Camps and Prisoners-of-War in Namibia, 1904–08* (Leiden: African Studies Centre, 2005).

Errell, L. *Kleine Reise zu schwarzen Menschen* (Berlin: Brehm, 1931).

Esche, Jan. *Koloniales Anspruchsdenken in Deutschland im Ersten Weltkrieg, während der Versailler Friedensverhandlungen und in der Weimarer Republik (1914 bis 1933)* (PhD diss., University of Hamburg, 1989).

Eskildsen, U., and D. Wiethoff. *Lotte Errell: Reporterin der 30er Jahre* (Essen: Museum Folkwang, 1997).

Ettighoffer, Paul C. *Eine Armee meutert. Schicksalstag Frankreich 1917. Ein Bericht* (Gütersloh: Bertelsmann, 1937).

Fabian, Johannes. *Time and the Other: How Anthropology Makes Its Object* (New York: Columbia University Press, 1983).

*Farbe bekennen. Afro-deutsche Frauen auf den Spuren ihrer Geschichte*, ed. by Katharina Oguntoye, May Opitz and Dagmar Schultz (Berlin: Orlanda, 1986).

Faulstich, Werner. *Medienwandel im Industriezeitalter* (Göttingen: Vandenhoeck & Ruprecht, 2004).

Fenske, Hans. "Die Deutsche Auswanderung in der Mitte des 19. Jahrhunderts— Öffentliche Meinung und amtliche Politik." In *Preussentum und Liberalismus. Aufsätze zur preussischen und deutschen Geschichte des 19. und 20. Jahrhunderts*, ed. by Hermann Hiery (Dettelbach: Röhl, 2002), pp. 415–28.

Fenske, Hans. "Imperialistische Tendenzen in Deutschland vor 1866. Auswanderung, überseeische Bestrebungen, Weltmachtträume." *Historisches Jahrbuch*, 97–8 (1978), 336–83.

Fenske, Hans. "Ungeduldige Zuschauer. Die Deutschen und die europäische Expansion 1815–1880." In *Imperialistische Kontinuität und nationale Ungeduld im 19. Jahrhundert*, ed. by Wolfgang Reinhard (Frankfurt/M.: Fischer, 1991), pp. 87–123.

Fiedler, Matthias. *Zwischen Abenteuer, Wissenschaft und Kolonialismus: Der deutsche Afrikadiskurs im 18. und 19. Jahrhundert* (Cologne: Böhlau, 2005).

Fisch, Jörg. "Imperialismus." In *Geschichtliche Grundbegriffe*, ed. by Reinhard Koselleck et al., 8 vols (Stuttgart: Kleff, 1972–97), vol.3, pp. 171–5.

Fischer, Fritz. *Griff nach der Weltmacht* (Düsseldorf: Droste, 1961).

Fleming, Michael. "Holocaust and Memory." *Ethnopolitics*, 4.1 (2005), 115–23.

Foerster, Wolfgang, Helmuth Greiner and Hans Witte (eds). *Kämpfer an vergessenen Fronten: Feldzugsbriefe, Kriegstägebücher und Berichte* (Berlin: Neufeld & Henius, 1931).

Föllmer, Wilhelm. "Die Schutz- und Polizeitruppe in Deutsch-Ostafrika." *Die Deutschen Kolonien*, 9.13 (1913), 71.

Forgey, Elisa. "'Die große Negertrommel der kolonialen Werbung.' Die Deutsche Afrika-Schau 1935–1943." *WerkstattGeschichte*, 3.9 (1994), 25–33 (see also Joeden-Forgey).

Forster, Peter G. *The Esperanto Movement* (New York: Mouton, 1982).

Foster, Hal. "Preface." In *Vision and Visuality*, ed. by Hal Foster (Seattle: Bay, 1988), pp. ix–xiv.

Foucault, Michel. *The Order of Things: An Archaeology of the Human Sciences* (New York: Vintage, 1994).

Foucault, Michel. *Vom Licht des Krieges zur Geburt der Geschichte* (Berlin: Merve, 1986).

Freedberg, David. *The Power of Images: Studies in the History and Theory of Response* (Chicago: University of Chicago Press, 1989).

Frenssen, Gustav. *Peter Moors Fahrt nach Südwest. Ein Feldzugsbericht* (Berlin: Grote, 1906).

Frevert, Astrid, Gisela Rautenstrauch and Matthias Rickling. "Kolonialismus und Darstellungen aus den Kolonien." In *Neuruppiner Bilderbogen. Ein Massenmedium des 19. Jahrhunderts*, ed. by Stefan Brakensiek, Regina Krull and Irina Rockel (Bielefeld: Verlag für Regionalgeschichte, 1993), pp. 137–55.

Freytag, Gustav. *Soll und Haben*, 58th edn (Leipzig: Hirzel, 1902).

Friedrichsmeyer, Sara, Sara Lennox and Susanne Zantop (eds). *The Imperialist Imagination: German Colonialism and Its Legacy* (Ann Arbor: University of Michigan Press, 1998).

Frobenius, Leo. *Und Afrika sprach: Bericht über den Verlauf der dritten Reiseperiode der Deutschen Innerafrikanischen Forschungsexpedition in den Jahren 1910–1912*, 3 vols (Berlin, 1912).

Funke, Alfred. *Afrikanischer Lorbeer. Kolonialroman* (Berlin: Vita, 1907).

Funke, Alfred. *Carl Peters. Der Mann, der Deutschland ein Imperium schaffen wollte* (Berlin: Metten, 1937).

Furber, David. *Going East: Colonialism and German Life in Nazi-Occupied Poland* (PhD diss., State University of New York at Buffalo, 2003).

Gann, L.H., and Peter Duignan. *The Rulers of German Africa 1884–1914* (Stanford, CA: Stanford University Press, 1977).

Geary, Christraud, and Virginia-Lee Webb. "Introduction: Views on Postcards." In *Delivering Views: Distant Cultures in Early Postcards*, ed. by Christraud Geary and Virginia-Lee Webb (Washington: Smithsonian, 1998), pp. 1–12.

Gewald, Jan-Bart. "The Funeral of Samuel Maharero and the Reorganisation of the Herero." In *Genocide in German South-West Africa. The Colonial War of 1904–1908 and Its Aftermath*, ed. by Jürgen Zimmerer and Joachim Zeller (Monmouth: Merlin, 2008), pp. 207–16.

Gewald, Jan-Bart. "Herero Genocide in the Twentieth Century: Politics and Memory." In *Rethinking Resistance: Revolt and Violence in African History*, ed. by Jon Abbink, Mirjam de Bruijn and Klaas van Walraven (Leiden: Brill, 2003), pp. 279–304.

Gewald, Jan-Bart. *Herero Heroes: A Socio-Political History of the Herero of Namibia, 1890–1923* (Oxford: Currey; Athens: Ohio University Press, 1999).

Gewald, Jan-Bart. *"We Thought we would be Free . . .": Socio-Cultural Aspects of Herero History in Namibia 1915–1940* (Cologne: Köppe, 2000).

Gewald, Jan-Bart, and Henning Melber. "Genozid, Herero-Identität(en) und die Befreiungsbewegung an der Macht." In *Genozid und Gedenken: Namibisch-deutsche Geschichte und Gegenwart*, ed. by Henning Melber (Frankfurt/M.: Brandes & Apsel, 2005), pp. 79–102.

Gilman, Sander. *Difference and Pathology: Stereotypes of Sexuality, Race, and Madness* (Ithaca, NY: Cornell University Press, 1985).

Gilman, Sander, and Zhou Xun (eds). *Smoke* (London: Reaktion, 2004).

Goltz, Joachim von der. *Der Baum von Cléry. Roman* (Berlin: Büchergilde Gutenberg, 1934).

Gombrich, Ernst Hans. "The Cartoonist's Armoury." In *Meditations on a Hobby Horse*, ed. by Ernst Hans Gombrich (London: Phaidon, 1963), pp. 127–42.

Graichen, Gisela. *Deutsche Kolonien: Traum und Trauma* (Berlin: Ullstein, 2005).

Grosse, Pascal. *Kolonialismus, Eugenik und bürgerliche Gesellschaft in Deutschland 1850–1918* (Frankfurt/M.: Campus, 2000).

Grosse, Pascal. "What Does German Colonialism Have to Do with National Socialism? A Conceptual Framework." In *Germany's Colonial Pasts*, ed. by Eric Ames, Marcia Klotz and Lora Wildenthal (Lincoln: University of Nebraska Press, 2005), pp. 115–34.

Grossmann, A. *Reforming Sex: The German Movement for Birth Control and Abortion Reform 1920–1950* (New York: Oxford University Press, 1995).

Gründer, Horst. *Geschichte der deutschen Kolonien*, 5th edn. (Paderborn: Schöningh, 2004).

Hagenbeck, Carl. *Von Tieren und Menschen* (Berlin: Vita, 1909).

Harder, Conrad. *In Busch und Steppe. Erlebnisse eines Kamerunkämpfers aus den letzten Jahren unserer Kolonie* (Berlin: Weltenberg, 1925).

Hargreaves, John D. *The End of Colonial Rule in West Africa* (London: Macmillan, 1979).

Hartenstein, Michael A. *Neue Dorflandschaften: nationalsozialistische Siedlungsplanung in den "eingegliederten Ostgebieten" 1939 bis 1944* (Berlin: Köster, 1998).

Hartwig, Helmut. "Weiter nichts neues andermal mehr—Kommunikation per Postkarte." In *Massenmedium Bildpostkarte*, vol. 1, ed. by Karl Riha (Siegen: Forschungsschwerpunkte Massenmedien und Kommunikation, 1979), pp. 1–42.

Harvey, Elizabeth. *Women and the Nazi East: Agents and Witnesses of Germanization* (New Haven, CT: Yale University Press, 2003).

Hauer, August. *Kumbuke: Erlebnisse eines Arztes in Deutsch-Ostafrika* (Berlin: Schneider, 1923).

Hayes, Patricia, et al. (eds). *Namibia Under South African Rule. Mobility & Containment 1915–1946* (Oxford: Currey; Windhoek: Out of Africa; Athens: Ohio University Press, 1998).

Heine, Peter, and Ulrich van der Heyden (eds). *Studien zur Geschichte des deutschen Kolonialismus in Africa: Festschrift zum 60. Geburtstag von Peter Sebald* (Pfaffenweiler: Centaurus, 1995).

Henderson, W.O. *The German Colonial Empire 1884–1919* (London: Cass, 1993).

Herzog, Jürgen. *Geschichte Tansanias* (Berlin: Deutscher Verlag der Wissenschaften, 1986).

Heye, Artur. *Vitani: Kriegs- und Jagderlebnisse in Ostafrika, 1914–1916* (Leipzig: Grunow, 1922).

Hiery, Hermann. "Der Kaiser, das Reich und der Kolonialismus. Anmerkungen zur Entstehung des deutschen Imperialismus im 19. Jahrhundert." <http://www.uni-bayreuth.de/departments/neueste/Imperium-Beitrag-Hiery.htm> [accessed 26 June 2006].

Higonnet, Anne. *Pictures of Innocence: The History and Crisis of Ideal Childhood* (New York: Thames & Hudson, 1998).

Hildebrand, Klaus. *Vom Reich zum Weltreich. Hitler, NSDAP und koloniale Fragen 1919–1945* (Munich: Fink, 1969).

Hillebrecht, Werner. "'Certain Uncertainties' or Venturing Progressively into Colonial Apologetics?" *Journal of Namibia Studies*, 1.1 (2007), 73–95.

Hobley, C.W. *Bantu Beliefs and Magic* (London: Witherby, 1922).

Hollmann, Helga, et al. (eds). *Das frühe Plakat in Europa und den USA*, vol. 3: *Deutschland* (Berlin: Mann, 1980).

Honold, Alexander, and Klaus R. Scherpe. "Einleitung." In *Das Fremde. Reiseerfahrungen, Schreibformen und kulturelles Wissen*, ed. by Alexander Honold et al. (Bern: Lang, 1999), pp. 7–11.

Honold, Alexander, and Klaus R. Scherpe. "Einleitung: Für eine deutsche Kulturgeschichte des Fremden." In *Mit Deutschland um die Welt. Eine Kulturgeschichte des Fremden in der Kolonialzeit*, ed. by Alexander Honold and Klaus R. Scherpe (Stuttgart: Metzler, 2004), pp. 1–25.

Honold, Alexander (ed.). *Mit Deutschland um die Welt. Eine Kulturgeschichte des Fremden in der Kolonialzeit* (Stuttgart: Metzler, 2004).

Höpker, L. *Als Farmerin in Deutsch-Südwest. Was ich in Afrika erlebte* (Minden: Köhler, 1936).

Höpker, L. *Um Scholle und Leben. Schicksale einer deutschen Farmerin in Südwest-Afrika* (Minden: Köhler, 1927).

House, Jim, and Neil MacMaster. *Paris 1961: Algerians, State Terror, and Memory* (Oxford: Oxford University Press, 2006).

House, Jim, and Neil MacMaster. "'Une journée portée disparue': The Paris Massacre of 1961 and Memory." In *Crisis and Renewal in France 1918–1962*, ed. by Kenneth Mouré and Martin S. Alexander (Oxford: Berghahn, 2002), pp. 267–90.

Hübbe-Schleiden, Wilhelm. *Deutsche Colonisation* (Hamburg: Friederichsen, 1881).

Hübner, Rudolf (ed.). *Johann Gustav Droysen. Briefwechsel*, 2 vols (Stuttgart: Deutsche Verlags-Anstalt, 1924).

Hunt, T., and M. R. Lessard (eds). *Women and the Colonial Gaze* (Basingstoke: Palgrave, 2002).

Hüppauf, Bernd. "Modernity and Violence: Observations Concerning a Contradictory Relationship." In *War, Violence and the Modern Condition*, ed. by Bernd Hüppauf (Berlin: de Gruyter, 1997), pp. 1–27.

JanMohamed, Abdul R. "The Economy of Manichean Allegory: The Function of Racial Difference in Colonialist Literature." In *"Race," Writing and Difference*, ed. by Henry Louis Gates, Jr. (Chicago: University of Chicago Press, 1985), pp. 78–106.

Jay, Martin. "Vision in Context: Reflections and Refractions." In *Vision in Context: Historical and Contemporary Perspectives on Sight*, ed. by Teresa Brennan (New York: Routledge, 1996), pp. 3–12.

Jelen, Brigitte. "17 octobre 1961–17 octobre 2001: Une commémoration ambiguë." *French Politics, Culture & Society*, 20.1 (2002), 30–43.

Joeden-Forgey, Elisa von. *Nobody's People: Colonial Subjects, Race Power, and the German State, 1884–1945* (PhD diss., University of Pennsylvania, 2004).

Joeden-Forgey, Elisa von. "Race Power in Postcolonial Germany: The German Africa Show and the National Socialist State, 1935–1940." In *Germany's Colonial Pasts*, ed. by Eric Ames, Marcia Klotz and Lora Wildenthal (Lincoln: University of Nebraska Press, 2005), pp. 167–88.

Johann, Ernst (ed.). *Reden des Kaisers: Ansprachen, Predigten und Trinksprüche Wilhelms II.* (Munich: DTV, 1966).

Johanna Watzinger-Tharp. "Turkish-German Language: An Innovative Style of Communication and its Implications for Citizenship and Identity." *Journal of Muslim Minority Affairs*, 24.2 (2004), 285–94.

Johnson, Sally. "The Cultural Politics of the 1998 Reform of German Orthography." *German Life and Letters*, 55.1 (2000), 106–25.

Junker, Wilhelm. *Im Sudan: In der libyschen Wüste und an den Quellen des Nil: Reisen 1875–1878* (Leipzig: Fock, 1889).

Kandetu, Vezera. "Namibia Cold Discourse Upon Chronic Pain." *New African*, 436 (January 2005), 64–6.

Karasek, Erika, Jane Redlin, et al. *Schilder, Bilder, Moritaten. Sonderschau des Museums für Volkskunde im Pergamonmuseum* (Berlin: Staatliche Museen, 1987).

Katz, Steven T. *The Holocaust and Comparative History* (New York: Leo Baeck Institute, 1993).

Kerbs, Diethart, and Jürgen Reulecke (eds). *Handbuch der deutschen Reformbewegungen 1880–1933* (Wuppertal: Hammer, 1998).

Kieser, Hans-Lukas, and Dominik J. Schaller (eds). *The Armenian Genocide and the Shoah* (Zürich: Chronos, 2002).

Klampen, Erich zu. *Carl Peters. Ein deutsches Schicksal im Kampf um Ostafrika* (Berlin: Siep, 1938).

Klotz, Marcia. "Global Visions: From the Colonial to the National Socialist World." *European Studies Journal*, 16.2 (1999), 37–68.

Knoll, Arthur J. *Togo Under Imperial Germany 1884–1914* (Stanford, CA: Hoover Institution, 1978).

Knoll, Arthur J., and Lewis H. Gann (eds). *Germans in the Tropics: Essays in German Colonial History* (Westport, CT: Greenwood, 1987).

Koch, Carl W.H. *Im Tropenhelm. Kriegstagebuch eines Kamerunkämpfers. Bearbeitet von Carl W.H. Koch* (Düsseldorf: Floeder, 1931).

Koch, Carl W.H. *Kamerun. Erlebtes und Empfundenes* (Leipzig: Voigtländer, 1924).

Kohlmann, Theodor. *Neuruppiner Bilderbogen* (Berlin: Staatliche Museen, 1981).

Koller, Christian. *"Von Wilden aller Rassen niedergemetzelt": Die Diskussion um die Verwendung von Kolonialtruppen in Europa zwischen Rassismus, Militär- und Kolonialpolitik (1914–1930)* (Stuttgart: Steiner, 2001).

Koltermann, Till Philip. "Zwischen Amnesie und Quellenfälschung: Defizite der neuesten Historiographie zum Herero-Deutschen Krieg 1904/05." *Nachrichten, Wissenschaftliche Gesellschaft Swakopmund*, 38.2 (2006), 24–42.

Kopp, Kristin. "Cartographic Claims: Colonial Mappings of Poland in German Territorial Revisionism." In *The Text as Spectacle: Visual Culture in Twentieth-Century Germany* ed. by Gail Finney (Bloomington: Indiana University Press, 2006), pp. 199–213.

Kopp, Kristin. "Constructing Racial Difference in Colonial Poland." In *Germany's Colonial Pasts*, ed. by Eric Ames et al. (Lincoln: University of Nebraska Press, 2005), pp. 76–96.

Kopp, Kristin. "'Ich stehe jetzt hier als einer von den Eroberern': *Soll und Haben* als Kolonialroman." In *150 Jahre "Soll und Haben" (1855)*. *Studien zu Gustav Freytags kontroversem Roman*, ed. by Florian Krobb (Würzburg: Königshausen & Neumann, 2005), pp. 225–37.

Köppen, Manuel. "Im Krieg mit dem Fremden. Barbarentum und Kulturkampf." In *Kolonialismus als Kultur. Literatur, Medien, Wissenschaft in der deutschen Gründerzeit des Fremden*, ed. by Alexander Honold and Oliver Simons (Tübingen: Francke 2002), pp. 263–87.

Koselleck, Reinhard, et al. (eds). *Geschichtliche Grundbegriffe*, 8 vols (Stuttgart: Klett, 1972–97).

Kössler, Reinhart. "Facing a Fragmented Past: Memory, Culture and Politics in Namibia." *Journal of Southern African Studies*, 33 (2007), 361–82.

Kössler, Reinhart. "From Genocide to Holocaust? Structural Parallels and Discursive Continuities." *Afrika Spectrum*, 40.2 (2005), 309–17.

Kössler, Reinhart. *In Search of Survival and Dignity: Two Traditional Communities in Southern Namibia under South African Rule* (Frankfurt/M.: IKO, 2006).

Kössler, Reinhart. "La fin d'une amnésie? L'Allemagne et son passé colonial depuis 2004." *Politique Africaine*, 1.102 (2006), 50–66.

Kössler, Reinhart. "Public Memory, Reconciliation and the Aftermath of War: A Preliminary Framework with Special Reference to Namibia." In *Re-examining Liberation in Namibia. Political Culture since Independence*, ed. by Henning Melber (Uppsala: Nordic Africa Institute, 2003), pp. 99–112.

Kössler, Reinhart, and Henning Melber. "Völkermord und Gedenken: Der Genozid an den Herero und Nama in Deutsch-Südwestafrika 1904–1908." In *Völkermord und Kriegsverbrechen*, ed. by Fritz Bauer Institut, Irmtrud Wojak and Susanne Meinl (Frankfurt/M.: Campus, 2004), pp. 37–75.

Kreutzer, Leo. *Literatur und Entwicklung. Studien zu einer Literatur der Ungleichzeitigkeit* (Frankfurt/M.: Fischer, 1989).

*Kriegsakten betreffend SMS Königsberg*. BA Militärarchiv, N 103/91: Marineabteilung.

Krüger, Gesine, *Kriegsbewältigung und Geschichtsbewusstsein. Realität, Deutung und Verarbeitung des deutschen Kolonialkriegs in Namibia 1904 bis 1907* (Göttingen: Vandenhoeck & Ruprecht, 1999).

Kulczycki, John J. *School Strikes in Prussian Poland, 1901–1907: The Struggle over Bilingual Education* (New York: Columbia University Press, 1981).

Kundrus, Birthe. "From the Herero to the Holocaust? Some Remarks on the Current Debate." *Afrika Spectrum*, 40.2 (2005), 299–308.

Kundrus, Birthe. "Grenzen der Gleichsetzung. Kolonialverbrechen und Vernichtungspolitik." *iz3w* 275 (2004), 30–3.

Kundrus, Birthe. *Moderne Imperialisten. Das Kaiserreich im Spiegel seiner Kolonien* (Cologne: Böhlau, 2003).

Kundrus, Birthe (ed.). *Phantasiereiche: Zur Kulturgeschichte des deutschen Kolonialismus* (Frankfurt/M.: Campus, 2003).

Kundrus, Birthe. "Von Windhoek nach Nürnberg? Koloniale 'Mischehenverbote' und die nationalsozialistische Rassengesetzgebung." In *Phantasiereiche. Zur Kulturgeschichte des deutschen Kolonialismus*, ed. by Birthe Kundrus (Frankfurt/M.: Campus, 2003), pp. 110–31.

Lacan, Jacques. *Écrits: A Selection* (New York: Norton, 2002).
Lamberty, Christiane. *Reklame in Deutschland 1890–1914. Wahrnehmung, Professionalisierung und Kritik der Wirtschaftswerbung* (Berlin: Duncker & Humblot, 2000).
Langheld, W. "Ueber einen Zug nach Ruanda." *Deutsches Kolonialblatt*, 2 (1895), 71–4.
Langsdorff, Werner von. *Deutsche Flagge über Sand und Palmen. 53 Kolonialkrieger erzählen* (Gütersloh: Bertelsmann, 1936).
Laplanche, Jean, and Jean Bertrand Pontalis. "Fantasy and the Origins of Sexuality." In *Formations of Fantasy*, ed. by Victor Burgin, James Donald and Cora Kaplan (London: Methuen, 1986), pp. 5–34.
Lau, Brigitte, "Uncertain Certainties." *Mibagus*, 2 (1989), pp. 4f. and 8.
Laumann, Dennis. "A Historiography of German Togoland, or the Rise and Fall of a 'Model Colony'." *History in Africa*, 30 (2003), 195–211.
Laumann, Dennis. *Remembering the Germans in Ghana* (New York: Lang, forthcoming).
Lebeck, Robert. "Die Postkarte im Spiegel der Kultur und Gesellschaft." In *Viele Grüße . . . : Eine Kulturgeschichte der Postkarte*, ed. by Robert Lebeck and Gerhard Kaufmann (Dortmund: Harenberg, 1985), pp. 399–437.
Lebzelter, Gisela. "Die 'Schwarze Schmach.' Vorurteile—Propaganda—Mythos." *Geschichte und Gesellschaft*, 11 (1985), 37–58.
Leclerc, Herbert. "Ansichten über Ansichtskarten." In *Archiv für Postgeschichte*, 2 (1986), 5–65.
Lefranc, Sandrine. *Politiques du pardon* (Paris: Presses universitaires de France, 2002).
Lenman, Robin. "Control of the Visual Image in Imperial Germany." In *Zensur und Kultur*, ed. by John McCarthy and Werner von der Ohe (Tübingen: Niemeyer, 1995), 111–22.
Lester, Rosemarie K. *"Trivialneger": Das Bild des Schwarzen im westdeutschen Illustriertenroman* (Stuttgart: Heinz, 1982).
Lettow-Vorbeck, Paul von. *Afrika, wie ich es wiedersah* (Munich: Lehmann, 1955).
Lettow-Vorbeck, Paul von. *Heia Safari! Erinnerungen aus Ostafrika* (Leipzig: Hase & Koehler, 1920; Biberach: Koehler, 1952).
Lettow-Vorbeck, Paul von. *Mein Leben* (Biberach: Koehler, 1957).
Levy, Daniel, and Natan Sznaider. *The Holocaust and Memory in the Global Age* (Philadelphia: Temple University Press, 2006).
Lewerenz, Susann. *Die "Deutsche Afrika-Schau." Rassismus, Kolonialrevisionismus und postkoloniale Auseinandersetzungen im nationalsozialistischen Deutschland* (Frankfurt/M.: Lang, 2006).
Lewinski, Agnes von. *Unter Kriegswettern in Ostafrika* (Leipzig: Frankenstein & Wagner, n.d.).
Linne, Karsten. *"Weiße Arbeitsführer" im "Kolonialen Ergänzungsraum". Afrika als Ziel sozial- und wirtschaftspolitischer Planungen in der NS-Zeit* (Münster: Monsenstein & Vannerdat, 2002).
Lipski, John M. "'Me Want Cookie': Foreigner Talk as Monster Talk." Lecture of 29 March 2005. <http://www.personal.psu.edu/jml34/monster.pdf> [accessed 30 August 2007].
Liulevicius, Vejas Gabriel. *War Land on the Eastern Front. Culture, National Identity, and German Occupation in World War I* (Cambridge: Cambridge University Press, 2000).
Lorenz, Detlef. *Reklamekunst um 1900* (Berlin: Reimer, 2000).
Lower, Wendy. *Nazi Empire-Building and the Holocaust in Ukraine* (Chapel Hill: University of North Carolina Press, 2005).
Lü, Yixu. "German Colonial Fiction on China: the Boxer Uprising of 1900." *German Life and Letters*, 59.1 (2006), 78–100.

Lü, Yixu. "Geschichte und Fiktion: Der Boxer-Aufstand in der zeitgenössischen deutschen Kolonialliteratur." *Jahrbuch für internationale Germanistik*, Series A 84 (2007), 229–34.

Lundtofte, Henrik. "'I believe that the nation as such must be annihilated . . .'—The Radicalization of the German Suppression of the Herero Rising in 1904." In *Genocide: Cases, Comparisons and Contemporary Debates*, ed. by Steven L.B. Jensen (Copenhagen: Danish Center for Holocaust and Genocide Studies, 2003), pp. 15–53.

Lusane, Clarence. *Hitler's Black Victims. The Historical Experiences of Afro-Germans, European Blacks, Africans, and African Americans in the Nazi Era* (London: Routledge, 2002).

Maase, Kaspar. *Grenzloses Vergnügen: Der Aufstieg der Massenkultur, 1850–1970* (Frankfurt/M.: Fischer, 1997).

Mackaman, Douglas, and Michael Mays. "The Quickening of Modernity, 1914–1918." In *World War I and the Cultures of Modernity*, ed. by Douglas Mackaman and Michael Mays (Jackson: University Press of Mississippi, 2000).

Madajczyk, Czesław (ed.). *Vom Generalplan Ost zum Generalsiedlungsplan* (Munich: Saur, 1994).

Madley, Benjamin. "From Africa to Auschwitz: How German South West Africa Incubated Ideas and Methods Adopted and Developed by the Nazis in Eastern Europe." *European History Quarterly*, 35 (2005), 429–64.

Maier, Hans. *Die christliche Zeitrechnung*, 5th edn (Freiburg/Br.: Herder, 1991).

Mankell, Henning. "Zeigt das wahre Afrika! Nur Elend und Sterben—warum die westlichen Medien ein falsches Bild vom schwarzen Kontinent zeichnen." *Die Zeit*, 12 January 2006, p. 45.

Marks, Sally. "Black Watch on the Rhine: A Study in Propaganda, Prejudice and Prurience." *European Studies Review*, 13 (1983), 297–334.

Martin, Peter. "Anfänge politischer Selbstorganisation der deutschen Schwarzen bis 1933." In *Die (koloniale) Begegnung. AfrikanerInnen in Deutschland 1880–1945. Deutsche in Afrika 1880–1918*, ed. by Marianne Bechhaus-Gerst and Reinhard Klein-Arendt (Frankfurt/M.: Lang, 2003), pp. 193–206.

Martin, Peter. "Die Kampagne gegen die 'Schwarze Schmach' als Ausdruck konservativer Visionen vom Untergang des Abendlandes." In *Fremde Erfahrungen. Asiaten und Afrikaner in Deutschland, Österreich und in der Schweiz bis 1945*, ed. by Gerhard Höpp (Berlin: Das Arabische Buch, 1996), pp. 211–24.

Martin, Peter. *Schwarze Teufel, edle Mohren. Afrikaner in Bewußtsein und Geschichte der Deutschen* (Hamburg: Junius, 1993).

Martin, Peter, and Christine Alonzo (eds). *Zwischen Charleston und Stechschritt. Schwarze im Nationalsozialismus* (Munich: Dölling & Galitz, 2004).

Marx, Christoph. "Entsorgen und Entseuchen. Zur Diskussionskultur in der derzeitigen namibischen Historiographie—eine Polemik." In *Genozid und Gedenken. Namibisch-deutsche Geschichte und Gegenwart*, ed. by Henning Melber (Frankfurt/M.: Brandes & Apsel, 2005), pp. 141–61.

Maß, Sandra. *Weiße Helden, Schwarze Krieger. Zur Geschichte kolonialer Männlichkeit in Deutschland 1918–1964* (Cologne: Böhlau, 2006).

Massing, Jean Michel. "From Greek Proverb to Soap Advert: Washing the Ethiopian." *Journal of the Warburg and Courtauld Institutes*, 58 (1995), 180–201.

Mazrui, Ali A. "The African University as a Multinational Corporation: Problems of Penetration and Dependency." *Harvard Educational Review*, 45 (1975), 191–210.

Mehnert, Wolfgang. "Education Policy." In *German Imperialism in Africa*, ed. by Helmuth Stoecker (London: Hurst, 1986), pp. 216–29.

Mehnert, Wolfgang. "The Language Question in the Colonial Policy of German Imperialism." In *African Studies—Afrika-Studien*, ed. by Thea Büttner and Gerhard Brehme (Berlin: Akademie, 1973), 383–97.

Melber, Henning (ed.). *Genozid und Gedenken: Namibisch-deutsche Geschichte und Gegenwart* (Frankfurt/M.: Brandes & Apsel, 2005).

Melber, Henning. "How to Come to Terms with the Past: Re-visiting the German Colonial Genocide in Namibia." *Afrika Spectrum*, 40.1 (2005), 139–48.

Melber, Henning. "Kontinuitäten totaler Herrschaft: Völkermord und Apartheid in 'Deutsch-Südwestafrika:' Zur kolonialen Herrschaftspraxis im Deutschen Kaiserreich." In *Jahrbuch für Antisemitismusforschung*, vol. 1, ed. by Wolfgang Benz (Frankfurt/M.: Campus, 1992), pp. 91–116.

Melber, Henning. "'Namibia, Land of the Brave': Selective Memories on War and Violence within Nation Building." In *Rethinking Resistance: Revolt and Violence in African History*, ed. by Jon Abbink, Mirjam de Bruijn and Klaas van Walraven (Leiden: Brill 2003), pp. 305–27.

Melber, Henning (ed.). *Re-examining Liberation in Namibia: Political Culture since Independence* (Uppsala: Nordic Africa Institute, 2003).

Melber, Henning, "'We never spoke about reparations.' German–Namibian Relations between Amnesia, Aggression and Reconciliation,' in *Genocide in German South-West Africa: The Colonial War of 1904–1908 and Its Aftermath*, ed. by Jürgen Zimmerer and Joachim Zeller (Monmouth: Merlin, 2008), pp. 259–73.

Meskimmon, M., and S. West (eds). *Visions of the "Neue Frau": Women and the Visual Arts in Weimar Germany* (Aldershot: Scolar, 1995).

Meyer, Hans. "Verfügung des Gouverneurs über das Neger-Englisch (pidgin-english)." *Amtsblatt für das Schutzgebiet Kamerun*, 6.14 (May 1913), 165–8.

Miaso, Jozef. "Educational Policy and Educational Development in the Polish Territories under Austrian, Russian and German Rule, 1850–1918." In *Schooling, Educational Policy and Ethnic Identity*, ed. by Janusz J. Tomiak (New York: New York University Press, 1991), pp. 163–84.

Michels, Stefanie. "Askari—treu bis in den Tod? Vom Umgang der Deutschen mit ihren schwarzen Soldaten." In *AfrikanerInnen in Deutschland und schwarze Deutsche. Geschichte und Gegenwart*, ed. by Marianne Bechhaus-Gerst and Reinhard Klein-Arendt (Münster: LIT, 2004), pp. 171–86.

Michels, Stefanie. "Deutsch-ostafrikanische Mythen: General Lettow-Vorbeck und die 'treuen Askari'." Unpublished paper presented at the Neue Gesellschaft, Hamburg, 6 December 2005.

Mitchell, W.J.T. *Picture Theory* (Chicago: University of Chicago Press, 1994).

Möhle, Heiko. "Betreuung, Erfassung, Kontrolle. Afrikaner aus den deutschen Kolonien und die 'Deutsche Gesellschaft für Eingeborenenkunde'." In *Die (koloniale) Begegnung. AfrikanerInnen in Deutschland 1880–1945. Deutsche in Afrika 1880–1918*, ed. by Marianne Bechhaus-Gerst and Reinhard Klein-Arendt (Frankfurt/M.: Lang, 2003), pp. 225–36.

Moyd, Michelle. "'Auch sie starben für Kaiser und Reich': The 'Loyal Askari' in Interwar German Discourse." Unpublished paper presented at the conference *Koloniale und postkoloniale Konstruktionen von Afrika und Menschen afrikanischer Herkunft in der deutschen Alltagskultur*, Königswinter near Bonn, 13–16 October 2004.

Mühleisen, Susanne. "Emil Schwörers *Kolonial-Deutsch* (1916). Sprachliche und historische Anmerkungen zu einem 'geplanten Pidgin' im kolonialen Deutsch Südwest Afrika." *Philologie im Netz*, 31 (2005), 30–48. <http://web.fu-berlin. de/phin/phin31/p31t3.htm> [accessed 30 August 2007].

Müller, Frank Lorenz. "Imperialist Ambitions in *Vormärz* and Revolutionary Germany: the Agitation for German Settlement Colonies Overseas, 1840–1849." *German History*, 17.3 (1999), 346–68.

Müller, Michael G., et al. *Die "Polen-Debatte" in der Frankfurter Paulskirche. Darstellung, Lernziele, Materialien* (Frankfurt/M.: Diesterweg, 1995).

Nachtigal, Gustav. *Sahara und Sudan: Ergebnisse sechsjähriger Reisen in Afrika*, 3 vols (Berlin: M.B.H, 1879–89).

Nagl, Tobias. "Kolonien des Blicks. Louis Brody und die schwarze Präsenz im deutschsprachigen Kino vor 1945." *jungle world*, 20 (2002). <http://www.nadir.org/nadir/periodika/jungle_world/_2002/20/15a.htm> [accessed 31 December 2008].

*Namibia—Deutschland: Eine geteilte Geschichte.Widerstand—Gewalt—Erinnerung*, ed. by Larissa Förster, Dag Henrichsen and Michael Bollig (Cologne: Minerva, 2004).

Ndumbe III, Kum'a. "Zur Problematik der Deutschlandstudien in der afrikanischen Germanistik." In *Deutschlandstudien international*, vol. 1, *Dokumentation des Wolfenbütteler DAAD-Symposiums 1988*, ed. by Hans J. Althof (Munich: iudicium, 1990), pp. 167–75.

Nederveen Pieterse, Jan. *White On Black. Images of Africa and Blacks in Western Popular Culture* (New Haven, CT: Yale University Press, 1992).

Nelson, Keith S. "Black Horror on the Rhine: Race as a Factor in Post–World War I Diplomacy." *Journal of Modern History*, 42 (1970), 606–27.

Newton, Gerald. "Deutsche Schrift: The Demise and Rise of German Black Letter." *German Life and Letters*, 56.2 (April 2003), 183–204.

Nolden, Thomas. "On Colonial Spaces and Bodies: Hans Grimm's *Geschichten aus Südwestafrika*." In *The Imperialist Imagination: German Colonialism and its Legacy*, ed. by Sara Friedrichmeyer, Sara Lennox and Susanne Zantop (Ann Arbor: University of Michigan Press, 1998), pp. 125–40.

Norris, Edward Graham, and Arnold Beuke. "Kolonialkrieg und Karikatur in Deutschland." In *Studien zur Geschichte des deutschen Kolonialismus in Afrika*, ed. by Peter Heine and Ulrich van der Heyden (Pfaffenweiler: Centaurus, 1995), pp. 377–98.

Novick, Peter, *The Holocaust in American Life* (Boston: Houghton Mifflin, 2000).

Noyes, John K. *Colonial Space. Spatiality in the Discourse of German South West Africa 1884–1915* (Chur et al.: Harwood, 1992).

Nussbaum, Manfred. *Togo, eine Musterkolonie?* (Berlin: Rutten & Loening, 1962).

Oguntoye, Katharina. *Eine afro-deutsche Geschichte. Zur Lebenssituation von Afrikanern und Afro-Deutschen in Deutschland von 1884 bis 1950* (Berlin: Hoho Verlag Christine Hoffmann, 1997).

Olden, Balder. *Ich bin ich. Der Roman Carl Peters* (Berlin: Wegweiser, 1927).

Orosz, Kenneth J. *Religious Conflict and the Evolution of Language Policy in German and French Cameroon, 1885–1939* (New York: Lang, 2008).

Otto Pentzel, *Buschkampf in Ostafrika* (Stuttgart: Thienemann, 1935).

Pallesker, Richard. "Kolonial-Deutsch." *Zeitschrift des Allgemeinen Deutschen Sprachvereins*, 31.10 (1916), 324.

Pàttaro, Germano. "The Christian Conception of Time." In *Cultures and Time*, ed. by Louis Gardet et al. (Paris: Unesco, 1976), pp. 169–97.

Penny, H. Glenn, and M. Bunzl (eds). *Worldly Provincialism: German Anthropology in the Age of Empire* 4th edn (Ann Arbor: University of Michigan Press, 2006).

Perl, Matthias. "Kolonial-Deutsch as Restructured German." In *"Was ich noch sagen wollte ...": A Multi-Lingual Festschrift for Norbert Boretzky on Occasion of His 65th Birthday*, ed. by Birgit Igla, Thomas Stolz and Norbert Boretzky (Berlin: Akademie, 2001), pp. 237–47.

Perras, Arne. *Carl Peters and German Imperialism 1856–1918. A Political Biography* (Oxford: Oxford University Press, 2004).

Perraudin, Michael. "Babekan's *Brille*, and the Rejuvenation of Congo Hoango. A Re-Interpretation of Kleist's Story of the Haitian Revolution". *Oxford German Studies*, 20 (1992), 85–103.

Peters, Carl. *England und die Engländer* (Berlin: Schletske, 1904).

Peters, Carl. *Gesammelte Schriften*, 3 vols, ed. by Walter Frank (Berlin: Beck, 1943–4).

Philburn, Elke. "Rechtschreibreform Still Spells Controversy." *Debatte* 11.1 (2003), 60–9.

Planert, Ute. "Vater Staat und Mutter Germania: Zur Politisierung des weiblichen Geschlechts im 19. und 20. Jahrhundert." In *Nation, Politik, und Geschlecht. Frauenbewegungen und Nationalismus in der Moderne*, ed. by Ute Planert (Frankfurt/M.: Campus, 2000), pp. 15–65.

Pogge von Strandmann, Hartmut. "Imperialism and Revisionism in Interwar Germany." In *Imperialism and After: Continuities and Discontinuities*, ed. by Wolfgang Mommsen and Jürgen Osterhammel (London: Allen & Unwin, 1986), pp. 90–119.

Pollig, Hermann. *Exotische Welten: europäische Phantasien* (Stuttgart: Cantz, 1987).

Pommerin, Reiner. *Sterilisierung der Rheinlandbastarde. Das Schicksal einer farbigen deutschen Minderheit 1918–1937* (Düsseldorf: Droste, 1979).

Preisendörfer, Bruno. *Staatsbildung als Königskunst: Ästhetik und Herrschaft im preußischen Absolutismus* (Berlin: Akademie, 2000).

Preston, Diana. *The Boxer Rebellion* (New York: Berkeley, 2000).

Puschner, Uwe (ed.). *Handbuch zur "Völkischen Bewegung" 1871–1918* (Munich: Saur, 1999).

Rapaport, Herman. *Between the Sign & the Gaze* (Ithaca, NY: Cornell University Press, 1994).

Reagin, Nancy. "The Imagined *Hausfrau*: National Identity, Domesticity, and Colonialism in Imperial Germany." *Journal of Modern History*, 73.1 (2001), 54–86.

Reck, Hans. *Buschteufel. Deutsch-Ostafrikanisches* (Berlin: Reimer/Vohsen, 1926).

*Record of the 3rd Battalion the Kings African Rifles during the Great Campaign in East Africa 1914–18*. Public Record Office, London, WO 106/273.

Record of Vizefeldwebel der Reserve Pfeiffer der 8. Feldkompagnie. In *Kämpfer an vergessenen Fronten: Feldzugsbriefe, Kriegstagebücher und Berichte*, ed. by Wolfgang Foerster, Helmuth Greiner and Hans Witte (Berlin: Neufeld & Henius, 1931), p. 82.

Reed-Anderson, Paulette. *Rewriting the Footnotes. Berlin und die afrikanische Diaspora—Berlin and the African Diaspora* (Berlin: Die Ausländerbeauftragte des Berliner Senats, 2000).

*Reklame: Produktwerbung im Plakat 1890 bis 1918*, DVD-Rom (Berlin: Deutsches Historisches Museum, 2005).

Roehl, Karl. *Ostafrikas Heldenkampf: Nach eigenen Erlebnissen dargestellt* (Berlin: Warneck, 1918).

Rohlfs, Gerhard. *Angra Pequena: Die erste deutsche Kolonie in Afrika* (Bielefeld: Belhagen & Klafing, 1884).

Rohlfs, Gerhard. *Quer durch Afrika: Die Erstdurchquerung der Sahara vom Mittelmeer bis zum Golf von Guinea 1865–1867*, ed. by Herbert Gussenbauer (Stuttgart: Thienemann, 1994).

Rohrbach, Paul. *Das deutsche Kolonialwesen* (Leipzig: Gloeckner, 1911).

Rommelspacher, Birgit. *Dominanzkultur: Texte zu Fremdheit und Macht* (Berlin: Orlanda, 1995).

Rorty, Richard. *Philosophy and the Mirror of Nature* (Princeton, NJ: Princeton University Press, 1979).

Rosenhaft, Eve. "Afrikaner und 'Afrikaner' im Deutschland der Weimarer Republik. Antikolonialismus und Antirassismus zwischen Doppelbewusstsein und Selbsterfindung." In *Phantasiereiche. Zur Kulturgeschichte des deutschen Kolonialismus*, ed. by Birthe Kundrus (Frankfurt/M.: Campus, 2003), pp. 282–301.

Rüger, Adolf. "Imperialismus, Sozialreformismus und antikoloniale demokratische Alternative. Zielvorstellungen von Afrikanern in Deutschland im Jahre 1919." *Zeitschrift für Geschichtswissenschaft*, 23 (1975), 1293–1308.

Ryan, James. *Picturing Empire: Photography and the Visualization of the British Empire* (Chicago: University of Chicago Press, 1997).

Rydell, Robert. "Souvenirs of Imperialism. World's Fair Postcards." In *Delivering Views: Distant Cultures in Early Postcards*, ed. by Christraud Geary and Virginia-Lee Webb (Washington: Smithsonian, 1998), pp. 47–63.

Sadji, Amadou B. "Deutschunterricht und Germanistik in Senegal." *Jahrbuch Deutsch als Fremdsprache*, 10 (1984), 75–85.

Salburg, Edith. *Carl Peters und sein Volk. Der Roman des deutschen Kolonialgründers* (Weimar: Duncker, 1929).

Salzmann, Oswald. *Das vereinfachte Deutsch: Die Sprache aller Völker* (Leipzig: Salzmann, 1913).

Sammartino, Annemarie. "The Frustration and Failures of Border Control in Early Weimar Germany." Unpublished paper presented at the German Studies Association Conference, Pittsburg, 2006.

Schaller, Dominik J., "Der Völkermord an den Armeniern und der Holocaust. Grenzen und Möglichkeiten eines Vergleichs." In *Zum 90. Gedenkjahr des Völkermordes an den Armeniern 1915–2005. Stimmen aus Deutschland*, ed. by Ischchan Tschiftdschjan (Beirut: Druckerei des Armenischen Katholikosats, 2005), pp. 196–201.

Schaller, Dominik J. "From Conquest to Genocide: Colonial Rule in German Southwest Africa and German East Africa." In *Empire, Colony, Genocide. Conquest, Occupation, and Subaltern Resistance in World History*, ed. by A. Dirk Moses (New York: Berghahn, 2008), pp. 296–324.

Schaller, Dominik J., and Jürgen Zimmerer. "Late Ottoman Genocides: the Dissolution of the Ottoman Empire and Young Turkish Population and Extermination Policies." *Journal of Genocide Research*, 10.1 (2008), 7–14.

Schauwecker, Franz. *Aufbruch der Nation* (Berlin: Frundsberg, 1930).

Schiffers, Heinrich (ed.). *Im Sattel durch Nord- und Zentral-Afrika 1849–1855* (Stuttgart: Thienemann, 2000).

Schivelbusch, Wolfgang. *Die Geschichte der Eisenbahnreise: Zur Industrialisierung von Raum und Zeit im 19. Jahrhundert*, 2nd edn. (Frankfurt/M.: Fischer, 2000).

Schmitt-Egner, Peter. *Kolonialismus und Faschismus: Eine Studie zur historischen und begrifflichen Genesis faschistischer Bewusstseinsformen am deutschen Beispiel* (Gießen: Achenbach, 1975).

Schmitt-Egner, Peter. "Wertgesetz und Rassismus: Zur begrifflichen Genesis kolonialer und faschistischer Bewußtseinsformen." *Gesellschaft. Beiträge zur Marxschen Theorie*, 8–9 (1976), 350–404.

Schmokel, Wolfe W. *Dream of Empire: German Colonialism, 1919–1945* (New Haven, CT: Yale University Press, 1964).

Schnee, Ada Adeline. *Meine Erlebnisse während der Kriegszeit in Deutsch-Ostafrika* (Leipzig: Quelle & Meyer, 1918).

Schnee, Heinrich. *Deutsch-Ostafrika im Weltkriege—wie wir lebten und kämpften* (Leipzig: Quelle & Meyer, 1919).

Schnee, Heinrich. *Die koloniale Schuldlüge* (Munich: Süddeutsche Monatshefte, 1924).

Schnee, Heinrich. *East Africa Diary of Dr. Schnee. Governor of German East Africa.* Public Record Office, London, WO 106/1460.

Scholz-Hänsel, Michael. *Das exotische Plakat* (Stuttgart: Cantz, 1987).

Schorn, Hans Traugott. *Dr. Carl Peters. Ein Lebensbild* (Hamburg: Rüsch, 1922).

Schubert, Michael. *Der schwarze Fremde. Das Bild des Schwarzafrikaners in der parlamentarischen und publizistischen Kolonialdiskussion in Deutschland von den 1870er bis in die 1930er Jahre* (Stuttgart: Steiner, 2003).

Schulte-Varendorff, Uwe. *Kolonialheld für Kaiser und Führer: General Lettow-Vorbeck—Mythos und Wirklichkeit* (Berlin: Links, 2006).

Schütt, Peter. "Der Denkmalssturz." *die Tageszeitung*, 7 August 1992. <http://www.taz.de/pt/1992/09/07/a0223.1/textdruck> [accessed 4 January 2008].

Schwarz, Jürgen. *Bildannoncen aus der Jahrhundertwende* (Frankfurt/M.: Kunstgeschichtliches Institut, 1990).

Schwarz, Thomas. "'Die Tropen bin ich!' Der exotische Diskurs der Jahrhundertwende." *KultuRRevolution*, 32–3 (1995), 11–21.

Schweinfurth, Georg. *Im Herzen von Afrika* (Stuttgart: Erdmann, 1985).

Schwörer, Emil. *Kolonial-Deutsch: Vorschläge einer künftigen deutschen Kolonialsprache in systematisch-grammatikalischer Darstellung und Begründung* (Diessen: Huber, 1916).

Schwörer, Emil. "Zur künftigen Sprachenfrage in den deutschen Kolonien." Parts 1 and 2, *Deutsche Kolonialzeitung*, 33.1 (20 January 1916), 10–12, and 33.2 (20 February 1916), 25.

Sebald, Peter. *Togo 1884–1914: Eine Geschichte der deutschen "Muster-kolonie" auf der Grundlage amtlicher Quellen* (Berlin: Akademie, 1988).

Shaviro, Steven. *The Cinematic Body* (Minneapolis: University of Minnesota Press, 1994).

Siegert, Bernhard. *Relais: Geschichte der Literatur als Epoche der Post, 1751–1913* (Berlin: Brinkmann & Bose, 1993).

Simons, Oliver. "Dichter am Kanal." In *Kolonialismus als Kultur. Literatur, Medien, Wissenschaft in der deutschen Gründerzeit des Fremden*, ed. by Alexander Honold and Oliver Simons (Tübingen: Francke, 2002), pp. 243–62.

Simons, Oliver. "Heinrich von Stephan und die Idee der Weltpost." In *Mit Deutschland um die Welt: Eine Kulturgeschichte des Fremden in der Kolonialzeit*, ed. by Alexander Honold and Klaus Scherpe (Stuttgart: Metzler, 2004), pp. 26–35.

Smith, Helmut Walser. *German Nationalism and Religious Conflict* (Princeton, NJ: Princeton University Press, 1995).

Smith, Woodruff D. *The German Colonial Empire* (Chapel Hill: University of North Carolina Press, 1978).

Smith, Woodruff D., *The Ideological Origins of Nazi Imperialism* (New York: Oxford University Press, 1986).

Sow, Alioune. *Germanistik als Entwicklungs-Wissenschaft? Überlegungen zu einer Literaturwissenschaft des Faches "Deutsch als Fremdsprache" in Afrika* (Hildesheim: Olms, 1986).

Speitkamp, Winfried (ed.). *Denkmalsturz: Zur Konfliktgeschichte politischer Symbolik* (Göttingen: Vandenhoeck & Ruprecht, 1997).

Speitkamp, Winfried. *Deutsche Kolonialgeschichte* (Stuttgart: Reclam, 2005).

Stephan, Heinrich von. *Geschichte der preußischen Post von ihrem Ursprung bis auf die Gegenwart* (Berlin: Decker, 1859; reprint: Heidelberg: Decker, 1987).

Stöber, Rudolf. *Deutsche Pressegeschichte. Einführung, Systematik, Glossar* (Konstanz: UVK Medien, 2000).

Stoecker, Helmuth (ed.). *German Imperialism in Africa: From the Beginnings until the Second World War* (London: Hurst, 1986).

Stoler, Laura Ann. *Race and the Education of Desire: Foucault's History of Sexuality and the Colonial Order of Things* (Durham, NC: Duke University Press, 1995).

Stora, Benjamin. *La Gangrène et l'oubli: la mémoire de la guerre d'Algérie* (Paris: La Découverte, 1991).

Stuhlmann, Franz. *Mit Emin Pascha ins Herz von Afrika: Ein Reisebericht mit Beiträgen von Emin Pascha*, 2 vols (Berlin: Reimer, 1894).

Stumpf, Rudolf. *La Politique Linguistique au Cameroun de 1884 à 1960* (Bern: Lang, 1979).

Surén, Hans. *Kampf um Kamerun. Garua* (Berlin: Scherl, 1934).

Swett, Pamela E., S. Jonathan Wiesen and Jonathan R. Zatlin (eds). *Selling Modernity: Advertising in Twentieth-Century Germany* (Durham, NC: Duke University Press, 2007).

Tafel, Theodor. "Von der Schutztruppe in Ostafrika." *Deutsche Kolonialzeitung*, 31.28 (1914), 417.

Thompson, Kristin. "The Concept of Cinematic Excess." In *Film Theory and Criticism*, ed. by Leo Braudy and Marshall Cohen, 5th edn (Oxford: Oxford University Press, 1999), pp. 487–98.

Timm, Uwe. *Deutsche Kolonien* (1981) (Cologne: Kiepenheuer & Witsch, 2001).

Timm, Uwe. *Heißer Sommer* (1974) (Munich: DTV, 1998).

Timm, Uwe. *Rot* (Cologne: Kiepenheuer & Witsch, 2001).

Trampedach, Tim. "'Yellow Peril'? German Public Opinion and the Chinese Boxer Movement." *Berliner China Hefte*, 23 (2002), 71–81.

Trotha, Trutz von. "Genozidaler Pazifizierungskrieg: Soziologische Anmerkungen zum Konzept des Genozids am Beispiel des Kolonialkriegs in Deutsch-Südwestafrika, 1904–1907." *Zeitschrift für Genozidforschung*, 4.2 (2003), 31–58.

Unverricht, Astrid. "Zwischen Propaganda und Heimatgefühlen: Deutsch-Südwestafrika in der Kolonialliteratur." In *Afrika—Kultur und Gewalt. Hintergründe und Aktualität des Kolonialkriegs in Deutsch-Südwestafrika. Seine Rezeption in Literatur, Wissenschaft und Populärkultur (1904–2004)*, ed. by Christof Hamann (Iserlohn: Institut für Kirche und Gesellschaft, 2005), 105–26.

Usborne, C. *The Politics of the Body in Weimar Germany: Women's Reproductive Rights and Duties* (Basingstoke: Macmillan, 1991).

van der Heyden, Ulrich. "Die 'Hottentottenwahlen' von 1907." In *Völkermord in Deutsch-Südwestafrika*, ed. by Jürgen Zimmerer and Joachim Zeller (Berlin: Links, 2003), pp. 97–102.

van der Heyden, Ulrich, and Joachim Zeller (eds). " . . . *Macht und Anteil an der Weltherrschaft": Berlin und der deutsche Kolonialismus* (Münster: UNRAST, 2005).

*Verhandlungen der Germanisten zu Lübeck am 27., 28. und 30. September 1847* (Lübeck: Boldemann, 1848).

Vick, Brian E. "Arndt and German Ideas of Race: Between Kant and Social Darwinism." In *Ernst Moritz Arndt (1769–1860): Deutscher Nationalismus—Europa—Transatlantische Perspektiven*, ed. by Walter Erhart and Arne Koch (Tübingen: Niemeyer, 2007), pp. 65–76.

Vick, Brian E. *Defining Germany: The 1848 Frankfurt Parliamentarians and National Identity* (Cambridge, MA.: Harvard University Press, 2002).

Viera, Josef. *Maria in Petersland. Roman* (Breslau: Bergstadt, 1937).

Vollmer, Jörg. *Imaginäre Schlachtfelder. Kriegsliteratur in der Weimarer Republik* (PhD diss., Free University of Berlin, 2003). <http://www.diss.fu-berlin.de/2003/232/indexe.html> [accessed 31 December 2008].

Walgenbach, Katherina. *Die weisse Frau als Trägerin deutscher Kultur. Koloniale Diskurse über Geschlecht, "Rasse" und Klasse im Kaiserreich* (Frankfurt/M.: Campus, 2005).

Wassink, Jörg. *Auf den Spuren des deutschen Völkermordes in Südwestafrika. Der Herero-/Nama-Aufstand der deutschen Kolonialliteratur. Eine literarhistorische Analyse* (Munich: M-Press, 2004).

Wehler, Hans-Ulrich. *The German Empire 1871–1918* (Leamington Spa: Berg, 1985).

Wehner, Joseph Magnus. *Sieben vor Verdun. Ein Kriegsroman* (Hamburg: Deutsche Hausbücherei, 1930).

Weindling, Paul. *Health, Race and German Politics between National Unification and Nazism 1870–1945* (Cambridge: Cambridge University Press, 1989).

Weisser, Michael. *Cigaretten-Reclame* (Münster: Coppenrath, 1980).

Wenig, Richard. *Kriegs-Safari: Erlebnisse und Eindrücke auf den Zügen Lettow-Vorbecks durch das östliche Afrika* (Berlin: Scherl, 1920).

Wentzcke, Paul, and Wolfgang Klötzer (eds). *Deutscher Liberalismus im Vormärz. Heinrich von Gagern: Briefe und Reden 1815–1848* (Göttingen: Musterschmidt, 1959).

Werther, C. Waldemar. *Zum Victoria Nyanza: Eine Anti-Sklaverei-Expedition und Forschungsreise* (Berlin: Paetel, 1894).

Wichterich, Richard. *Dr. Carl Peters. Der Weg eines Patrioten* (Berlin: Keil, 1934).

Wieland, Rudolf. *Schutztruppe für Deutsch-Ostafrika. Erlebnisse und Eindrücke vom Bekanntwerden des Waffenstillstandes bis zur Heimkehr der letzten 25 Lettow-Krieger.* BA Militärarchiv, N 103/91.

Wielandt, Ute, and Michael Kaschner, "Die Reichstagsdebatten über den deutschen Kriegseinsatz in China: August Bebel und die 'Hunnenbriefe'." In *Das deutsche Reich und der Boxeraufstand*, ed. Susanne Kuß and Bernd Martin (Munich: iudicium, 2002), pp. 183–202.

Wiener, Michael. *Ikonographie des Wilden. Menschen-Bilder in Ethnographie und Photographie zwischen 1850 und 1918* (Munich: Trickster, 1990).

Wigard, Franz. *Stenographische Berichte über die Verhandlungen der deutschen konstituierenden Nationalversammlung zu Frankfurt a. M.*, 9 vols (Frankfurt/M.: Sauerländer, 1848–9).

Wigger, Iris. *Die "Schwarze Schmach am Rhein". Rassistische Diskriminierung zwischen Geschlecht, Klasse, Nation und Rasse* (Münster: Westfälisches Dampfboot, 2006).

Wild, Reiner (ed.). *Geschichte der deutschen Kinder- und Jugendliteratur* (Stuttgart: Metzler, 1990).

Wildenthal, Lora. *German Women for Empire, 1884–1945* (Durham, NC: Duke University Press, 2001).

Wilke, Jürgen. *Grundzüge der Medien- und Kommunikationsgeschichte: Von den Anfängen bis ins 20. Jahrhundert* (Cologne: Böhlau, 2000).

Wilkending, Gisela. *Mädchenliteratur der Kaiserzeit. Zwischen weiblicher Identifizierung und Grenzüberschreitung* (Stuttgart: Metzler, 2003).

Williams, Linda. *Film Bodies: Gender, Genre, and Excess*, in *Film Genre Reader*, vol. 2, ed. by Barry Keith Grant (Austin: University of Texas Press, 1995), pp. 140–58.

Witte, Arnd. "Germanistik und DaF in Afrika (Subsahara)—Geschichte, Bestandsaufnahme, Aussichten." *Acta Germanica*, 30–1 (2003), 169–79.

Wittek, Erhard. *Durchbruch anno achtzehn. Ein Fronterlebnis*, 3rd edn (Stuttgart: Franckh, 1933).

Wojtczak, Maria. *Literatur der Ostmark: Posener Heimatliteratur, 1890–1918* (Poznan: Wydawnictwo Naukowe Uniwersytetu im. Adama Mickiewicza, 1998).

Wollstein, Günter. *Das "Grossdeutschland" der Paulskirche. Nationale Ziele in der bürgerlichen Revolution 1848/49* (Düsseldorf: Droste, 1977).

Woody, Howard. "International Postcards: Their Histories, Production, and Distribution (circa 1895 to 1915)." In *Delivering Views: Distant Cultures in*

*Early Postcards*, ed. by Christraud Geary and Virginia-Lee Webb (Washington: Smithsonian, 1998), pp. 13–45.

Wynn, Wynn E. *Ambush* (London: Hutchinson, 1937).

Young, Robert J.C. *Colonial Desire: Hybridity in Theory, Culture and Race* (London: Routledge, 1995).

Zantop, Susanne. *Colonial Fantasies: Conquest, Family, and Nation in Precolonial Germany 1770–1870* (Durham, NC: Duke University Press, 1997).

Zantop, Susanne. "Race, Gender, and Postcolonial Amnesia." In *Women in German Yearbook 17: Feminist Studies in German Literature & Culture*, ed. by Patricia Herminghouse and Susanne Zantop (Lincoln: University of Nebraska Press, 2001), pp. 1–13.

Zeller, Joachim. "Genozid und Gedenken. Ein dokumentarischer Überblick." In *Genozid und Gedenken*, ed. by Henning Melber (Frankfurt/M.: Brandes & Apsel, 2005), pp. 163–88.

Zeller, Joachim. "Images of the South West African War: Reflections of the 1904–1907 Colonial War in Contemporary Photo Reportage and Book Illustration." In *Hues Between Black and White*, ed. by Wolfram Hartmann (Windhoek: Out of Africa, 2004), pp. 309–23.

Zeller, Joachim. *Kolonialdenkmäler und Geschichtsbewußtsein: Eine Untersuchung der kolonialdeutschen Erinnerungskultur* (Frankfurt: IKO, 2000).

Zimmerer, Jürgen. "The Birth of the 'Ostland' out of the Spirit of Colonialism: A Postcolonial Perspective on Nazi Policy of Conquest and Extermination." *Patterns of Prejudice*, 39.2 (2005), 197–219.

Zimmerer, Jürgen. "Colonial Genocide and the Holocaust. Towards an Archaeology of Genocide." In *Genocide and Settler Society: Frontier Violence and Stolen Indigenous Children in Australian History* ed. by A. Dirk Moses (New York: Berghahn, 2004), pp. 49–76.

Zimmerer, Jürgen. *Deutsche Herrschaft über Afrikaner: Staatlicher Machtanspruch und Wirklichkeit im kolonialen Namibia* (Münster: Lit, 2001).

Zimmerer, Jürgen, "Entschädigung für Herero und Nama." *Blätter für deutsche und internationale Politik*, 50.6 (2005), 658–60.

Zimmerer, Jürgen. "Rassenkrieg und Völkermord: Der Kolonialkrieg in Deutsch-Südwestafrika und die Globalgeschichte des Genozids." In *Genozid und Gedenken: Namibisch-deutsche Geschichte und Gegenwart*, ed. by Henning Melber (Frankfurt/M.: Brandes & Apsel, 2005), pp. 23–48.

Zimmerer, Jürgen, "War, Concentration Camps and Genocide in South-West Africa. The First German Genocide." In *Genocide in South-West Africa. The Colonial War of 1904–1908 and its Aftermath*, ed. by Jürgen Zimmerer and Joachim Zeller (Monmouth: Merlin, 2008), pp. 41–63.

Zimmerer, Jürgen, and Joachim Zeller (eds). *Völkermord in Deutsch-Südwestafrika: Der Kolonialkrieg 1904–1908 in Namibia und seine Folgen* (Berlin: Links 2003; updated English version, Monmouth: Merlin 2008).

Zimmerman, Andrew. *Anthropology and Antihumanism in Imperial Germany* (Chicago: University of Chicago Press, 2001).

Zimmermann, Peter (ed.). *"Interkulturelle Germanistik"—Dialog der Kulturen auf Deutsch?* (Frankfurt/M.: Lang, 1989).

Zöberlein, Hans. *Der Glaube an Deutschland. Ein Kriegserleben von Verdun bis zum Umsturz* (Munich: Eher, 1931).

Zollmann, Jakob, "Polemics and Other Arguments—A German Debate Reviewed." *Journal of Namibia Studies*, 1.1 (2007), 109–30.

# Index

Compiled by Bernhard Feistel